TEACHERS AND THE LAW

By the same author:

LEGAL CASES FOR TEACHERS

TEACHERS
AND THE LAW

G. R. BARRELL, B.Sc.(Econ.), F.C.P., F.R.S.A.

Head Master, Sir John Cass's Foundation and
Red Coat Church of England Secondary School, London

With a Foreword by
THE LATE
MR JUSTICE VAISEY
D.C.L.

METHUEN & CO LTD
11 NEW FETTER LANE LONDON EC4

First published 1958 by Methuen & Co Ltd, 11 New Fetter Lane,
London EC4P 4EE
Fourth edition (completely revised and rewritten) 1975
© 1975 G. R. Barrell
Printed in Great Britain by
Richard Clay (The Chaucer Press), Ltd.,
Bungay, Suffolk

SBN hardback 416 15190 6
SBN paperback 416 82610 5

CONTENTS

TABLE OF FIGURES

FOREWORD

BY THE LATE MR JUSTICE VAISEY D.C.L.

This book covers a very wide field. Its author is well qualified, both by knowledge and by experience, to deal in a practical way with the many problems which arise in that field, and to get together a great deal of information not readily obtainable elsewhere. The work should prove both interesting and useful, not only to members of the great teaching profession, but to many others who would like to know more about its subject. To all such persons I would commend it. For whether Education is regarded as an art or as a science (and of course it is both), it is admittedly of the highest importance, and here is much valuable material for a better appreciation and understanding of what it means.

H. B. VAISEY

Royal Courts of Justice

ACKNOWLEDGEMENTS

I am indebted to Mr Justice Vaisey, not only for contributing the foreword to this book, but also for his characteristic interest and kindly encouragement. The whole book has been read in manuscript by Mr Hugh Leslie Watkinson, M.A., B.Sc., formerly Headmaster of Mexborough Grammar School and for many years a member of the Legal Committee of the Incorporated Association of Headmasters, by Captain G. Howard Walker, M.C., M.A., LL.B., of Barnsley, and by Mr A. J. C. Gooding, of Ealing, all of whom have made a number of most helpful comments. Mr Gooding has also assisted me with the reading of the proofs. The chapter on the juvenile courts was read by Mr A. Wallich-Clifford, of the London Probation Service, and advice on the subject of armorial bearings was given by Chester Herald of Arms. Dr F. A. Cockin, the Bishop of Bristol, has kindly given me permission to quote his definition of the aim of religious education. Last, but by no means least, I must mention the debt which I owe to the knowledge and experience of the staff of Messrs Methuen and Co., not only in the field of publishing, but also of education.

Quotations from, and references to, material in which Crown copyright subsists have been made with the permission of the Controller of Her Majesty's Stationery Office.

I am most grateful to all those who, by their advice and help, have enabled me to remove many imperfections from this book; for any which remain I, alone, am responsible.

As I am the Headmaster of a school which is aided by the London County Council, it is necessary to state that the Council is in no way responsible for any opinions or conclusions contained in this book.

G.R.B.

NOTE TO FOURTH EDITION

Vast changes have taken place in educational law, and in the thinking which goes to make law, since the last edition of this book was published nine years ago. This edition has been revised to take account of those which have occurred up to October 1974.

Once again, I am greatly indebted to many people who have assisted me in the preparation of material. The officers of some organizations are mentioned in footnotes: in addition I am grateful to Richmond Herald for bringing the section on school badges up to date, and to Mr Geoffrey Crabb, the Rights Fellow of the Council for Educational Technology, for his valuable comments on the chapter dealing with the intricacies of copyright.

Many heads up and down the country owe a great debt of gratitude to Mr C. C. Tipper, B.Sc., F.C.P., the Professional Consultant of the National Association of Head Teachers. Those of us who have also enjoyed his personal friendship through the years are keenly aware of the distinguished service he has rendered to education, and freely acknowledge his influence on our own thinking. No one is more closely in touch with legal and administrative developments in this field and, by the many kindnesses he has shown me, he has ensured that the chapters on salaries and superannuation are updated as much as possible at a rapidly changing time; he has also read the whole book at proof stage. To him I offer special thanks.

Quotations from, and references to, material in which Crown copyright subsists have again been made with the permission of the Controller of Her Majesty's Stationery Office, and quotations from the reports are printed with the permission of Butterworths (*All England Law Reports*) and Charles Knight & Co, Ltd (*Local Government Reports*).

28 October 1974   G.R.B.

PREFACE

This book is intended to help the teacher through some of the many legal pitfalls which beset his path today. It is hoped, also, that it may be of some use to students in colleges of education so that they may be both forewarned and forearmed. Whilst much of the subject matter is primarily the concern of heads, a great deal more is part and parcel of the everyday life of the assistant teacher. Furthermore, managers and governors often have to deal with matters of a legal nature and, in any case, need some knowledge of the structure of the educational system in which they may well play an increasingly important part in years to come. The book has been so arranged that it provides a quarry of material to which quick and easy reference may be made by those whose concern with education is limited to their spare time, and whose training is in other disciplines.

The first part of the book is devoted to a simple outline of the educational system of England and Wales as established by law. Teachers often have hazy ideas about those parts of the national system of education with which they are not in close contact, and of their own place, rights and responsibilities within it. A teacher's employment is subject to the terms of his contract and this, in turn, depends upon the common law, statutes and a host of regulations made under the authority of those laws. Whilst it is hardly possible to commend Statutory Instruments as soothing bedside reading, it is highly desirable that teachers should understand the conditions upon which they are employed.

A teacher is *in loco parentis* and, whilst a child is in his care, some of the privileges of the natural parent are transferred to him in order that he may carry out his duties. In return, the teacher must assume certain responsibilities and must recognize that these obligations, partly legal and partly moral, rest upon him in every aspect of his work. The second part of the book deals with the way in which some of these matters affect the teacher in his professional capacity.

The law requires that, since the teacher is *in loco parentis*, he should, quite naturally, take such care of his pupils as a prudent father would take. It does not demand more; it will not be satisfied with less. Most of us would agree that caring for other people's children is morally a greater burden than looking after our own. The law does not take this view, but it does expect that we should take the same care.

Many of the problems covered in this book are illustrated by actual cases which have been before the courts. It should be remembered that the law, as promulgated in Acts of Parliament, is stated in very general terms for it would be quite impossible to frame a statute which would meet every conceivable set of circumstances – and some circumstances are almost inconceivable. It is the duty of the courts to apply the test of law to the facts of a particular case and the decisions thus made, provided they have not been appealed against successfully, become case law and may be quoted as precedents in similar proceedings.[1]

It would be foolish to pretend that the aim of this book is to make every teacher his own lawyer. No two cases are exactly alike in their circumstances, and the differences are often so subtle that only a trained legal mind can recognize them. It is intended as a general guide to help teachers to unravel some of the simpler problems, and to warn them of the existence of some of the graver dangers. Most teachers manage to pass from college to retirement without being personally concerned in any major legal problems; others are not so fortunate, and may become involved in wrangling over the tenure of their appointment or a complaint by a contentious parent which has arisen through no fault of their own. If serious trouble threatens, a wise teacher will take two precautions.

First, he should immediately inform his superior and discuss the matter fully and frankly with him. For assistants this means the head; a head will go to the chairman of his governors or managers and, if he deems it wise, to the local education author-

---

[1] For an outline of the doctrine of the binding force of precedent, see the author's *Legal Cases for Teachers* (Methuen, 1970), pp. 11–12.

ity. If legal action is probable, a superior has a right to be forewarned. Moreover, such action is in the teacher's own interest
since he is much less likely to receive sympathetic treatment
when concealed trouble bursts like a bolt from the blue or when
the passage of time has seriously restricted the help which can be
given to him. It is useless and unwise for an assistant teacher
to try to persuade a complaining parent to drop a matter he is
threatening to report. If the teacher has acted reasonably, he
has little to fear from an investigation; if, on the other hand, the
parent suspects that he fears any probing into his work, it is
highly probable that the same complaint, or another, will be
raised at a later date. Almost inevitably the teacher's earlier
attempt to hush things up will then be revealed, with disastrous
effects on his professional reputation.

The second precaution is to report the whole affair to his professional association. Some teachers will say that they are not
'union minded' and that they prefer not to join such an organization. Quite apart from the fact that many of the privileges of the
profession are due to the activities of the associations there are
many practical advantages to be gained from membership, and
not the least of these is the provision of legal advice to members
faced with litigation. When an important issue is at stake the
associations will spare no time, trouble or money to safeguard
their members' interests.[1] The case of *Lewis* v *Carmarthenshire
County Council*[2] is an outstanding example. This book is not
intended as a substitute for service of this kind; the teacher faced
with a lawsuit should consult his association at once and, having
received advice, he should follow it. This applies even when the
advice is unpalatable, and the member is advised not to pursue a
line of action which he was proposing to take. Only the association's
solicitor, in possession of all the facts of the case and with records
of many more relevant cases than could be included in a book of

---

[1] It should be remembered that professional associations will undertake
to defend their members only in connection with matters arising after
they join. It would be unfair to other members if it were possible to take up
membership because it is already certain that free assistance is needed.

[2] See pages 261–2.

this scope, can weigh the various factors and advise the member how best he can act in his own interests.

A teacher charged with an offence before the courts should seek the advice of his professional association before entering any plea. Even though the nature of the charge may not be such that the association can accept responsibility for fighting the teacher's case, it will put him in touch with a solicitor if necessary, and will be ready to deal with any professional implications which may arise should he plead or be found guilty. The teacher may, for example, be asked to show cause why the Secretary of State should not withdraw his recognition as a qualified teacher. In some instances this result would be inevitable, but there is an undefined area where a person is not necessarily unfit to be a teacher merely because he has been convicted of an offence, and his professional association may be able to plead extenuating circumstances. The author has personal knowledge of a young teacher who pleaded guilty to a charge of possessing drugs, and whose career was saved by representations made by a solicitor. In this case the teacher did not belong to an association, and had, therefore, to bear her own legal costs. Had she been in membership the service would have been provided free of charge.

This is not intended to be a standard work on the law of education so much as a hand-book of professional advice on points at which the law touches teachers. Therefore, where it has seemed worthwhile to do so, the opportunity has been taken of including some material which is purely professional in character, but which has a bearing on the main theme.

Finally, for the benefit of the ladies, I should add that section 1 (2) of the Interpretation Act 1889 applies to this book with the effect that, 'unless the contrary intention appears, words importing the masculine gender shall include females'.

INTRODUCTION

STATUTORY AND COMMON LAW

The law affects teachers at practically every turn in their professional lives, whether they realize it or not. There are two main strands in English law: the older, the common law, and the newer statutory law, that is Acts of Parliament, and it is important to understand the way in which those two strands follow teachers into school each day.

So far as statutory law is concerned, the basis is the Education Act 1944, to which has been added a number of amending Acts. No statute can take account of every single set of circumstances which can possibly arise, and Parliament has never striven to achieve this detailed perfection. It would be quite foolish, even presumptuous, because conditions vary from one part of the country to another and from time to time during the currency of an Act. Therefore a statute is cast in very general terms. But most statutes, including the Education Act 1944, give the power to competent authorities to make regulations; and these regulations, if they are made within the powers given by the Act, and if they are neither contrary to law nor repugnant to public policy, have the force of law and form part of the statutory law of the realm.

This is what is called delegated legislation, and the Act naturally gives power in the first instance to the Minister (now the Secretary of State)[1] to make such regulations. For example, there are the Schools Regulations 1959 which lay down in a little more detail how schools which are within the maintained system shall be governed. It is the Schools Regulations, for example, which include, amongst many other things, the rules relating to holidays

---

[1] See page 34.

and occasional closures. Then there are the regulations dealing with special schools and handicapped pupils which are similar requirements dealing with special education. There are the Direct Grant Schools Regulations, and there is quite a sheaf dealing with independent schools. These are made by the Secretary of State, Parliament has the opportunity of questioning them before they are put into force, and they then have the effect of law. There should be a copy in every school; all too often there is not.

The second level to which legislation in education is delegated is the local education authority and, within the framework of the Act and the Secretary of State's regulations, a local education authority may make regulations in more detail dealing with the conduct of its schools. Once again, if they are not repugnant to law or public policy, they have the force of law, and these regulations vary quite considerably from one authority to another. This is part of the wisdom of Parliament in that, having given the provision of the public sector of education into the hands of local education authorities, it then leaves to those authorities quite a wide discretion as to how the duties bound upon them by the Act are to be carried out to take account of local needs.

There is, however, another level at which there is a delegation of the authority to make regulations and this is an important one from the teacher's point of view. Under section 17 of the Act of 1944 it is provided that every primary school shall be conducted in accordance with rules of management, and every secondary school shall be conducted in accordance with articles of government. The rules of management or articles of government define the relationship and the duties of the local education authority, the managers or governors, and the head of the school. There are references in them to the appointment and dismissal of the teaching staff, and there is a standard provision that the assistant staff shall have an opportunity to make their views known, but the functions and the duties of the staff, other than the head, are not dealt with in the rules or articles. In law they are appointed to assist the head.

One of the standard provisions is that the headmaster 'shall control the internal organization, management and discipline of the school, shall exercise supervision over the teaching and non-teaching staff, other than the clerk to the governors, and shall have the power of suspending pupils'. This places the whole burden of running the school professionally in the hands of the head and of no one else; and it is part of the recognized system of natural justice in this country that if you place a duty on someone you must give him the necessary discretion to carry it out. There is no point in binding an obligation on any person, and preventing him from discharging it by bonds which cannot be broken.

To carry out his duty the head of a school must have a code of rules. These may be formulated in different ways: they may not be called rules in every school; they may be written, or they may be the accumulation of a large number of oral precepts which become, so to speak, the tradition of the school. No matter what form the rules take, they are part of the system by which the head discharges his legal obligation to control the internal organization, management and discipline of the school and they have, for the members of that school, the force of law. School rules have been upheld in courts of justice.

In 1929 there was a rule at Newport Grammar School in Shropshire that pupils of the school should not smoke within the school precincts or in public during term time. One afternoon, two boys left school and smoked as they strolled through the streets. They were seen by prefects who reported them to the head master, and the head master decided that they should be caned for breach of a school rule. One boy took his punishment 'like a man', but the other objected. He said that his father had given him permission to smoke, it was no concern of the head whether he did or not, and that the head could not make a rule which flouted the father's authority. Moreover it had happened away from the school premises, and after school hours. The head got two masters to hold the boy down and administered the beating. The father thereupon summoned the head master before the magistrates, and the case was dismissed. The father then asked the justices to state a case for the consideration of the Divisional Court of the King's Bench Division. The justices at first refused, holding the application to be frivolous, but in due course they had to comply. The

Lord Chief Justice, Lord Hewart, said at the hearing in the King's Bench Division:[1]

There was at the school a school rule forbidding smoking by pupils at the school during the school term and on the school premises and in public. That, he said, was a reasonable rule. The boy deliberately broke the rule, being aware of it, and the head master caned him. Such punishment was a reasonable punishment for the breach of the school rule, and the father's application to the court must be dismissed. The court was quite clearly upholding a school rule, whether the members of that court approved of smoking or not.

Some years later, in the early 1950s, came the case of *Spiers* v *Warrington Corporation*.[2] A thirteen-year-old girl named Eva Spiers was a pupil at a secondary school in Warrington, and failed to turn up at school in clothing which the headmistress considered suitable. She came, in fact, in jeans. There was a school rule relating to the suitability of clothing in the school. The mother's excuse was that the girl had had two bouts of rheumatic fever. She had been advised by a doctor that the girl's kidneys should be kept warm, and believed that jeans keep kidneys warmer than skirts. The headmistress thereupon asked the mother to produce a medical certificate to this effect.

No such certificate was forthcoming, and the headmistress put her up repeatedly for medical examinations in school, but Eva failed to turn up. The headmistress then decided to take a well-charted but fairly exceptional course. Every time Eva came to school in slacks the headmistress said to her, in effect: 'Now run along home dear and come back properly dressed. As soon as you do, you can come into school.' But Eva stayed at home for the morning and arrived at school again in the afternoon. The same conversation would take place and Eva would return the next morning. This went on for some months until the County Borough of Warrington decided to prosecute the father for failing to send his child to school as was his duty. The magistrates found him guilty and fined him ten shillings.

[1] *R* v *Newport (Shropshire) Justices* ex parte *Wright* [1929] 2 KB 416; LCT 237.   [2] [1954] 1 QB 61; LCT 165.

Mr Spiers appealed, maintaining that the magistrates were wrong in law, that he had sent his child to school; and that it was the perversity of the headmistress which was preventing Eva from receiving her education, the education to which she was entitled.

The West Derby Quarter Sessions Appeal Committee quashed the conviction, believing that the parents were acting reasonably in the interests of their child. The local education authority thereupon appealed to the Queen's Bench Division, which did not agree.

Lord Chief Justice Goddard considered the clause in the articles of government quoted above: 'The Head Mistress shall control the internal organization, management and discipline of the school.' He commented: 'The Head Mistress obviously has the right and the power to prescribe the discipline for the school. . . . There must be somebody to keep discipline, and of course that person is the Head Mistress . . . The question is: was the Head Mistress in communicating her refusal to allow the girl to come to school in this way acting within her rights? We hold that she was not only within her rights, but that it was her duty; and the parent, knowing that the child would not be admitted, and insisting on her being dressed in this way . . . committed an offence.'

Once again, the court upheld the school rule, and said that for Eva Spiers the rule relating to dress was part of the law of the land and judiciable before the courts.

Turning to the common law, it must be noted that much of the education of children is entrusted to the schoolmaster and, if he is to carry out his obligations, some of the rights and some of the duties of the natural parent must be transferred to him so far and for so long as may be necessary for him to carry out his duty. In other words the schoolmaster is said, to that extent, to be *in loco parentis*. He may chastise the child; if he does so unreasonably he is accountable to the law. He must take care of the child, and if he fails to do so reasonably he is accountable to the law. Indeed, this question of the care of children really lies at the root of many of our problems, because a large number of the restraints which we place on children are placed upon them for their own good, or for the good of other pupils. In the late nineteenth century there was a case in what we should now call an independent boarding school where some boys exploring the school conservatory found some phosphorus and started to play about with it. They had an accident, and one boy was very badly burnt. The parent brought a successful action for damages for negligence against the school,[1] and in the course of the hearing Mr Justice Cave asked: 'What is the duty of a schoolmaster?' 'The duty of a schoolmaster,' he continued, 'is to take such care of his boys as a careful father would take of his boys.'

That is the basic duty *in loco parentis*, and the courts have generally borne in mind that wise, prudent and careful parents do not have forty children. But there has been a tendency in the courts since the war to raise the standard of care in all cases of negligence. So far as educational cases are concerned this trend started with a case in Middlesex in 1962[2] arising out of an incident when two boys had been playing a game of ring-a-ring o' roses round the changing rooms of the gym, until one put his fist through a pane of glass and cut his arm badly. Mr Justice Edmund Davies considered the schoolmaster's duty of care in *Williams* v *Eady* to take such care of his boys as a careful father would take of his boys; and decided that this was not a careful father thinking in relation to events at home, but a careful father applying his mind to school life where there is 'more skylarking and a bit of rough play', and he awarded very heavy damages to the boy.

There have been other cases in which the standard of care has been raised but one of the most important was one in which the learned judge restated the rule in *Williams* v *Eady* in more specific terms, and then inquired into the school's disciplinary system in detail.[3]

As has been said earlier, a head must make rules in order to perform his duty to control the discipline of the school under the rules of management or articles of government. These rules form part of the school's system, one of the functions of which is to take all reasonable steps to prevent any untoward event which a

[1] *Williams* v *Eady* (1893) 10 TLR 41; LCT 240.
[2] *Lyes* v *Middlesex County Council* (1963) 61 LGR 443; LCT 198.
[3] *Beaumont* v *Surrey County Council* (1968) 66 LGR 580; LCT 246.

reasonable person might foresee, or which is preventable, and which might cause injury to any person. There must be, of course, the provision of an adequate degree of supervision to make the system work. This, in turn, will usually necessitate a requirement that the assistant staff will assist the head by undertaking such duties as he may require.

When it is alleged that a school has been negligent in caring for its pupils, the court examines the system in detail. Having first satisfied themselves that the school has an adequate system, the court will then inquire whether, on the occasion in question before them, the system at that particular point was being maintained at full efficiency.

In *Beaumont* v *Surrey County Council* it was established that during break there were two masters on duty, four prefects, four sub-prefects and four monitors – fourteen people. It should have been adequate. On the day in question, when an accident happened, the two masters (whose duty it was also to clear the school at the beginning of break) did not, in fact, emerge into the playground until about eight minutes after the break began. The accident had already happened. This was a break-down of the system, with the result that the decision went against the Authority.

In his judgment Mr Justice Geoffrey Lane said that the duty of a headmaster is to protect his pupils from inanimate objects, from the actions of their fellow pupils or from a combination of the two.

So the two strands of the law meet. On the one hand there is the statutory duty under the articles of government or the rules of management; on the other, duty at common law. In all that is being written about the excessive powers of the head, one must never forget, as the law stands at present, the inescapable burden of duty and responsibility placed upon him and, to a lesser degree, upon every teacher. No one can continue to carry out that duty or exercise that responsibility unless he has the necessary discretion: so one must talk in terms of the discretion necessary to carry out a duty, rather than in terms of power. Without it a teacher cannot fulfil his obligations in law.

Part One

TEACHERS AND THEIR EMPLOYERS

I

THE ORGANIZATION
OF EDUCATION

1 Statutory provisions

The organization of the public system of education in England and Wales is laid down in detail in the Education Act 1944, commonly called the 'Butler' Act after Lord Butler who, as President of the Board of Education, piloted it through Parliament and subsequently became the first Minister of Education.

The Act of 1944 is cited as the principal Act. It has, however, been amended by the Education Act 1946, the Education (Miscellaneous Provisions) Acts of 1948 and 1953, the Education Acts of 1959, 1962 and 1964, the Remuneration of Teachers Act 1965, the Education Acts of 1967 and 1968, the Education (No. 2) Act 1968, the Education (School Milk) Act 1970, the Education (Milk) Act 1971, the Education (Work Experience) Act 1973 and the Education Act 1973. These later statutes were designed to make amendments in the light of experience of the working of the principal Act. The fourteen statutes are cited as the Education Acts, 1944 to 1973. The Education (Handicapped Children) Act 1970 is no longer included among the Education Acts.[1]

In addition, there are other Acts which affect the administration of the educational system, either by specific reference or because their provisions apply across the whole spectrum of society. Examples of the first category are the London Government Act 1963 which included educational reorganization in the general reconstruction of the capital's local government, and the Local Government Act 1972 which did the same in the rest of England and Wales. In the second group are such measures as the Con-

[1] Education (Milk) Act 1971, s. 2 (1).

33

tracts of Employment Act 1972 and the Race Relations Act 1965 to 1968.

2 The Secretary of State

The 1944 Act provided that there should be a Minister of Education 'to promote the education of the people of England and Wales and the progressive development of institutions devoted to that purpose, and to secure the effective execution by local authorities, under his control and direction, of the national policy for providing a varied and comprehensive educational service in every area'.[1]

The Minister replaced the former President of the Board of Education and took over all the functions formerly exercised by him. The Secretary of State for Education and Science Order, 1964,[2] transferred the functions of the Minister of Education and Science to a Secretary of State, and the Ministry of Education became the Department of Education and Science (commonly called the DES).

The Secretary of State is a member of the government of the day and is answerable to Parliament for the actions of his department.[3] He is assisted by subordinate Ministers of State.

3 The Department of Education and Science

The DES has a large permanent staff under the control of the Secretary of State and carries on the day-to-day routine of the latter's functions as laid down in the Act, in accordance with the wishes of Parliament. It correlates the work of the various education authorities and examines their schemes involving capital expenditure. Regulations made by the Secretary of State in accordance with the powers given by the Act are prepared, in the first instance, by the permanent staff.

All teachers in schools within the statutory system of education must be recognized by the DES, which is the keeper of their professional records. Modern statistical methods have enabled the

[1] Education Act 1944, s 1 (1).   [2] S.I. 1964, no. 490.
[3] Education Act 1944, s. 5.

DES to replace teachers' service books by service cards, which contain all the information previously contained in book form relating to qualifications, details of service from year to year, and matters concerning salary and superannuation. Arrangements are being made for teachers to obtain copies of their service cards. In the meantime, the employing authority will provide a certified statement of service at a nominal charge.

The Act provides that the Secretary of State shall 'cause inspections to be made of every educational establishment at such intervals as appear to him to be appropriate, and to cause a special inspection of any such establishment to be made whenever he considers such an inspection to be desirable'.[1] For this purpose he recommends to the Crown the appointment of inspectors whose duties are to visit the schools in order to consider whether they are complying with the regulations, and to report upon their general efficiency.

Her Majesty's Inspectors (commonly known as HMIs) deal with a wide range of subjects including not only the actual teaching work of the school but also the state of the buildings and the provision of facilities generally. They may not inspect religious education of a denominational character in voluntary schools. They make periodic routine visits to the schools under their care and, although regular full inspections have been discontinued, they may still take place from time to time. Over the years the HMI's function has changed in emphasis, and greater stress is now laid on the advisory side of his work. Although the inspectoral element has diminished, however, it still remains a basic part of HMIs' duties when appropriate. A review of the functions of the inspectorate may be found in *HMI Today and Tomorrow*.[2]

It is an offence to obstruct any person authorized to make an inspection, the penalty being a fine not exceeding £20 for the first offence or, for subsequent offences, a fine not exceeding £50 with or without a maximum of three months' imprisonment.[3]

The Act also set up two advisory councils, one for England,

[1] Education Act 1944, s. 77.
[2] HMSO, (1970).
[3] Education Act 1944, s. 77.

the other for Wales and Monmouthshire.[1] The function of these bodies is 'to advise on educational theory and practice as they think fit and on any questions referred to them' by the Secretary of State. Members of the councils are appointed by the Secretary of State and must include persons with educational experience outside the statutory system. They replace the former Consultative Committee which issued such far-reaching documents as the Hadow Report on *The Education of the Adolescent*[2] and the Spens Report on *Secondary Education*,[3] the Crowther Report on *Secondary Education*[4] and the Plowden Report on *Children and their Primary Schools*.[5] The Councils may investigate subjects which they have chosen for themselves, in addition to dealing with those referred to them by the Secretary of State.

4 Local education authorities

It is a characteristic British anomaly that, although there is a statutory system of education, there are no state schools. The actual provision and administration of education, other than universities and voluntary establishments, is in the hands of local education authorities.[6] The whole structure of local government in England and Wales has, however, been altered since the passage of the 1944 Act, and little remains of the local education authorities established at that time. In 1944 the local administration of education was entrusted to the councils of counties and county boroughs; and the county authorities, other than London, were required to prepare schemes for dividing their areas into smaller units each with a divisional executive committee. In addition, some non-county boroughs and urban districts were given the status of an excepted district which enabled them to act as the divisional executive committee for their areas.

Reorganization of local government in Greater London took effect in 1964; and a decade later county boroughs, divisional executives and excepted districts were swept away by the Local

[1] Education Act 1944, s. 4. The constitution of the Advisory Councils is laid down in the Central Advisory Councils for Education Regulations, 1945 and 1951.

[2] HMSO (1926).　　　[3] HMSO (1938).　　　[4] HMSO, (1959).
[5] HMSO, (1967).　　　[6] Education Act 1944, s. 6 (1) and (2).

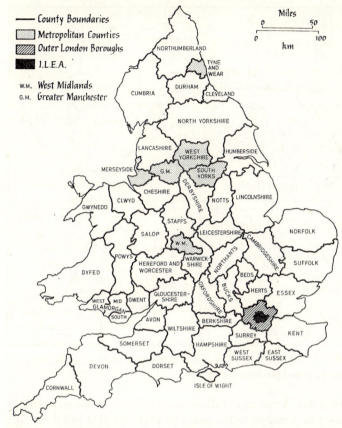

Fig. 1. – *Local Education Authorities: Counties. In the metropolitan counties (shaded on the map) education is the responsibility of the metropolitan districts.*

Government Act 1972 which came into force in 1974. As a result, thirty-nine authorities with populations below 100,000 disappeared, together with all statutory intermediate bodies between the authority's education committee and the managing and governing bodies of schools.

Local education authorities appoint education committees to discharge their functions under Part II of the first schedule to the

Fig. 2. – *Local Education Authorities: metropolitan districts within the metropolitan counties*

1944 Act. A majority of the members of the education committee must be members of the authority itself, but it is laid down that the composition must include persons of experience in education and persons acquainted with the educational provisions prevailing in the area for which the committee acts.

Local education authorities are required to provide an adequate number of school places, a sufficient supply of teachers in the various categories, and the books and equipment needed for their work. Their duties are bound upon them by the Act.[1]

Non-metropolitan counties – There are forty-seven non-metropolitan counties, of which thirty-nine are in England and eight in

---

[1] Education Act 1944, ss. 8 and 41.

Fig. 3. – *Local Education Authorities: Greater London. The Inner London Education Authority is responsible for education in the central, shaded area; each of the outer boroughs is a separate local education authority.*

Wales. The counties are divided into districts, but the latter have no powers in relation to education.[1]

Metropolitan counties – Six areas of dense population – Tyne and Wear, Merseyside, Greater Manchester, West Yorkshire, South Yorkshire and West Midlands – have been designated as metropolitan counties. They are divided into metropolitan districts which are the local education authorities in these areas. The metropolitan county councils have no educational functions.

Greater London – The London Government Act 1963, which abolished at a blow the London and Middlesex County Councils, introduced a unique system for the administration of education in the Greater London area. Since its provisions took effect, the whole of the area until then administered by the London County Council has been controlled by the new Greater London Council,

[1] Local Government Act 1972, s. 192.

acting by means of a special committee. Each of the new outer London boroughs became a local education authority in its own right. The special committee for the central area consists of the members of the Greater London Council for that area, one representative of each inner London borough council appointed by that council from among its members, and one representative of the Court of Common Council of the City of London appointed from among its members. When acting in this capacity the body is known as the Inner London Education Authority, usually referred to as ILEA. The Act provided that the Secretary of State should review the situation by 1970 to determine whether all or part of this service should be transferred to the City and the inner London boroughs,[1] but Mr Anthony Crosland announced on 18 November 1965 that legislation would be introduced to repeal this section. This was done, and London's educational administration has survived the Local Government Act 1972.

In addition to schools, local education authorities provide a wide range of ancillary services ranging from school meals to libraries, grants for further education, and the service of youth. They must make provision for the education of children who are handicapped physically or mentally, and for those who are deprived of a normal home environment or who are maladjusted. They may appoint their own inspectorate to advise and report on the work of their schools.[2] The penalties for obstructing these officers are the same as in the case of HMIs.

Some local education authorities maintain colleges for the training of teachers. Entry to such colleges is not restricted to those living in the authority's area, neither are those trained in them necessarily employed later in the service of that authority.

One of the duties of a local education authority is the appointment of a Chief Education Officer.[3] This official is responsible for the administration of the authority's education service under the direction of the committee. The requirement that the authority

---

[1] London Government Act 1963, ss. 30–4.
[2] Education Act 1944, s. 77 (3) and (4).
[3] Education Act 1944, s. 88.

should consult the Secretary of State before making an appointment has been repealed.[1]

Local education authorities may make such rules as they consider necessary for the good conduct of their schools and the guidance of those who work in them. These regulations must not conflict with the provisions of the Acts, nor with any rules made by the Secretary of State under the Acts.

The revenue necessary for meeting an authority's liabilities is derived partly from local rates levied by the finance committee of the council for the area concerned, and partly from government grants.

5 Diocesan education committees

Voluntary schools are provided, so far as the buildings are concerned, by various bodies. In the case of Church of England schools, however, the close relationship between Church and State has involved the creation of Diocesan Education Committees by a Measure of the former Church Assembly which gives them a statutory existence.[2] This Measure provides for the creation of such committees in every diocese except that of Soder and Man.

The majority of Church schools were once parochial in character and were provided out of funds raised in the parish. Before the war, many of these buildings had long ceased to conform to modern standards and the cost of putting them in order was far beyond the means of the ordinary parish.

Moreover, in large cities the shift of population and the development of local authorities' housing schemes meant that some Church schools were no longer required, whereas neighbouring parishes badly needed new schools. So long as the trusts were on a parochial basis, it was almost impossible to close down a school in one place and apply its funds elsewhere.

The diocesan education committees can redeploy the educational resources of a whole diocese in accordance with an overall plan. This enables the most urgent modernizations to be carried

---

[1] Local Government Act 1972, schedule 30.
[2] Diocesan Education Committees Measure 1955.

out, and many new schools have been built which would not have been possible before the creation of the committees. The value of the diocesan education committees has been particularly evident in the establishment of new Church secondary schools which, by their nature, usually serve a much wider area than one parish.

The functions of the diocesan education committees are laid down as follows:[1]

(*a*) to take such steps as may appear to the Committee to be conducive to the promotion of religious education according to the faith and practice of the Church of England, and to watch the interest of Church schools;

(*b*) to take such action as may appear desirable to provide new schools;

(*c*) to promote, and to co-operate with other religious bodies and with local education authorities in promoting, religious education within the diocese;

(*d*) to give advice, as and when the committee thinks fit, to trustees or owners, and managers or governors, of church schools and others concerned as to any matters affecting Church schools within the diocese, and also to the governing bodies of Church educational endowments as to any matters affecting Church educational endowments within the diocese;

(*e*) to make plans calculated, in the opinion of the Committee, to further the development and organization of religious education in the diocese, and in particular of instruction in religious education according to the faith and practice of the Church of England, after consultation with such trustees or owners and managers or governors of Church schools within the diocese and with such other persons as, in the opinion of the Committee, are interested or as may be in any way affected thereby.

Trustees or owners and managers of Church schools are required to consult the diocesan committee before concluding any agreement dealing with the restoration, rearrangement, continuance, discontinuance, closing, sale or lease of any Church school.

[1] Diocesan Education Committees Measure 1955, s. 2 (1).

The constitution of the committees is laid down in a schedule to the Measure.

A Church school is now defined as a voluntary school, including its site and buildings, which is held on trust for the purposes of primary or secondary education together with instruction (whether as part of, or in addition to, such primary or secondary education) in accordance with the principles and practice of the Church of England. A school may fall within this definition by statute or charter, by a scheme, order, or other instrument deriving from a statute or other authority, by usage or repute, or by any combination of these authorities.[1]

Providing bodies other than the Church of England have their own arrangements which are determined by the varying structures of the bodies concerned.

6 Age, ability and aptitude

The 1944 Act states that 'the schools available for an area shall not be deemed to be sufficient unless they are sufficient in number, character and equipment to afford for all pupils such variety of instruction and training as may be desirable in view of their differing ages, abilities and aptitudes'.[2] In addition, 'the Secretary of State and local authorities shall have regard to the principle that, so far as is compatible with the provision of efficient instruction and training and the avoidance of unreasonable public expenditure, pupils are to be educated in accordance with the wishes of their parents'.[3]

The organization of schools to meet these needs is laid down as follows: 'The statutory system of public education shall be organized in three successive stages to be known as primary education, secondary education and further education.'[4]

The primary stage of education covers nursery schools or

[1] Diocesan Education Committees Measure 1955, s. 3 (1).

[2] Education Act 1944, s. 8 (1).

[3] Education Act 1944, s. 76. See also the section on parental choice (pages 45–50), and *Choice of Schools* (Manual of Guidance – Schools No. 1, first issued by HMSO 23 August 1950, and reprinted with minor amendments September 1960).

[4] Education Act 1944, s. 7.

classes, infants' schools and junior schools. It is defined as 'full-time education suitable to the requirements of junior pupils who have not attained the age of ten years and six months, and full-time education suitable to the requirements of junior pupils who have attained that age and whom it is expedient to educate together with junior pupils who have not attained that age'.[1] A junior pupil is a child who has not attained the age of twelve years.[2]

At the secondary stage there are several different kinds of schools. Secondary education is 'full-time education suitable to the requirements of senior pupils, other than such full-time education as may be provided for senior pupils in pursuance of a scheme made under the provisions of this Act relating to further education, and full-time education suitable to the requirements of junior pupils who have attained the age of ten years and six months and whom it is expedient to educate together with senior pupils'.[3] A senior pupil is a person who has attained the age of twelve years, but has not attained the age of nineteen years.[4]

During the first twenty years following the passage of the 1944 Act many local education authorities found the somewhat precise definition of the frontier between primary and secondary education unduly restrictive. In some areas it was difficult to move towards comprehensive secondary education and, at the same time, to make an economical use of the existing buildings. Some educationalists questioned whether the statutory age of transfer was psychologically the best time for transition to a new school environment. Both these considerations pointed towards the development of middle schools which would cater for pupils at the upper end of the primary and the lower end of the secondary categories as defined in the 1944 Act.

The 1964 Act met these difficulties by permitting proposals to be put forward, either for county or voluntary schools, which specify that a school will provide full-time education for pupils

---

[1] Education (Miscellaneous Provisions) Act 1948, s. 3 (2).

[2] Education Act 1944, s. 114 (1). The Education Act 1964 provided that schools might be established at which the age of transfer does not correspond to the ages laid down in the 1944 Act.

[3] Education Act 1944, s. 8 (1) (b) and Education (Miscellaneous Provisions) Act 1948, s. 3 (3).   [4] Education Act 1944, s. 114 (1).

below the age of ten years and six months and over the age of twelve. The upper and lower age limits must be precisely stated. The Secretary of State, when giving his approval to any particular application, will specify whether the school is to be a primary or a secondary school.[1]

Further education comprises all vocational and non-vocational education provided for young people after they have left school, and for adults. Until 1944, this field was not among those where authorities were bound to act; all had some system of further education, and provision of this type is now compulsory. Vocational education is covered by technical, commercial and art courses, many non-vocational courses are arranged,[2] county colleges will eventually be established and the service of youth provides a wide range of recreational facilities. Children in their last year of compulsory education at school may attend a college of further education in the evenings with their head's permission.

7 Parental choice

Parliament has provided that pupils are to be educated in accordance with the wishes of their parents.[3] This general principle is subject to the proviso that such education shall be compatible with efficient instruction and training, and that it shall not cause unreasonable public expenditure.

It has been held that this section does not inhibit a local education authority from modifying its development plan, nor from changing the fundamental character of its schools by introducing a system of comprehensive education. When the officer of the Joint Parents Committee of the Ealing Grammar Schools asked the courts to restrain comprehensive reorganization of secondary education in the borough, Mr Justice Goff said:

There is, in my judgment, no *prima facie* case of a breach of section 76, since in administrative matters the obligation means no more than that the authority must take into account

[1] Education Act 1964, s. 1.

[2] Some idea of the remarkable variety of the non-vocational courses can be gained from a study of *Floodlight*, the annual prospectus of courses published by the Inner London Education Authority.

[3] Education Act 1944, s. 76.

the general principle, weighing it in the balance against other considerations'. . . . Moreover, I cannot find anywhere in the Act any obligation on the local education authority to consult parents on the revision of the development plan. . . . The general principle is confined to the wishes of particular parents in respect of their own particular children. . . . In my judgment, education in section 76 must refer to the curriculum, and if it includes any, and if so what, religious instruction, and whether coeducational or single-sex, and matters of that sort, and not to the size of the school or the conditions of entry.[1]

The DES has given advice on the application of section 76.[2] After stressing the fact that the parent has not a complete freedom of choice, the Manual of Guidance lists six reasons for the choice of an alternative school to that which a particular child would normally attend:

(*a*) denominational religious grounds;

(*b*) educational considerations, e.g. the provision of a particular kind of advanced work or, in Wales, the linguistic character of the instruction;

(*c*) convenience of access, and the avoidance of traffic dangers;

(*d*) the existence of special facilities; e.g. the provision of school meals in the case of a pupil both of whose parents go out to work;

(*e*) preference for a single-sex or a mixed school;

(*f*) family association with a particular school;

(*g*) medical reasons.

It is not enough, however, for a parent to express a preference in one of these categories. The local education authority or, in the case of an appeal, the Secretary of State must balance the request against the proviso of section 76. It would not, for example, be compatible with the provision of efficient instruction and training if the class which a pupil would enter in the school of the parents'

[1] *Wood and others* v Ealing London Borough Council [1967] Ch 364; LCT 143.

[2] *Manual of Guidance Schools No. 1* (23 September 1950; reprinted with minor amendments, September 1960).

choice were full. Similarly, undue travelling strains would prevent a child from profiting fully from his education. It is suggested that a journey, from door to door, of more than forty-five minutes for primary pupils or seventy-five minutes for secondary pupils is a reasonable limit. In terms of mileage the DES considers that such journeys would, in general, limit the catchment area of a primary school to five or six miles, and of a secondary school to its defined catchment area of ten miles, whichever is the less.

A further consideration is the avoidance of unreasonable public expenditure such as would be implicit in journeys of greater length; although it is recognized that in such cases parents may opt to pay the fares themselves where there is no other objection to the choice. It would also be unreasonable to take up places at independent schools either where the requisite educational facilities can be provided in grant-aided schools, or where an independent school would not provide an education suitable to the needs of the child.

The right of a parent under section 76 of the 1944 Act to choose a particular school for his children was the subject of a lawsuit in 1955.[1] The Watt twins passed the eleven-plus examination and, as there was no grammar school in their part of the county, the local education authority offered to pay their fees at Stamford School, an independent Church of England foundation. The boys were Roman Catholics and the father sent them to Roman Catholic schools in Monmouthshire and Northamptonshire, demanding from the Council payment of the full fees. He based his claim on the authority's duty to educate children in accordance with the wishes of their parents as laid down in section 76. The Court of Appeal upheld the decision of Mr Justice Ormerod that the Council had not failed to comply with the section by refusing to pay. Section 76 did not give a parent the right to choose his children's school at the public expense, subject to two conditions; it only laid down a general principle. In this particular case the public expenditure would have been unreasonable. Leave was given to appeal to the House of Lords, but the parent dropped the case at this point.

[1] *Watt* v *Kesteven County Council* [1955] 1 All ER 473; LCT 136.

Another case connected with section 76 of the Act came before Lord Chief Justice Parker, Mr Justice Ashworth, and Mr Justice Hinchcliffe in the Queen's Bench Division in 1962.[1] The Hertfordshire local education authority had decided that Bonnygrove Primary School, Cheshunt, was overcrowded, and that the six-year-old children concerned must attend Burleigh Primary School. The parents wished their children to attend the former school, which was only a hundred yards from their homes, whereas the school named by the authority was a mile away, and involved crossing the Great Cambridge Road.

Mrs Darling and Mrs Jones persuaded their husbands to make them the temporary heads of their families, and kept the children away from school after the Minister had made a School Attendance Order under section 37 of the Act.[2] In November 1961 both mothers were fined ten shillings for failing to send their children to school. They had arranged for three hours' tuition a week, which was all they could afford.

In the Queen's Bench Division they applied for an extension of time for leave to apply for an order of *certiorari* to quash the decision of the Minister. For the parents, Mr R. K. Brown QC agreed that section 37 (3) of the Act gave the Minister the power to name a school if he considered the school chosen by the parent to be unsuitable or to involve unreasonable public expense, but pointed out that overcrowding was not mentioned as a ground for this action.

Lord Parker asked what the Minister could do if the nearest school was overcrowded, and Mr Brown replied that the authority could adjust its pupils' list so that children could be moved to another school. The Court granted the extension of time, but refused leave to apply for the order of *certiorari*. The effect of this decision is to limit the parent's right to choose the school at which his child is to be educated if the Minister deems the school so selected to be overcrowded. Moreover, the Minister's decision cannot be challenged in the courts.

The denominational problem was thrown into sharp relief in

[1] *Darling* v *Minister of Education; Jones* v *Minister of Education* (1962) *The Times* 7 April; LCT 139.   [2] See pages 210–11.

Birkenhead through the authority's fear that, unless all the first-year places in Roman Catholic secondary schools were taken up, there would be a serious shortage of places in other secondary schools. Accordingly, circulars were issued to the parents of children preparing to leave Roman Catholic junior schools restricting their choice to Roman Catholic schools, but adding that re-allocation would be considered in special cases. In the High Court action which followed, it was claimed that the authority had acted *ultra vires* in issuing the circulars, that the plaintiffs had a right to express a preference unfettered by any question of religious affiliation, and that the authority was in breach of its duty under sections 8 and 76 of the 1944 Act.[1]

Mr Justice Ungoed Thomas did not agree. Rejecting the plaintiffs' claim, he held that the authority's duty was to provide 'sufficient schools', not to pay regard to religious differences, and the only remedy lay in appeal to the Secretary of State under section 99 for default of statutory duty by the authority. The limiting factor was a lack of places in county schools, except for pupils leaving Church of England or county primary schools.

In a judgment in the Court of Appeal the Master of the Rolls, Lord Denning, upheld this decision. The authority had the power and duty to allocate children, and must exercise a proper administrative discretion in doing so:

> If this education authority were to allocate boys to particular schools according to the colour of their hair, or, for that matter, the colour of their skin, it would be so unreasonable, so capricious, so irrelevant to any proper system of education that it would be altogether *ultra vires*, and this court would strike it down at once. But if there were valid educational reasons for a policy as, for instance, in an area where immigrant children were backward in the English tongue and needed special teaching, then it would be perfectly right to allocate those in need to special schools where they would be given extra facilities for learning English. . . . [The authority's action] is a sound administrative policy decision to which no objection

[1] *Cumings and others* v *Birkenhead Coporation* (1971) 69 LGR 47, 444.

can be taken, especially when it is realized that in exceptional cases the authority are ready to reconsider the position of any particular pupil. In my opinion, there is no ground for saying that the education authority have acted beyond their powers. If they have done anything wrong at all – and I do not suggest that they have – it is not a matter which comes within the jurisdiction of these courts. If complaint is to be made, it should be made to the Minister, and not to us.

An unusual objection by a parent was revealed when a Muslim father pleaded guilty to a charge of failing to cause his daughter to receive efficient full-time education suitable to her age, ability and aptitude.[1] The family lived in Blackburn, where all the secondary schools are co-educational, and the father believed that, having regard to the tone of present-day society, she would lose her virtue and become unmarriageable under Muslim law. The court imposed a fine of £5.

8 The primary stage

Nursery schools – Nursery schools are designed for children under five. Nothing approaching formal education is contemplated in these communities where the principal aim is to let children learn to live and play together. They are happy, active places which help the child to learn to curb his own desires for the benefit of others. Where it is not expedient to provide a separate school, nursery classes may be formed within the framework of a larger primary school.

Infants' schools – Between the ages of five and seven the child passes through the infants' school where, although there is still a good deal of play, the beginnings of work are to be seen. By the time they leave, most children can read simple books fluently and have acquired a reasonable facility in the use of number.

Junior schools – The real foundations of later education are laid at this stage which caters for children between the ages of seven and eleven. There is more formal work, but there are now few parts of the country where the junior school curriculum is still dominated by a rigorous selection procedure to determine the

[1] Reported in the *Daily Mail*, 3 November 1972. See also pages 438–9.

kind of secondary education most suitable for each individual child. Consequently, there is a greater flexibility of approach than was once the case. Where grammar schools remain there is still some form of selection; but this is more flexible than it was a few years ago, and is increasingly dependent on the record of a child's whole primary school career rather than on the result of a single day's examination.

Junior mixed and infants' schools – Many primary schools provide both for the infants' and junior stages so that children have an unbroken career in one school from the age of five until they pass to a secondary school. Some of these schools also have their own nursery class.

9 The secondary stage

Secondary school provision is historically of three kinds – grammar, technical and modern. These distinctions, however, were not legislative. Contrary to popular opinion, the 1944 Act made no stipulation as to the structure of secondary education. For a time after 1944 most children were drafted at the age of eleven plus to a grammar school or a modern school, but within a short time some local education authorities began to experiment with various forms of comprehensive school designed to accept all secondary pupils from a given area. The move towards comprehensive secondary education gathered momentum in the 1950s and 1960s and, in principle, gained official support from both sides of the House of Commons. Nevertheless, at the time of writing (October 1974), many grammar schools and modern schools remain, and the reorganization of secondary education on comprehensive lines is by no means complete.

Grammar schools – These include the ancient foundations and also the schools (variously known as secondary schools, county high schools, etc.) established under the Education Act of 1902. They provide a five-year basic course leading to the Ordinary level of the General Certificate of Education and continuing, for selected pupils, to two or three years' sixth form studies for the Advanced level. The schools are designed for the top academic flight of children and were the principal means of entry to the universities and professions. This is still, to a large extent, true in those areas where comprehensive schools exist side by side with grammar schools.

Modern schools – In the 1940s and 1950s some 80 per cent of children went at eleven plus to secondary modern schools. These schools, first envisaged in the Hadow Report,[1] soon began to find their feet. The courses were designed for children whose intelligence was, at best, not greatly above the average and which was often well below. Consequently, they were more practical in their approach. The whole character of secondary modern schools changed rapidly, and the distinction between the various kinds of schools for children over eleven became increasingly blurred. Many pupils stayed on beyond the end of the basic four-year course, and a large proportion of such children showed themselves capable of taking a limited number of subjects at the Ordinary level of the General Certificate examination – though perhaps a year later than their contemporaries in the grammar schools. There was an increasing development in the use of external examinations in schools of this kind, some of them at the end of the fourth year. The Beloe Report[2] recommended the introduction of a fifth-year Certificate of Secondary Education to be conducted by regional boards composed largely of teachers, and this new examination was first held in some areas in 1965. Fourth year examinations have disappeared finally with the raising of the school-leaving age to sixteen.[3]

Comprehensive schools – The protagonists of comprehensive schools claim that there are advantages in a more homogeneous unit, and that the majority of children will not be written off as failures because they 'only went to a modern school'. Many of

[1] *The Education of the Adolescent* (HMSO, 1926).

[2] *External Examinations in Secondary Schools* (HMSO, 1960). This report has been followed by the fourth and fifth reports of the Secondary School Examinations Council – *The Certificate of Secondary Education: A Proposal for a New School Leaving Certificate other than the GCE* (HMSO, 1961) and *The Certificate of Secondary Education: Notes for the Guidance of Regional Examining Bodies* (HMSO, 1962).

[3] J. Vincent Chapman: *Your Secondary Modern Schools* (College of Preceptors, 1959) contains a full account of the work of secondary modern schools in the late 1950s.

these schools are streamed, and for many years it was maintained that it is easier to move a child from one stream to another in the same school than to arrange a transfer from one school to another. More recently there has been a tendency to advocate the abolition of streaming on the ground that this is a survival of selectivism. As these schools have developed, ways have been found of overcoming what seemed at first to be a serious disadvantage – the size of the schools – by breaking them down into smaller vertical or horizontal units such as houses or year groups. In some areas junior high schools are provided for pupils until they reach the upper age limit of compulsory education, whilst those who plan to stay at school longer go on to senior high schools.

The organization of secondary education remains an area of controversy. In 1965 the DES issued *The Organization of Secondary Education*[1] asking local education authorities to amend their development plans with a view to ending selective secondary education by the universal establishment of comprehensive schools. Some authorities showed a tendency to drag their feet, however, and two attempts were made to introduce legislation designed to outlaw all forms of selection for various kinds of secondary schools. A general election resulting in a change of government frustrated these intentions, and Circular 10/70 stated that the Secretary of State would adopt a more flexible attitude towards the organization of secondary education. Reorganization has continued during the seventies, but the tempo has slowed appreciably.

10 Further education

The term 'further education' comprises:

(*a*) full-time and part-time education for persons above the upper limit of compulsory education, and

(*b*) leisure-time occupation in such organized and cultured training and recreative activities as are suited to their requirements, for any persons over compulsory school age who are able and willing to profit by the facilities provided for the purpose.[2]

[1] Circular 10/65.   [2] Education Act 1944, s. 41.

The pattern of further education establishments has changed considerably since the passage of the Act. The county colleges have failed to materialize: successive governments have paid lip-service to their importance, but the heavy cost and the consider-able administrative needs of implementing the more urgent requirements of the 1944 Act in respect of primary and secondary education make it seem unlikely that these sections[1] will ever be implemented, at any rate in the form in which they were envisaged.

Instead, a four-tiered structure of further education institu-tions developed. The most advanced work was undertaken by the Colleges of Advanced Technology which were removed from the control of local education authorities as direct grant establish-ments. These ten colleges prepared students for external univer-sity degrees, and also for the Diploma in Technology introduced in 1956 as the equivalent of a first honours degree. Four years later the Membership of the College of Technologists was estab-lished as the equivalent of a lower doctorate, but in 1964 the Council for National Academic Awards was established by royal charter as 'an autonomous body with powers to award first and higher degrees, diplomas, and other academic distinctions to persons who have successfully pursued courses or undertaken research work approved by the Council at an educational or research establishment other than a university'. The work of the CNAA continues in other fields, but eight of the colleges of advanced technology have become universities, and the other two are now constituent colleges of the Universities of London and Wales respectively.

The second group consisted of some twenty-five regional colleges, also concerned with preparation for external degrees, the Diploma in Technology, and the Higher National Certificates and Diplomas. In addition to full-time students, the regional colleges also undertook sandwich courses whose students spent alternate periods, usually of six months each, in employment and at college. By a process of amalgamation, sometimes with another regional college and sometimes with an area college, the regional colleges have now become the major part of the new system of

[1] Education Act 1944, ss. 43–6.

thirty polytechnics which with a recruitment partly national, partly local, provide full-time and part-time courses leading to degrees and other advanced qualifications. The polytechnics are aided by local education authorities.

The two remaining tiers – the area and the local colleges – were designed to recruit their students from within the area of the local education authority where they were situated. The area colleges provided courses for the Ordinary National Certificates and the examinations of the City and Guilds of London Institute, whilst the local colleges were designed to handle more elementary studies in a restricted area. Although a variety of names is still in vogue, these colleges are now generally known as colleges of further education, and provide a wide range of courses for full-time, day-release and evening students.

The curricula of the colleges of further education are as varied as the needs of the students who attend them. Some of the courses are designed to lead to vocational qualifications, many are cultural and recreational. For example, students may wish to learn German because they will need it in their work, or to use it on holiday, or just out of interest. Evening courses may include such diverse subjects as oil-painting, local history, flower-arrangement and yoga.

The number of students undertaking further education has increased beyond all expectation, and this applies particularly to day-time courses. As Professor H. C. Dent has said, one of the most significant changes in the structure of further education that has been taking place since the second world war is 'the transfer of studies related to vocation from the evening to the working day'.[1]

In addition to the provision of local education authorities, non-vocational education is undertaken by 'responsible bodies', HM Forces and a number of voluntary organizations. A 'responsible body'[2] is recognized for grant-aid by the DES, and must be a university, a national association principally devoted to promoting liberal adult education (such as the Workers' Educational

---

[1] H. C. Dent: *The Educational System of England and Wales* (ULP 5th edition, 1971) page 170.

[2] Further Education (Grant) Regulations 1959, no. 19.

Association), or a joint body representative of universities, recognized national associations and local education authorities approved by the Secretary of State.

The aims and structure of adult education were examined between 1969 and 1973 by a committee under the chairmanship of Sir Lionel Russell, formerly Chief Education Officer for Birmingham. The report[1] saw three needs:

(a) a continuation of formal education, including remedial education, second-chance education and up-dating;

(b) self-fulfilment centred on creative and artistic expression, or physical or intellectual activity;

(c) helping the individual to contribute more fully in the life of the community.

The report advocated a continuation of the partnership between local education authorities and voluntary bodies, monitored by local, regional and national development councils. At the time of writing (October 1974) the Government has made no pronouncement on the report.

11 The universities
Before the Second World War there were twelve universities in England and Wales, only two of which were founded before the nineteenth century. There are now thirty-five, including the Open University.

It is practically impossible to state precisely what constitutes a university, since many of those created since 1948 are very different in character from those founded earlier. Two common ingredients, however, seem to remain: they 'must be incorporated by the highest authority, i.e. by the sovereign power, succeeding, no doubt, to the Papal privilege which was exercised in Christendom in the middle ages by the proper and, indeed, only body which could incorporate and give authority to a great teaching institution.'[2] Secondly, it is a common feature of all universities

[1] *Adult Education: A Plan for Development* (HMSO, 1973).
[2] *per* Vaisey, J. in *St David's College, Lampeter* v *Ministry of Education* [1951] 1 All E.R 559; LCT 370.

that the right to grant degrees is included in their royal charters of incorporation. The Council for National Academic Awards[1] is the only body other than the universities with the power to award these distinctions.

There is no space in a work of this nature to describe in detail the varied pattern of these institutions, which are independent, self-governing corporations acting within the terms of their charters. Readers who are interested are referred to the appropriate chapter in Professor Dent's book,[2] or to the longer study by Dr V. H. H. Green.[3]

Two points, however, should be understood. Universities are not merely teaching institutions, but also places of research, and the degree of importance attached to each of these functions varies from university to university. Secondly, although the degree structure may seem complicated, there are, in fact, four essential levels of degrees in England and Wales; in ascending order those of Bachelor, Master, Doctor of Philosophy and the higher doctorate. The last named is awarded to distinguished scholars who have made significant contributions to knowledge. There is, incidentally, no Bachelor's degree (other than the Bachelor of Education) in Scotland.

A new educational experiment began on 1 June 1969 with the grant of a charter to the Open University. Eighteen months later the University began its first courses in humanities, social sciences, mathematics and sciences. Tuition is by correspondence, television and radio programmes and seminars. There are no formal entry qualifications, but it is a requirement that the standard of the degree shall be equivalent to those of other universities.

12 Special education

Local education authorities have a duty to provide facilities for children who need specialized treatment in some form or another.

[1] See page 54.
[2] H. C. Dent: *The Educational System of England and Wales* (ULP 5th edition, 1971) pages 190–211.
[3] V. H. H. Green: *The Universities* (Penguin, 1969).

In many cases these arrangements have been made by the provision of special schools, e.g. 'ESN' schools for the mentally retarded, open air schools for the delicate, and special provision for the physically handicapped. A number of authorities maintain boarding schools for pupils whose well-being will be promoted by residential school life. Special schools are also provided for maladjusted children. Special education, however, need not take place in a special school, or even in school at all.[1] There is a growing belief among many educationalists that handicapped children need to grow up among normal classmates, and there is evidence that some local education authorities are considering reducing the number of their special school places in order to provide for handicapped children in ordinary schools. Special units, e.g. for partially-hearing children, may be attached to ordinary schools, and individual tuition provided for severely handicapped children.

The various categories of handicap are defined by regulation,[2] as are the requirements for the education of handicapped children in ordinary schools.[3]

New duties were placed upon local education authorities in 1970. Until then a local education authority was under a statutory duty to ascertain what children were suffering from a disability of mind of such a nature as to make them unsuitable for education at school. There were provisions for appeal against any decision.[4] If no successful appeal was made, the local health authority became responsible for the training of the child.[5] On the other hand, handicapped children deemed suitable for special educational treatment in ordinary or special schools were dealt with under a different section of the Act,[6] and remained the responsibility of the local education authority. The Education (Handi-

[1] Education Act 1944, ss. 33 and 56.

[2] Handicapped Pupils and Special Schools Regulations 1959, no 4. See pages 185-7.

[3] Handicapped Pupils and Special Schools Regulations 1959, no 20.

[4] Education Act 1944, s. 57 as amended by the Mental Health Act 1959, which substituted new ss. 57, 57A and 57B.

[5] Health Services and Public Health Act 1968, s. 12.

[6] Education Act 1944, s. 34.

capped Children) Act 1970 repealed sections 57, 57A and 57B of the 1944 Act as amended, and directed that in future all children should be dealt with under the section 34 procedure. The powers and duties of the local health authorities in this matter were abolished, and the responsibility for training such children has now passed to the local education authorities. Buildings and staff have also been transferred.

A further statute of the same year[1] applies to any person undertaking the provision of a university, a college, a school within the meaning of the Education Act 1944,[2] or an institution for providing further education in accordance with the Act,[3] or an educational establishment within the meaning of the Education (Scotland) Act 1962. The section requires that such a building shall include such facilities for the disabled as are practicable and reasonable in respect of means of access to and within the building, parking facilities and sanitary conveniences. The Act does not refer specifically to new buildings.

The same Act requires that, so far as is practicable, a local education authority must arrange for special educational treatment, for the deaf–blind, the autistic (and those with other forms of early childhood psychosis) and the acutely dyslexic, in any school which it maintains. The Secretary of State for Social Services may require information about provision of this kind which is being made by the authority.[4]

13 Direct grant schools

Schools which receive financial aid directly from the Secretary of State, and not from a local education authority, are known as direct grant schools. Many of the public schools fall into this cate-

[1] Chronically Sick and Disabled Persons Act 1970, s. 8.

[2] The Education Act 1944, s. 114 defines a school as 'an institution for providing primary or secondary or both primary and secondary education, being a school maintained by a local education authority, an independent school, or a school in respect of which grants are made by the Minister to the proprietor of the school; and the expression 'school' where used without any qualification includes any such school or all such schools as the context may require.'

[3] Education Act 1944, s. 42.

[4] Chronically Sick and Disabled Persons Act 1970, ss. 25–7.

gory. To be included in the direct grant list, a school must comply with the relevant regulations,[1] must submit to inspection by HMIs, and must reserve one quarter of its places for pupils nominated by the local education authority (or authorities) whose area it serves. Such pupils are selected through the normal procedure for transferring children at the end of their primary school courses, and their fees are paid by the nominating authority.

14 Independent schools

The independent schools stand outside the statutory system of education. They range from those well-known public schools which are administered under a trust deed, but which have not been placed on the direct-grant list, to small schools conducted for private profit. Parliament has now taken cognizance of the existence of all such schools.[2] Formerly they were liable to inspection only if they asked for grant aid. In all other cases inspection was voluntary. Section 70 of the Act, which provides for the registration and inspection of all independent schools, was implemented in the autumn of 1957.

The Independent Schools Tribunal has discretion to disqualify a person from being a proprietor of an independent school, without disqualifying that person from being a teacher in any school. This was held by the Queen's Bench Division in 1968. A husband and wife were equal shareholders and directors of an independent school near Salisbury. When the husband was jailed for assault and cruelty to his pupils, the Secretary of State served a notice of complaint on the wife, alleging that as a director she was responsible for her husband's employment and for his conduct as headmaster. The Independent Schools Tribunal disqualified her from being the proprietor of any independent school, but did not disqualify her from being a teacher. The Divisional Court held that she was an equal party in running the school, and responsible for what had happened. There was some evidence she had contributed to the good academic record which, in some respects, the school had, and it was unnecessary to bring her teaching career

[1] Direct Grant Schools Regulations 1959, as amended.
[2] Education Act 1944, ss. 70-5.

to an end provided that the management of any school in which she was a teacher was in other hands.[1]

In April 1970 Mr Chaim Grunhut and Mr Mervyn Warner were charged with conducting an unregistered school on premises disqualified under the Education Act 1944. In 1968 a notice of complaint had been served because of the inadequate secular education at the school. Religious lessons were given in the mornings by three rabbis, and Mr Warner, the headmaster, gave secular instruction to thirty-five boys in the afternoons. A notice of closure in August 1969 was ignored. Mr Grunhut, a member of the managing committee, maintained that he had resigned before the offences were committed, and was acquitted. Mr Warner said he believed that an appeal was still possible after the notice had been served, so he had continued to work part-time although he no longer considered himself responsible for the running of the school. He was fined £5 on each summons.[2]

15 The service of youth
It is the duty of every local education authority to secure the provision of adequate facilities for 'leisure-time occupation, in such organized cultural training and recreative activities as are suited to their requirements, for any persons over school age who are able and willing to profit by the facilities provided for that purpose'.[3] The Service of Youth is statutorily a part of further education, with its own Division at the DES, and sub-committees of the local education authority. The main function of the authority is to encourage the development of leisure-time activities in its area, to establish youth centres, to maintain liaison with the voluntary youth organizations, to provide financial aid, and to recruit and train instructors and youth leaders. In 1960 the Government accepted the report of the Albermarle Committee[4] which criticized the neglect of this aspect of education, and called for a ten-year development plan.

[1] *Byrd* v *Secretary of State for Education and Science; Secretary of State for Education and Science* v *Byrd* (1968) *The Times*, 22 May.
[2] *The Times Educational Supplement*, (1970) 3 April.
[3] Education Act 1944, s. 41.
[4] *The Youth Service in England and Wales* (HMSO, 1960).

During the sixties the National College for the Training of Youth Leaders produced nearly 1,000 trained youth leaders, and there are now (1974) fifty-three colleges of Education offering courses in youth leadership at various levels. The National College closed in 1970, its work being transferred to six existing colleges where it could be undertaken in a more broadly-based context.

Other developments have included a vast extension of community service by young people through such agencies as the Community Service Volunteers and Task Force, in addition to those organizations which have always encouraged this form of service.[1] In 1967 the Young Volunteer Force Foundation was set up to stimulate and co-ordinate voluntary community service. There has also been increasing co-operation between the service of youth and the schools: teacher/youth leaders have been appointed, and youth wings have been added to school buildings. The British Youth Council, the British committee of the World Assembly of Youth, is financed by the Foreign and Commonwealth Office, and is largely concerned with the international aspect of youth work.

16 The National Health Service

The 1944 Act required local education authorities to establish a comprehensive school health service which included medical and dental inspection and treatment. These duties were swept away on 1 April 1974 on the grounds that those who provide health services for schoolchildren need to work closely not only with the education service, but also with the hospital and personal health services for families and children.

The National Health Service Reorganisation Act 1973 laid down the pattern of a new structure responsible to the Secretary of State for Health and Social Services. Regional health authorities are responsible for overall planning and large hospitals, but the key bodies are the area health authorities which, in general, are coterminous with the new local government authorities. In Greater London each area authority is responsible for two or three London boroughs.

[1] *Service by Youth* (HMSO, 1966).

Fig. 4. – *The National Health Service: regional and area health authorities.*

Local education authorities retain the responsibility for the ascertainment and education of children needing special education, for social work and educational psychology, but the remainder of their functions have been transferred to the area health authorities.

It is the duty of the Secretary of State for Health and Social Services to make arrangements for medical and dental inspection

Fig. 5. – *The National Health Service: area health authorities in the metropolitan counties.*

and treatment of pupils at maintained schools.[1] By arrangement with the local education authority he may make similar arrangements for senior pupils at maintained educational establishments providing full-time education other than schools, but only with the agreement of the governors of that institution. He may also make similar arrangements with the proprietor of an educational establishment not maintained by a local education authority, and in such cases the proprietor may be required to pay for the services provided.

Local education authorities and the managers or governors of

[1] It must be remembered that voluntary schools are 'maintained'.

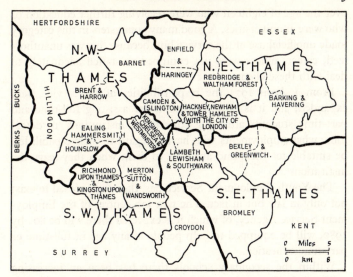

Fig. 6. – *The National Health Service: area health authorities in those parts of the four 'Thames' regional authorities which lie within Greater London.*

voluntary schools must provide suitable accommodation for this purpose.[1]

Joint consultative committees, consisting of representatives of the area health authorities and the local authorities they serve (including, where appropriate, the Inner London Education Authority) have been set up to ensure co-operation 'and advance the health and welfare of the people of England and Wales'.[2]

17 The careers service

Local education authorities were, until March 1974, required to provide a careers service for persons under the age of eighteen, and for those over that age who are for the time being attending school.[3] The service had no functions in relation to young people

[1] National Health Service Reorganisation Act 1973, s. 3.
[2] National Health Service Reorganisation Act 1973, s. 10.
[3] Employment and Training Act 1948, s. 7.

over the age of eighteen who were receiving further education or who were at universities. A good many youngsters in this category made unofficial use of the service but, because this was unauthorized, careers offices were not equipped or staffed adequately to deal with these clients.

From 1 April 1974 the responsibilities of the service were expanded, and it is now responsible for assisting full-time and part-time students attending educational institutions 'to determine what employments will, having regard to their capabilities, be suitable for them and available to them when they leave the institutions'.[1]

The Youth Employment Service has, therefore, ceased to exist not only in law but in fact. The new job centres of the Employment Service Agency, of which it is expected there will be 800 by 1980, will be equipped to help people of any age in full-time or part-time education.

Within the secondary schools there has been an increasing tendency in recent years to appoint members of staff with the special responsibility of advising pupils about careers, the opportunities available to them and the qualifications they need. In many schools, however, provision of this kind is given inadequate preparation and thought. In colleges of further education even less formal help is given and, although some have counsellors, much of the internal advice is given on an *ad hoc* basis by students' personal tutors.

To some extent the work of the careers officer in the school is helped or hindered by the quality of the careers teacher. Ideally, much of the careers education should be undertaken by the teacher, the careers officer's educational function being largely consultative in this field, leaving him more free for interviews and individual counselling. It remains to be seen how effectively the new organization will work, but the indications are that success will depend on a trained, dedicated and sympathetic careers teacher whose teaching load is light enough to enable him to give sufficient time and energy to his vocational guidance.

Whereas the former Youth Employment Service was adminis-

[1] Employment and Training Act 1973, s. 8.

tered by local education authorities on behalf of the Department of Employment, the new Careers Service is entirely the responsibility of the local education authorities. Advice given by the Secretary of State for Employment will be of a general character.

18 The school milk and meals service

Under the 1944 Act a local education authority was required to establish a milk and meals service by which all pupils at school and students in county colleges could obtain daily one-third of a pint of milk free. In 1969 regulations[1] prescribed that local education authorities had no duty to provide milk for pupils other than pupils in attendance at primary schools or special schools. The Education (School Milk) Act 1970 added junior pupils at middle schools (which included pupils both of primary and secondary ages to the list) of those eligible to receive free milk.

By the Education (Milk) Act 1971 local education authorities are not required to provide a pupil with milk after the end of the end of the summer term following his seventh birthday unless he is in attendance at a special school or, if he attends an ordinary primary school or is a junior pupil at a middle school, the competent medical officer has certified that his health requires him to be provided with milk at school. The cost of milk provided by local education authorities for any other pupils must be defrayed by the pupils receiving it, or their parents.

Some general-purpose local authorities have taken over the provision of free milk now that education authorities can no longer supply it. Most of the Inner London boroughs have made arrangements on these lines.

Pupils at non-maintained schools may not be provided with milk by a local education authority beyond the end of the summer term following their seventh birthday unless the school is a special school.

Local education authorities are also required to provide a midday meal and such other refreshment as may be necessary for

---

[1] Provision of Milk and Meals Regulations 1969.

pupils at a small charge. Teachers can no longer be required to supervise the midday meal.[1]

19 Provision of clothing

A local education authority may provide clothing, including boots or shoes, for any pupil who is maintained as a boarder at an educational institution by the authority, or who is a pupil in a maintained nursery school or class, or for a pupil for whom they are providing board and lodging otherwise than at an educational institution if that pupil is receiving special educational treatment.

If it appears to the local education authority that any pupil not falling within the categories listed above, and who is a pupil of a maintained school or of a special school (whether maintained or not), is unable to take full advantage of his educational opportunities because of inadequate or unsuitable clothing, the authority may provide necessary clothing to remedy the deficiency.

Physical education clothing may be provided for pupils in schools, at county colleges, or taking advantage of other physical education facilities provided by the authority.

The authority may determine whether it confers a right of property, or of user only, when providing such clothing. The authority may require a parent to pay such sum as he is able to find without hardship.[2]

20 Non-maintained schools and ancillary services

A local education authority may, with the consent of the proprietor of any school not maintained by the authority,[3] make arrangements for the provision of milk (within the limitations outlined above), meals and other refreshment for pupils at that school, and for the supply of clothing for the benefit of registered pupils at that school. The financial arrangement must be such that the cost to the authority is no greater than it would have been if the

---

[1] For a discussion on the position of teachers in relation to dinner duty, see pages 370–4.

[2] Education (Miscellaneous Provisions) Act 1948, s. 5, as amended by the Education (Miscellaneous Provisions) Act 1953, s. 17 and Schedule I.

[3] E.g. a direct grant or an independent school.

service were being provided for a pupil in one of its own schools.[1]

As has already been noted, the Secretary of State for Health and Social Services may charge for the provision in such schools of medical and dental inspection and treatment.[2]

21 The Council of Europe

In Britain great stress is laid on the sovereignty of Parliament and the rule of law. For many Britons the age of legal idealism dawned at Runnymede in 1215, and they sometimes forget that the privileges of freedom and of equality before the law have not been shared so widely, or for so long, in some other countries.

Moreover two world wars have drawn the nations of Europe more closely together. Britain's entry into the European Economic Community (EEC) in 1973 is still hotly debated, and one of the favourite arguments of opponents of the Common Market is the loss of Parliamentary sovereignty. The Council of Europe, which was born in London on 5 May 1949, 'to achieve a greater unity among its members for the purpose of safeguarding and realizing the ideals and principles which are their common heritage' is conveniently forgotten. At present there are seventeen member nations,[3] and throughout its history the Council has striven to ensure that fundamental human rights are secured to every citizen in each of the member states.

The principles which lie behind these rights are enshrined in the European Convention on Human Rights, which came into force on 3 September 1953, together with its watchdogs, the European Commission of Human Rights and the European Court of Human Rights. The Convention has been ratified by all the member states except France and Switzerland, and eleven members (including the United Kingdom) have recognized the

[1] Education Act 1944, s. 78 (2) and Education (Miscellaneous Provisions) Act 1948, s. 5 (4).

[2] National Health Service Reorganisation Act 1973, s. 3 (3).

[3] Austria, Belgium, Cyprus, Denmark, the Federal Republic of Germany, France, Iceland, Ireland, Italy, Luxembourg, Malta, the Netherlands, Norway, Sweden, Switzerland, Turkey and the United Kingdom. Greece withdrew in December 1969.

competence of the Commission to receive individual as well as inter-state applications.

There have been five Protocols (supplementary conventions), and education is dealt with in the first of these which was signed in Paris on 20 March 1952, ratified by the United Kingdom on 3 November in the same year, and entered into force in 18 May 1954. Article 2 provides:

No person shall be denied the right to education. In the exercise of any functions which it assumes in relation to education and to teaching, the State shall respect the right of parents to ensure such education and teaching in conformity with their own religious and philosophical convictions.

Quite clearly, the United Kingdom, as a signatory, can neither make a new law nor attempt to enforce existing law in a way which is contrary to the spirit of this article. Indeed, for the individual, this safeguarding may be of greater importance now, in an increasingly multicultural society (where, for example, strict Muslims refuse on religious grounds to send their daughters to co-educational schools) than it was when it was drafted.

Three educational issues have been referred to the Commission. Between 1962 and 1964, six groups of francophone residents in Flemish Belgium and the Brussels area claimed that the linguistic system for education in Belgium was incompatible with the Convention. The court found that there had been discriminatory treatment, and new legislation was introduced in Belgium. Of four other linguistic cases, two were declared inadmissible.

In *Karnell and Hardt* v *Sweden*, filed in 1971, members of the Evangelical–Lutheran Church of Sweden complained that parents of children belonging to that Church were prevented from giving their children appropriate religious instruction as the children were obliged to attend religious instruction in school. The Church had been refused permission to provide alternative religious instruction. The application was eventually withdrawn following a decree by the King-in-Council that, at their parents' request, children belonging to the Evangelical–Lutheran Church could be exempted from compulsory religious instruction, which should not take place in classes where they were present, and that such pupils should not suffer any disadvantage.

In *Kjeldsen* v *Denmark*, the parents of a ten-year-old girl complained that a law making sex education compulsory was a violation of their right not to have their daughter educated contrary to their religious and philosophical convictions. Optional sex education had been common in Denmark for many years; the new law made it obligatory, not as a separate subject but integrated with the teaching of other subjects. The Danish government maintained that the parents had not exhausted all the domestic remedies (which must be done before a case is referred to the Commission), that they could legally educate her at home (which they had been doing for some time), and that there were plenty of private schools near the parents' home. The case is not yet decided.[1]

In the mid-seventies, the world is shrinking, there is greater mobility between countries, economic ties are being more closely bound and there is a wider appreciation of human dignity and human rights. The privileges which for centuries the Britisher has enjoyed before the law are now much more universally accepted. Before long, the EEC will have to consider the validation of academic qualifications among its members. English educational organization is still basically the concern of Westminster, but Parliament in its turn must ensure that its legislation and practice are acceptable not only in these islands, but also in a wider context.

[1] Readers who are interested in this subject are recommended to read Edward Wall: *Europe – Unification and Law* (Penguin, 1969).

II

THE CONDUCT OF SCHOOLS

1 Primary schools

Primary schools are conducted by a body of managers[1] who are appointed under an instrument of management which is made by the local education authority in the case of county schools and by the Secretary of State for voluntary schools.[2] Their powers are defined by rules of management drawn up by the local education authority. The principal executive officer of the managers is known as the correspondent.[3]

2 Secondary schools

Secondary schools are conducted by a body of governors[4] who are appointed under an instrument of government which is made by the local education authority in the case of county schools and by the Secretary of State for voluntary schools.[2] Their powers are defined by articles of government which are made by the local education authority (with the Secretary's approval) for county schools, and by an order of the Secretary of State for voluntary schools. Such articles determine the respective functions of the local education authority, the board of governors and the head of the school. The principal executive officer is known as the clerk to the governors.[3]

3 All-age schools

All-age schools, containing pupils of both primary and secondary

[1] Education Act 1944, s. 17.

[2] See Figure 7 (page 80).

[3] In county schools this is normally the Chief Education Officer, who may perform the duties by deputy.

[4] Education Act 1944, s. 17.

school ages, are conducted administratively in all respects as though they were primary schools.[1]

4 Middle schools

The Education Act 1964 enabled the establishment of schools which would include pupils both of primary and secondary school age.[2] The Act provides that, when giving his approval of an application to set up such a school, the Secretary of State will designate it as a primary or secondary school. Such an institution will, therefore, have managers or governors as may be appropriate.

5 Maintained and other schools

Maintained schools are those which are maintained by local education authorities, and both county and voluntary schools are in this sector. The whole cost of running a maintained school, including the salaries of the staff, is met by the authority. County schools are provided by a local education authority and voluntary schools by a voluntary body which may be a religious denomination, a city company or an educational trust. An incorrect distinction is often made between 'maintained' and 'voluntary', instead of between county and voluntary, schools.

Direct grant and independent schools are outside the maintained sector. The former receive grants from the DES; but the latter (sometimes called 'private' schools, and including some of the 'public' schools) receive no grants from public funds. Independent schools must rely entirely upon their fees and any endowments which they may have for their income.

6 County schools

In county primary schools, two-thirds of the managers are appointed by the local education authority and one-third by the minor authority where there is one.[3]

The governors of county secondary schools are appointed in accordance with the instrument of government.[4]

[1] Education Act 1944, s. 31 (2).
[2] Education Act 1964, s. 1, see pages 44–5.
[3] Education Act 1944, s. 18 (1) and (2).
[4] Education Act 1944, s. 19 (1).

The whole cost of the provision and maintenance of county schools falls to the charge of the local education authority. Religious education and worship must be undenominational in character, and in accordance with the agreed syllabus.[1]

7 Aided schools

An aided school is a voluntary school, that is, one not established by a local education authority, in which the managers or governors are able and willing to find 15 per cent of the cost of improving or enlarging the school to bring it up to the standards laid down. If it be a new school the managers or governors are required to find 15 per cent of the cost of building.

Two-thirds of the managers of an aided primary school are appointed by the voluntary body providing the school, and are called foundation managers. Their particular duty is to ensure that the school is conducted in accordance with the terms of any trust deed. Of the remaining managers, not less than one-third nor more than one-half are appointed by the minor authority, if any. The remainder are appointed by the county authority.[2]

The governors of an aided secondary school are appointed in the proportions of two-thirds foundation governors to one-third local education authority representatives.[3]

The cost of improving or enlarging the school building,[4] including the cost of a new site, is the responsibility of the managers or governors,[5] subject to a maintenance contribution of 85 per cent from the Secretary of State.[6] Other buildings or capital expenditure, e.g. playing fields, canteens, kitchens, etc., must be

[1] Education Act 1944, s. 26.

[2] Education Act 1944, s. 18 (3).

[3] Education Act 1944, s. 19 (2) (b).

[4] School buildings are defined as any building, or part of a building, forming the school premises except those required *only* as a caretaker's dwelling, in connection with school playing fields, for medical purposes or for the provision of milk, meals or other refreshment. (Education Act 1946, s. 4 (2).)

[5] Education Act 1944, s. 15.

[6] Education Act 1944, ss. 102, 103 and 105, as amended by the Education (Miscellaneous Provisions) Act 1953, s. 8, the Education Act 1967, s. 1, and the Education Act 1968, Schedule 2.

provided by the local education authority: in such cases, all additions to the site (other than playing fields) must be conveyed to the trustees.[1] New voluntary-aided secondary schools, designed to accommodate children who have attended primary schools belonging to the same religious denomination, were envisaged by the Education Act 1959. Popularly known as 'matching schools', they also rank for a maintenance grant of 80 per cent.[2]

Religious education is under the control of the managers or governors, and must be in accordance with the trust deed or, where there is no deed, in accordance with the practice in the school before it became aided. Agreed syllabus instruction must be provided for children who cannot be conveniently educated elsewhere, if their parents request it.[3] The secular instruction in an aided primary school is under the control of the local education authority, in secondary schools of the governors.[4]

Teachers are appointed by the managers or governors[5] subject to the establishment and educational qualifications prescribed by the local education authority, which may prohibit the appointment of any particular person to be employed for giving secular instruction, or require his dismissal if, in the authority's opinion, he is unsuitable for that purpose. Teachers are the servants of the managers or governors and not of the authority,[6] although, since their salaries form part of the authority's liability in maintaining an aided school, they are usually paid direct by the authority.

The schoolkeeping staff is appointed by the managers or governors, subject to the general requirements of the authority.[7] The school meals staff is appointed by the local education authority in accordance with the Secretary of State's regulations. The appointment of secretarial staff is in accordance with the rules of management or articles of government.

[1] Education Act 1946, s. 3 and Schedule I.

[2] The provisions of the 1959 Act have been superseded by the enlarged powers of the Secretary of State to make grants under the Education Act 1967, s. 1. as amended by the Education Act 1968, Schedule 2.

[3] Education Act 1944, s. 28.

[4] Education Act 1944, s. 23 (1) and (2).

[5] Education Act 1944, s. 24 (2).

[6] *Crocker* v *Plymouth Corporation* [1906] 1 KB 494, LCT 69.

[7] Education Act, 1944 s. 22 (4).

In general, the managers or governors are responsible for the exterior maintenance and repair of the building (with an 85 per cent maintenance contribution from the Secretary of State), the local education authority for the interior. The local education authority maintains the playground and playing fields.[1]

The local education authority may require the free use of the buildings for any educational purpose or for the welfare of the young on not more than three days in any week, when they are not in use as a school, provided that no other suitable accommodation is available.[2]

8 Controlled schools

The term 'controlled school' is not defined in the Act, but it may be said to be a voluntary school which is neither an aided nor a special agreement school. It is a voluntary school – that is, a school not provided by a local education authority – where the managers or governors are unable or unwilling to find the required proportion of the cost of improving or enlarging the school,[3] or of building a new voluntary school to provide for the closure or reorganization of existing voluntary schools.[4]

One-third of the managers of controlled primary schools are foundation managers; of the remainder, not less than one-third nor more than one-half are appointed by the minor authority, if any, the remainder by the local education authority.[5]

One-third of the governors of controlled secondary schools are foundation governors; the remainder are appointed by the local education authority.[6]

The local education authority bears the whole cost of improvements and additions to the school[7] and, if these are on the original site, their ownership must be vested in the trustees. This need not be done, however, in the case of a new controlled school.

---

[1] Education Act, 1944 s. 15 (3).
[2] Education Act 1944, s. 22 (2), and Education Act 1967, ss. 2 and 3.
[3] Education Act 1944, s. 15 (3).
[4] Education (Miscellaneous Provisions) Act 1953, s. 2, as amended by the Education Act 1968, Schedule 2.
[5] Education Act 1944, s. 18 (3).   [6] Education Act 1944, s. 19 (2) (a).
[7] Education Act 1944, s. 15 (3).

Religious education must be in accordance with an agreed syllabus,[1] but denominational instruction must be provided, for not more than two periods a week, for those pupils whose parents request it.[2] The nature of the daily act of worship is not specified but, unless the Secretary of State makes a direction to the contrary, it may be in accordance with the trust deed or, if there is no deed, in accordance with the practice in the school before it became controlled.

Teachers are appointed by the local education authority which must, however, consider representations from the foundation managers or governors in appointing the head. Reserved teachers must be appointed.[3]

The whole cost of the maintenance of the school and the buildings is borne by the local education authority,[4] which also appoints the non-teaching staff.[5]

The use of the school is reserved to the foundation managers on Sundays, and on Saturdays if it is not required by the local education authority for the purposes of the school or the welfare of the young.[6]

9 Special agreement schools

The constitution of managing and governing bodies is the same as in the case of an aided school.[7]

In the case of a new school, capital expenditure on the building is met by the voluntary body with a grant of not more than 85 per cent from the local education authority.[8] Where the special agreement school is to provide accommodation for displaced pupils, the cost is met by the voluntary body with a grant of not more than 85 per cent from the Secretary of State towards such

[1] Education Act 1944, s. 27 (6).
[2] Education Act 1944, s. 27 (1).
[3] Education Act 1944, s. 27 (2) to (5). For a discussion of the position of reserved teachers, see pages 110–11.
[4] Education Act, 1944, s. 15 (3).
[5] Education Act 1944, s. 22 (4).
[6] Education Act 1944, s. 22 (1).
[7] See page 74.
[8] Education Act 1944, Schedule III, 4 and 5, as amended by the Education (Miscellaneous Provisions) Act 1948, s. 11 (1) and Schedule I.

part as he may determine to be attributable to the provision of places for displaced pupils.[1]

The provisions for religious instruction are as in the case of an aided school.[2] The position with regard to worship, however, is the same as in a controlled school.[3] Except as may be otherwise provided in the articles of government, secular instruction is under the control of the local education authority.[4]

The teaching staff is appointed under the same conditions as in a controlled school,[5] with similar provisions regarding the appointment of the head and of reserved teachers. The proportion of reserved teachers, however, is not fixed by the Act, and is determined jointly by the proposers of the school and the local education authority. Seventy-five per cent is a usual figure.

The non-teaching staff is appointed by the local education authority.[6]

The arrangements for the maintenance of the premises are the same as in the case of an aided school.[7]

The local education authority may require the use of the premises for educational purposes or for the welfare of children when they are not in use as a school. Such use is limited to not more than three days in any one week, and conditional upon there being no suitable alternative accommodation available.[8]

10 Minor authorities

A minor authority, in relation to a school maintained by a local education authority[9] is one of the following:

(a) the parish council (in England) or the community council (in Wales) which appears to the local education authority to be the council of the area served by the school;

(b) the parish meeting where a school is situated in a parish which has no council;

(c) the district council where a school is situated in a com-

---

[1] Education Act 1967, s. 1., as amended by the Education Act 1968, Schedule 2.
[2] See page 75. [3] See page 77. [4] Education Act 1944, s. 23 (1).
[5] See page 77. [6] Education Act 1944, s. 22 (4).
[7] See page 76. [8] Education Act 1944, s. 22 (2). [9] See page 73.

munity (in Wales) which has no council, or (in England) neither in a parish nor a metropolitan county;

(*d*) the parish or community council or councils, the parish meeting or meetings, or the district council or councils acting jointly where a school appears to serve more than one minor authority area[1]

It is not necessary that a representative manager or governor should be a member of the body which appoints him.

11 Grouping of schools
A number of schools may be grouped together under the same body of managers or governors.[2] Where this is done, the schools are generally, though not necessarily, of a similar kind. Primary and secondary schools are not usually grouped together although the Act expressly states that this may be done. As a rule, it is not practicable to group county and voluntary schools under the same body, and such a scheme requires the consent of the local education authority, the Secretary of State and the managers or governors of the schools concerned. Community homes and remand homes are maintained by an authority by virtue of its powers under the Children and Young Persons Acts, and are therefore not the responsibility of the education committee.

12 Instruments of management or government
The instrument defines the constitution of the managing or governing body and lays down the procedure by which its members are appointed. Instruments vary somewhat to suit particular circumstances but, in general, the following matters are included:

1. Constitution, including *ex-officio* members, if any. The total membership in the case of a voluntary primary school, or of a county school where there is a minor authority, must be not less than six, and must be a multiple of three. If there is no minor authority the local education authority may determine the number of managers of a county primary school. In county secondary schools the number is determined by the

[1] Local Government Act 1972, s. 192 (4).
[2] Education Act 1944, s. 20.

local education authority, and in voluntary secondary schools by the local education authority in consultation with the Secretary of State. In the case of voluntary secondary schools the total must be a multiple of three.[1]

Fig. 7. – *Responsibility under the Education Act 1944 for making instruments of management and government and rules of management or articles of government.*

	Instrument	Rules or Articles
PRIMARY:		
County	LEA	LEA
Voluntary:		
Controlled	S of S	LEA
Special Agreement	S of S	LEA
Aided	S of S	LEA
SECONDARY:		
County	LEA	LEA*
Voluntary:		
Controlled	S of S	S of S
Special Agreement	S of S	S of S
Aided	S of S	S of S

* With the Secretary of State's approval.

2. Terms of office of managers or governors.

3. Prohibition of the appointment as managers or governors of any person having a financial interest, except as a trustee, in the school.

4. Provision for the determination of membership through failure to attend meetings, bankruptcy, incapacity or resignation.

5. Provision for competent bodies to appoint new members, to fill seats vacated by their representatives.

6. Method of appointment of chairman and vice-chairman.

[1] For the proportions in which foundation, local education authority, and minor authority managers are appointed, see Figure 8 (page 81).

Fig. 8. – *Composition of managing and governing bodies.*

	Foundation	*Representatives* LEA	*Minor Authority (if any)*
PRIMARY:			
County	—	Two-thirds	One-third
Voluntary:			
Controlled	One-third	One-third – Four-ninths	One-third – Two-ninths
Special Agreement	Two-thirds	One-sixth – Two-ninths	One-sixth – One-ninth
Aided	Two-thirds	One-sixth – Two-ninths	One-sixth – One-ninth
SECONDARY:			
County	—	As determined by the LEA	
Voluntary:			
Controlled	One-third	Two-thirds	—
Special Agreement	Two-thirds	One-third	—
Aided	Two-thirds	One-third	—

7. Procedure for summoning and adjourning meetings and rescinding resolutions.

8. Frequency of meetings. These must, by law, be held at least once a term.[1]

9. Provision for keeping a record of the attendance of members.

Until quite recently most, if not all, instruments included a clause prohibiting the appointment of teachers as managers or governors of the school in which they were serving. During the last few years there has been a growing body of opinion favouring the view that the body immediately responsible for the conduct of a school should be more formally representative both of the

[1] Education Act 1944, Schedule IV, as amended by the Education (Miscellaneous Provisions) Act 1948, Schedule I, Part I.

school as a community and of the school in a community. This has led to demands that managing and governing bodies should include representatives of the parents, the teaching staff and, possibly, the non-teaching staff and pupils.

This development has led local education authorities to a good deal of heart-searching, and has raised a number of legal issues. In the first place, the manner of appointment must be kept within the law, and the Act makes no provision for representation of these groups as such. Consequently, such representation can be made only by the local education authority undertaking that a number of appointments in its gift will be made on the nomination of the parents or the teaching staff, as the case may be. The term of office of such members raised a further problem, since it would clearly defeat the purpose of representation of this kind if these managers or governors were to remain in office after their children had left the school or, in the case of teachers, they had left the staff before the expiry of their full term of office.

A third difficulty arose in connection with eligibility for election and, indeed, with the manner of election. Many schools have part-time and temporary members of the staff. Was there to be any restriction on such persons becoming managers or governors, or in helping to choose them? Should elections of parent-managers be by the parent–teacher association; or by the whole parent body, many of whom may not know each other?

Another issue, still not satisfactorily resolved, concerns the status of these categories of managers or governors. Are they purely representatives, acting individually after appointment; or are they delegates taking instructions from, and reporting back to, those who have nominated them? The former view seems preferable on two grounds, one constitutional, the other practical. Such managers and governors are nominated by their fellow parents or colleagues; but they are appointed by the local education authority. It is, therefore, to the authority, not to the nominating body, that they owe the duties arising from appointment. Secondly, a great deal of confidential matter comes within the knowledge of managers and governors as, for example, when dealing with the suspension of pupils and the appointment, promotion and discipline of staff. If there were a duty to report back there would be a grave risk that personal and confidential matters could be bruited about, causing unnecessary suffering and loss of confidence in these bodies with no compensatory public advantage.

It is a matter of public policy that those who receive their salaries from public funds should not be members of the bodies from which they hold their appointments. In county schools this does not necessarily present a grave problem, as appointments are generally in the gift of the local education authority. It is otherwise in voluntary-aided schools, where appointments are made by the managers or governors, subject to the authority's consent, and this is one reason that the aided schools have not moved so far in this direction as the county schools.

Many authorities have now amended the instruments of county schools to provide for representation of some of the groups mentioned above. In Inner London, for example, the head is now *ex officio* a manager or governor, there is one representative of the teaching staff and one representative of the parents. The National Association of Governors and Managers reported in May 1973 that thirty-two authorities had made moves in this direction. Twenty-three had appointed teachers, and thirty had appointed parents. In Sheffield, Brent and Ealing the non-teaching staff were also represented.

It is doubtful, however, if the issue has passed beyond the controversial stage. In reply to questions in the House of Commons, the Secretary of State for Education and Science said that the appointment as governors of persons under the age of eighteen would appear to be unlawful. She added, 'I have under consideration the question whether teachers ought to be able to serve as governors of their own schools, but there would appear to be a legal as well as other problems there.'[1]

Nevertheless, according to the report quoted above, seven authorities have found ways of admitting pupils to governors' meetings. In Derby, Warley and Ealing, pupil governors over the age of eighteen are elected by all pupils aged sixteen and over. In Ealing

[1] (1972) *The Times*, 16 June.

a pupil under eighteen may be elected, but he is officially an 'observer'. 'Observers' are also appointed in Sutton, Rochdale and Nottingham, and in Brighton pupil governors may be co-opted.

13 Rules of management and articles of government

These are rules for the general guidance of managers and governors in the conduct of schools.[1] They define the functions of managers or governors, the relationship between the governing body, the local education authority and the head, and between the governing body and the school. Rules and articles vary somewhat from place to place and according to the type of school, but the following are among the matters usually included:

1. The management of the school must be in accordance with the Education Acts, the appropriate regulations of the Secretary of State and, except in the case of voluntary-aided schools, the regulations of the local education authority.

2. The managers or governors are responsible for certain matters connected with maintenance and for obtaining the necessary estimates.

3. The respective functions of the managers or governors and the local education authority in connection with the appointment and dismissal of teaching and non-teaching staff are defined.

4. In county and controlled schools the correspondent or clerk to the governors is appointed by the authority; in aided and special agreement schools, the governing body may appoint.

5. The managers or governors have general control of the school and must take appropriate action within their powers; in matters where they have no power to act they must notify the local education authority of anything requiring attention.

6. The educational character of the school is determined by the local education authority.

7. Responsibility for the internal organization, management

[1] Education Act 1944, s. 17 (3) and Schedule IV, as amended by the Education (Miscellaneous Provisions) Act 1948, s. 11 (1) and Schedule I, Part I. See also, *Principles of Government in Maintained Secondary Schools* (HMSO, 1944).

and discipline of the school is vested in the head, together with the supervision of both teaching and non-teaching staff, and the power to suspend pupils from attendance.

8. Provision is made for full consultation between the head, the managers or governors and the local education authority; and opportunity is given for the assistant staff to make representations either through, or with the knowledge of, the head.

9. The head is entitled to attend throughout the meetings of managers or governors unless excluded for good cause during the discussion of specific business.

10. Holidays are, in general, determined by the local education authority; the granting of occasional closures[1] being within the discretion of the managers or governors.

11. The managers or governors must furnish the local education authority with such returns as may be required.

12. A copy of the rules of management or articles of government must be given to every teacher on appointment, or he must be given facilities for acquainting himself with them.

Where proposals for a significant change in the character of a school are approved under the Education Act 1944, s. 13, the Secretary of State may make such variations of the articles of government (if the school is a secondary school) or modifications of the trust deed which appear to him to be required. In such a case the rights of interested parties to make representations has been removed.[2]

[1] See pages 181–2.
[2] Education Act 1968, s.1. Reorganization of secondary education in Enfield placed HM Government in an embarrassing situation when it was held in the courts that both the local education authority and the Secretary of State had acted *ultra vires*. This provision validated retrospectively other actions which might have been challenged, and diminished the possibility of local objections. See *Bradbury and others* v *London Borough of Enfield* [1967] I WLR 1311, LCT 39; *Lee and Another* v *London Borough of Enfield* (1968) 66 LGR 195, LCT 46; and *Lee and Others* v *Secretary of State for Education and Science* (1968) 66 LGR 211, LCT 23.

III

THE STATUS OF TEACHERS

1 Duties of local education authorities

The Secretary of State's requirements concerning the staffing of schools are binding upon all maintained schools as follows:[1]

(a) every school must have a head who takes part in the teaching; and

(b) every school must have a qualified teaching staff which is adequate in all respects having regard to the ages, abilities and aptitudes of the pupils.

The regulation provides that, having regard to the number of teachers available in England and Wales as a whole, the Secretary of State may fix the maximum number to be employed by any authority.

The teachers employed must be qualified, but the regulation provides for certain relaxations:

(a) unqualified teachers in service before 1 April 1945 in schools maintained or aided by a former authority may continue to be employed, subject to the approval of Her Majesty's Inspector if there has been a break in service;

(b) student teachers and 'instructors' may be employed in accordance with the regulations;[2]

[1] Schools Regulations 1959, no 16.

[2] Schools Regulations 1959, nos 17 and 18 as amended by the Schools (Amendment) Regulations 1968 no 2 (a) and (b). The effect of the amendment is to replace the words 'temporary assistant teacher' by the words 'student teacher' in Regulation 17 (1). The amending regulations substitute a new category in place of the occasional teachers in the original Regulation 18: these persons are commonly known as instructors, and this term is employed in this book, although another reference to

86

(c) a person who is not a qualified teacher may, with the permission of the Secretary of State, be appointed to the assistant staff of a nursery school or class if she has satisfactorily completed a course of instruction in the care of young children.

2 Qualified teachers

The Schools (Qualified Teachers) Regulations 1969 replace the definition of 'qualified teacher' previously laid down in the Schools Regulations 1959, No 16 (2) to include persons accepted as qualified teachers by the Secretary of State in the following categories:

(a) a person who has completed a course of initial training for persons training to be teachers in schools in accordance with the Secretary of State's regulations, or approved by him as comparable;

(b) a person who possesses a special qualification approved by the Secretary of State. In the case of primary schools the special qualification must have been obtained before 1 January 1970. The regulation is concerned only with the date when the qualification was awarded, and a person who was eligible for qualified teacher status by virtue of such a qualification may still take up a first teaching appointment. Later regulations[1] made a similar provision in the case of secondary school teachers in respect of special qualifications (which include degrees).[1] In secondary schools persons are eligible for qualified teacher status in respect of qualifications gained before 1 January 1974. The regulations give the Secretary of State power to recognize a special need for teachers of certain subjects (which are not specified); and, in such cases, untrained teachers may take up first employment in a secondary school (other than a special school) notwithstanding the fact that they gained their special qualifications after 31 December 1973; for the time being,

---

them in the Regulations speaks of persons 'employed by virtue of Regulation 18'. See sections 10 and 11, pages 96–7.

[1] Schools (Qualified Teachers) Regulations 1973.

teachers of mathematics and science are so exempted. Making the announcement, the Secretary of State hoped that the shortage of teachers of these subjects will allow the exemption to be removed as quickly as possible;

(*c*) a person recognized, or eligible to be recognized, as an uncertificated teacher by the Board of Education, and who has completed twenty years' service as a teacher;

(*d*) a supplementary teacher with twenty years' service as a teacher;

(*e*) a person with such a qualification as may on the recommendation of a local education authority be approved by the Secretary of State, and who has completed ten years' service (or less if approved for special reasons);

(*f*) a person who has obtained the Training Council's[1] Diploma and has subsequently completed five years' service in training children classified as unsuitable for education at school,[1] or as a teacher in a special school or partly in each;

(*g*) a person who has obtained the Training Council's[2] Diploma through having been awarded a diploma in teaching mentally handicapped children by the National Association of Mental Health, or the Middlesex County Council, followed by service such as that described in the preceding paragraph;

(*h*) a person who has obtained the Training Council's[2] Declaration of Recognition of Experience, and has subsequently completed five years' service in a special school. The Declaration was awarded in recognition of service in training centres and hospital schools for the mentally handicapped.[3]

The regulations are amplified in *The Qualification of Teachers*[4], issued by the DES.

[1] Under the Education Act 1944, s. 57.

[2] The Training Council for Teachers of the Mentally Handicapped, Alexander Fleming House, Elephant and Castle, London, SE1. Holders of the earlier diplomas granted by the National Association for Mental Health or the Middlesex County Council are eligible to receive the Training Council's Diploma.

[3] Schools Regulations 1959, no 2 (*a*) and (*b*), as amended by the Schools (Qualified Teachers) Regulations 1969, no 2 (1).

[4] Circular 10/71, revised 31 January 1972.

Additional requirements in respect of teachers in special schools are given below.[1]

3 Approved courses of training

The Area Training Organizations are responsible for the examination and assessment of students who have taken one of the approved courses of training, and the Secretary of State awards qualified status when a student has been recommended by the appropriate Area Training Organization.

Such a course may be taken in a college of education, a department of education in a polytechnic or a university department of education.

If, in exceptional circumstances, a course is not under the supervision of an Area Training Organization, the body providing the course submits the results to the Secretary of State.

In England and Wales, courses recognized by the General Teaching Council for Scotland are accepted as approved initial training; and the following courses approved by the Ministry of Education for Northern Ireland and leading to recognition as a teacher in primary, intermediate or grammar schools in that country are also recognized by the Secretary of State:

Queen's University, Belfast

New University of Ulster, Coleraine

Stranmillis College, Belfast

Saint Joseph's College of Education, Belfast

Saint Mary's College of Education, Belfast

Ulster College of Physical Education, Jordanstown, Co. Antrim

Belfast Training College for Teachers of Domestic Economy[2]

Initial training courses are conducted in accordance with the Training of Teachers Regulations 1967.

The whole question of teacher training is under review. A committee under the chairmanship of Lord James, the Vice-Chancellor of the University of York, reported in January 1972.[3]

[1] See pages 94–6.
[2] Circular 10/71, Appendix 2.
[3] *Teacher Education and Training* (HMSO, 1972).

The report attacked the present system as no longer adequate, largely because of its excessive preoccupation with initial training and the separate graduate and non-graduate routes.

The report recommended the establishment of a national council which, working through regional councils, would have the power to determine conditions of entry and to award diplomas in education.

The report envisaged teacher education in three cycles. The first, not necessarily committing the student to teaching would consist of a two-year course leading to a diploma in higher education or a first degree. The successful student would then begin the second cycle, aimed specifically at preparation for teaching, spending one year in full-time study followed by a period as a 'licensed teacher' during which he would be released for study for at least one day a week. This cycle would lead to the degree of Bachelor of Arts (Education). The third cycle would offer a compulsory term's release for study every seven years, and a wide range of in-service training courses.

There is no indication, after three years, of acceptance or rejection of the report in part or as a whole.

4 Special approved qualifications

Graduates of universities within the British Isles, holders of degrees granted by the Council for National Academic Awards;[1] and those who (subject to any conditions therein mentioned) possess any of the qualifications listed in Appendix 3 of Circular 10/71 are regarded as holders of special approved qualifications.

They can, however, no longer take up a first appointment in a primary school unless they gained their special qualification before 1 January 1970; nor in a secondary school unless it was awarded before 1 January 1974.[2]

Teachers already in service on the relevant date are not affected by the restriction.

[1] See page 54.

[2] As already noted, there is a temporary respite for teachers of Mathematics and Science in secondary schools.

The grant of qualified status by virtue of qualification through one of the certificates listed in the appendix does not limit the particular form of instruction which the teacher may give. It is for the employing authority to decide whether a teacher is qualified to give instruction in a particular subject or to be appointed to a particular post.

5 Special cases

If an authority wishes to appoint as a qualified teacher a person who does not possess an approved qualification, the DES must be consulted; and the approach must be made by the local education authority, not by the teacher. To be granted qualified status, such a person must possess a combination of qualifications and experience. The latter must include at least ten years' teaching experience unless there are special reasons for making an exception. The probation for such teachers cannot be extended.

6 Overseas qualifications

The Secretary of State is prepared to recognize courses and qualifications taken in the British Commonwealth and in other countries if they appear to be of a standard equivalent to British qualifications. The length of the list precludes the publication of details of all the courses which have been so recognized and employing authorities should consult the DES about all qualifications, including degrees, obtained overseas.

7 Verification of qualifications

An employing authority is required to verify without delay the qualifications of teachers appointed to its service.

The DES issues a notification to teachers who complete satisfactorily the courses of training which are subject to assessment by the Area Training Organizations. This states the date from which the teacher is recognized as qualified.

In cases submitted for the DES's confirmation, salary is not payable at the qualified rate until the approval of the DES has been notified to the employing authority.

8 Probation

The initial period of service as a qualified teacher in a maintained school[1] is probationary in character and, during it, the teacher must satisfy the Secretary of State of his practical proficiency as a teacher.[2]

The probationary period is designed not only to test the teacher, but also to give him a chance to 'run-in'. Local education authorities are asked to ensure that the schools in which teachers serve their probation offer favourable working conditions and the opportunities for advice and help from the head or an experienced assistant. In particular authorities are asked not to appoint probationers to their supply staff where this would involve working in a number of schools. On the other hand a transfer should be possible if the teacher is not making the progress expected of him.

There are two categories of probationary service. Procedure A applies only to full-time teachers who have successfully completed an approved course of training. The period of probation is one year, and the main responsiblity for its supervision rests with the local education authority which before the end of that period may recommend either that probation has been satisfactorily completed, or that a further period of six months should be served, or that the person should no longer be employed as a qualified teacher. It is the authority's responsibility to advise the teacher if the probationary period is successful; if extension or termination is recommended, the teacher should be informed of the contents of a special report to the Secretary of State, who will make the decision. If a second, or further, extension, or termination is recommended, the Secretary of State will give the teacher an opportunity to make representations before the decision is reached.

Procedure B is used for all other persons eligible for recognition as qualified teachers, including those serving on a part-time basis. For full-time teachers the period is two years, but this may be reduced or waived by the Secretary of State in exceptional cases;

[1] For a definition of the term 'maintained school', see page 73.

[2] Schools Regulations 1959, Schedule II. 2, as amended by the Schools Amendment Regulations 1968, no 4; see also Administrative Memorandum 10/68 which contains the Department's guidance to local education authorities on this subject.

the Secretary of State will determine a longer period in each individual case for part-time teachers, but this will not exceed four years. Supervision of the probation is shared between the local education authority and HMIs. In the first place the local education authority recommends, as in the case of trained teachers, to an HMI. The authority does not have to submit a report if an extension is recommended, but the teacher should be given reasons. Extension cannot be considered in the case of 'exceptional recognition as a qualified teacher'.[1] If termination is advised, a special report must be made, and the teacher informed of its contents. The form is returned to the DES by the HMI, and, as with trained teachers, the person concerned is given the opportunity to make representations to the Secretary of State before a decision is taken on an adverse report.

For a teacher whose first appointment is in a direct-grant or independent school, in a college of further education, or in any establishment other than a maintained school, probationary service does not begin unless and until the teacher transfers to the maintained sector. The Secretary of State has, however, advised local education authorities that if such a teacher has good experience and substantial service reliably vouched for, it would be unreasonable to require the full, or in some cases any, period of probation. An authority can, in such cases, make an early application even at the time of appointment for a reduction or waiver of probation. In suitable instances this might apply to teachers with experience overseas.

The Secretary of State has also said that if an untrained qualified teacher quickly satisfies the HMI of his practical proficiency, he should not be expected to serve the full probationary period of two (or, for part-time teachers, three or four years). It is not expected, however, that such a teacher will normally be recommended for completion of probation in less than one year.

Quite apart from the probationary period required by the Secretary of State, it was once the practice of some local education authorities to require experienced teachers, even heads, to serve their own 'local authority probation' on entering their service

[1] See Section 5, page 91.

from elsewhere. This practice has now more or less disappeared, although it is probable that, strictly, the managers or governors of a voluntary-aided school could ask teachers to sign a clause accepting such a condition under the general law relating to master and servant.

9 Special schools

Special requirements are laid down in respect of teachers in special schools.[1]

Each special school must have a head who takes an appropriate part in the teaching of the school and a staff of assistants suitable and sufficient in number to provide full-time education suitable to the ages, abilities, and aptitudes of the pupils.

All members of the staff must be qualified teachers within the meaning of the Schools Regulations 1959, no. 16 (2) as amended, and, if they are teaching blind, deaf or partially-hearing children, they must have such further qualifications as may be required by the Secretary of State. Nevertheless,

(a) a teacher recognized by the Board of Education before 1 April 1945 may continue to be employed in the same capacity and kind of special school and, if he was recognized as a teacher of the blind, he may also be employed in any school for parti-ally-sighted pupils;

(b) any person who taught in a secondary school for blind pupils before 1 April 1945 may be employed in any school for blind pupils;

(c) a person who holds the Diploma or the Declaration but has not completed five years' experience in a special school, or training children classified as unsuitable for education at school, may be employed in any special school.

The following may also be employed:

(a) a person employed before 1 April 1971 by or under a local health authority or regional hospital board in training, or

[1] Handicapped Pupils and Special Schools Regulations 1959, nos 15 and 16, as amended by the Qualified Teachers and Teachers in Special Schools Regulations 1971, no 3.

assisting a person training children classified under the Education Act 1944;

(*b*) a person who, by virtue of his qualifications and experience (or otherwise), the authority or, in the case of a non-maintained school, the managers or governors, are satisfied is competent to teach pupils requiring special educational treatment, provided no person authorized under any of the preceding categories is available.

Student teachers and instructors may be employed as in ordinary schools.

The following are the special requirements at present laid down by the Minister for teachers of blind, deaf or partially-hearing children:

(*a*) Teachers of these categories of children shall not teach in such schools for more than three years (without special permission of the Secretary of State in a particular case) without obtaining one of the following qualifications:

(i) *in schools for the blind* either the School Teacher's Diploma of the College of Teachers of the Blind, or the one-year course for teachers of the blind at the University of Birmingham;

(ii) *in schools for the deaf or partially-hearing* the Teacher's Diploma of the National College of Teachers of the Deaf or the one-year course for teachers of the deaf at the University of Birmingham;[1]

(iii) *in classes for those who are blind and deaf or partially-hearing* one of the examinations prescribed in the last subsection.

(*b*) These special requirements do not apply to those engaged solely in teaching crafts, domestic, or trade subjects, or to such other teachers as the Secretary of State may, in special circumstances, determine.

[1] The Schools Regulations 1959, no 20 (3) provide that teachers of classes of partially deaf children in ordinary schools must obtain their qualification *before* taking up employment, and are not allowed to teach for up to three years before qualifying, as are teachers in special schools.

Before 1971 some unqualified teachers worked in training centres for the mentally handicapped, but are now in special schools, having been transferred[1] or re-employed after a break in service. There are also unqualified persons, newly recruited because of their qualifications, experience or other qualities for work with pupils requiring special treatment. There is no separate category, under the Education Acts, of mentally handicapped (as distinct from educationally sub-normal) pupils; therefore it is not possible to restrict teaching by these persons to the mentally handicapped. It is suggested, however, that such teachers should work with sub-normal pupils as far as possible.[2]

10 Student teachers

A person who is eighteen years of age, and who holds one of the qualifications required for admission to an approved course of training,[3] or possesses some other qualification acceptable to the Secretary of State, may be appointed as a student teacher.[4] A student teacher is not counted against the teaching establishment of a school. He should intend to proceed to qualified teacher status, and should not be given the responsibilities of a class or subject teacher. Initial approval is for two years as a maximum. Extension is possible only for those who, having undertaken a course of approved training, have not completed their training satisfactorily, and is limited to the time needed for an opportunity to retrieve the failure.

11 Instructors

It sometimes occurs that no qualified teacher is available to teach some of the specialist skills which are now included in the school curriculum, e.g. playing musical instruments, office arts and skills, sports, games and pastimes, and technical skills, some of which may be vocational in character. It is now possible to appoint an instructor who is not a qualified teacher to undertake this work,

[1] Education (Handicapped Children) Act 1970.

[2] Circular 10/71, paragraph 33.

[3] Training of Teachers Regulations 1967, Schedule 2, II.

[4] Schools Regulations 1959, no 17, as amended by the Schools (Amendment) Regulations 1968, no 2 (a); see also Circular 15/68.

provided that no specialist teacher is available. An instructor may not be employed in a more general capacity.[1]

12 Health

Subject to the provisions of the Disabled Persons (Employment) Acts, a teacher must satisfy the Secretary of State of his health and physical capacity for teaching unless he has already done so for the purposes of the Teachers (Superannuation) Acts. This must be done at the outset of his first employment as a qualified or temporary assistant teacher.[2]

13 Professional register

The Education (Administrative Provisions) Act, 1907, established a Council representative of the teaching profession with the power to form and keep a register of qualified teachers. Registration was voluntary and subject to the payment of a life membership fee. At no time did the register contain the names of more than a small minority of teachers.

Before the passage of the 1944 Act the Board of Education had recognized only teachers in public elementary schools. From 1 April 1945, however, all teachers in maintained and assisted schools became subject to recognition by the ministry, and in 1948 the Royal Society of Teachers ceased to accept new members. It was incorporated in the Ministry of Education, the interests of existing members being safeguarded.

In 1969 the Secretary of State, at that time the Rt Hon. Edward Short, himself a former schoolmaster, set up a working party consisting of representatives of the local education authorities and the teachers' professional associations under the chairmanship of Mr J. R. Weaver[3] of the DES. The function of the committee was to formulate proposals for the formation of a council through which teachers in England and Wales could exercise a measure of professional self-government, and for

[1] Schools Regulations 1959, no 18, as amended by the Schools (Amendment) Regulations 1968, no 2 (*b*); see also Circular 15/68.
[2] Schools Regulations 1959, Schedule II, 1.
[3] Now Sir Toby Weaver.

national arrangements to advise the Secretary of State on the training and supply of teachers. The working party reported within seven months.

In brief, the report recommended the establishment of a council of forty members, of whom twenty-five would be appointed by the Secretary of State on the nomination of the teachers' professional associations, and fifteen appointed by the Secretary of State to represent the views of such bodies as the local authority associations, the universities and the public at large. The inclusion of the College of Preceptors, in view of its long association with efforts to enhance the status of the profession, was specifically mentioned.

The report suggested that the functions of the council would be the maintenance of a register of qualified teachers, the recommendation to the Secretary of State of standards of entry to the profession, the control of probation and the discipline of registered teachers.

The report was referred to the professional associations for comment. There was some adverse criticism, and some praise, but little has been heard of the scheme since a general election swept the Government which Mr Short represented from power.

14 Professional conduct

As there is at the moment no professional council to determine the standards of conduct expected of teachers in professional matters, some of the professional associations have drawn up codes specifying actions which have already been declared by them to be unprofessional, and have set up the necessary machinery for dealing with allegations that their code has been broken. The code applies, of course, only to members of the association concerned.

The code of the National Union of Teachers declares it to be unprofessional:

1. For any teacher to take an appointment from which, in the judgment of the NUT Executive, a member of the Union has been unjustly dismissed;

2. For any teacher[1] to make a report on the work or conduct of another teacher without at the time acquainting the teacher concerned with the nature of it, if it be a verbal report, or without showing it, if it be written, and allowing the teacher concerned to take a copy of it;[2]

3. In any case of dispute between members of the NUT settled by arbitrator under Rule 48 for any member not to abide by the decision;

4. For any teacher systematically to detain scholars in primary schools for extra tuition;

5. For any teacher to canvass for scholars either personally, by means of the school staff, by circular, or otherwise;

6. For any teacher systematically, and in his professional capacity, to instruct scholars on the school premises, before or after school hours, for the purpose of outside competitive examinations;

7. For any teacher to censure other teachers or to criticize their work in the hearing of the scholars;

8. For any teacher to seek to compel another teacher to perform outside the ordinary school hours any task which is not essentially connected with the ordinary work and organization of the school;

9. For any teacher to impose upon another teacher, out of the ordinary school hours, an excessive and unreasonable amount of work of any kind;

10. For any teacher to be found guilty of conduct detrimental or injurious to the interests and/or honour of the profession;

11. For any teacher to disregard any lawful instruction of the Union.

[1] Although the use of the word 'teacher' in the second Article of the code is primarily applicable to serving teachers and those actively and professionally engaged in education, the Professional Conduct Committee reserves the right to examine matters referred to it concerning members of the Union who are not so engaged.

[2] Where a teacher gives the name of another teacher or member as a referee, he takes, in accordance with normal practice, a risk as to the nature and contents of the reference which the referee may give. Accordingly, any reference so given is not regarded by the Executive as a report within the meaning of the above Article. See pages 407–10.

Members of the Union who are found guilty of a breach of professional honour may be warned, censured, fined, suspended or expelled.

Since the beginning of 1973 members of the Association of Teachers in Technical Institutions have not automatically and individually been members of the NUT. They may, however, join a local association of the Union, in which case they are bound by its code. Apart from this, the Association can take action against any member whose conduct has been detrimental to its interests.

The only other code is contained in a resolution of the Incorporated Association of Assistant Masters in Secondary Schools, whose council has declared the following acts to be injurious to the interests or objects of the Association:

1. for any member to take an appointment from which, in the judgment of the executive committee, a teacher has been unjustly dismissed;

2. for any member to take an appointment in any school where, in the opinion of the executive committee, the conditions or terms of service are unsatisfactory;

3. in the case of a dispute with an employer, for any member to refuse to act on a direction from the executive committee concerning his conduct towards that employer;

4. for any teacher to make a report on the work or conduct of another teacher without at the time acquainting the teacher concerned with the nature of it, if it be an oral report, or without showing it, if it be written, and allowing the teacher concerned to take a copy of it;[1]

5. for any teacher to censure or criticize another in the presence of pupils.

The executive committee of the Association has power to suspend any member guilty of conduct injurious to the interests or objects of the Association, subject to the member's right of appeal to the council.

[1] Unlike the NUT, the Assistant Masters Association extends this provision to references given in the course of seeking employment, whether the referee has been named by the candidate or not.

15 Aides

In 1967 the Plowden Committee on primary education recommended the employment of aides to undertake some of the routine work which is necessary to support the teaching itself.

The aides in primary schools correspond, in some degree, to the technicians used for many years in secondary school laboratories and workshops.

The professional associations are naturally concerned that ancillary staff shall not be used either to dilute the quality of the teaching profession, or to affect pupil teacher ratios adversely. In general it is felt that one aide could be shared by two infants', or four junior classes.

As distinct from welfare helpers, the aides work in the classroom situation under the control of a qualified teacher; but they do not assume control of the class as a teaching unit.

In delegating responsibilities to aides and helpers it is important that they should not be assigned duties which might be considered exclusively those of a professional teacher. Many teachers are concerned about their personal responsibility for accidents arising from the negligence of ancillary staff to whom they have delegated duties which involve the care of pupils. This responsibility is neither greater nor less than is involved in any delegation, and is considered in a later chapter.[1]

[1] See pages 269–71.

IV

CONDITIONS OF SERVICE

1 Types of appointment

Teachers may be appointed to full-time service in a number of ways:

(a) *to the staff of a school* – It is not normally possible to transfer teachers so appointed to the staff of another school without their consent.

(b) *to the service of an authority* – In such cases the teacher must be prepared to serve in any school and in any teaching capacity which the employing authority may determine. An example of this kind of appointment is the London divisional staff whose members may be used anywhere in the division to which they are appointed. In practice, however, they are normally left for considerable periods in one school.

(c) *to the authority's unattached staff* – These appointments are similar to those in the last category but the teachers concerned are really 'permanent supply' teachers and are used to fill vacancies caused through the absence of regular members of the staff of a school. Some authorities also maintain a small staff of unattached heads who can be used in a similar way during the absence of the permanent head of a school.[1]

In addition to full-time service, authorities may make appointments on a permanent part-time, terminal, or supply basis.

2 Appointment

Most vacancies are advertised in the educational press. The majority are for open competition and any suitably qualified

[1] See page 138.

teacher may apply. In some areas, however, certain promotion appointments are limited to a particular range of candidates.

Applications must usually be made on a form provided by the authority. When a form is not issued the particulars should be tabulated by applicants in such a way that they may be read easily.[1] The information given must be accurate since it will form the basis of the contract between the authority and the successful candidate. The suppression of material facts or the inclusion of information which is false within the candidate's knowledge may lead to the withdrawal of an offer, to dismissal if the appointment has been taken up, or even to prosecution.[2]

A teacher[3] appealed against her dismissal by an authority which claimed that her application had been false within her knowledge through wilful omissions and the suppression of material facts. In giving judgment for the Council, Mr Justice McCardie said that the authority was right in requiring high standards from its teachers because, otherwise, the children would suffer.

The DES requires a medical examination before a first appointment is taken up.[4] Some local authorities also require a medical check-up including, in some cases, a satisfactory chest X-ray examination when a serving teacher enters their service from the area of another authority or returns after a long absence.

Sometimes an appointing committee merely has the power to recommend an appointment to the local education authority, subject to a satisfactory medical report, and a candidate may be told that it will not be possible to confirm the offer for some weeks. It may be that this delay will mean that the candidate will have

[1] It should be superfluous to add that the writing should be legible, but every head has suffered much from badly written applications. Unless there is a specific instruction to the contrary, it is now generally accepted that applications may be typewritten. In such cases a brief covering letter may be enclosed in the candidate's own hand.

[2] The inclusion of false testimonials may lead to a prosecution under the Servant's Characters Act 1792. The whole question of testimonials and references is dealt with on pages 402–10.

[3] *Watts* v *London County Council* (1932), *The Times*, 9 December; LCT 95.

[4] See page 97.

to resign an existing appointment before the new one is confirmed, if he is to be free to join his new school when required. It is then reasonable to ask whether it is safe to resign. Usually it is, but there must always remain the risk that the appointment may not be confirmed.

In one case the managers of a school passed a resolution appointing a candidate. This fact was not officially communicated to the teacher but was casually mentioned to him by a manager. At a later meeting the resolution was rescinded and another candidate was appointed. The rejected candidate claimed damages for breach of contract[1] but the court held that, as the appointment had not been properly communicated, there was no concluded contract to break.

The first appointment of a qualified teacher in a maintained school is subject to probation.[2]

3 Conditions of tenure

Teachers will find that, if they move from one part of the country to another, their terms of service will be similar. The conditions of tenure at present in force were agreed in 1946 by a conference of the principal associations representing teachers and their employing authorities. They were up-dated in 1950, 1958, 1968 and 1972.

When the conditions were first considered there were considerable variations in practice: there were variations in the period of notice required by different authorities and in the incidence of holidays. This could lead to loss of salary in moving from one school to another, and the first major issue to be defined was contained in a recommendation that, for the purposes of notice and salary, the calendar year was to be regarded as consisting of three equal terms of four months. As a corollary teachers would be paid one-third of a year's salary for a third of a year's work.

The various provisions of the conditions of tenure are included at appropriate points throughout the relevant chapters.

[1] *Powell* v *Lee* (1908) 72 JP 353; LCT 68.
[2] See pages 592–4.

4 The agreement

When the appointment has been confirmed, the teacher will generally receive two copies of an agreement, one of which must be signed and returned to the authority. Alternatively, he may receive a notification of appointment under minute. A teacher must be furnished with a copy of the agreement or minute under which he is appointed, together with any regulations referred to therein, unless he is given an opportunity of acquainting himself with the rules in some other way.[1]

The candidate should read the agreement carefully before signing it, and be certain that he understands its terms since they form the contract between him and his employer. The principal points covered in an agreement are:

(*a*) Date of commencement of appointment;

(*b*) School (if applicable) and capacity in which the teacher is to be employed, whether as head or assistant, whether full- or part-time, and whether partly as a teacher and partly in some other capacity;

(*c*) Reference to the regulations under which the teacher is employed;

(*d*) Provision for termination of the agreement by either side on giving:

(i) two months' notice[2] terminating on 31 December or 30 April;[3]

(ii) three months'[2] notice terminating on 31 August;[4]

(*e*) Unless the teacher is employed partly as a teacher and partly in some other capacity (or in a boarding school), he may

[1] Schools Regulations 1959, Schedule II. 3.

[2] For heads the period of notice is one month longer than for assistants.

[3] When the teacher's resignation is to take effect in April there is normally a provision that, if his new school begins the summer term before 1 May, the teacher will be released from such earlier date.

[4] In accordance with the agreed national conditions of tenure most local education authorities include a clause providing for automatic retirement at the end of the term in which the teacher attains the age of sixty-five. Service may be extended beyond this age by mutual agreement between the teacher and the local authority and, during such an extension, all other terms of the agreement will remain in force.

not be required to perform any duties except such as are connected with the work of a school; nor may he be required to
abstain, outside school hours, from any occupations which do
not interfere with the due performance of his duties;[1]

(*f*) Reference to the salary scales and the frequency of payment of salary;

(*g*) Provision for the suspension and dismissal of the teacher;

(*h*) In the case of a reserved teacher[2] in a controlled or special
agreement school, a reference to this fact and the requirements
contingent upon it.

Full-time permanent teachers in voluntary-aided schools are
appointed by the managers or governors and the agreement is
therefore made with them and not with the local education authority which maintains the school. The rules of management or
articles of government normally provide that such appointments
are subject to the consent of the authority.

Occasionally an authority issues revised agreements in respect
of all its teachers. This is done to bring existing teachers into line
with new terms of service which have been agreed nationally
between the local education authorities and the professional
associations. Refusal to sign could be followed by dismissal which
might, though not necessarily, be accompanied by an offer to
re-appoint in accordance with the new terms. Teachers should
not sign substituted agreements unless advised to do so by their
professional associations.

5 Contracts of Employment Act 1972
Under the Contracts of Employment Act, every employer is required to give to each of his employees a statement of certain
terms of the contract, and this must be provided within thirteen
weeks of the commencement of employment.[3] The statement
may, for all or some of the required particulars, refer to a document which the employee has reasonable opportunities to read.

[1] This clause *must* be included, in compliance with the Schools Regulations 1959, Schedule II. 3 (c).

[2] For a definition of the term 'reserved teacher', see page 110.

[3] Contracts of Employment Act 1972, s. 4 (1).

A statement is not required in connection with service for less than twenty-one hours weekly.

Some authorities and voluntary school bodies incorporate the information in their agreements or letters of appointment, others issue a separate document. When the latter is done, it must be remembered that this by itself is no more than the statement required by the Act, and is not a contract.

Information relating to pensions need not be given in respect of a statutory scheme such as that provided by the Teachers Superannuation Act, and, if there is no information to be given under any other head, this fact should be stated. Reference to specific schemes and documents such as the Burnham salary scales, the authority's staff code and so forth is sufficient.

The statement must include the date of commencement of employment and, if it is for a fixed term, the date of expiry.

6 Married women

The 1944 Act removed the disqualification which was at one time imposed on married women as full-time teachers. No woman may now be disqualified or dismissed from appointment by reason only of marriage.[2]

7 Race Relations Act 1968

It is illegal for an employer, or any person concerned with the employment of others to discriminate[3] against any other person by refusing or omitting to employ him on any available work for which he is qualified; by not offering work on the same terms and conditions as it is offered to others; or by dismissing that person in circumstances when others would not be dismissed.[4]

It is also unlawful for a trade union or an employers' or trade association to discriminate against a person by refusal of member-

[1] Contracts of Employment Act 1972, s. 6.

[2] Education Act 1944, s. 24 (3).

[3] For this purpose 'to discriminate' means to treat a person less favourably than others on the ground of colour, race, or ethnic or national origins – Race Relations Act 1968, s. 1.

[4] Race Relations Act 1968, s. 3.

ship or the benefits of membership on the same terms as are accorded to others.[1]

It is also contrary to the Act to publish any advertisement which is, or appears to intend, an act of discrimination. It is possible, however, to advertise appointments for Commonwealth citizens, or any class of such citizens, outside Great Britain; or for non-Commonwealth citizens in Great Britain.[2]

There are certain exceptions. Section 3 of the Act does not apply to employers of not more than ten persons in addition to those employed in his private household: this exception could not apply to a local education authority, but it might in the case of a very small voluntary-aided primary school where the whole staff, including the non-teaching staff, does not exceed ten.

Also excepted is the employer who is attempting, in good faith, to preserve a reasonable balance of persons of different racial groups. What is a reasonable balance is a matter of fact in each case, and for this purpose persons wholly or mainly educated in Great Britain are treated as belonging to the same racial group.

It is also permissible to select a person of a particular nationality or descent if the employment requires attributes possessed particularly by persons of that group.[3]

The Race Relations Acts do not seek to place anyone in a privileged position, and it is unfortunate that situations sometimes arise where an employer feels inhibited because, when acting from perfectly proper motives, he is told that the issue will be treated as a matter for complaint under this legislation. In simple terms, the test to be applied is: 'In the same situation would I treat a person of the same colour as myself, or who is of the same race, or ethnic or national origin, as myself in precisely the same way?'

The Queen's Bench Divisional Court has held that, within the circumstances of the case before it, there had been no discrimination at Walbrook College, London, in connection with promotion. Mr Selvarajan, who had been a Grade I lecturer at the college for

---

[1] Race Relations Act 1968, s. 4.
[2] Race Relations Act 1968, s. 6.
[3] Race Relations Act 1968, s. 8 (1) (*a*), (2), (3) (4) and (11).

at least ten years, applied for promotion to a Grade II vacancy. It was unusual for a lecturer at that college to remain on Grade I for so long a period and the candidate suspected discrimination when he was not successful. The Race Relations Board rejected his complaint, as did the divisional court.[1]

8 Condition of premises

The Offices, Shops and Railway Premises Act 1963, which lays down standards for accommodation, lighting, sanitary provision and so forth, does not apply to the teaching rooms in schools nor to pupils' lavatories and toilets. It does apply, however, to the administrative parts of the school building.[2]

9 Indemnity against assault

The national conditions of tenure recommend local education authorities to indemnify members of their teaching staff or, in the event of death, their dependants, against financial loss caused by violence or criminal assault in the course of, or as a consequence of, their employment.

In the event of death within twelve months of the assault the recommended figure is £200 if the employee has no dependants. If, however, he has one or more dependants the suggested sum is two years' salary subject to a ceiling of £7,500.

For total disablement preventing continuation in employment as a teacher the compensation recommended is the equivalent of the gross weekly remuneration at the time of the assault for each week until the teacher reaches the age of sixty-five, less any compensation received; National Insurance benefits; sick pay, pension or gratuity from the employing authority; and any earnings in other employment. This is subject to a maximum of £2,000 in any year, and a time limit of ten years.

10 Crimes of violence

If a teacher is absent because of injuries for which he may make a claim to the Criminal Injuries Compensation Board, and is

---

[1] *R* v *Race Relations Board* ex parte *Selvarajan* (1974) *The Times*, 12 February.
[2] See also page 131.

qualified to receive sick pay, it is recommended in the national conditions of tenure that such sick pay should be granted without any requirement of a refund of any part of this in the event of an award by the Board.

If an award has been made, it is recommended that the authority should be at liberty to discount all or part of the sick leave, as may seem fit, in calculating the teacher's entitlement to such leave.

11 Personal property

Local education authorities are asked, in the national conditions of tenure, to consider sympathetically loss of, or damage to, a teacher's personal property when such losses are suffered during duty at school or whilst taking part in out-of-school activities, and there has been no negligence on the teacher's part.

It is recognized that the authority may have no legal liability in this matter, but some take out insurance against such contingencies whilst others make an *ex gratia* payment.

The code does not suggest full compensation, and teachers would be well advised to cover any valuable property they may have in school by private insurance. In some cases membership of a professional association carries a limited degree of indemnity. Insurance companies, however, are reasonably careful in dealing with such claims, and frequently reject those where there is an element of negligence on the owner's part. It is therefore important to take all reasonable care of personal belongings in school.

12 Reserved teachers

In controlled and, normally, in special agreement schools a certain proportion of the staff must be appointed as reserved teachers. These are persons specially selected for their fitness to give religious instruction according to the tenets of the providing body.[1]

In controlled schools reserved teachers must form not more than one-fifth of the total teaching staff; when the establishment

[1] Education Act 1944, s. 27 (2) to (5) and s. 28 (3) and (4).

is not a multiple of five it is, for this purpose, treated as though it were the next highest multiple. The head is not a reserved teacher, but is included in the staff for the purpose of calculating the number of reserved teachers.

In special agreement schools, the agreement will state whether reserved teachers are to be appointed, and will specify the proportion of the staff to be reserved. Seventy-five per cent is a usual figure.

Although the local education authority appoints the whole teaching staff of such schools, the foundation managers or governors must be consulted before a reserved teacher is appointed. The foundation managers or governors may also require the local education authority to dismiss a teacher from being a reserved teacher in their school on the grounds that he is not competent to give the religious instruction for which he was appointed. This does not, however, preclude the authority from appointing the same person as a non-reserved teacher in the same school.

13 Corruption in office

If an officer of a local authority, under colour of his employment, exacts or receives any fee or reward whatsoever other than his proper remuneration, he is liable on summary conviction to a fine not exceeding £200.[1]

14 Pecuniary interest

If an officer of a local authority knows of a contract in which he has any pecuniary interest, whether direct or indirect, which has been (or is proposed to be) entered into by the authority, or any of its committees in office, he must, as soon as practicable, give notice of his interest to the authority in writing. The penalty for failing to do so is a fine not exceeding £200.[1]

15 Membership of public bodies

A paid officer of a local authority who is employed in an office to which appointment is, or may be, made or confirmed by that

[1] Local Government Act 1972, s. 117.

authority, or any of its committees or sub-committees, or by a joint board on which it is represented, or by any person who is himself employed by the authority, is disqualified from being elected, or being a member of that authority.[1] Neither may a person be appointed to the service of any authority whilst he is a member of that authority, nor for twelve months afterwards.[2]

The only exceptions are a paid chairman, vice-chairman or deputy chairman of the authority.

Teachers in schools maintained, but not established, by the authority (i.e. voluntary schools) are subject to the same disqualification.[3]

A teacher employed by a county authority may be a member of a district council, even though that council nominates members of the county education committee. Similarly, a teacher employed by a metropolitan district council may be a member of the county council, even though the county council nominates members of the district education committee.[4]

The special exception provided for teachers in Greater London by Schedule 4 (10) of the London Government Act 1963 was repealed by the Local Government Act 1972.

16 Religious opinions

No teacher may be disqualified or dismissed from appointment, receive less emolument or be deprived of promotion, purely on the grounds of holding any particular religious opinions, or because he attends (or fails to attend) any particular place of worship.[5]

This does not apply to the staffs of aided schools; nor to reserved teachers in controlled and special agreement schools who are selected for their fitness to give denominational instruction.

In spite of this clause it is still not unknown for teachers to be

[1] Local Government Act 1972, s. 80 (1) (a).
[2] Local Government Act 1972, s. 116.
[3] Local Government Act 1972, s. 80 (3).
[4] Local Government Act 1972, s. 81 (4).
[5] Education Act 1944, s. 30.

asked questions of this character at an interview. Whatever the candidate says, he is at a disadvantage. The safest course is to reply that the question is highly personal and, therefore, irrelevant. Strictly speaking, the managers or governors of a county school have no right to question a candidate on his religious beliefs, even when he has applied for appointment as a scripture specialist.

17 Accidents to teaching staff

In English law the relationship between master and servant does not involve a guarantee that the former will never expose his employees to danger or risk. In accepting employment the servant willingly undertakes the risks ordinarily involved in the work, and the employer is not required to indemnify him against these.

Even where negligence is proved, there is no case against the employer if the servant continues in a place where he is aware of danger. In one case a man continued to work for a railway company for a fortnight after he learned that there was danger due to the negligence of the employer. His action failed.[1]

In any case, the duties of a teacher are not always very clearly defined: he is expected to do whatever he considers to be necessary for the welfare of the pupils, and this will involve many things besides teaching. Indeed, the risk of accident is often greater outside the normal work of the classroom. It is possible, for a small premium, to insure against injury and the teacher may well consider it wise to make this provision.

By the doctrine of common employment, it was once held that an employer was not liable for injury to an employee through the negligence of a fellow servant, unless he had retained the servant in his employ knowing him to be incompetent. Under the Law Reform (Personal Injuries) Act 1948, this defence has now been abolished, and all contracts or agreements are void in so far as they exclude or limit the liability of an employer by the doctrine of common employment. This applies not only to new contracts or agreements, but also to those made before the passage of the Act.

The employer's duty is not clearly defined, but he is bound to

[1] *Woodley* v *Metropolitan District Railway Co.* (1877) 2 Ex. D. 384.

use reasonable care to provide safe premises and appliances. The common law right to compensation requires proof of negligence, or continuation in common employment after proof of incompetence.

In county, controlled and special agreement schools, the local education authority is the employer of the teacher. In aided schools the teachers are appointed by the managers or governors and there is no privity of employment between the teacher and the authority. Teachers in an aided school have, therefore, no claim against the authority as employer since there is no relationship as between master and servant. The authority may, however, be liable in respect of failure to carry out repairs for which it is responsible or for dangerous apparatus which it has installed. An employer is not liable if the defective nature of the apparatus is due to the negligence of a servant.

It is probable that the success of an action would not be prejudiced by the fact that the teacher was performing a voluntary duty at the time of an accident.

18 The grievance procedure

By section 4 (2) (b) of the Contracts of Employment Act every employee must be given a note specifying, by description or otherwise, a person to whom he can apply to seek redress of any grievance, and the manner in which he should apply. The note should indicate what steps will follow such an application or, alternatively, it should state where such information is reasonably accessible to the employee in documentary form. Discussions between, substantially, the same bodies which drew up the recommended conditions of tenure have resulted in a standard form of grievance procedure which, with small local variations, is likely to be applied throughout the country.[1]

The procedure is designed to deal with the grievances of individual teachers, and does not apply to collective disputes. It recognizes that grievances may arise between assistant teachers, or between assistants and the head; that they may be simple or fundamental; and that they may involve the managers or governors

[1] See page 75.

and the local education authority. The scheme sets out an informal procedure which would not involve recourse to any subsequent stage, and a formal procedure for use when the simpler form has failed. Modified procedures are outlined for heads, and a note sets out the matters which need to be taken into account in dealing with grievances in voluntary schools.

Assistants: informal procedure – If an assistant's grievance is against his managers, governors or local education authority, he should (without involving any other member of the staff) approach the chief education officer or the managers or governors, as may be appropriate. If his grievance involves other members of the staff, he may resolve the matter by direct approach to that person, or by discussion with the head of department concerned, some other senior colleague or the head. If a request for a discussion with one of these senior staff is received, a personal interview should be granted within five days. The senior colleague should try to resolve the matter personally, or by mutual agreement, in consultation with other members of the staff. If the head is asked to intervene he may, with mutual agreement, consult the chairman of the managers or governors, officers of the local education authority or representatives of the appropriate professional associations.

Assistants: formal procedure – If informal discussions fail, the person aggrieved should submit a formal notice of grievance to the head and the other teacher concerned. The head should make a formal written report to the managers or governors, and send a copy to the chief education officer. The managers or governors, in consultation with the chief education officer (if appropriate) should, with all relevant documents available, seek to settle the issue. If they wish, the parties should have an opportunity to make submissions, each being accompanied (if desired) by a friend or official representative of his professional association. This meeting should take place within ten days.

Assistants: appellate procedure – The appellate procedure should be settled between the local education authority and the professional associations. All relevant documents should be submitted to the appellate body, which should then meet within ten days. Submissions and the presence of 'friends' should be permitted as at the original hearing.

Heads: informal procedure – A head who has a grievance should try to settle it with the person concerned and, if this fails, he should discuss the matter with an advisory or administrative member of the local education authority's staff. If the problem cannot be settled in this way, the head should discuss it with the chief education officer (or his representative) who may, by mutual agreement, consult the chairman of the managers or governors or representatives of any professional association concerned.

Heads: formal procedure – If the informal procedure is unsuccessful, the head should submit a formal written notice of the grievance to the managers or governors and/or to the chief education officer. The managers or governors, if the grievance lies against them, should arrange a meeting within ten days, at which the parties may make submissions and be accompanied by 'friends'. If the grievance lies against the local education authority, the chief education officer should refer it to the authority's appropriate committee, whether or not the head has sought the support of the managers or governors. The committee should meet within ten days, the parties being given an opportunity to make submissions and to be accompanied by 'friends'.

Heads: appellate procedure – This is the same as for assistants.

Application to voluntary schools – Subsequent discussions with the Church of England and Roman Catholic educational bodies produced agreement on a number of points which take account of the fact that teachers in voluntary-aided schools are the employees of the managers or governors, but that many of their conditions of employment stem from the local education authority. The modifications might also be helpful in dealing with grievances in other voluntary-aided schools, e.g. those established by City livery companies. The question of applying the modifications to controlled or special agreement schools depends on the rules of management or articles of government.

Any procedures adopted must not conflict with the rules of management or articles of government. The appropriate voluntary school authorities should be concerned in the establishment of any appellate body. In making an informal approach, heads should, unless it is inappropriate, consult the chairman of the managers or governors, rather than the chief education officer. Similarly, in moving to the next informal stage, a head should discuss the matter with his chairman before going to the chief education officer. The head of a voluntary school should normally submit a written grievance to his managers or governors; if circumstances make this inappropriate, he must send them a copy of any written notice of grievance he sends to the chief education officer. Similarly, if the grievance lies against the authority, the head should report the matter to the chief education officer, and inform his chairman. There is no procedure for submitting a complaint against the managers or governors to the authority.

For the purpose of the grievance procedure, a teacher in a voluntary-aided school is regarded as an employee of the local education authority.[1]

19 Resignation

Notice of resignation should be served on the employer[2] in accordance with the terms of the agreement. Sometimes an employer will release a teacher if notice is not given by the specified date, but it should be remembered that this is an act of grace and not of right.

20 Suspension of teachers

The terms under which teachers may be suspended are contained in the rules of management or articles of government, and are usually set out fully in the agreement, if one is concluded.[3]

A teacher has the right to be present, accompanied by a 'friend' if he so desires, at any meeting of managers, governors or the local education authority at which his suspension or dismissal is considered. He must be given seven days' clear notice of such meet-

[1] Trade Union and Labour Relations Act 1974, Schedule 1.27.
[2] The managers or governors in aided schools; the local education authority in others.
[3] In the case of teachers appointed under a minute, the letter of appointment will refer to the appropriate staff code where these conditions are set out.

ings. In the case of dismissal following suspension, for misconduct or other urgent cause, the teacher is not entitled to the usual notice and salary is stopped from the date of suspension.

Where, following suspension, a teacher is reinstated, arrears of salary accruing from the date of suspension to the date of reinstatement will normally be paid to the teacher. The conditions of tenure recommend, however, that payment of full salary during suspension should be regarded as the normal procedure from which departures should be made only when the employing authority decides that there is a compelling reason for so doing.

21 Dismissal

A teacher may be dismissed on the usual notice being given at any time. For misconduct or other urgent cause he may be dismissed on the terms laid down or referred to in his agreement.

In principle, a dismissal may be challenged generally only on the grounds that it is *ultra vires* or in bad faith. Lord Sumner stated that 'where discretion is given to a local authority, it is for the authority to exercise it, provided that it is not *ultra vires*, nor its power exercised corruptly or *mala fide*. When the exercise of a discretion is challenged it is for the plaintiff to prove a duty in the courts to interfere.'[1]

A headmaster was given notice of dismissal by a local education authority following an action against him for excessive corporal punishment.[2] The magistrates had held that the punishment was excessive, although there had been great provocation, and the headmaster was bound over under the Probation of Offenders Act. His appeal to Quarter Sessions was allowed with costs. His case against the Council was that, in view of the successful appeal, the dismissal was invalid and inoperative, and he sought an injunction against the Council to prevent them from acting on the notice. He also asked for costs. The Corporation maintained that the dismissal was a valid and effective exercise of discretion and that there was no liability for restraint or damages.

[1] *Roberts* v *Hopwood* [1925] AC 578.
[2] *Gill* v *Leyton Corporation* (1933) *Education*, 14 April; LCT 103.

Giving judgment for the Corporation, Mr Justice Clauson said that the education committee had considered whether the educational machine would not function more satisfactorily without the plaintiff. There was a difference of opinion, which went against the headmaster. There had been no suggestion of corruption and he could see no evidence of bad faith.

It will be seen from this that a breach of the local education authority's discipline, which has not involved breaking the law, may be a valid ground for dismissal.

In recent years there has been a tendency on the part of those appealing to the courts against dismissal to claim that their employers have acted 'contrary to the principles of natural justice'. These principles are not formulated in any code but are a compound of common sense and the basic principles of the common law. In ordinary speech we call them 'fair play'.

Hannam v *Bradford Corporation* – A master in a voluntary school was dismissed by his governors, and the local education authority decided not to exercise its statutory power to prohibit the dismissal.[1] This decision was taken by the authority's staff sub-committee, three members of which at the meeting were governors of the school, but they had not attended the governors' meeting. In the county court the authority's decision was condemned, but the Court of Appeal found otherwise. Lord Justice Sachs said: 'It is not conceivable that any properly constituted sub-committee of the authority could have decided to prohibit the dismissal.' Lord Justice Cross added: 'The question is not whether the tribunal will in fact be biased, but whether a reasonable man with no inside knowledge might well think it might be biased.' The court held that the plaintiff's right to be heard did not stem from his contract, but from the articles of government; consequently he could not bring an action for breach of contract against the authority.[2]

Malloch v *Aberdeen Corporation* – An important Scottish case reached the House of Lords in 1971, when one of thirty-seven teachers who had been dismissed for refusing to register with the

[1] Education Act 1944, s. 24 (2) (*a*)
[2] *Hannam* v *Bradford Corporation* (1970) 68 LGR 498.

Scottish Teachers Council won a majority decision. The plaintiff had not been present at the meeting which decided to dismiss him; and Lord Reid thought that, had he been, there was a substantial possibility that 'he might have influenced enough of the members to prevent a two-thirds majority from voting for his dismissal. . . . If an employer failed to take the preliminary steps which the law regarded as essential, he had no power to dismiss, and any purported dismissal was a nullity.'[1]

Gorse v *Durham County Council* – In 1967, before the withdrawal of the regulations which made supervision of school meals mandatory,[2] over 400 teachers in Easington refused to carry out this duty. They were told that they had repudiated their contracts, and were excluded from their schools until they agreed to carry out all duties. Four days later they returned, but the authority refused to pay their salaries for the period of suspension. The court held that the teachers had refused a lawful order, that their conduct amounted to a repudiation of their contracts, and it was open to the authority to act if they wished – either by treating the contracts as at an end, or by regarding them as continuing and taking some action in respect of the breach. 'The truth is that neither side intended any final rupture in the relations.' Four points emerged:

(a) that in tenure cases local education authorities must act strictly in accord with the contracts they have made;

(b) that if a teacher refuses a legal and reasonable requirement, it is open to the authority to treat the contract as at an end;

(c) that it is equally open to the authority to treat the contract as continuing, and to take action in respect of the breach;

(d) that if the authority choose the latter alternative, they are still bound by the terms of the contract, and cannot plead the original repudiation by the teacher as an excuse for a further breach by the authority.[3]

It is, of course, also possible for a teacher to claim before an

---

[1] *Malloch* v *Aberdeen Corporation* [1971] 2 All ER 1278.
[2] See pages 370–74.
[3] *Gorse* v *Durham County Council* (1971) 69 LGR 452.

industrial tribunal that he has been unfairly dismissed and that his employer is therefore guilty of an 'unfair industrial practice'.[1] In such cases the burden of proof on the employer to justify the dismissal under Schedule 1.6 requires acceptable evidence that the dismissal was related to the capability or qualifications of the employee to perform the work he was required to do, to the conduct of the employee, to redundancy, or to the fact that it would be contrary to statute to continue the employment. 'Capability' in this context is assessed by reference to skill, aptitude, health or any other physical or mental quality, and 'qualifications' include any relevant degree, diploma or other academic, technical or professional qualifications.

Weddell v *Newcastle-upon-Tyne Corporation* – The pattern is still to be set, but an industrial tribunal has decided that it was not an unfair industrial practice to dismiss a teacher with fourteen years' experience who had become increasingly desperate because of his inability to control a class or to get to school on time, and whose pupils were lounging about, laughing, talking and listening to the Derby on a radio set. The chairman said: 'We are not satisfied that Mr Weddell was a bad teacher, but there were ample grounds for dismissal for unpunctuality. Also, his powers of discipline in a pretty tough class were well below average.'[2]

Newbigin v. *Lancashire County Council* – It was also not an unfair industrial practice to dismiss the head of a remedial department who believed that it was her responsibility to encourage children to find out about life by acting among themselves. The headmaster had found a thirteen-year-old girl lying flat on her back across two desks, whilst a boy lay on top of her simulating sexual intercourse. One of the bystanders, a girl, was screaming. It was also complained that the teacher allowed boys to touch her breasts and permitted them to put their hands up girls' skirts.[3]

Summary dismissal may take place for wilful disobedience of a

[1] Trade Union and Labour Relations Act 1974, Schedule 1.4.

[2] *Weddell* v *Newcastle-upon-Tyne Corporation* (1973), *Daily Telegraph*, 8 November.

[3] *Newbigin* v *Lancashire County Council* (1973) *Daily Mail*, 14 November.

lawful order, misconduct, incompetence, permanent disability or gross moral misbehaviour which is inconsistent with the fulfilment of the conditions of service. A member of a university staff took a student into a dark lecture room where he put his arm round her and kissed her. He was dismissed by the university authorities and subsequently brought an action against them.[1] Judgment, with costs, was given for the university.

In aided schools, where the managers or governors are the employers, there is a clause in the rules of management or the articles of government requiring them to dismiss teachers when directed to do so by the local education authority, and prohibiting the dismissal of teachers without the consent of the authority except in any cases where the managers or governors are expressly given this power.[2] If the managers or governors of an aided school dismiss a teacher on the instructions of the authority, any complaint of unfair dismissal, and any remedy, will lie against the local education authority.[3]

22 Redundancy payments

Employers are required to make lump sum payments to men under sixty-five and women under sixty who are dismissed because of redundancy. The amount of the payment is related to the employee's age, pay, and length of service with the employer. The test of redundancy is that the employer needs fewer people to do work of a particular kind.

Liability to the payment is excluded if the employee is dismissed either with normal, shorter or no notice, in circumstances which would justify dismissal without notice, i.e. in cases of grave misconduct. It is also avoided if, before the notice takes effect, the employer in writing offers re-engagement without a break in service of more than four weeks. The employment offered must be suitable in relation to the employee, and liability to make the redundancy payment is only avoided if the offer is accepted or refused unreasonably.

[1] *Jones* v *University of London* (1922) *Times*, 22 March.
[2] Education Act 1944, s.24.
[3] Trade Union and Labour Relations Act 1974, Schedule 1.27.

The detailed provisions of the scheme are complex, and readers who are interested, should study the relevant legislation and official guide.[1]

Taylor v *Kent County Council* – In 1968 the Kent County Council decided to amalgamate a boys' secondary school with a similar school for girls. The appointment of the headmaster, who had held office for ten years, was terminated. The local education authority wrote to him, stating that his salary had been safeguarded; and that, as he had refused a post (which was not offered in writing) in the new school, he was offered a post in the mobile pool of teachers. This meant he might be required to serve in any capacity in such schools as the authority might require, but probably in a different part of the county from that where he was actually living.

The industrial tribunal rejected the headmaster's application for a redundancy payment, basing their decision on his age, qualifications, experience, loss of status, the safeguarding of his salary and his 'unfortunate showing at the interview'. 'The fact that the offer made was less suitable does not necessarily make it unsuitable.'

The Queen's Bench Division allowed the headmaster's appeal. The Lord Chief Justice, Lord Parker, said:

'Suitability is almost entirely a matter of degree and fact for the tribunal, and not a matter with which this court would wish to or could, interfere, unless it was plain that they had misdirected themselves in some way in law, or had taken into consideration matters which were not relevant for the purpose. It is to be observed that so far as age was concerned, so far as experience was concerned, they negative the suitability of this offer, because the appellant is going to be put into a position where he had to go where he is told at any time for short periods, to any place, and be put under a headmaster and assigned duties by him.

'The only matter which can be put against that as making this offer suitable is the guarantee of salary. One would think, speaking for myself, that a headmaster of this experience would think an offer which, while guaranteeing him the same salary, reduced his status, was quite unsuitable. To go to quite a different sphere of activity, a director under a service agreement is offered on dismissal a job as a navvy, and it is said: but we will guarantee you the same salary as you have been getting. I should have thought such a salary was plainly unsuitable.

'Here one wonders whether one of the matters which affected the tribunal was this reference to the words "Not forgetting the unfortunate showing at the interview". That is a reference to when he was interviewed, not by the respondents, but by the governors of the school with a view to taking on the headmastership of the new school. One really wonders what the relevance of that was unless it be that the tribunal felt from what they had heard that he was not up to a headmastership at all. But at once one says to oneself: if that was in their minds, it was not evidence on which they could properly act, having regard to the fact that the appellant had given satisfaction for some ten years, and if he was not up to his job he could have been dismissed for that reason, and no question of redundancy would have arisen.'

Mr Justice Melford Stevenson and Mr Justice Willis agreed.[1]

23 Withdrawal of recognition

If a teacher's appointment is terminated for grave professional default, misconduct or conviction of a criminal offence, the facts must be reported to the Secretary of State. It is immaterial whether the teacher has resigned or been dismissed.[2]

If the Secretary of State, after giving the teacher every chance of refuting the charges, declares him to be unsuitable for employment as a teacher on grounds of grave professional default, or misconduct, he shall not be so employed. This prohibition also

[1] *Taylor* v *Kent County Council* [1969] 2 All ER 1080; LCT 398.
[2] Schools Regulations 1959, Schedule II, 4.

extends to those similarly disqualified by the President of the Board of Education before 1 April 1945.[1]

If the Secretary of State determines that a teacher shall be employed to a limited extent only, he may be employed only to that extent.[1]

After giving the teacher every chance of making representations the Secretary of State may, on educational or medical grounds, require that the employment of a teacher be terminated or made subject to such conditions or qualifications as he may impose.[2]

In an answer in the House of Commons,[3] the Under Secretary of State said that decisions on withdrawal of recognition are taken personally by the Secretary of State, and, also, that about eighteen teachers are reinstated each year. The number of those who again fall from grace does not exceed one a year:

> The concern of successive Secretaries of State has been to regard the safety of the children as the paramount consideration but, subject to that, to temper justice with mercy and, in particular, to avoid either vindictiveness or undue moral rigidity. It seems to me to be an essential part of the reinstatement procedure that no black mark should be permanently made against a reinstated teacher in any departmental record made available to employing authorities.

24 Part-time teachers

The conditions of tenure suggest that when teachers are appointed on a part-time basis, their appointments being in all other repects comparable to those of their full-time colleagues, their tenure should be on a comparable basis:

(a) Letters or contracts of appointment, setting out the detailed terms, should be supplied before the teacher takes up service;

(b) The periods of notice should be the same as for full-time teachers;

[1] Schools Regulations 1959, Schedule II. 5.
[2] Schools Regulations 1959, Schedule II. 6.
[3] *Hansard*, 13 April 1970.

(*c*) The general conditions should be as for full-time teachers, including the right to a hearing in case of termination otherwise than for redundancy. If particular hardship is claimed in a case of redundancy, the teacher should be able to make representations to the local education authority.

25 Car mileage

It is recommended in the conditions of tenure that when teachers use their cars, at the request of the head, to facilitate official duties, the employing authority should pay a mileage allowance to cover running costs, depreciation and insurance on a scale to be negotiated between the professional associations and the individual local education authorities. In fixing the scale the current local casual user rate should be taken into account.

26 Industrial action

In common with all other employees, teachers have the right to belong to a trade union, to seek and hold office in it, and to take part in its activities. Subject to certain limitations they may not be excluded or expelled from such membership by way of arbitrary discrimination.[1] They may, however, terminate their membership on giving reasonable notice.[2]

The position of teachers' professional associations with regard to membership of the TUC and registration under the Act is indicated in Appendix I.

Strikes and other practices such as 'working to rule' are relatively infrequent in the teaching profession, but there has been a tendency for them to increase in number recently. Working to rule is, in any case, a difficult procedure to define in a vocation which has no rule book; the general interpretation is a refusal to take part in out-of-school activities, most of which are, in any case, voluntary.

There have been several instances where teachers belonging to some of the professional associations have withdrawn their services for a day or half a day during the past few years. The In-

[1] Trade Union and Labour Relations Act 1974, s. 5.
[2] Trade Union and Labour Relations Act 1974, s. 7.

dustrial Court which excluded the jurisdiction of the High Court over such matters under the Industrial Relations Act 1971, has now been abolished.[1] So have the provisions which made it an offence for anyone (other than a registered trade union or one of its officials) to induce another person to break a contract. No court can now compel an employee to do any work, or to attend at any place of work.[2]

27 The European Economic Community

It is a basic principle of the Common Market that there should be complete freedom for firms, branches, agencies and individuals, belonging to any of the member states, to set up in business or practice anywhere within the EEC.[3]

This provision is intended to apply to members of the professions, as well as to those engaged in business. At present, little progress has been made, however, because of the wide variations in training, qualifications and practice in the member states. Shortage of staff is said to be one reason for the delay, but there are many problems concerned with the recognition by the member states of each other's qualification equivalents.

28 Independent schools

Lying outside the maintained and direct grant sector, the independent schools are largely free to devise their own conditions of service. The terms of notice may be different, the conditions of tenure do not apply, and the avenues of promotion are not the same. Some adhere to the Burnham Scale for the payment of salaries, some pay more, others less. In many boarding schools a lower salary is paid, but the staff enjoy residential emoluments.

There is a growing concern on the part of the Government to regulate certain aspects of the relationships between employers and those who work for them; where this has been done, the

[1] Trade Union and Labour Relations Act 1974, s. 1(3).
[2] Trade Union and Labour Relations Act 1974, s. 16.
[3] Treaty of Rome (25 March 1957), Articles 52 to 58; Treaty of Accession (January 1972).

statutory provisions apply with equal force in independent schools. The provision of a statement complying with the requirements of the Contracts of Employment Act 1972, the right to belong to a union or an organization of workers under the Industrial Relations Act 1971, and the entitlement to a redundancy payment in appropriate circumstances under the Redundancy Payments Act 1965, apply to independent schools with the same force as to maintained establishments.

29 Secondment for service overseas

British Commonwealth – The Commonwealth Education Conference which was held at Oxford in 1959 drew attention to the desperate shortage of teachers in the less developed parts of the Commonwealth. Following this, the Government agreed to stimulate recruitment for periods of teaching service overseas.

Teachers intending to participate in this scheme may apply for secondment by their local education authority or governing body for a period of one year. Provision has been made for teachers to be reinstated as far as possible in posts as nearly equivalent to their appointments on secondment.

Teachers taking part in the scheme should be between the ages of twenty-five and forty-five, with at least five years' experience of which at least two years should have been with their current local education authority. Teachers are required to sign an undertaking to return to service with the same employing authority in the United Kingdom.

The scheme is administered for the DES and overseas education authorities by the League for the Exchange of Commonwealth Teachers.[1] The League also operates on behalf of the education authorities for Scotland and Northern Ireland.

Europe and the United States of America – The European scheme is intended mainly for teachers of modern languages. Post-to-post exchanges, usually for a term but occasionally for a year, are available with Austria, France, Germany and Spain. There are also arrangements which permit the unilateral exchange of

[1] Ord Marshall House, 124 Belgrave Road, London, SW1V 2BL.

teachers: in such cases teachers are paid by the authorities in the host country, and teachers should write to the pensions branch of the DES to make arrangements to safeguard their pension rights.[1] The unilateral exchanges are usually of one year's duration and involve the teaching of English as a foreign language. The participating continental countries are Austria, Denmark and the Federal Republic of Germany.

Exchanges with the United States are available for a period of one year to teachers with at least three years' experience. Salary is paid by the 'home' authority and British teachers receive a tax-free grant to offset the higher cost of living in the United States.

The European and United States schemes are operated on behalf of the DES, the Scottish Education Department and the Ministry of Education by the Central Bureau for Educational Visits and Exchanges.[2]

Other schemes – Projects both for pupils and adults on a wide front are planned by the Educational Interchange Council[3], a representative body established in 1947 to promote and assist educational visits and exchanges of all kinds. It is particularly concerned with experimental schemes in countries where economic, political and other factors have made contacts difficult.

Health – The United Kingdom has reciprocal arrangements with a number of overseas countries intended to protect the interests of its citizens working abroad, but these agreements do not necessarily give complete cover. Teachers can obtain Leaflet NI 38 from the local office of the Department of Social Services. Full details of agreements with individual countries can be obtained from the Department's overseas group.[4]

The benefits conferred by the various agreements are set out in the table on the previous page.

[1] Department of Education and Science, Pensions Branch, Mowden Hall, Staindrop Road, Darlington, Co. Durham.

[2] 43 Dorset Street, London W1H 3FN.

[3] 43 Russell Square, London, WC18 5DG.

[4] Department of Social Services, Overseas Group, Newcastle-upon-Tyne, NE98 1YX.

Fig. 9 – SOCIAL SECURITY RECIPROCAL AGREEMENTS

Benefits available to citizens of the United Kingdom by various reciprocal agreements.

1 *Sickness Benefit*
2 *Industrial Injuries*
3 *Unemployment Benefit*
4 *Maternity Benefit*
5 *Guardian's Allowance*
6 *Retirement Pension*
7 *Death Grant*
8 *Widow's Benefit*
9 *Family Allowances*

European Economic		Malta, G.C.[2]	123 56 8
Community:		Norway[3]	123456789
Belgium	123456789	Sweden[3]	123456 89
Denmark[3]	123456789	Switzerland	12 456789
France	12 4 678	Turkey	12 45678
German Federal			
Republic	123456789	Other countries:	
Irish Republic	12345678	Australia[1,2]	1 3 56 89
Italy	123456 8	Bermuda[2]	2 6 8
Jersey & Guernsey[2]	12 456789	Canada[2]	3 6 9
Luxembourg	12 45678	Finland	123456 89
Netherlands	123456 8	Israel[4]	12 456 8
		New Zealand[1,2]	1 3 56 89
Other members of the		United States of	
Council of Europe:		America	6 8
Cyprus[2]	12345678	Yugoslavia[3]	1234 6789

[1] Some benefits are subject to a means test.
[2] Members of the British Commonwealth of Nations.
[3] Visitors and tourists may not have to bear the full cost of treatment.
[4] Sickness benefit is limited.

NOTE:

Condition of premises (see also page 109)

Whilst this book was in the press, the Health and Safety at Work Act 1974 received the royal assent. A Health and Safety at Work Commission has been set up to receive complaints from those who have failed to persuade their employers to bring their physical working conditions up to standard. The Act applies to all places of work, and a spokesman for the Association of Metropolitan Authorities has estimated that the application of the Act to schools might, at a conservative estimate, cost £22 million.

V

SALARIES AND INCOME TAX

***

1 The salary committees

It is the duty of the Secretary of State to secure the appointment of one or more committees consisting of an independent chairman, one or more persons representing the Secretary of State, together with representatives of local education authorities and of organizations appearing to the Secretary of State to represent local education authorities, teachers, or particular descriptions of teachers. The committees must submit proposals for suitable salary scales to the Secretary of State when they think fit, or when he so requires. After the scales have received his approval, the Secretary of State makes an order binding them upon the local education authorities.[1]

In 1961 the Minister refused to accept the proposals of the Burnham Committee, and insisted on the submission of new scales within a specified global figure. His successor, Sir Edward Boyle, also rejected the recommendations made in January 1963 which provided for an identical cash increase at each point of the scale, a small addition to the good honours allowance, and the assimilation of the two-year trained teachers to the three-year scale. The Committee refused to submit further proposals, whereupon the Minister announced that he intended to initiate legislation to provide for a new scale dating from 1 April 1963 which would give greater increases to teachers with greater experience, qualifications, and responsibility.

The Remuneration of Teachers Act 1963 gave the Secretary of State power to fix salaries until 31 March 1965 by means of the

***

[1] Remuneration of Teachers Act 1965, ss. 1 and 2.

Remuneration of Teachers Order 1963 which amended the existing reports.

The present statute, the Remuneration of Teachers Act 1965, replaced and repealed s. 89 of the Education Act 1944 and the interim Act of 1963. The independent chairman is appointed by the Secretary of State, and there is provision for arbitration in default of agreement in committee. It also allows, for the first time, decisions to be retrospective.

When a review of salaries is projected, the Burnham Main Committee considers the salaries of teachers in primary and secondary schools. After these have been agreed, the committees dealing with other institutions meet to revise the scales for which they are responsible. These are to some extent geared to the primary and secondary scales.

After both panels of the committee have agreed on a decision the scales are referred to the various bodies represented on the committee, and are then submitted to the Minister. His approval is given in a letter to the chairman of the committee and the scales are printed for the guidance of all concerned.[1]

2 Duration of the scales

The 1925 scales continued in operation, subject to war allowances, until 1945. New scales, each for a period of three years, were introduced in 1945, 1948, 1951 and 1954. The rapidly rising cost of living caused the Minister, early in 1956, to use his power under the former section 89 of the 1944 Act to ask the committees to consider new scales to be introduced not later than 1 October 1956.

The scales were again revised with effect from 1 October 1959 for a period of two and a half years. In 1961, however, the Minister agreed that the new scales should commence on 1 January, three months earlier than the date originally set for the termination of the 1959 scales. He also stated that negotiations could be reopened not later than the summer of 1962 for a further revision to take effect from the beginning of April 1963. New

[1] The printed Reports are published by Her Majesty's Stationery Office.

proposals were agreed in January 1963 for a scale to last for two years until 31 March 1965.

Further Reports were approved periodically. The 1971 Report provided a completely new structure of teachers' salaries, but only after the Burnham Committee had failed to agree, and therefore had to submit to arbitration. The arbitral body reported in July 1971, and its findings formed the Burnham Report for that year. There were no structural changes in the 1972 and 1973 Reports, but important changes were made in the 1974 regulations.

3 Primary and secondary schools

General structure – The basic scale for full-time teachers is a salary increasing by annual increments to a prescribed maximum. There are five scales of salaries for assistant teachers, a scale for deputy heads, and a further scale for heads. Appointments are made within the various scales according to the responsibility demanded by the post. Very broadly they correspond to the former 'head of department' and 'graded' posts of previous reports, but they permit a much greater flexibility in determining the staffing structure of any particular school.

Allowances for qualifications are made by determining a position on the incremental scale, so that they are, in effect, increments rather than separate allowances. Above Scale 3 certain of these allowances become absorbed in the scales.

Equal pay – Until 1954 the salaries of women teachers were somewhat lower than those of men. From that year a scheme was introduced to raise women's salaries by seven annual stages to the men's level. Since 1 April 1961 there has been no difference.

Approved study and training – Teachers who have completed more than the minimum period of training by further full-time study or training receive an addition of not more than three increments, at the rate of one increment for each year of such training.

The graduate allowance – Graduates of English, Scottish, Welsh or Irish universities, of St David's College, Lampeter (or of Commonwealth or other universities if, in the opinion of the Secretary of State, their standards approximate to those of an

English university), are eligible for payment of the graduate allowance. Many other qualifications, including the final examinations of many professional bodies, are also accepted for this purpose. A complete list is published in an appendix to the current Report. Possession of the qualification is a sufficient ground for payment of the allowance; it is not necessary that the teacher should be engaged in teaching the subjects in which it was taken. A teacher may hold only one graduate allowance. Possession of an additional degree (unless it be a higher degree awarded by examination to a teacher whose first degree does not qualify for the good honours addition) does not entitle a teacher to a further increase in salary.

The good honours allowance – A further allowance is payable to the holder of a higher degree, or of a first degree in first or second class honours of one of the universities listed in the appendix to the Report. Where a teacher holds an unclassified honours degree of a university in the United Kingdom of Great Britain and Northern Ireland or the Republic of Ireland, the employing authority, in consultation with the university concerned, may determine whether or not it should be deemed a good honours degree. Higher degrees recognized for this purpose must have been obtained by examination, or by research work or some other post-graduate achievement.

The London allowances – A new scheme of allowances for teachers in and around Greater London was introduced in 1974. This provides for graduated additions to the scales to avoid the creation of a salary 'cliff' around the capital. The tiers are:

(*a*) Inner London Education Authority, Barking, Brent, Ealing, Haringey, Merton and Newham.

(*b*) Outer London boroughs not included above.

(*c*) *Buckinghamshire*: Chiltern and Beaconsfield;
Berkshire: Windsor, Slough, Maidenhead and Bracknell;
Essex: Basildon, Brentwood, Epping Forest, Harlow and Thurrock;
Hertfordshire: Broxbourne, Dacorum, Hatfield, St Albans, Watford and Welwyn;

Kent: Dartford and Sevenoaks.

Surrey: the whole county;

West Sussex: Crawley.

Teachers already serving in the Metropolitan Police District, but outside area (*a*), i.e. those who received the former London allowance, are safeguarded at the highest rate.

Experience before qualification – Subject to the limitations contained in the appropriate appendix to the report, certain additions may be made to the minimum of the scale. It should be noted that these merely affect the teacher's placing on the scale and are not continued through the maximum. Their effect is to secure that the teacher reaches the maximum earlier than he would purely in respect of service as a qualified teacher.

Qualification after twenty-one – Teachers who qualified after attaining the age of twenty-one qualify for an addition of one increment in respect of each period of three years' experience after the age of eighteen in teaching, industrial, professional, clerical, social or other gainful employment. No service regarded by the Secretary of State as part of the qualification for the status of qualified teacher may be included under this head.

For unqualified teaching service the addition is at the rate of one increment for every three years; other service may be reckoned at the rate of one increment for one, two or three years' service (up to a maximum of twelve years) at the discretion of the local education authority.

Unqualified teachers – Unqualified teachers receive salaries based on a lower scale than that for their qualified colleagues. These scales apply to student teachers and instructors.

Heads' allowances – Since 1965 heads have been paid on a 'consolidated' scale based on the size of their schools. They receive no personal allowances, and normally the only permitted addition is the London area allowance. For the calculation of heads' salaries, schools are divided into a number of groups based on a 'unit total', each pupil on the roll counting as a number of units according to age on 31 March:

Aged under 13	.	.	.	.	$1\frac{1}{2}$ units
Aged 13–14 .	.	.	.	.	2 units
Aged 15	.	.	.	.	4 units
Aged 16	.	.	.	.	6 units
Aged 17 or over	.	.	.	.	10 units

The group in which a school is placed is determined by the unit total. Special schools for handicapped pupils have a different group scale and a different unit value for their pupils.

Deputy heads – In all schools with a unit total of 151 or above the authority must appoint a deputy head, who is paid, like the head, on a consolidated scale based on the school's unit total. In a mixed school in Group 7, or above, the authority must designate an additional post of second master or second mistress: these appointments rank for payment on the same scale as a deputy head. The authority has a *discretion* to appoint a deputy head in a school with a unit total below 151; and to appoint a second deputy in a school in Group 10 or above.

Tenure of allowances – When a review results in a school being placed in a lower group, the allowances payable to the head and the deputy head are safeguarded in accordance with the terms of the Burnham Report. It is within the discretion of the local education authority to make appointments for varying responsibilities within a school; the scale applicable to the post being evaluated on the basis of the responsibility entailed. The total number of such appointments must come within the points score range of the school, as set out in the Report. Teachers holding former posts of responsibility were transferred to the appropriate new scale in 1971 and they, together with those appointed above Scale 1 since that date, will continue to receive their salaries on that scale even though the points score range of the school falls below the number of appointments made. This provision continues only so long as they remain on the staff of the same school, and no new appointments may be made above Scale 1 unless the points score permits this action to be taken.

Temporary allowances – If an assistant takes charge of a school during the absence of the head or pending a new appointment, the salary must be that which would be payable if the teacher concerned were appointed as the permanent head of the school. It is payable only during such periods as the assistant is actually in charge of the school. A local education authority may make an additional payment to a teacher in certain categories when it is considered that the salary or the scale properly payable under the Report is inadequate having regard to the special circumstances of the teacher's duties and responsibilities. A teacher whose appointment is temporary, pending the reorganization of his school, is entitled to a safeguarding of his salary from 1 July 1967.[1]

Unattached heads – Local education authorities may retain on their permanent staffs one or more unattached heads, paid at salaries appropriate to Groups 1, 2 or 3, who are available to fill temporary vacancies in headships.

Educational priority areas – The Plowden report on primary education suggested that local education authorities should consider designating as educational priority areas those parts of their territories which, for one reason or another, appeared to be educationally disadvantaged and where there is difficulty in recruiting sufficient teachers of high calibre. Teachers in some schools in these areas receive an additional payment, subject to annual review, so long as they are in a school which has been designated. It should be noted that designation refers to an area, but it does not necessarily follow that all schools in an educational priority area are nominated for additional assistance.

Supply teachers – It is recommended that teachers appointed on a day-to-day or other short notice basis should be paid, according to their qualifications and experience, by reference to the number of days or weeks for which the school is open during the year. Thus, if the school is open for two hundred days during forty weeks, the daily rate would be one two-hundredth, the weekly rate one-fortieth, of the annual rate. A teacher employed throughout the year would thus receive the same salary as he would if employed under contract. It is recommended that a teacher who is employed continuously for a term or more should not be paid on

[1] *Stott* v *Oldham Corporation* (1969) 67 LGR 520; LCT 393.

a short notice basis, but should be regarded as a 'regular part-time teacher', and paid monthly.

4 Special schools and classes
Teachers (whether qualified or unqualified), receive an addition to the salary which would be payable in ordinary schools, and this is payable throughout the scale.

There are separate scales for the heads and deputy heads of special schools.

5 Other educational establishments
Separately negotiated salary scales are published in respect of:

Universities
Technical colleges
Farm institutes
Colleges of education
Youth service organizers
Specialist organizers
Educational psychologists
General inspectors and organizers.

6 Income tax
There is not space, in a book of this scope, to deal with the various complexities of the income tax regulations. Small hand-books which explain the current provisions are easily obtainable from any bookseller.

It should be noted that the rule which makes allowances for expenses 'necessarily and exclusively' incurred in following one's occupation is strictly interpreted and there are few claims open to teachers under this head. Books, for example, are not regarded as a necessary expense since they are supplied by the local education authority. A typewriter is likely to be regarded as neither necessarily nor exclusively obtained for the following of the profession of a teacher.

7 Tax allowances on professional subscriptions
Members of professional associations and learned societies may

now claim income tax allowances against their subscriptions. These include not only annual fees which are payable as a statutory condition of exercising a profession, but also subscriptions to bodies which have been approved by the Commissioners of Inland Revenue. It is required that the activities of the body should be relevant to the profession concerned.

NOTE:

The Houghton Committee

As this book reaches the proof stage (October 1974) a committee is considering representations, both by the teachers' professional associations and by the employing authorities, that educational salaries have fallen far below the relative position in the national spread of incomes which they occupied several years ago. It is understood that that committee is also examining the structure of teachers' salaries, and changes in differentials within the profession. The committee was set up in May 1974, and was allowed until December to complete its work. Any recommendations for increases may be made retroactive to the date of the committee's appointment. It is possible, therefore, that the whole structure described in this chapter will have passed into history before publication.

VI

LEAVE OF ABSENCE

1 Sickness

According to Halsbury's *Laws of England* a servant is entitled to his wages during temporary illness, provided that the contract of service remains in existence throughout that time and that he is ready and willing to carry out his duties save for the incapacity produced by the sickness. On the other hand, it has been held[1] that permanent illness is a good ground for the termination of the contract.

Sickness has been defined by Mr Justice McNaghten as 'any morbid condition, without paying any attention to the cause'[2] and therefore includes incapacity due to accident. It comprises not only the illness itself but also approaching illness and the subsequent convalescence, and was described by Mr Justice Channell as 'not a breach of contract but an act of God'.[3]

It should be noted that the contract of employment must subsist throughout the illness. A servant who is unable to commence fresh employment through illness is not entitled to salary from his new employer, even though he has left the employ of his former master.[4]

2 Sick pay regulations

Sick pay allowances are granted by local education authorities under schemes which have, in general, been agreed between them

---

[1] *Cuckson* v *Stones* (1858) 28 JP 25.
[2] In *Maloney* v *St Helens Industrial Co-operative Society, Ltd* (1932), 49 TLR 22.
[3] *Davies* v *Ebbw Vale UDC* (1911) 75 JP 533; LCT 75.
[4] *R.* v *Wintersett* (1783) Cald MC 298.

and the teachers' professional associations. The schemes vary somewhat from authority to authority, but service in one area is recognized for the calculation of benefits on transfer to another in accordance, of course, with the scheme of the new authority.

The nationally agreed minimum rates of sick pay are as follows:

Year of Service	Working days' pay	
	Full	Half
First	25	25[1]
Second	50	50
Third	75	75
Fourth (and successive)	100	100

When an illness extends over more than three working days, a medical certificate must be submitted to the authority. It is also necessary, in order to claim benefit, to send a 'National Health' medical certificate to the local office of the DHSS within six days. If a certificate cannot be obtained within that time, the teacher should write to the Social Security office, quoting his full name, address, date of birth and National Insurance number. The letter should state that benefit is being claimed, and the medical certificate should be sent on as quickly as possible.

Some local education authorities are prepared to accept the National Health certificate and, after recording the details, to forward it to the department. There is, however, a risk in following this procedure: if, through postal or administrative delays, the certificate is not received at the Social Security office within the prescribed time there may be a loss of benefit. Teachers may consider it worthwhile to pay for a private medical certificate for their employing authority, and to send the official certificate themselves to the Social Security office.

If the certificate states that the teacher will be fit to return to work within a week, no further certificate is necessary before returning to work. If the certificate is for a longer period, it must either be renewed on expiry, or a 'fit' certificate obtained before

[1] Eligibility for half pay does not begin until the completion of four months' service.

returning to work. Teachers in hospital are normally required to send a certificate only on admission and discharge.

Teachers are strongly recommended to obtain particulars of their authority's sick pay procedure as early as possible after entering service.

3 Infectious illness

All teachers who are in contact with infectious illness at home should notify the authority. As a rule they are not excluded from school except when the illness is of an exceptionally serious character such as smallpox or poliomyelitis. If, however, they are excluded, they should forward a certificate to this effect from the Medical Officer of Health or, if this cannot be obtained quickly, from their own doctor. Full pay should be allowed, and the absence should not prejudice future entitlement to sick pay.

When a teacher himself contracts an infectious illness which the authority's medical officer certifies to have been, in all probability, caught in school, full salary is allowed for the necessary absence and neither the time nor the sick pay is counted against the teacher's entitlement.

4 Accidents during teaching duty

If a teacher's absence is certified to be due to an accident arising out of, and in the course of, his duty, he will be entitled to industrial injury benefit for a period of twenty-six weeks' incapacity. He cannot draw sickness benefit at the same time; but, if the incapacity extends beyond twenty-six weeks, sickness benefit (or invalidity benefit) will be payable. Injury benefit qualifies for an earnings-related supplement in the same way as sickness benefit.

The accident should be recorded immediately it is reported in the book provided by the Department of Health and Social Security.

Where an authority makes up the salary of a teacher receiving benefit as the result of an accident sustained at school, this is without prejudice to the authority's liability in the case of negligence. Any amount so paid, however, would be deducted from an award of damages.

The model sick pay scheme recommends that, subject to the production of medical certificates, full pay should be allowed for a period of up to six months, at the end of which an extension should be considered. Absence resulting from accidents during teaching duty should not count against future sick pay claims. Accidents arising from extra-curricular or voluntary activities connected with the school should be classified under this head.

5 Accidents outside teaching duty

If a teacher's absence is due to the actionable negligence of a third party[1] he should advise the authority accordingly. The authority may advance sick pay on the basis of a loan, pending the result of any action taken by a teacher to obtain compensation, but may then claim a sum to the extent of the damages recovered, not exceeding the allowances paid in respect of sick pay. If the claim be settled on a proportionate basis between the parties, the authority will determine the proportion to be refunded by the teacher.

In one case, a teacher was prevented from carrying out her duties following an accident when she was returning from her holidays. She claimed that she was entitled to her full salary for the three weeks that she was absent. The authority's case was that the sick pay regulations conferred eligibility, but not a right, to allowances as there was a clause which allowed the withholding of payments in a specific case. Judgment in the Bury County Court was given for the teacher.

6 Tuberculosis

Special arrangements are usually made for teachers who contract pulmonary tuberculosis, and those who suspect that they have developed this illness should consult the authority immediately. Full pay is normally paid for twelve months.

---

[1] This might cover a whole range of accidents including, for example, being knocked down by a careless motorist, illness arising from food poisoning which can be traced to actionable negligence, etc.

7 Maternity leave

The standard scheme for maternity leave applies to married women with at least twelve months' continuous service immediately prior to the commencement of the maternity leave, though not necessarily with one authority. An authority can, at its discretion, apply the scheme in whole or in part to unmarried women.

The teacher must apply for leave not less than sixteen weeks before the date of the expected confinement. She must, unless the authority agrees, absent herself from duty for a period of eighteen weeks, commencing eleven weeks before the confinement. If the child does not live, she may return to duty four weeks after the confinement.

Full pay is allowed for the first four weeks, and for any additional period earlier than eleven weeks before the confinement during which the authority may require the teacher to absent herself from duty. Half pay is allowed for the remainder of the leave, the national maternity allowance being deducted only if this allowance and half pay, together, exceed the teacher's salary. Married women who do not pay contributions[1] are deemed to do so, and the benefits to which they would have been entitled are deducted during the period of full pay.

Subject to the provision of a medical certificate, any absence due or attributable to the pregnancy, absence due to miscarriage, and any extension of maternity leave, are treated as sick leave. If a teacher returns to part-time duty for a period before resuming full-time service, that period is treated as leave without pay.

Payment during maternity leave is conditional on the teacher returning to full-time duty for at least thirteen weeks, which runs from the date of return or from the date when she is certified to be fit for duty if that occurs during a holiday. Payment of any sums due in respect of leave following the confinement, or of salary in respect of a holiday period following immediately on maternity leave, may be withheld until the teacher actually returns. If the teacher does not return, the authority may require a refund of such proportion of the payments made as it deems appropriate.

[1] See pages 147–8.

8 Holidays

When a teacher is on sick leave at the end of term he will normally be paid at the rate to which he is entitled (full or reduced pay) for the whole of the holiday period. If, however, he obtains a certificate of fitness during the holiday, sick pay ends from the date of that certificate and he is treated as having returned to service, provided that he is in school on the first day of term.

Similarly, a teacher who falls sick during the holidays should report the matter to the local education authority and the DHSS. Benefits are payable, and deductions are made, as in term time.

9 Suspension of sick pay

Most authorities include in their schemes a provision that if sickness is due to the teacher's misconduct, failure to observe the conditions of the scheme or conduct prejudicial to recovery, benefits may be suspended. When this is done, the teacher is informed of the fact and may then make representations to the authority.

10 Deductions from sick pay

In accordance with general practice in public employment, no teacher, during sickness, may receive from public funds an amount in excess of his full salary. When a teacher is absent on full or half pay which, together with benefits receivable from other sources, would exceed full pay, deductions are made in respect of allowances to which the teacher is eligible under the National Insurance Acts, the National Insurance (Industrial Injuries) Acts, the Workmen's Compensation Acts (where the right to compensation stems from an accident sustained before 5 July 1948), and the dependency element (but not the disability element) of any treatment allowance.

Since 1948 teachers have been required to contribute for benefits under the National Insurance Acts and it should be particularly noted that the deductions from sick pay are made by the authority if the teacher is entitled to benefit, *whether he has claimed the benefit or not*. It is important, therefore, that claims to full entitlement, including any benefits payable in respect of dependants, should be submitted promptly. Otherwise the teacher will suffer loss of income.

11 Saturdays and Sundays

Saturdays and Sundays falling within a period of sick leave normally count against the sick pay entitlement, unless they immediately precede or follow a period of leave. Exceptions may be made when a week-end comes in a period of unpaid leave of less than a week's duration.

12 Graduated contributions

When graduated contributions were introduced by the National Insurance Act 1959, teachers in general were contracted out of the scheme. They paid only the employee's share of the basic contribution to which the employer added his proportion, and bought an appropriate stamp to affix to the employee's card.

The National Insurance Act 1966 introduced a scheme of earnings-related supplements to the various benefits, financed by additional graduated contributions. These must be paid by all employees between the age of eighteen and the minimum pensionable age if their earnings exceed £9 a week. The employer collects his servants' contributions through the pay-as-you-earn tax system, adds an equal contribution of his own, and forwards it to the Collector of Inland Revenue.

Part-time and supply teachers, who do not contribute to the teachers' superannuation scheme, are liable for the full graduated contribution, not simply that part which is in respect of the earnings-related supplement.

13 Declaration as to National Insurance entitlement

All teachers are required to notify the authority of their entitlement to benefit under the National Insurance Acts. Such entitlement is related to the number of dependants, of whom only one may be an adult.

14 Married women

Married women must notify their entitlement to the authority, even though they have elected to be exempted from the payment of contributions other than those which they cannot avoid (industrial injuries and, if their pay in any week exceeds £9, graduated contributions).

A married woman who elects, as above, for exemption, will not be entitled on the basis of her husband's insurance to sickness benefit, unemployment benefit, maternity allowance or a full retirement pension. Nevertheless, the Teachers' Sick Pay Regulations provide that, if she is ill, the authority will deduct from her salary the full amount of the benefit to which she would have been entitled if she had paid the full contributions.

A married woman can, of course, opt to pay contributions in full, in which case she will be entitled to full benefits. She may be entitled to claim benefits for as long as two years after exemption, in virtue of contributions previously paid or credited, and should therefore continue to submit claims until she is notified that her entitlement has expired.

Married women who pay only industrial injuries contributions are regarded by employing authorities as though they were fully insured and deductions are made from their sick pay accordingly.

15 First appointments
Teachers leaving college become entitled to sickness benefit shortly after starting work, and should claim benefit immediately if they are ill. The Ministry requires this evidence, even though benefit may not be immediately payable, in order to grant credits for contributions in respect of complete weeks of absence.

16 Leave for reasons other than personal illness
Leave of absence may sometimes be granted for reasons other than the personal illness of the teacher. Except in grave emergencies, such leave should be requested in advance through the head of the school. The question of payment of salary is at the discretion of the authority and varies widely in practice.

It has been held in the courts that a dismissal is not valid if a teacher is absent for urgent cause without the permission of the authority but with the permission of the head.[1]

[1] *Martin* v *Eccles Corporation* [1919] 1 Ch. 387.

Some of the grounds on which leave of absence is sometimes granted are noted below, but these must not be regarded as more than a general guide to the sort of application which may be considered by an authority. Because of the considerable differences in the practice of the local education authorities, only a general indication has been given as to whether salary is payable in any particular instance. For detailed information, the teacher must consult the rules of his own authority.

(a) *Serious illness of relative* – The usual degrees of relationship which are accepted are husband, wife, father, mother, child, brother, sister, a child of whom the teacher is guardian and, in exceptional circumstances, other persons. It is generally a condition that a doctor should certify that the illness involves serious domestic difficulties which require the teacher's presence.

(b) *Death and funeral* of members of the family in the categories listed above.

(c) *Weddings* of relatives in the same degrees.

(d) *Private or family business* – usually without pay.

(e) *Holiday with husband or wife* – This is primarily intended for cases where the teacher's spouse is serving in HM Forces or is compelled to take the main annual leave in term-time. Such leave is normally without salary.

(f) *Blood transfusions* – Teachers may be allowed to act as donors provided that they keep themselves fit for normal duties.

(g) *Conferences* on purely educational matters to which the teacher is a delegate, or of which he is a permanent official.

(h) *Courses of training* approved by the authority. Some authorities will allow leave for the final months of study for a degree.

(i) *Examinations and private study* – Most authorities pay for leave for an examination which would improve the teacher's educational qualifications, but this is not universal. Salary is not paid for private study at home without attendance at a recognized institution.

(j) *Honours, decorations and degrees* – Leave is usually granted for the ceremony of presentation to a teacher or the teacher's wife, child or ward.

(*k*) *Inquests, witness and jury service* – Leave is normally with pay but any fee received should be handed to the authority which will then refund out-of-pocket expenses which are not in excess of the fee.

(*l*) *Days of religious obligation* – Leave is usually granted with pay on condition that the teacher may be required to make up the time in another school on a day on which his own is closed.

(*m*) *Interviews for appointments* – Some authorities limit the number of days' paid leave which may be granted for this purpose in a year. In some cases salary is not paid when the post sought is outside the profession.

(*n*) *Public duties* – Special leave may be granted for teachers who are candidates at parliamentary or local elections, who are justices of the peace or who have other public duties, including attendance at national conferences of political parties, trade unions or Whitley conferences.

(*o*) *Sport and out-of-school activities* – Leave may be granted to act in a responsible capacity at sports meetings, musical festivals, etc., promoted by schools or associations of schools. Occasionally, leave may be granted to enable teachers to represent their country in international sports events or trials.

(*p*) *National service* – Members of the Territorial Army, the Auxiliary Air Force, the Officers' Training Corps, the Royal Naval Volunteer Reserve or the Air Training Corps may be allowed leave for annual training. Pay may be allowed for part of the absence on proof that the whole period of training has been completed.

(*q*) *Visits to other schools* – Leave for a limited number of days a year may be granted for purposes of observation.

VII

SUPERANNUATION

1 Statutory provisions

Until 1972 the statutory provisions for teachers' superannuation were to be found in the Teachers Superannuation Acts. These have been repealed, and the legal basis of the scheme is now to be found in the Superannuation Act 1972. which applies to a wide range of persons employed in the public service.

Section 9 of the Act empowers the Secretary of State for Education and Science to make regulations dealing with teachers' pensions, allowances or gratuities, with the consent of the Minister for the Civil Service. The regulations also prescribe the conditions under which such benefits may be paid.

The various matters which may be included in any regulations are specified in schedule 3 to the Act. The Secretary of State is required, before making any regulations, to consult with the representatives of local education authorities, of teachers, and of anyone else he deems appropriate.

For the purposes of this section the word 'teachers' includes persons employed, otherwise than as teachers, in educational work which involves a substantial control or supervision of teachers, and those employed in connection with the provision of education or its ancillary services.

All teachers employed in maintained or direct grant schools must participate in the scheme. 'Accepted schools' are independent schools operating the scheme in the same way as grant-aided schools: full-time service in these establishments is counted as reckonable service.

Independent schools operating a modified form of the scheme are called 'admitted schools'. Service in such schools places a teacher in a position somewhat different from that in grant-aided or accepted schools, and is described in a leaflet obtainable from the DES, and known as 430 Pen.[1]

2 Contributions

Teachers in contributory service pay a contribution of 6 per cent of their salary during such service, and at least an equal amount is paid by the employing authority.[2] Contributions are not funded but are appropriated in aid of the vote of the DES. An actuarial inquiry into the scheme is held every five years and, should this reveal a deficiency, supplementary contributions are payable by the employers. The contributions cover both personal and family benefits.

No contributions are payable in respect of service exceeding forty-five years' pensionable service, nor after the age of seventy.

In cases where a teacher's salary is reduced, he may opt to continue paying contributions on his previous higher rate of salary. This procedure is dealt with in section 16 of this Chapter.[3]

Contributions are deducted from salaries by the employer, who remits them to the Treasury. They are allowed as a deduction from income for tax purposes.

3 Pensionable service[4]

Pensionable service is, in general, all full-time service as a teacher in schools not conducted for private profit and, in certain cases, as an educational organizer or full-time youth leader employed by a local education authority. Such service falls into four categories:

(a) *Recognized service* is full-time service as a teacher, rendered between the ages of eighteen and sixty-five, before

[1] All correspondence with the DES in connection with superannuation should be addressed to: The Department of Education and Science, Pensions Branch, Mowden Hall, Staindrop Road, Darlington, Co. Durham, DL3 9BG.

[2] From 1 April 1972, teachers paid 6·75% of their salary, but this reverted to six per cent from 1 December 1973.

[3] See page 163.

[4] This is now referred to as *reckonable service.*

1 April 1926 in schools grant-aided by the Board of Education, in approved schools and certified institutions under the Mental Deficiency Act 1913, or (except in the case of elementary and approved schools) schools which, although not grant-aided at the time of the service, became so before 1 April 1924;

(b) *Contributory service* includes full-time service, up to his seventieth birthday, of a teacher in a maintained or grant-aided school, training college, county college, or place of further education in England and Wales. It may include periods as an educational organizer with responsibility for the control or supervision of teachers, or organizing or advisory work in connection with the services ancillary to education such as School Meals or Youth Service. Full-time service may include 'class supervision and subsidiary duties such as corrections, preparations, and supervision'. It may be divided between two schools under the same control or management. In general, it is held to be sufficient for the teacher to be on contract as a full-time teacher with a full-time salary;[1]

(c) *Qualifying service* is employment, whether or not as a teacher, which is accepted by the Treasury for qualification for a pension. Service in independent schools which do not operate the government's superannuation scheme may be so counted, as may certain periods of service abroad. War service which does not count as recognized or contributory service is always included under this head. An application for the recognition of qualifying service should be made within three months of:

(i) entry into contributory service by a person who has not previously been so employed, or

(ii) entry into qualifying service from contributory service;

[1] Where, with the consent of the Secretary of State, a teacher pays contributions during a break in contributory service, the contributions are assessed on the probable salary he would have received had he remained in the same (or similar) contributory service. This does not apply to allowances which began to accrue before 10 November 1965, or to a gratuity payable before that date. If the Secretary of State's consent to payment was given before 10 November 1965, the teacher could elect to pay under the 'probable salary' clause from any date not earlier than 1 January 1962. This, however, did not apply to any period of absence falling partly or wholly before that date.

(*d*) *Approved external service* may be counted in establishing a claim to a retirement pension, but is not in itself pensionable under the teachers' superannuation scheme. It includes teaching service in Scotland and Northern Ireland, service in universities in the United Kingdom and many parts of the Dominions, employment in the Civil Service which is not integrated with teaching service, work as an educational officer of the British Broadcasting Corporation, employment as an educational administrator, or service recognized under the National Health Service (Superannuation) Regulations.

4 Supplementary service

Service as a supplementary teacher was not pensionable. In the case, however, of those in such employment on 1 April 1945 (or re-employed after that date) the following provisions have been made:

(*a*) Teachers who, within a year of being employed as supplementary teachers, were not subject to the Local Government Superannuation Act 1937, are automatically in contributory service. They may opt to count all, or part of their previous service on payment of the appropriate contributions;

(*b*) Teachers who, within a year of being employed as supplementary teachers, were subject to the Local Government Superannuation Act 1937, could remain in that scheme if they chose, or withdraw their contributions, with compound interest, and join the teachers' scheme with the option to count all, or part, of their previous service on payment of the appropriate contributions.

5 Overseas service

A teacher who has been in contributory service in this country may count a period of teaching overseas as pensionable service on payment of the appropriate contributions. Such service is normally limited to five years, but the period may be extended by the Secretary of State. Teaching in schools maintained by other Commonwealth countries in Britain may be counted similarly.

To facilitate the recruitment of staff to schools overseas in which it is desirable that British teachers should be employed, a similar provision can be made, even if there is not any previous service in this country. Such service will normally be allowed for a period of up to five years, provided that the teacher enters contributory service within two years of the end of overseas service. Contributions for the period spent abroad will, in the case of teachers with no previous contributory service, be based on the salary they would probably have received under the Burnham Scale if they had been teaching in this country. The contributions payable include both the teacher's and the employer's share.

6 'Buying in' service

New regulations have extended the provisions for purchasing added years so that a teacher may, within certain limits, buy-in, at full cost, any period after the age of twenty which would not otherwise count as reckonable.

In order to be able to buy-in such periods, a teacher must have entered reckonable service before the age of fifty-five, and he must be employed in reckonable service at the time he elects to buy-in.

Not more than thirty years' service may be bought-in and, unless the teacher is buying-in the maximum period possible, only complete years may be so treated. A teacher may not buy-in more than will allow him to acquire forty years of reasonable service on reaching the age of sixty. Teachers entering reckonable service for the first time after attaining the age of fifty may buy in only a limited number of years:

Age of entry	*Maximum number of years*
50	23
51	16
52	9
53	2
54	Twice the period from date of entry to the teacher's 55th birthday.

The number of years will also be restricted if a teacher has received, is receiving, or will receive, superannuation benefits from another scheme.

Payment may be made by deduction from salary, a single payment, or on an actuarial basis, by uniform monthly instalments calculated as follows:

Method 1

Payment of periodical contributions (i.e. by deduction from salary) until sufficient have been paid to buy-in all the service which the teacher elected to purchase. In the event, however, of a teacher's death or retirement on ill-health grounds with an award of infirmity benefits before payment has been completed he will be credited with the full amount of service he elected to purchase at the outset. If a teacher leaves reckonable service for any other reason before payment has been completed then, generally speaking, he will be credited with only so much service as he has paid for at that time or will be given the opportunity to pay off the amount outstanding in one sum.

The rate of payment is to be chosen by the teacher, but must be either 1 per cent or any multiple of 1 per cent (being a whole number) subject to a maximum of 9 per cent and the following conditions:

(a) except where the highest rate of 9 per cent is chosen, the percentage rate must be sufficient to complete payment by the age of sixty;

(b) except where the lowest rate of 1 per cent is chosen, the percentage rate must not be such that payment will be completed within five years;

(c) where a teacher is already paying additional contributions over and above his normal contributions of 6 per cent total additional contributions including those for 'buying-in' service must not exceed 9 per cent;

(d) where a teacher has elected to bring in reckonable service before 1 April 1972 to count for family benefits he will not be debarred from purchasing additional service under these arrangements which will count for both personal and family benefits but he will have to select a single combined contribution rate not less than the rate at which he has elected to purchase earlier reckonable service to count for family benefits; he will be able to reduce the number of years for which he elected to purchase back service for family benefits provided this is not reduced below five years;

(*e*) a teacher will be able to increase (but not decrease) his chosen rate of payment. The increased rate of contributions will become payable on 1 April in the year following that in which he makes an amending election.

Special overriding conditions will apply to older teachers:

(*a*) a teacher over the age of sixty will have to pay at the rate of 9 per cent;

(*b*) a teacher over the age of fifty-five but not yet sixty will have to pay at the percentage rate which will complete payment at the earliest possible date after, but not before his sixtieth birthday (unless, even by choosing the minimum rate of 1 per cent payment would be completed before the age of sixty is reached).

Method II
A single payment at the outset which, generally speaking, will be a percentage (according to age) of salary at the time of the acceptance of a teacher's election by the DES.

Method III
A teacher will be able to elect to pay the lump sum determined under Method II by actuarially calculated uniform monthly instalments to be deducted from his salary. Contribution rates are set out in Leaflet 374.

Payment may be made by one of the three methods, partly by Method I and partly by Method II, or partly by Method I and partly by Method III.

Income tax relief will normally be given on contributions paid under Methods I and III provided payments are in accordance with Inland Revenue requirements. The lump sum payment under Method II or any other lump sum payment will not attract income tax relief.

7 War service

War service by a teacher who left contributory service for this purpose is counted as contributory service. If the authority supplemented the service pay or if the service pay was equal to, or higher than, the teacher's salary, normal contributions were paid by both teacher and employer on the full teaching salary.

If the authority did not supplement the service pay, and the latter was less than the teaching salary, no contributions are payable and the service is treated as fully contributory.

In cases where a teacher in training, or a trained teacher who had not yet entered contributory service, undertook war service, such service is treated as contributory without payment of contributions unless the service pay equalled or exceeded the amount he would have received as a teacher.

Service recognized during the war of 1914–18 included service with HM Forces, full-time service in military or VAD hospitals, and service abroad with the Red Cross or the Friends' Ambulance Units. Other work, as in munitions, was recognized only if the teacher had special qualifications for the work he was doing. During the 1939–45 war the scope of recognized war service was extended to any form of work which the Secretary of State considered appropriate, and included not only HM Forces, but also the Civil Defence, National Fire Service, War Relief Police, Hospital services, and a wide variety of occupations.

Teachers in service, or who commenced certain courses of training before specified dates in 1950 are now treated (as to one half) as being in reckonable service in respect of service in HM Forces, and certain auxiliary services, undertaken before 1 April 1949. Contributions are deducted from the lump sum. There is no entitlement to family benefits in respect of this service. The scheme applies to existing pensioners at, but not to those who died before, 1 September 1974, nor to anyone who has transferred out of the teachers' superannuation scheme.

8 Residential and other emoluments

Emoluments in kind form part of a teacher's contributory salary only if the Secretary of State is satisfied that it is impracticable or inconvenient to convert their value into cash salary. In such cases the Secretary of State must be satisfied that there is an actual legal obstacle to conversion (such as a clause in a trust regulating a school foundation which requires a teacher to occupy a rent-free house by virtue of office and not as a tenant). A contract or agreement, which may be altered or cancelled during the tenure of employment, is not usually sufficient to satisfy the Secretary of State.

Board and lodging may not normally be treated as an emolument which may be included in a teacher's contributory salary.

Emoluments in kind which are a reward for duties beyond those of a full-time teacher (such as boarding-house supervision) are not pensionable.

9 Leave of absence

Absence on sick leave is not treated as contributory service:

(*a*) after continuous sick leave of more than twelve months, or eighteen months in the case of tuberculosis;

(*b*) after the issue of a medical certificate of permanent incapacity for further contributory service;

(*c*) when on less than half-pay.

Periods of leave, other than sick leave, may be treated as contributory service up to a maximum of thirty days in any financial year. If a teacher is seconded on full pay for a longer period (e.g. for further training), the time limit of thirty days does not apply.

Leave without pay, or other unpaid service, up to a maximum of one year may be counted as contributory service with the Secretary of State's permission. In this case the teacher will be required to pay both his own and the employer's share of the contributions for the period concerned, and to satisfy the Secretary of State that he intends to return to contributory service. Application for permission should be made as early as possible.

10 Re-employment after retirement

If a teacher retires, even for one day, he is entitled to claim his lump sum and to receive a pension for the period of retirement. Should he return to contributory service, or to service which would be contributory if he were under the age of seventy, his pension may be suspended if his annual salary on re-employment is as great as it would have been had he remained in service. If his salary during re-employment is less, he may receive enough of his pension to make it up to the salary at the date of retirement. If he has allocated part of his pension, the salary before retirement is considered to be reduced by the amount which is equal to the allocated part of the pension.

Re-employment for a period, or periods, amounting to a full year may be taken into account for the reassessment of superannuation benefits, so however that the teacher's pension is not thereby reduced. Service after the age of seventy cannot be allowed for reassessment. If the service after retirement does not qualify for reassessment, the contributions are returned to the teacher.

A teacher can be re-employed on a *part-time* basis permanently without loss of pension, provided that his earnings plus his pension in any particular quarter do not exceed the quarterly rate of his equivalent salary on retirement.

11 Application for pension

Four months before retirement a teacher should write to the Department of Education and Science (Pensions Branch),[1] asking for the appropriate forms for application for allowances. After completion they should be sent to the employing authority who will forward the application to the DES.

The DES will not notify an assessment of the allowances before the formal date of retirement, that is, the last day on which salary is paid or, if the teacher has already retired, his sixtieth birthday.

12 Qualification for allowances

Retirement is optional at sixty and contributory service cannot

[1] The address of the Pensions Branch is given in a footnote on page 152.

continue beyond the age of seventy. With the approval of the local education authority, however, a teacher may continue in non-contributory service beyond the latter age. Most local education authorities, in compliance with the national conditions of tenure, include a clause in their conditions of service, providing for automatic retirement at the end of the term in which a teacher attains the age of sixty-five, and for extension beyond that age by mutual agreement.

Allowances are based on the number of years of pensionable service, up to a maximum of forty-five, and on the teacher's highest salary for any successive 365 days during the last three years of service. To qualify for allowances, a teacher must have completed five years' pensionable service. They are not payable before the age of sixty, except in the case of an infirmity allowance.

All service, including odd days, is taken into account in determining a teacher's entitlement to a pension.

13 The annual allowance (pension)

The annual allowance is a sum equal to one-eightieth of the highest salary for any successive 365 days during the last three years' service, for each year of pensionable service. This is subject to a limit of forty-five years, of which not more than forty may be service before the age of sixty.

Teachers who are entitled to receive a modified pension under the National Insurance scheme receive a reduced pension to which they become entitled on reaching the age of sixty in the case of women, or sixty-five for men. The amount of the reduction varies according to the amount of modified service, but the maximum is £67·75 a year, and this applies only where a teacher has completed forty years' modified service.[1]

The pension may be paid by draft which may be cashed at any bank, proof of life and identity being required when payment is due. Payment may, alternatively, be made by credit to the pensioner's account.

Pensions are treated as earned income for tax purposes,[2] and

[1] See Section 24 below.
[2] Contributions made during service are exempted from tax.

assessments in this connection are made by HM Inspector of Taxes, Public Departments (3), Ty Glas Road, Llanishen, Cardiff, to whom all correspondence on the subject should be addressed.

14 The additional allowance (lump sum)

The lump sum is equal to three-eightieths of the highest salary for 365 consecutive days during the last three years of service, for each year of pensionable service. This is subject to a limit of forty-five years.

In the case of teachers with pensionable service before 1 October 1956, the service before that date is calculated at the rate of one thirtieth for each year. The limitation which applies to the pension requiring not more than forty of the qualifying years to have been completed before the age of sixty does not apply to the lump sum, but the amount attributable to service before that pensionable age must not exceed one and a half times the salary.

The lump sum is payable on application to HM Paymaster General immediately after the notification of the award.

15 Allocation of part of pension

On reaching the age of sixty, or on retirement, a teacher in good health who has qualified for a pension may, subject to certain conditions, surrender up to one-third of his pension for actuarially equivalent benefits payable to his wife or other dependant after his death. This may now be done without interrupting service by temporary retirement, but the terms offered to 'continuing teachers' are less favourable than those for 'retiring teachers'.

A teacher may not allocate more than a third of his pension, or such an amount as would make his pension smaller than that payable to his beneficiary after his death. Neither may he allocate so small an amount that the beneficiary will receive less than a quarter of his reduced pension after his death. There are two ways of doing this.

Option A permanently reduces the teacher's pension by the amount of the allocation and secures a pension for the beneficiary on the teacher's death.

Option B also permanently reduces the teacher's pension, but he also receives an annuity during the lifetime of the spouse. On the teacher's death the spouse receives a pension which is double the annuity.

16 Safeguarding of amount of pension

If a teacher continues in service, but at a lower rate of salary, he may safeguard his pension at the higher rate, but only with the consent of the Secretary of State. To do so he must continue to pay contributions at the rate of 6 per cent on the higher salary, and also pay the appropriate part of the related contribution by the authority.

17 Breakdown allowance

A teacher with a minimum of five years' pensionable service may, on the grounds of permanent incapacity, receive an infirmity allowance and lump sum. If the service amounts to less than twenty years it is calculated as though twenty years had been completed provided that the teacher could, had he remained in pensionable service, have served for this length of time before reaching the age of sixty-five. If he could not have done so, the pension is based upon the number of years he could have completed before reaching that age.

Lump sums paid on disablement are calculated at the rate of three-eightieths of the average salary for each year of service since 1 October 1956, and one-thirtieth for each year of contributory service before that date.

If a teacher's health breaks down before the completion of five years' service he is entitled, provided that one year has been completed, to a short service gratuity amounting to one-twelfth of his average salary for each completed year of service.

An application for a disablement allowance or short service gratuity should be made within six months of the end of a teacher's contributory sick leave. In this case, twelve months' continuous absence on not less than half pay (or as a special case, eighteen months in the case of tuberculosis) is treated as contributory sick leave. The Secretary of State has, however, the power to accept later applications.

Teachers who return to contributory service after receiving a breakdown allowance will not have their pensions reduced on retirement, but the lump sum in respect of the whole period of service will be reduced by the amount already received.

It has been held that the acceptance of a short service gratuity by a teacher automatically frustrates his contract of service without the need for notice.[1]

18 Death gratuity

When a teacher dies in reckonable service, a death gratuity equivalent to the best consecutive 365 days' salary during the last three years, or the lump sum which would have been payable if the teacher had retired on an infirmity allowance at the time of his death, will be paid. This is conditional upon death taking place in contributory service or within twelve months of leaving such service, and the completion of five years' reckonable service.

There are arrangements for men who die before completing five years' reckonable service, and for temporary payments to a male teacher's widow for a period of three months. These payments are equivalent to the teacher's qualifying salary.

19 Note on will

Every teacher should enclose with his will a note to his executors quoting his DES reference number and instructing them to write, claiming any allowances payable at his death to the Department of Education and Science (Pensions Branch), Mowden Hall, Staindrop Road, Darlington, Co. Durham, DL3 9BG. This note should not be attached with a pin or paper clip. In one case a teacher had pinned such a note to his will, but when his executors sought to obtain probate they had to swear an affidavit to the effect that the pin-holes and the rusty marks were not caused by any attempt to tamper with the testator's wishes.

[1] *Watts* v *Monmouthshire County Council* and *another* (1968) 66 LGR 171; LCT 77.

20 Annuities

A teacher who, under the Elementary School Teachers (Super-annuation) Act 1898, paid contributions before 1 April 1919, is entitled at the age of sixty-five or, if he continues in employment after that age, on retirement to an annuity in accordance with the Annuity Tables of March 1899.

21 Widows, widowers, orphans and other dependants

The integrated scheme introduced in 1972 includes provision for dependants. If a teacher's contributions cover dependants, either because they have been paid since 1 April 1972, or because all previous service has been bought-in, the widow is entitled to half the pension the teacher would have received, or has received. If all previous service has not been bought-in, the dependants' allowances are reduced proportionately. These pensions commence on the conclusion of the temporary pension referred to in section 18 above.

The pension for one dependent child is one-half of the widow's pension; if there are two or more dependent children, the pension is equal to the widow's pension.

If there are dependent children, but no widow, one child qualifies for two-thirds of the teacher's pension; if there are two or more children, the amount payable is four-thirds.

A woman teacher may nominate any financially dependent close relative (including a dependent husband) to receive these benefits. An unmarried man may similarly nominate an adult dependant, but this nomination lapses on his marriage.

22 Return of contributions

Where a teacher fails to qualify for the payment of allowances before reaching the age of seventy, or ceases to be employed in pensionable service without having so qualified, all contributions paid may be returned with compound interest at the rate of 3 per cent after three months' continuous absence from contributory service. A similar provision exists for women who marry, provided that they cease to be employed in pensionable service within one year of marriage – subject, where appropriate, to deductions in lieu of graduated contributions to the National Insurance scheme. Such payments are subject to deductions for income tax. No contributions may be returned to a teacher who has left the profession and is employed in approved external service.

The former provision by which teachers could return their repaid contributions if they returned to reckonable service has been generally withdrawn. It remains open, however, for those who applied to withdraw their contributions before 1 June 1973.

23 Effect of dismissal

The Secretary of State may refuse altogether, or grant at a reduced rate, any allowances when a teacher's service has ceased through grave misconduct. It would appear that in such cases the decision is at the Secretary of State's discretion and it is immaterial whether the service has been concluded by dismissal or by resignation.

24 National Insurance

Since 1948 all teachers have been required to pay National Insurance contributions. Qualification under the National Insurance Acts is additional to any benefits receivable under the Teachers (Superannuation) Acts for 'existing teachers' who opted to continue payment of the full contributions under the Teachers (Superannuation) Acts as well as those to which they are liable under the National Insurance scheme.[1]

'New entrants' to the profession after 1 July 1948 (with the exception of those classified as 'existing teachers' although they had not commenced contributory service) pay modified con-

---

[1] 'Existing teachers' are those who on 1 July 1948:

(a) were in contributory service, or

(b) had completed an approved course of training, or

(c) had entered an approved training college, or

(d) had been accepted for an approved course of training, or

(e) had applied for admission to an approved course of training and, as a result of that application, later began such a course, provided that they entered contributory service within six months of completing that training.

tributions which are lower than the normal six per cent of the gross salary[1] by £2·40 a year for men, and £2·95 a year for women. The authority's contribution is reduced by the same amounts. There is a corresponding reduction in the pension or disability allowance by an amount which depends on the teacher's age at the date of modification, but which cannot exceed £67·75 a year.

'Existing teachers' who were not over the age of fifty-five, in the case of men, or fifty, in the case of women, could opt to pay the modified contributions. In their case the reduction of pension applies only to that part for which they have qualified in the years subsequent to modification, and not at all for any years in excess of forty years of pensionable service.

Most teachers are contracted out of the graduated scheme, but have to pay contributions at the lower rate applicable to contracted-out employees. These contributions earn units of graduated pension, but do not affect contributions or benefits under the teachers' superannuation scheme.

Those entering service too late to qualify for benefits under the teachers' superannuation scheme before they reach the National Insurance retirement age[2] must pay the full graduated contributions. They pay lower contributions under the teacher's scheme, and these pensions are reduced by approximately the amount of their graduated pension.

25 Transferability

Under certain conditions it is possible to transfer pensionable service between various sectors of the public service provided there is no more than a very limited break. Unless the DES is notified within three months of any change of employment, the right to transfer may be lost.

The principal services between which transferability arrangements may, at present, be made are the teaching profession, the Established Civil Service, and pensionable employment in local government, the National Health Service and some public boards.

[1] 5 per cent before 1 October 1956.
[2] Sixty for women, sixty-five for men.

The Department hopes, in the future, to increase these facilities, and to include moves to and from private employment.

26 The Pensions (Increase) Act 1971

The Pensions (Increase) Act 1971 repealed the previous Acts passed between 1920 and 1969. The purpose of this legislation is to keep pensions in the public service more or less in step with decreases in the value of money through the effect of inflation. The earlier Acts had added specific amounts or percentages to pensions commencing before particular dates, and further increases could be secured only by a further Act.

After setting out the percentages to be added to pensions beginning before 1 April 1971,[1] the 1971 Act provides that the Minister for the Civil Service shall make a biennial review of official pensions against any rise in the cost of living during the review period.[2] The first review was to take place as soon as possible after 31 March 1973. If the review disclosed a rise of at least four per cent, the Minister must make an order raising pensions beginning before the review period by the percentage disclosed. *Pro-rata* increases must be applied to pensions commencing after the beginning of the review period.[3]

[1] Pensions (Increase) Act 1971, s. 1.
[2] This review must now be made annually.
[3] Pensions (Increase) Act 1971, s. 2.

Part Two

TEACHERS AND THEIR EMPLOYMENT

VIII

ROUTINE ADMINISTRATION

1 Obligatory records

Both the Department of Education and Science and the local education authorities require certain records to be kept in schools. This chapter deals principally with those required by the DES, since the local authorities' forms differ widely. The keeping of such documents is an essential part of a teacher's work and it should be done with care. Some of the records, or certified extracts from them, are admissible as evidence in the courts and it is vital that they should be accurate. It is a serious reflection on a teacher when, for example, an attendance register for which he is responsible is kept with a degree of carelessness which he would not tolerate from his pupils.

The DES requires that in every grant-aided school,[1] or every department of such a school organized under a separate head, the following records should be kept by, or under the supervision of, the head.[2]

(a) an admission register;

(b) attendance registers;

(c) the school annals (formerly known as the log book or school record);

(d) a punishment book in which all cases of corporal punishment must be recorded.

Entries in these documents must be written in ink. They must

[1] This requirement applies to schools which are maintained, i.e. those which receive grants from a local education authority (county and voluntary schools); and to those which receive grants from the DES (direct grant schools).

[2] Administrative Memorandum no 531 (10 May 1956).

171

be originals and not copies, and all alterations should be made so that both the original entry and the correction are clearly distinguishable.

Admission and attendance registers must be preserved for at least three years from the date on which they were last used. The same requirement applies to the punishment book. The school annals should be preserved at least during the life of the school.

2 Admission of pupils

The rules of management or articles of government normally provide that the admission of pupils is under the control of the managers or governors, subject to any general requirements of the DES or the local education authority.

A pupil may not be refused admission to, or be excluded from, a school on other than reasonable grounds.[1] It has been held that it is not reasonable to refuse a child admission to a voluntary school merely because he does not belong to the religious persuasion providing the school. Other grounds which have been held to be unreasonable are that the child has previously been untaught, that he is shoeless and neglected, that he has been irregular in attendance or that his brothers and sisters do not attend the school.

The Race Relations Act 1968 provides that it is unlawful for anyone concerned with the provision of any goods, facilities or services for the public, to discriminate against any person seeking to obtain those goods or services by refusing, or deliberately omitting to provide, them on the grounds of colour, race or ethnic or national origins. No person may on these grounds be treated less favourably than anyone else; and segregation for any of these reasons is regarded as discrimination. Facilities for education, instruction or training are included amongst those where discrimination is illegal.[2]

Refusal to admit, or a decision to exclude, has been held to be

[1] Schools Regulations 1959, no 7 (1), and Handicapped Pupils and Special Schools Regulations 1959, no 11 (3).
[2] Race Relations Act 1968, ss. 1–3. The Act does not prohibit, where necessary, the segregation of persons on educational or religious grounds, e.g. if one group requires a particular form of remedial teaching, or a special diet which can be provided only by segregation.

reasonable if a child does not live in the area served by the school, if he has been persistently insubordinate after suffering the usual punishments, or if there has been a refusal to submit to a medical examination in connection with the cleansing of a verminous child.

A pupil may not be admitted to, or retained in, a special school unless it is suitable for him, having regard to age, sex, and the nature of the handicap. In cases of doubt, a pupil may be admitted for a trial period. The roll of a special school must not exceed that approved by the Secretary of State.[1]

An admission register, which may be of loose-leaf or card-index form, must be kept in which the name of every pupil is entered on the day he first attends the school. The details required are:

(a) the full name of the pupil;

(b) sex;

(c) the name and address of the parent or guardian;

(d) the date of the pupil's birth, verified if necessary by reference to the birth certificate;

(e) the date of admission or re-admission;

(f) the name and address of the last school attended;

(g) in the case of schools taking boarders, a statement as to whether the pupil, if of compulsory school age, is a boarder or a day-pupil.

A child whose name is entered in the admission register becomes a registered pupil of that school,[2] and his name must be deleted only when one of the grounds noted in the following section has become applicable.[3]

Children may be admitted only to schools for which they are qualified by age, ability and aptitude. A child of primary school age may not be admitted to a secondary school,[4] and only those qualified by the selection procedure may be admitted to secondary grammar schools. The development of middle schools permitted

[1] Handicapped Pupils and Special Schools Regulations 1959, no 11.

[2] Education Act 1944, s. 114 (1).

[3] Education (Miscellaneous Provisions) Act 1948, s. 4 (6).

[4] Except in certain cases between the ages of ten and a half and twelve. See page 30.

by the Education Act 1964 has blurred the former distinction between primary and secondary schools. For administrative purposes, however, each middle school is specifically designated by the Secretary of State as either a primary, or a secondary, school.[1] Similarly, a child ascertained as educationally sub-normal must not be admitted to an ordinary school if the local education authority has required his admission to a special school.

Children must not be admitted to nursery schools before they attain the age of two. In the case of nursery classes forming part of a larger school, the lower age limit is three. They must not be retained after the end of the term in which they reach the age of five. These limits may be varied if there are exceptional circumstances in the case of any pupil.[2]

3 Removal from roll

The name of a pupil must be removed from the roll of a school on any of the following grounds becoming applicable:[3]

If still of compulsory school age:

(*a*) if the pupil is registered at the school through the requirements of a school attendance order, and the order is amended by the substitution of another school or revoked because arrangements have been made for the child to receive suitable education otherwise than by attendance at school;

(*b*) in any other case where the child has become a registered pupil of another school;

(*c*) in any case not falling within (*a*) above when the pupil has ceased to attend the school and the parent has satisfied the authority that he is receiving efficient full-time education suitable to his age, ability and aptitude otherwise than by attendance at school;

---

[1] See pages 44–5 and 73.

[2] Schools Regulations 1959, no 7 (2).

[3] Pupils' Registration Regulations 1956, no 4. It is important that the name should not be removed until there is evidence that one of the conditions has been fulfilled. When a pupil's name has been removed, he ceases to be a registered pupil of that school and, should the parent fail to cause him to be admitted to another school, the local education authority might be considerably embarrassed in proceedings for failure to attend school.

(*d*) when, being a day-pupil, he has removed to a place from which the school cannot be reached with reasonable facility;

(*e*) when the pupil is certified by the school medical officer as unlikely to be fit to attend school before becoming exempt from the obligation to do so;

(*f*) when the pupil has been continuously absent for at least four weeks and reasonable inquiries have failed to elicit the cause of absence;

(*g*) when the pupil is known to have died;

(*h*) in the case of a boarder, or a pupil in a school not maintained by a local education authority, when the child has ceased to be a pupil of the school;

(*i*) when the pupil will cease to be of compulsory school age before the next meeting of the school and it is known that he intends to leave;[1]

(*j*) when the pupil has been permanently excluded by the local education authority or by the managers or governors of a maintained school.[2]

If not of compulsory school age:

(*a*) if the pupil has ceased to attend the school or, if a boarder, he has ceased to be a pupil of the school;

(*b*) when the pupil has been continuously absent for at least four weeks and reasonable inquiries have failed to elicit the cause of absence;

(*c*) when the pupil is known to have died.

When a pupil of compulsory school age, who is not the subject of a school attendance order, has become a registered pupil at a special school under arrangements made by a local education authority, his name must not be removed from the roll of that school without the consent of the authority or, if this be refused, without a direction by the Secretary of State.

[1] The names of these pupils should be removed on the last day of term: Administrative Memorandum no 531 (10 May 1956).
[2] If the Secretary of State as the result of an appeal by the parent, determines that the child has been excluded unreasonably, the name must be restored to the roll.

4 Suspension and expulsion of pupils

The procedure to be followed is laid down in the rules of management or articles of government and in the regulations of the local
éducation authority. Suspension is within the jurisidiction of the
head and is usually the limit of his power, but there are some
schools where the head is authorized by the articles of government, to expel. It cannot be too strongly urged that, even where
this is so, it is always wiser to choose the less final course. Suspension gives the pupil and his parent the opportunity of a constitutional inquiry, whereas there is an administrative difficulty[1]
connected with expulsion which might mean that the decision
would have to be revoked, with consequent embarrassment to all
concerned, except, possibly, the pupil.

Even the right of suspension should be used with the greatest
discretion, and only for serious and urgent cause. When a head has
decided to pursue this course he should explain carefully to the
pupil that he may not attend school again until the matter has
been fully considered. The suspension should be communicated
at once, in writing, to the parent and to the local education
authority. In the case of voluntary-aided schools the head should
notify the correspondent or clerk whose duty it then becomes to
inform the authority.

The parent must be given an opportunity of attending any
meeting at which the suspension is to be considered. At this meeting, unless there are cogent reasons to the contrary, it should be
decided, subject to any consents which may be necessary, either
to fix a date from which the suspension will be lifted on such
conditions as may seem desirable, or to confirm the suspension and
expel the pupil.

It is the duty of the head to tell the parents that they have a
right to appeal. In the first instance they may address their appeal
to the managers or governors and, if this prove unsuccessful, they
may also state their case to the Secretary of State. If the child is
expelled, they may request that he should continue as a pupil of
the same school and should the Secretary of State decide that the
expulsion is unreasonable, the child must be readmitted by the

[1] See page 177.

school.[1] Herein lies the danger of expulsion from an administrative point of view. If the Secretary of State's decision were to be against the managers or governors there would be considerable loss of face by all concerned, and the force of expulsion as an ultimate sanction would be lost.

When a pupil has been expelled from a particular school, the local education authority is not relieved of its duty to provide an education for the child suitable to its age, ability and aptitude. Normally, no proceedings for non-attendance can be taken in the courts in respect of any child who is suspended or who, being expelled, has not been admitted as a registered pupil at another school. Where, however, suspension is due to the parent's encouragement of his child's disregard of the school rules, a prosecution of the parent may be successful, as was the case in *Spiers* v *Warrington Corporation*.[2]

In view of what has been written in the last paragraph, local education authorities are naturally not over-enthusiastic about the expulsion, or even the suspension, of pupils from a maintained school. With the recent tendency towards the reduction or elimination of corporal punishment, there has been a tendency for suspensions to increase in numbers. Some local education authorities have shown a corresponding tendency to advise and sometimes to exert pressure on heads not to suspend pupils. During the past few years there has also been a growing feeling that violence, insubordination and other forms of anti-social behaviour have increased among pupils. As a result heads sometimes find themselves faced with a staff demand that a pupil should be suspended. It is also implicit in such a demand that the managers or governors will support the head and the staff, so that expulsion will follow as a matter of course. In such a situation the head may well find himself subjected to opposing pressures from the authority and the staff.

[1] Pupils' Registration Regulations, 1956, no. 4 (x). The Secretary of State might make such a decision if, for example, the parents stated that the school in question was the only voluntary school within reasonable distance to provide religious education in accordance with their own beliefs.

[2] See pages 26–7 and 206.

Suspensions fall into one of two broad groups, and may arise from a specific and serious breach of school order by a pupil or, alternatively, from the cumulative effect of a long series of disruptive acts.

In law, that is according to the rules of management or articles of government, the head's position has not changed: the decision to suspend, or not to suspend, remains his alone.

In order to avoid a large number of suspensions, it is not unknown for a local education authority to suggest that a head may consider keeping a pupil out of school for a specific period of, say, three or four days, or to surround the head's discretion with a range of the procedures described below before suspension takes place.

The rules or articles do not provide a head with the discretion to re-admit a pupil by ending a suspension. The first of these courses, therefore, needs great caution and, if it is employed, great care should be taken not to refer to suspension but to exclusion. The distinction was drawn by Lord Chief Justice Goddard in *Spiers* v *Warrington Corporation*.[1] Whereas suspension is a refusal to admit to the school, exclusion, a term not known to the law in this context nor indeed used by Lord Goddard, is a willingness to admit the child at all times subject to certain conditions being met. Such a condition may be, as in *Spiers* v *Warrington*, that the pupil shall be properly dressed or it may be a requirement that his father should visit the school before the pupil resumes his studies. The pupil must be re-admitted as soon as the condition is fulfilled. In view of the uncertainty as to the extent of the head's powers in this situation, exclusion should be used with the greatest of care if the head is not to be accused of denying a pupil his educational rights. The condition must be reasonable, and must be capable of being fulfilled. It is doubtful if the passage of time *per se* is sufficient; in other words, exclusion should be designed for the benefit of the child or the school, or both, and should not be used as a disciplinary procedure equivalent to rustication in the ancient universities. It will normally be preceded by endeavours to secure parental co-operation in the issue at stake.

[1] See pages 26–7.

The 'requirement' by some local education authorities that heads should enter into a long series of procedures before suspending any pupil, including such tactics as consultation and correspondence with the parents, seeking the advice of the educational welfare service, arranging for the services of the child guidance clinic, or discussing a transfer with a colleague in a neighbouring school, is appropriate to the cumulative variety of suspension. In such a case the relationships between pupil and staff may well have broken down to such an extent that it will be in the pupil's interest, as well as that of the school, that he should move elsewhere. There are occasions when in spite of his concern for the individual pupil, his dislike for handing on his professional failures to someone else, and his care not to seem merely to cast out a difficult member of the community, a head must ask: 'Have I now reached the stage where I must place the welfare of the school as a whole, and the other pupils as individuals, above my concern for this pupil?'

It is not, however, necessarily a justifiable criticism by parents that they knew nothing of any problems at school before a suspension. Sometimes a pupil commits some offence quite out of keeping with his character, for which there is no alternative to suspension without warning. Sometimes there may have been prior indications of a deterioration in character which were insufficient to cause enough concern to notify the parents. If, in these circumstances and with due consideration, a head considers that suspension is the only course, he has a duty to take this step as part of his legal responsibility under the rules of management or articles of government.

No one suggests that suspension is a procedure on which to embark lightly or prematurely. Professionally, however, delay can lead to a situation where it is difficult to distinguish one act of indiscipline from another in order to decide that suspension has become inevitable. In the end it is often staff strain which tells, and the offence which precipitates the suspension may be less serious than some of its predecessors which appear to have been condoned. It may also make justification of the suspension more difficult on the facts at law. Delay can also lead to an imperceptible deterioration in the behaviour of the pupil concerned and in the good order of the school.

As was said earlier in this section, the power of suspension should be used with great caution, it should be used only in the interests of the pupil concerned or those of the school as a whole, it must be firmly rooted in facts which can be established, and it must be exercised strictly in accordance with the rules of management or articles of government.

Finally, it must be remembered that in suspending a pupil a head revokes his jurisdiction to his managers or governors who have, subject to appeal, complete discretion. If they re-admit the pupil, even against his advice, he has no cause to complain nor have the other members of the staff.

5 Infectious illness

Pupils suffering from an infectious or contagious illness should be excluded from school in accordance with the regulations of the local education authority. Unless the notification comes from him, the medical officer should be informed of the illness. If a case of an unusually serious nature, such as smallpox, diphtheria, cholera, dysentery or poliomyelitis, occurs amongst the pupils of a school it is advisable to telephone the medical officer and ask for special instructions.

Children in contact with infectious illnesses at home are excluded in certain cases. Contacts should be carefully watched after their return to school, in case the disease develops at this later stage.

The medical officer should be informed of verminous children in order that he may take the necessary steps for cleansing them.

The closure of schools during an epidemic is now rare. Children running about and playing together are as dangerous to each other as they are in school. Moreover, during such periods, teachers can watch for the appearance of symptoms and do much to prevent the spread of the epidemic by prompt action. Closure is a matter for the medical officer and the advice of the DES in a pamphlet, now withdrawn, is that 'it is only in special and quite exceptional circumstances necessary to close a school in the interests of public health'.[1]

6 Records of individual development

The DES in a circular[2] issued in 1947, has made suggestions for the keeping of records concerning the progress of individual children. Such records are still in the experimental stage and it is suggested that they should cover not only attainment but also such matters as aptitudes, special interests and disposition. These documents are of particular value when filling in employment records for school leavers, and writing testimonials and references for pupils who have left. Where local education authorities have abandoned the more formal examination for selecting pupils for different kinds of secondary education, individual records play an important part in selection. Care should be taken to ensure that the records are factual, and as objective as possible.

7 Transfer of records

When a child ceases to attend a school and becomes a pupil at another place of education or training, such educational information as the local education authority considers reasonable shall be supplied to the new school if requested. In this regulation the term 'school' includes a special school.[3]

8 Educational year and holidays

A maintained school must meet, except for unavoidable cause, for not less than 400 sessions in each calendar year, from which may be deducted not more than twenty for closures during term.[4] A special school must meet on 200 days, from which not more than ten may be deducted for occasional closures.[5] The provi-

---

[1] *Memorandum on Closure of and Exclusion from School* (HMSO, reprinted 1953).

[2] *School Records of Individual Development* (Circular no 151, dated 18 July 1947).

[3] Schools Regulations 1959, no. 8; and Handicapped Pupils and Special Schools Regulations 1959, no. 10.

[4] Schools Regulations 1959, no. 11.

[5] Handicapped Pupils and Special Schools Regulations 1959, no. 11.

sion that an educational year, beginning on 1 August, shall be divided into three or four terms was removed in 1966 in order to permit more administrative flexibility in organization.[1]

Occasional closure, for half term or other purposes, *during* term may be granted in accordance with the rules of management or articles of government, provided that the limits described in the last paragraph are not exceeded. It should be noted that these holidays must be taken during the course of a term, and may not be added to the main holidays.

9 School sessions

The length of an individual session is no longer prescribed, but on every day on which a school meets, there must be provided in a maintained school:

(*a*) *in a nursery school or class* – at least three hours of suitable training and activities;

(*b*) *in a school or class mainly for pupils under eight years of age* – at least three hours of secular instruction;

(*c*) *in a class for pupils eight years of age and over* – at least four hours of secular instruction.

This must be divided into morning and afternoon sessions unless exceptional circumstances make this undesirable. If a school meets on six days in the week, one day may consist of a single session of half the length noted above. If pupils attend a nursery school or class for half a day only, the session may be of one and a half hours' duration.

The time set aside for registration is excluded from these periods, but the necessary time for recreation, and the medical examination, inspection, and treatment of pupils (including dental treatment) may be included. In a voluntary school the time required for the inspection of religious education[2] may also be included.[3]

[1] Schools Amending Regulations 1966, no. 2 (*b*); and Handicapped Pupils and Special Schools Amending Regulations 1966, no. 2.

[2] Education Act 1944, s. 77.

[3] Schools Regulations 1959, no. 10, and Handicapped Pupils and Special Schools Regulations 1959, no. 13.

10 Timetable

There must be a timetable for each maintained school on which the following information is shown:[1]

(a) the times of the beginning and end of the school session on any day;

(b) the place at which any instruction is given regularly elsewhere than on the school premises.

The timetable is, legally, the responsibility of the head. In large schools, in particular, it is a complicated document which attempts to resolve the various constraints (such as the number of teachers and rooms, the provision of specialist facilities, and the number of periods available) in such a way as to interpret the school's educational philosophy in terms of a number of periods each week. It is important that, although he must be prepared to justify the principles underlying a particular timetable, the head should recognize the value of contributions which can be made by the teaching staff, particularly in the early stages of preparation. Consultation often begins as early as December in connection with a timetable which will become effective ten months later. It is not always possible to meet all the requests made by the staff, but it is wise not to abandon them without explanation and further discussion. A timetable ruthlessly imposed can lead to considerable friction, and a staff which is accorded the courtesy of effective consultation will amost certainly co-operate still further by making their intentions known in such matters as changes of syllabus or impending resignation which affect the construction of the timetable.

It is important that the head should be advised of any deviations. Nothing is calculated to make him feel more foolish than occasions when after consulting the timetable, he steers an inspector towards a particular lesson only to discover that both teacher and pupils have migrated, even though for a perfectly valid reason.

11 Size of classes

Classrooms and other rooms used for instruction must not be overcrowded.[2]

[1] Schools Regulations 1959, no. 14.   [2] Schools Regulations 1959, no. 5.

The regulation which formerly stipulated the maximum number of pupils permitted on the roll of any class has been withdrawn.[1]

12 Temporary closure of schools

The HMI must be given seven clear days' notice of the closure of a school or the suspension of its ordinary work for holidays or any other cause. If, in the case of an emergency, this notice cannot be given, the closure should be notified by telegram to ARISTDIDES, AUDLEY, LONDON, whence the message will be transmitted to the inspector concerned.[2]

The purpose of this notification is twofold. It enables the DES to keep a check on the number of closures during the year, and it avoids fruitless visits by an inspector to a school which is closed.

13 School annals

This record should be kept by or under the supervision of the head, and it forms a permanent record of events connected with the history of the school. The actual form is not prescribed, but the following matters are amongst those which should be included:[2]

(*a*) matters of significance such as changes in the character, organization or curriculum of the school, alterations to the premises, substantial changes in equipment, visits of managers or governors, the illness or absence of members of the staff;

(*b*) the receipt of any report on the school sent by the DES to the authority, or to the managers or governors, and any remarks made by the DES thereon;

(*c*) the receipt of any report made to the authority by the committees or officers, if so directed by the authority;

(*d*) the reasons for a temporary closure of the school, a substantial variation in the routine or a marked change in the average attendance.

[1] Schools (Amendment no. 2) Regulations 1969, no. 2. For the maximum size of classes in special schools, see page 188.
[2] Administrative Memorandum no. 531 (10 May 1956).

14 Corporal punishment

All cases of corporal punishment must be entered immediately in a book which is kept for this purpose. The head is responsible for its completeness and accuracy.[1]

15 External examinations

The following regulations[2] govern the entry of pupils by maintained schools for external examinations:

(a) No pupil below the age of sixteen on 1 September in the year in which the examination is held may be entered by a school for any external examination other than the General Certificate of Education;

(b) A pupil below the age of sixteen on 1 September in the year in which the examination is held may be entered for the General Certificate of Education if the head certifies that it is desirable on educational grounds that he should be entered, and that it is probable that he will pass in the subject or subjects for which he is entered.

Care must be taken to ensure that examination results are notified accurately. A former student at the Technical College was awarded £50 in damages against the Canterbury City Council for shock when she learned, after five months, that she had failed all four subjects in the General Certificate of Education examination. She had previously been informed that she had passed in each.[3]

16 Handicapped children

Handicapped pupils are those who require special educational treatment because of some disability of mind or body. Their education may be provided in either a special school or an ordinary school, but it must be appropriate to the age, ability and aptitude of the pupil concerned, having regard to the nature of his disability. The requirements for the education of handicapped chil-

[1] Administrative Memorandum no. 531 (10 May 1956).

[2] Schools Regulations 1959, no. 15.

[3] *Hollands* v *Canterbury City Council and Hooke* (1966) *Kentish Gazette*, 30 September and 28 October; LCT 188.

dren in ordinary schools are set out in the Schools Regulations 1959, no. 20.

The increased provision of special schools in recent years has done much to help handicapped children to overcome their problems, and it is important to place them correctly as early as possible in their school lives.

The various categories of handicapped pupils are as follows:[1]

(a) *Blind* – those with no sight or who are, or probably will become, so defective in vision that they require to be taught by methods not involving the use of sight;

(b) *Partially-sighted* – those who cannot follow the normal school régime, but who can be educated by special methods involving sight;

(c) *Deaf* – those with impaired hearing who require methods appropriate for those with little or no naturally acquired speech or language;

(d) *Partially-hearing* – pupils with impaired hearing whose development of speech and language, even if retarded, is following a normal pattern, and who require special arrangements or facilities though not necessarily all the methods used for deaf pupils;

(e) *Educationally sub-normal* – those with limited ability or other educational retardation who require some specialized education wholly or partly in substitution for the normal education of ordinary schools;

(f) *Epileptic* – those who, because of this condition, cannot be educated under a normal régime without detriment to themselves or other pupils;

(g) *Maladjusted* – those with emotional instability or psychological disturbance which requires special treatment for their personal, social or educational readjustment;

(h) *Physically-handicapped* – pupils not suffering solely from a defect of sight or hearing who cannot be educated under a normal régime because of disease or crippling defect;

[1] Handicapped Pupils and Special Schools Regulations 1959, no. 4, as amended by the Handicapped Pupils and Special Schools Regulations 1962.

(*i*) *Pupils suffering from speech defect* which, whilst not due to deafness, requires special treatment;

(*j*) *Delicate* – those who do not fall under any other category but who, because of their impaired physical condition, need a change of environment or who cannot, without risk, be educated in ordinary schools;

(*k*) *Deaf-blind;*

(*l*) *Autistic and psychotic;*

(*m*) *Acutely dyslexic.*

Local education authorities have a duty to provide special facilities for pupils in each of the last three categories and, so far as is practicable, to make them available in any school which it maintains or assists.[1]

Until the beginning of April 1971 some children were classified as 'mentally handicapped' and regarded as unsuitable for education at school. Provision for their training was made by the public health authority, not by the local education authority. The responsibility for these children has now been transferred to the education service.[2]

17 Special schools

It is the duty of local education authorities to have regard to the need for securing that provision is made for pupils who suffer from any disability of mind or body by providing special educational treatment, either in special schools or otherwise.[3] Special schools are suited to the needs of children in the various handicapped categories and, in the nature of things, some of these are boarding schools whilst others cater only for day-pupils. The modified code for these schools is laid down in the Handicapped Pupils and Special Schools Regulations 1959, and the Special Schools and Establishments (Grant) Regulations 1959 as amended. Some of the principal provisions are noted below.

Staffing – The requirements of the Secretary of State regarding

[1] Chronically Sick and Disabled Persons Act 1970, ss. 25–27.

[2] Education (Handicapped Children) Act 1970.

[3] Education Act 1944 s. 8 (2) (*c*).

the staff of special schools have already been discussed in Chapter III.[1]

Terms – There is no longer any provision limiting the number of terms into which a year is divided.[2]

School Sessions – The day should be divided into two sessions, unless exceptional circumstances make this undesirable. There should be three hours' secular instruction each day for classes of pupils mainly under eight years of age, and four hours of such instruction for classes of pupils mainly over that age. The necessary time for recreation, and for medical examination, inspection and treatment, and dental treatment may be included.[3]

Size of Classes – The maximum number of pupils permitted on the roll of any given school is determined by the Secretary of State.[4] The number of pupils on the register of a class in a special school is limited to the following numbers:

(*a*) Pupils who are deaf, partially deaf[5] or suffering from a speech defect 10

(*b*) Pupils who are blind, partially sighted or maladjusted 15

(*c*) Pupils who are educationally sub-normal, epileptic or physically handicapped 20

(*d*) Pupils who are delicate 30

These numbers may be exceeded if this is desirable in the interests of the efficiency of the school as a whole, and the average number of children in all the classes does not exceed the number prescribed. If, because of a shortage of teachers or other unavoidable circumstances, it is not possible to comply with this regulation,

[1] See pages 94–6.

[2] Handicapped Pupils and Special Schools Regulations 1966, no. 2.

[3] Handicapped Pupils and Special Schools Regulations 1959, no. 13.

[4] Handicapped Pupils and Special Schools Regulations 1959 no. 11 (1).

[5] In the regulation dealing with the classification of handicapped pupils the term 'partially deaf' was replaced by 'partially hearing' – Handicapped Pupils and Special Schools Regulations 1962. The wording of the regulation dealing with the size of classes was not amended. The change in the classification was designed 'to take account of the greater use of residual hearing made possible by improved electronic aid and new techniques of special educational treatment'.

the number of pupils on the register of a class shall be such as is reasonable in all the circumstances.[1]

Hospital schools – The Secretary of State may approve such modifications of the general scheme as he may deem necessary in the case of a school held in a hospital.[2]

Further education – An establishment for the further education of the disabled must provide courses of vocational training suitable to the disability of the students, including their general education and appropriate physical education. Admission is normally limited to those over sixteen.[3]

18 Change of pupil's name

Teachers are asked from time to time to change a child's surname in the school records. This is often done when the parents are divorced and the mother, having the custody of the child, marries or lives with another man. Care is needed in dealing with such a request.

A case came before the Chancery Division on this point in 1962.[4] The mother had changed her child's name to that of her new husband, without informing the father. When she eventually told her former husband of her action he brought a lawsuit in order to restore the child's original surname. It was held that an adult can change his name at any time, but there is no magic in a deed poll which merely records the intention to change in a solemn form. If there is any power to change an infant's name it resides in the natural guardian, who is the father if he is still alive. An order for custody means no more than the name implies, and does not abrogate all the rights of the father. Mr Justice Buckley ordered the restoration of the father's name.

Requests of this kind should be referred to the local education authority for advice. In any case the entry in the admission and attendance registers should be in the form, '*Smith, otherwise*

[1] Handicapped Pupils and Special Schools Regulations 1959, no. 9. See also *Staffing of Special Schools and Classes* (Circular 47/73).
[2] Handicapped Pupils and Special Schools Regulations 1959, no. 26.
[3] Special Schools and Establishments (Grant) Regulations 1959, no. 8.
[4] T. (*Orse H.*) (*An Infant*) [1963] Ch. 238; LCT 133.

Jones', to enable quick cross-referencing, and to prevent, for example, the invalidation of a summons for failing to attend school.

The position is somewhat different where a child with a foreign name which is very difficult for his English classmates is known by an English name; sometimes the parents adopt an English forename without intending to make any legal or permanent change. In such cases no formality is required, but both names should appear in all registers. Entries for external examinations should always be made in the legally recognized name to facilitate the verification of qualifications against other documentation later in life.

19 Scientific dangers
Ionizing radiations – No instruction may be given in any school or other educational establishments involving:

(*a*) radio-active material other than a compound of potassium, thorium or uranium normally used as a chemical agent, or

(*b*) apparatus in which electrons are accelerated by a potential difference of five kilovolts or greater, other than apparatus used only for the purpose of receiving visual images by way of television,

unless the Secretary of State has given his approval, which may be withdrawn at any time.[1]

Carcinogenic amines – Naphthylamine and other known carcinogens should not be kept in schools. The risks are greatest with beta-naphthylamine and benzidine.[2]

Lasers – Under no circumstances should laser beams be viewed directly, and their use should accord with the Ministry of Technology's Code of Practice for Laser Systems (1969).[3]

20 Bombs and explosive devices
A feature of life in recent years has been the use of explosives in civil disturbances. In the train of this development has come the practical joker who gets some satisfaction out of giving false

[1] Circular 1/65.	[2] Circular 3/70.	[3] Circular 7/70.

warnings that a bomb has been placed in a particular building. Hundreds of hoaxes of this kind were perpetrated in London during the month following an explosion in the Post Office Tower.

Happily, so far, no devices of this nature have been placed in schools; and one would hope that it is unthinkable that anyone would risk the safety or lives of schoolchildren. Nevertheless, schools have had their share of false alarms and, unfortunately, there have been sufficient explosions elsewhere to make it imperative to treat every warning as genuine until all reasonable steps have been taken to establish its true nature.

In the first place, it must be remembered that pupils are in the care of the staff *in loco parentis*, and the precautions to be taken are those which a reasonable parent would take in similar circumstances. Safety is the paramount consideration.

The school's fire drill system may be sufficient as far as the pupils are concerned, but if a spate of warnings is received it may be necessary to devise a special scheme, possibly in consultation with the police.

Immediately a warning is received the school must be cleared and all pupils escorted to the safest available place where the register should be checked to ensure that no one has been left behind. The police should be informed immediately, with as much information about the nature of the call as possible.

Unless arrangements have been agreed with the police beforehand, a search of the premises should be deferred until the police arrive. This is essential if a particular call seems particularly significant, or any suspicious object has been noticed. Assistance in searching by teaching or non-teaching staff must be a matter for individual voluntary consent, and must not be given if it has been prohibited by the local education authority. No pupils, whatever their age, should be permitted to search.

The police can rarely, if ever, say that they are completely satisfied that there is no risk in returning to the building. The head will have to take this decision, basing his judgment on the facts available to him, such as whether the call is one of a series, whether a deadline was given, the nature of the search and so forth.

No amateur attempts should be made to touch any object which arouses suspicion.

If an external examination is interrupted by an evacuation, the examining board should be asked by telephone for instructions before it is resumed. A written report should also be sent.

Sometimes a public occasion, such as a concert or prizegiving, may be scheduled to take place during a period when a school is suffering a series of hoaxes. In such cases the advice of the police should be sought as to any special precautions to be taken.

21 Age of majority

Since the age of majority was reduced from twenty-one to eighteen, secondary schools have, for the first time, numbered adults among their pupils, and this has led to a considerable degree of uncertainty about the relationship between these pupils and the school organization.

The legislation provides that a person shall reach 'full age' on attaining the age of eighteen,[1] and applies to all statutory provisions and rules of law unless there is a contrary definition or expression of intent. It also applies to wills and other instruments made after the Family Law Reform Act came into force on 1 January 1970. As teachers are sometimes asked by pupils about their rights in law, a summary of the principal changes is given below, and the table on pages 194–5 sets out the minimum ages for a wide variety of acts.

It is now possible at the age of eighteen to marry without parental consent (section 2), to make a valid will and to benefit under intestacies occurring after 1 January 1970 (section 3). Various maintenance orders may be kept in force until attainment of the age of twenty-one, and a son may claim under the Inheritance (Family Provisions) Act 1938 until he reaches that age (sections 4 and 5).

Persons under the age of eighteen may be described as 'minors' instead of 'infants' (section 12).

A minor, having attained the age of sixteen, may give consent to any surgical, medical or dental treatment which would otherwise

[1] Family Law Reform Act 1969, s. 1.

constitute, without consent, a trespass to the person. This includes diagnostic procedures and ancillary acts including, particularly, the administration of an anaesthetic (section 8).

Schedule 2 of the Act sets out a number of miscellaneous changes effected by the Act. On attaining the age of eighteen it is now possible to become a member of the committee of a trade union,[1] a friendly society, or an industrial and provident society,[2] and also to vote and hold office in a building society. The powers of a guardian over the person and property of a minor[3] cease when the minor attains the age of eighteen. At the same age a person can apply income to maintainance and accumulate a surplus income; he may be hypnotized at a public entertainment; he may withdraw money from a trustee savings bank, and sue for wages; he may receive betting advertisements; and he may become a manager or governor of a school.

In certain matters, however, no change was made by the Act. Under Schedule 2 it is expressly provided that the Act does not affect the Representation of the People Act 1933, so that no person under the age of twenty-one may be a candidate at a parliamentary election. Neither can he be a candidate in a local government election.[1] Statutory provisions relating to taxes are also unaffected by the changes in the law.

It is still an offence for consenting males to commit an act of gross indecency together, even in private, if one of them is under the age of twenty-one.

So far as schools are concerned, the two problems which are most commonly raised are the duty of the schoolmaster *in loco parentis* towards pupils who are adults, and the power to exercise control over such pupils in cases of indiscipline.

No cases have so far come before the courts for decision on these points, and any consideration must therefore, to some extent, be a matter of conjecture. So far as the first issue is concerned, it would seem doubtful if the schoolmaster can be *in loco parentis*

---

[1] Membership of the trade union itself can begin at sixteen.
[2] Industrial and provident societies may be joined at sixteen.
[3] Under the Tenures Abolition Act 1660.
[4] Local Government Act 1972, s. 79.

Fig. 10. LEGAL AGE LIMITS
At the age shown in the left-hand column a person

	MAY	*MUST*

MINORS
Children

	MAY	MUST
0	Have a bank deposit account	
6w	Be handed to prospective adoptive parents	
$4\frac{1}{2}$m	Be adopted	
2	Join a nursery school	
3		Be paid for on public transport
5		Begin school
10	Be charged with a crime if in need of care or control	
12	Buy a pet	
13	Have a current bank account at the manager's discretion	
14	Go into a bar with an adult	Pay full fares on public transport

Young Persons

	MAY	MUST
	Consent to his fingerprints being taken Be fined up to £50 Be sent to a detention centre Be admitted to an 'AA' film Own an air-gun	
15	Own a shot-gun Join the Army, Navy, Royal Air Force or Women's Royal Army Corps with parental consent	
16	Drink cider or beer with a meal in a room with no bar Leave school Buy fireworks Fly a glider solo Marry, with parental consent	Pay National Insurance contributions Have own passport if travelling abroad (except when travelling on a collective passport)

194

16   Consent to medical treatment
Buy and smoke cigarettes and tobacco
Drive a motor-cycle or tractor

Young Persons

16½ Receive sickness and unemployment
benefit

17   Drive a car   Be tried on any charge in
Pilot a powered aircraft solo   an adult court
Be sentenced to imprisonment
Join the Women's Royal Naval Service
with parental permission

ADULTS

18   Not be adopted
Buy or consume alcohol in a bar
Become a blood donor
Own land
Be admitted to see 'X' films
Enter a betting shop
Marry without consent
Join the Women's Royal Air Force
Bring an action before the courts
Give a body organ or tissue for trans-
plant
Vote in a parliamentary or local election
Receive, personally, money under a will
Make a will

21   Drive a lorry or bus
Serve on a jury
Stand for election to Parliament or a
local authority

to an adult. Nevertheless, he owes a common law duty of care to everyone who comes to the school, as well as a duty under the Occupiers Liability Act 1957. To discharge these duties he must have an adequate, fully-maintained system, and in planning that system it would be prudent to remember that he has among his pupils a number of young adults and, usually, a large number of children on the premises. Any system he devises should aim to prevent injury to any person in either of those categories, and must be enforced.

There can be little doubt that the relationship between a pupil and the school changes immediately the former attains his majority. A possible basis for discipline seems to be the acceptance by both that the pupil remains at school voluntarily, and thereby agrees to abide by the rules of the school so far as they may reasonably be applied to him. It is most doubtful whether detention or corporal punishment may be used to deal with disciplinary offences by adult pupils, in view of what has been said in the last paragraph about the position of the schoolmaster *in loco parentis* to these members of the school. If, however, their behaviour merits it, they can be suspended and, if it seems right in all the circumstances, expelled.

Various subsidiary questions are raised from time to time. If an adult pupil wishes to be withdrawn from religious education should he not make the request himself? On the face of it, this seems reasonable, but the Education Act has not been amended at this point. Parents are still expected to contribute to the maintenance of their children until they are twenty-five (or twenty-one in the case of a married daughter) if they are students, unless they have been self-supporting for three years.

To whom should a report on the work of an adult pupil be given? It is probably wiser that this should be handed to the pupil, and not sent to the parents.

In general, the rights and obligations of a parent or guardian end when the child reaches the age of majority. A parent's rights and obligations would end on the child's earlier marriage, but this would not be so in the case of a guardian whose male ward married before the age of eighteen.

The problems are similar to those with which universities and colleges have had to deal for a very great many years. There is no indication that the difficulties of schools have been vastly increased merely because the age of majority has been lowered. As time goes by a corpus of practice will develop. In the meantime a working relationship may be founded on the acceptance that the pupil is continuing in attendance voluntarily, and voluntary membership of any organization implies an acceptance of its rules and customs.

22 School councils

The last decade has witnessed a considerable extension of what is sometimes called 'pupil power', accompanied by the formation of bodies such as the Schools Action Union and the National Union of School Students to campaign for an active role for pupils in the management of schools.[1]

Some schools have established councils, which include members of the staff, pupils and, sometimes, non-teaching staff. Insofar as these bodies can act in a consultative capacity to achieve desirable results which cannot be attained in some less formal way, there is something to commend them.

It must be pointed out however that, whatever the ideals which may lie behind the promotion of 'effective' school councils with a 'real' say in the running of a school, the law has not been changed, nor has the responsibility been shifted. Any head who allows a school council to be formed, and who gives the impression that he has abdicated his legal responsibilities to it, is encouraging the members to live in a fools' paradise. If the council is then adamant in proposing a course of action which he can reasonably foresee will lead to disaster, and disaster ensues, it will be the head and not the council which is held accountable.

23 Work experience

A pupil in his last year of compulsory schooling may be employed under regulations made by the local education authority with a

[1] The term 'management' is here used to describe all the organization of schools, and is not restricted to the functions of the manager of primary schools.

view to providing work experience as a part of education. Before 1973, this was possible only for those who had reached the upper age limit of compulsory education.[1]

Pupils may not be employed under this Act, in ships. Nor may they be employed contrary to any statute, by-law, regulation or other statutory provision which excludes young persons from any description of work or prescribes the conditions under which they may perform it.

24 Employment of children

Under the Employment of Children Act 1973, restrictions are placed upon the employment of children of compulsory school age with a view to safeguarding the health and well-being of those who have frequently proved a temptation to employers seeking cheap labour.

The Act has removed the power of local education authorities to make by-laws in respect of the employment of children, and placed the responsibility for making regulations in the hands of the Secretary of State. The supervision of the regulations remains with the local education authority.

A person who assists in a trade or occupation carried on for profit is deemed to be employed, even though he receives no reward for his labour.

Age limits – No child may be employed until he has attained the age of thirteen.

Time limit – On days on which he is required to attend school a child may not be employed before the end of school hours, nor for more than two hours. He may not be employed for more than two hours on a Sunday, nor before seven o'clock in the morning, nor after seven o'clock at night on any day. The nature of the employment must be such that he is not required to lift, carry or move anything so heavy as to be likely to cause him injury.

The Secretary of State's regulations may reduce the age limit for children employed by their parents in light agricultural or horticultural work and may permit employment for not more than one hour before the beginning of school hours. The regulations may

[1] Education (Work Experience) Act 1973.

also prohibit altogether the employment of children in certain occupations and may prescribe restrictions regarding the actual periods of employment, periods of rest and holidays. They may also prohibit employment except under and in accordance with a permit issued by the local education authority, and require employers to keep records of children so employed, and to furnish returns.

The regulations may not prevent a child from taking part in an entertainment under a licence granted in pursuance of the Children and Young Persons Act, nor in a performance where, by virtue of section 37 (3) of the Children and Young Persons Acts 1963, no licence is required. A licence is not required if a child has not taken part in a performance of the kind mentioned in the following paragraph on more than three days in the previous six months. Neither is a licence required for a performance under arrangements made by a school, or other organization approved for this purpose by the Secretary of State, provided no payment, other than for expenses, is made to him or any other person.

Entertainments – In general, children are not allowed to take part in any entertainment for which a charge is made, whether for admission or not, to any member of the audience. Neither may they perform in licensed premises, or take part in a broadcast performance, or any recorded performance made for exhibition to the public by broadcast or film. A local authority may, however, grant a licence for such performances (in accordance with any conditions and restrictions which may be made by the Secretary of State for Education and Science).

Children may not be allowed time off from school for unlicensed public performances in any medium. This applies also to auditions and rehearsals. The making of recordings (except for use in a broadcast or a film intended for public exhibition), and modelling, are subject to the ordinary law regulating the employment of children, and not to the provisions dealing with entertainments.

Dangerous performances – No person under the age of sixteen may take part in any performance endangering his life or limb, nor may he be trained for such performances if under the age of twelve.

Between the ages of twelve and sixteen a licence is necessary for such training.

Performances abroad – No person under the age of eighteen may be taken outside the United Kingdom and the Republic of Ireland for the purposes of singing, playing, performing or being exhibited for profit except under licence. Licences for this purpose are granted only by the Chief Magistrate at Bow Street. The prohibition does not apply to a person under the age of eighteen who is not permanently resident in the United Kingdom.

Absence from school – A licence may authorize absence from school: it is for the licensing authority to determine that the holder's education will not suffer thereby.

Age limits – A child who has attained the age of thirteen may be licensed for any kind of performance. A younger child may not be licensed unless:

    (*a*) for acting the part cannot be taken except by a child of about his age;

    (*b*) for ballet the part cannot be taken except by a child of about his age, and the programme consists entirely of ballet or opera;

    (*c*) the performance is wholly or mainly of music, opera or ballet, and the child's part is wholly or mainly musical.[1]

Street trading by young persons below the age of eighteen is controlled by regulations made by the local education authority in pursuance of the Children and Young Persons Acts as amended by the Education Acts. This includes the hawking of newspapers, matches, flowers or any other articles, singing or performing for profit, shoeblacking and other similar occupations carried on in public places.[2] Young persons below the age of seventeen are prohibited altogether from street trading, unless the by-laws permit them to be employed by their parents. Children may not be so employed in any circumstances.

Enforcement of the law relating to the employment of children and

[1] The Children (Performances) Regulations 1968. See also *The Law on Performances by Children* (HMSO, 1968), and page 343.

[2] The term 'public place' is defined in a footnote on page 336.

young persons is the duty of the local education authority, but often the first notice which an authority has of a suspected infringement comes from a school. Teachers should therefore remember that, though they have no power to act directly in this matter, they can help by bringing apparent breaches of the law to the attention of the local education authority.

Teachers can also help in cases where children who have a licence appear to be suffering as a result of their employment. A report that a licensed child is lethargic in school will enable the authority to submit him to a further medical examination with a view to considering whether it would not be in the child's best interests to withdraw the licence, or to make it subject to certain conditions.

IX

SCHOOL ATTENDANCE

1 Compulsory school age

The Education Act 1944 provided that a person who has attained the age of five years but has not attained the age of fifteen is deemed to be of compulsory school age.[1] The Act also required the Secretary of State, as soon as he was satisfied that it was practicable, to raise the upper limit to sixteen, and this has now been done.[2] A pupil may not, however, necessarily leave school immediately he passes his sixteenth birthday, as he is not deemed for this purpose to have reached the upper age limit of compulsory education until the appropriate school-leaving date.[3]

For children receiving special educational treatment in a school provided for this purpose the upper limit under the 1944 Act has always been sixteen. If a child becomes a registered pupil of such a school under arrangements made by a local education authority, the authority must give its consent before the child can be withdrawn from the school.[4] If the authority refuses, the parents may appeal to the Secretary of State.

2 Attainment of age

As the law stood until the end of 1969, a person attained a given age at the beginning of the day preceding the appropriate birthday.[5] Parliament has now acted to provide that since 1 January 1970 a particular age expressed in years is attained at the

[1] Education Act 1944, s. 35.
[2] Raising of the School Leaving Age Order 1972, S.I. 1972 no. 444.
[3] Education Act 1962, s. 9. See Section 3 below.
[4] Education Act 1944, s. 38.
[5] See Re Shurey: *Savorg* v *Shurey* [1918] 1 Ch. 263.

commencement of the relevant anniversary of the date of birth.[1]

3 Attainment of school leaving age

For the purpose of determining whether a pupil has attained the upper limit of compulsory education Parliament has fixed two school-leaving dates in the year, and a pupil may not leave until the relevant date in relation to his sixteenth birthday:

(a) for pupils born between 1 September and 31 January both dates inclusive – the end of the spring term at his school;

(b) for pupils born between 1 February and 31 August, both dates inclusive – the end of the summer term at his school.

This law applies to all children who are registered pupils at a school at the date of their sixteenth birthday, or who have been so registered at any school within the preceding twelve months. There are certain categories of young people, however, who attain the school leaving age immediately they reach their sixteenth birthday. Those who have attended a community home during the twelve months preceding attainment of the age of sixteen; and those who have left schools in Scotland or Northern Ireland, or HM Forces' or other schools abroad before reaching the school leaving age under English law, are examples. The exceptions apply, of course, only to those who have at no time been registered pupils at a school in England and Wales between their fifteenth and sixteenth birthdays.

It will be noted that pupils who reach the age of sixteen between the end of the summer term and 31 August are free to leave at the end of that term, even though the autumn term may begin before the beginning of September.

For the purposes of this section the spring term is deemed to be the last term ending before 1 May, and the summer term is the last term ending before 1 September.[2]

A child who has remained at school beyond the school leaving age may, of course, still leave at any time.

[1] Family Law Reform Act 1969, s. 9.

[2] Education Act 1962, s. 9. See also *The Education Act 1962* (Department of Education and Science Circular 4/62).

4 Presumption of age

In court proceedings for failure to attend school a child is presumed to be of compulsory school age unless the parent proves the contrary.[1]

5 Duties of parents

It is the duty of the parent[2] of every child of compulsory school age to cause him to receive efficient full-time education suitable to his age, ability and aptitude, either by attendance at school, or otherwise.[3]

There is no obligation on a school to admit a pupil except at the beginning of term unless the child was unable to start then because he was ill, or there were circumstances beyond the parent's control, or the parent was then resident at a place from which the school could not be reached with reasonable facility. Where, under the provisions of this section of the amending Act,[4] it is not practicable for a parent to arrange for his child to become a registered pupil at a school, he is relieved of his duty under section 36 of the principal Act until such time as he can secure admission of the child.

If a child of compulsory school age, who is a registered pupil of a school, fails to attend regularly, the parent is guilty of an offence.[5] The same section of the Act provides that the following grounds shall be a good defence in the case of day-pupils when action is taken:

> (a) that the child was absent with the leave of any person authorized by the managers, governors or proprietor of the school;

[1] Education (Miscellaneous Provisions) Act 1948, s. 9.

[2] The term 'parent' includes a guardian and every person who has the actual custody of a child or young person – Education Act 1944, s. 114 (1). Apparently, for this purpose, it may include the mother, even though the child is living with both parents.

[3] Education Act 1944, s. 36. For a definition of 'full-time education', see pages 213–14.

[4] Education (Miscellaneous Provisions) Act 1948, s. 4 (2).

[5] Education Act 1944, s. 39.

(*b*) that he was prevented from attending by sickness or other unavoidable cause;[1]

(*c*) that the child was absent on a day exclusively set apart for religious observance by the persuasion to which the parent belongs;[2]

(*d*) that the school is not within walking distance[3] of the child's home and the local education authority has failed to provide arrangements for transport, for admission to a school nearer home, or for admission to a boarding school. This defence does not hold when a child is proved to have no fixed address, unless the nature of the parent's occupation requires him to travel from place to place and the child has attended a school of which he is a registered pupil as regularly as the parent's occupation permits. In the case of a child who has attained the age of six this exception is no defence, unless the parent proves that the child has made 200 attendances during the twelve months prior to the commencement of proceedings.

Only the four statutory defences are acceptable. In *Jenkins* v *Howells*[1] the magistrates felt great sympathy with the parents, and Lord Goddard did not wonder at this: 'Parliament has not seen fit to provide that what may be called "family responsibilities" or "duties" can be relied on as an excuse for a child not attending school. . . . But I think "unavoidable cause" must be read in the present context as meaning something in the nature of an emergency.'[4]

[1] The child himself must be sick. A mother kept her daughter at home because she was herself ill. The justices acquitted her of a charge under this section. On a case being stated for appeal, the matter was remitted to the magistrates with a direction to find it proved. – *Jenkins* v *Howells* [1949] 2 KB 218; LCT 168.

[2] See pages 244–5.

[3] Two miles in the case of children under eight; three miles in all other cases, measured by the nearest available route – Education Act 1944, s. 39 (5). In *Shaxted* v *Ward* [1945] 1 All ER 336; LCT 193, it was held that distance and not safety is the test to be applied in defining the nearest available route. See also *Choice of Schools* (Manual of Guidance – Schools no. 1, first issued by HMSO, 23 August 1950, and reprinted with minor amendments, September 1960).

[4] For a discussion of the problems facing gypsies, see pages 437–8.

Drastic revision of the law relating to school transport was proposed late in 1973 by a working party established by the Secretary of State for Education and Science and the Secretary of State for Wales. The report[1] recommended that the link between school attendance and the obligatory provision of free school transport should be broken. The working party suggested that local education authorities should have a general duty to provide or arrange transport at the request of parents. These arrangements should take children to and from the nearest suitable school to their homes, and parents would be required to pay a flat-rate charge fixed nationally. Handicapped pupils would, where transport is necessary, be carried free of charge; and there would be remission of the charge for others in cases of hardship.

Exclusion by the school may not necessarily be a defence. A mother persisted in sending her daughter to school wearing slacks, maintaining that the girl's health demanded this costume. The headmistress refused to admit the girl in this attire unless the mother produced a medical certificate stating that it was necessary. Although the girl had been excluded, the mother was guilty of an offence.[2]

It is held that a boarder has failed to attend school regularly if he has been absent during any part of a school term when he was not prevented from attending by reason of sickness or other unavoidable cause.

6 Effect of truancy

Truancy is not a term known to English law. In common speech it is absence from school on the child's own initiative. It is the parent's duty to cause his child to receive full-time education in accordance with the requirement of section 39 of the 1944 Act, and it has been held that he is guilty even if he is unaware that his child is truanting.

In 1969 the Bracknell magistrates dismissed an information against the parents of a girl who had been away from school

---

[1] *School Transport* (HMSO, 1973).

[2] *Spiers* v *Warrington Corporation* [1954] 1 QB 61; LCT 165. See pages 26-7.

on twenty-three half-days in two and a half months. The justices found that there was no reasonable excuse for twelve of the absences, but that the parents were not aware of them. As soon as they knew, they obtained police assistance to find their daughter and thereafter ensured her regular attendance. On appeal,[1] Lord Parker, the Lord Chief Justice, held that the bench had erred in law. The offence is absolute and 'it is unnecessary in order to create the offence to show any knowledge on the part of the parents of the child's absence or any neglect on their part to ensure that the child did regularly attend. Those are matters which, as the justices' clerk appears to have advised them, were matters wholly in mitigation and did not affect the offence at all. The real and only question here is whether the twelve occasions out of a possible 114 when this little girl was not attending school, and had no reasonable excuse for not attending, amount to a failure to attend regularly. In my judgment they do, and what is more important I read the case stated as showing that the justices were of the same conclusion.'

7 Attendance registers

At one time a school's grant was based upon regularity of attendance, and the rules relating to the keeping of attendance registers were enforced with great care. Until 1956 the Minister of Education laid down detailed regulations for this purpose, but the new rules give much more discretion to the local education authorities as to the way in which registers should be marked. The Secretary of State's requirements[2] may be summarized as follows:

(a) There must be an attendance register for each class, form or group containing the names of all pupils in that class, form or group. The register must be marked at the beginnning of each morning or afternoon session at which secular instruction is given.

(b) Any pupil who is out of class for medical or dental inspection or treatment (unless he is in hospital or receiving

---

[1] *Crump* v *Gilmore* (1970) 68 LGR 56.
[2] Administrative Memorandum no. 531 (10 May 1956). See pages 26–7.

treatment at his home) must be marked present. It is immaterial whether the treatment is arranged through the National Health Service or privately.

(c) There must be a special register for secular instruction given elsewhere than on the school premises, but this requirement does not apply to classes forming an integral part of the school, even though they are in detached buildings or another school. If such classes are under the control of the head of the school to which the pupils belong, the attendances should be marked in the ordinary class register.

Apart from these requirements, the method of marking attendance registers is left to the discretion of the local education authority, whose regulations should be followed.

It is not necessary to record in an attendance register the presence or absence of any pupil who is a boarder in an independent school.[1]

Lest it should be thought that the fact that the Minister's less rigid requirements offer more scope for slackness in keeping registers, it should be stated that they are still important documents. They are open to inspection by HMIs, by persons authorized by the Secretary of State under section 77 (2) of the 1944 Act and by authorized officers of the local education authority, all of whom may make extracts therefrom for the purposes of the Act.[2]

Moreover, attendance registers are documents from which evidence may be required in a court of law and the registers, or certified extracts from them, may be vital in a prosecution for failing to attend school regularly. Periodic returns must be made of all day-pupils who fail to attend school regularly or who have been absent continuously for two weeks unless a medical certificate has been received. This return must give the full name and address of the pupils concerned, and the cause of absence if it is known.[3]

All entries in attendance registers must be originals and in ink;

[1] Pupils' Registration Regulations 1956, no. 3 (4).
[2] Pupils' Registration Regulations 1956, nos. 5 and 6.
[3] Pupils' Registration Regulations 1956, no. 7.

any alteration should be made in such a way that both the original entry and the correction are clearly distinguishable. Attendance registers must be preserved for three years from the date on which they are last used.[1]

8 Leave of absence

Leave of absence must not be granted to enable a child to be employed during school hours, or to take holidays during term time, subject to the exceptions noted below.[2] Employment includes assistance in any trade or occupation carried on for profit and it is immaterial whether the pupil receives any reward or not.[3]

The Secretary of State may make arrangements permitting such employment temporarily in the interests of the general welfare of the community. The employment of children in entertainments under a licence[4] is not subject to this regulation.

At the request of the parent, a child may be granted leave for not more than two weeks in any calendar year for the purpose of accompanying the parent on his annual holiday.[5]

9 Enforcement of school attendance

Once a local education authority has been notified of the irregular attendance of a pupil, the duty of enforcing attendance passes to the authority, which may institute proceedings against the parent. The courts may inflict a fine of £10 for a first offence; and £20 in the case of subsequent offences, or a month's imprisonment, or both.[6]

Such proceedings may be commenced only by a local education authority, which before deciding to prosecute must consider whether it is appropriate, alternatively or additionally to bring the child before a juvenile court under section 1 of the Children

[1] Pupils' Registration Regulations 1956, nos. 8 and 9.

[2] Schools Regulations 1959, No. 12, and Handicapped Pupils Regulations 1953, no. 37.

[3] Employment of Children Act 1973, s. 2 (6).

[4] Children and Young Persons Act 1933, s. 22.

[5] Schools Regulations 1959, no. 12, and Handicapped Pupils and Special Schools Regulations 1959, no. 14.

[6] Education Act 1944, s. 40 (1); as amended by the Criminal Justice Act 1967, Schedule 3.

and Young Persons Act 1969. If the authority merely proceeds against the parent, and there is a conviction, the court may direct the authority to bring the child before a juvenile court. If this happens, the authority must comply.[1]

The previous provisions by which proceedings could be instituted against a child for failure to attend school have been repealed.[2] Failure to attend school is now part of the care proceedings in juvenile courts.[3] The court may make one of five orders in respect of a child if 'he is of compulsory school age within the meaning of the Education Act 1944 and is not receiving efficient full-time education suitable to his age, ability and aptitude . . . and also that he is in need of care or control which he is unlikely to receive unless the Court makes an order under this section in respect of him'.[4]

Proceedings in cases where a school attendance order is in force are discussed below.[5]

10 School attendance orders

When a parent is apparently failing to perform his duty to ensure that his child is receiving education as required by the Act, the local education authority may require him to show that he is, in fact, fulfilling that duty. The notice served by the authority must specify the time within which the parent must reply, and this must not be less than fourteen days.[6]

If the parent then fails to satisfy the authority, the latter must serve a school attendance order in the prescribed form[7] requiring the parent to present the child for admission to the school named in the order. The parent must be given fourteen days to select a school but if, for good reason, the authority deems that the school chosen by the parent is unsuitable, it may appeal to the Secretary of State to name a school. Whilst the order remains in

[1] Education Act 1944, s. 40 (2) and (3).
[2] Children and Young Persons Act 1969, Schedule 6.
[3] See pages 389–90.
[4] See pages 390–91.
[5] Children and Young Persons Act 1969, s. 1 (2).
[6] Education Act 1944, s. 37.
[7] School Attendance Order Regulations 1944, s.R. & O. 1944, no. 1470.

force, the parent may request the authority to substitute another school, or to revoke the order on the grounds that the child is, in fact, receiving efficient full-time education suitable to his age, ability and aptitude.[1] This request must be complied with unless the authority is of the opinion that the change would be detrimental to the child's interests. In such cases an appeal lies to the Secretary of State.

Failure to comply with the requirements of a school attendance order is an offence unless the child is receiving suitable full-time education otherwise than by attendance at school.[2] A court before whom a parent appears for failing to comply with an order may revoke the order, but this does not preclude the authority from taking further action.

School attendance orders remain in force until the child ceases to be of compulsory school age, unless revoked by the local education authority or the courts.

11 Further education

A young person who is not exempted from compulsory attendance at a county college must comply with the requirements of any college attendance notice served upon him by the local education authority.[3] In the event of failure to do so, he may be charged before the juvenile court if under seventeen, or before the adult court if he is older.

The Act provides that the following grounds shall provide a good defence:

(a) that he was, at the material time, exempt from compulsory attendance;

[1] Education Act 1944, s. 40 (4) as amended by the Children and Young Persons Act 1969, Schedule 5. 13.

[2] Apparently, however, an offence would be committed by sending the child to a school not named in the order, in spite of the fact that suitable full-time education otherwise than by attendance at school is a statutory defence.

[3] Education Act, 1944, s. 44. This section remains on the statute book, although there is now little likelihood that any Order in Council for the establishment of county colleges will be made.

(*b*) that he was prevented from attending by sickness or other urgent cause;

(*c*) that the requirement does not comply with the provisions of the Education Acts.

The following persons are statutorily exempted from attendance for further education:

(*a*) those in full-time attendance at any school or educational institution other than a county college;

(*b*) those receiving suitable and efficient instruction, whether full-time or not, for at least 330 hours a year;

(*c*) those who, having been exempted under the preceding clauses, did not cease to be so exempt until they had attained the age of seventeen years and eight months;

(*d*) any person undergoing an approved course for the mercantile marine or the sea fishing industry or who, having completed such a course, is engaged in that industry;

(*e*) any person in the service of the Crown, persons of unsound mind and those detained by order of a court;

(*f*) any person who attained the age of fifteen before 1 April 1945 and who was not, immediately before that date, required to attend a continuation school under the terms of the Education Act 1921.

12 Documents receivable in evidence

The following documents may be received in the courts and deemed to be correct in every detail without proof of the identity, signature or official capacity of the persons by whom they purport to have been signed, unless the contrary be proved:[1]

(*a*) those issued by a local education authority and signed by an authorized officer;

(*b*) extracts from the minutes of the managers or governors of a school, signed by their chairman or clerk;

(*c*) certificates of attendance signed by the head of a school;

[1] Education Act s. 95 (2), importing into (*d*) the amended definition in s. 114 (1) of 'medical officer' required by the National Health Service Reorganisation Act 1973, Schedule 4. 8.

(*d*) certificates signed by a medical officer of a local education authority, or a medical officer whose services are made available to that authority by the Secretary of State for Social Services.

13 Lateness and full-time attendance

On 24 May 1960 the Birmingham magistrates imposed a fine of ten shillings in a case brought against a parent for failing to send his six-year-old son to school regularly. The father appealed to Quarter Sessions under section 39 (2) (*a*) of the Education Act 1944, which prescribes that no proceedings may be taken if a child is absent through sickness or other unavoidable cause. The child had been present on twenty-seven out of fifty-six occasions in a period of six weeks in a school where the registers were closed at 9.45 a.m. In reply to the Assistant Recorder a welfare and school attendance officer said that he knew of no regulation which entitles a particular school to decide on the time for closing its register, but technically it should be closed at the time of the school assembly.

In allowing the appeal, the Assistant Recorder said, 'When this certificate says weekly attendances, it means in fact weekly attendances by 9.45 a.m. I don't know if there is any authority under the Act whereby a local education authority is entitled to limit weekly attendances by failure to attend by a certain time. . . . Unless there is any authority under the Act to limit attendance to attendances by a certain time, the first point of the case – failure to attend school – has not been established. . . . This certificate sets out to show a fact which I now know is not the fact at all.'

The local education authority appealed against this decision, and the case was heard in the Queen's Bench Divisional Court before the Lord Chief Justice (Lord Parker), Mr Justice Winn, and Mr Justice Lawton. For the Corporation it was said that, if the Assistant Recorder's decision were allowed to stand, a boy who did not like spelling would be able to skip that lesson, but would still be entitled to have 'Present' against his name. The Lord Chief Justice said that the Assistant Recorder took the view that the headmaster's certificate was not evidence of non-attendance, although it might be evidence of unpunctuality. In the view of the Court the phrase 'full-time education' meant attendance for the period prescribed by the school authorities. The Assistant Recorder was wrong in ruling that there was no case to answer, and it would be remitted.[1]

When the case came before the Court of Quarter Sessions for the second time, the father said that he now wished to appeal, not against the conviction but against the sentence. The Recorder ordered the fine to stand but, because the father said he was unemployed, ordered it to be paid at the rate of one shilling a week.

This is an important decision which defines the term 'full-time education' as meaning exactly what it says. Some confusion exists in the minds of many teachers who remember that at one time registers were opened before the scripture period in the morning, and closed at the end of it. Under the Code for Public Elementary Schools, this subject was required to be placed at the beginning or end of the day, it did not form part of the period of secular instruction, and children who were exempted could not be held to be absent. It was, however, not intended that this should be a period of grace during which late-comers could slip into school without loss of attendance. There is now no regulation which requires the religious knowledge lesson to be placed at the beginning of the day, and the secular instruction may well begin immediately after assembly. A child who is late may miss part of the secular instruction required by the Schools Regulations, and may be marked as absent.

[1] *Hinchley* v *Rankin* [1961] 1 All E.R. 692; LCT 172.

X

RELIGIOUS EDUCATION

1 Freedom of conscience

In some countries, of which the United States of America is an
example, the educational system is purely secular and no religious
teaching is permitted in the state schools. This is not so in
England where the Church was a pioneer in the field of education,
and religious education is an essential part of the work of every
school. In a country where there are to be found many non-
Christian religions as well as many orders within the Christian
faith, it is essential that the freedom of the individual conscience
should be strictly safeguarded on lines such as those laid down in
the 1944 Act.

The provisions of the Act are designed to protect both pupil
and teacher. Although there must be religious education in all
schools, no child may be taught any doctrine or practice which
is repugnant to the wishes of his parent, even in a denominational
school. Parents may, if they wish, withdraw their children wholly
or partly from religious instruction.

Except in a limited number of cases,[1] a teacher's beliefs are his
own concern and he cannot be dismissed, deprived of promotion
or paid a lower salary because of his religious opinions. The
conscience clauses of the Act are characteristic of the English
attitude towards freedom of belief and must be strictly observed.

If the faith of a person involves limitations on food, these must
be strictly observed. Indeed, the whole question of what may be
called 'secondary' religious practices (practices which derive from
the teaching of a particular faith) is something with which the law

[1] The exceptions are the staffs of aided schools and reserved teachers in
controlled and special agreement schools.

215

will have to come to grips in a society which is increasingly multicultural. Examples may be found in the Sikh's insistence on wearing a turban and the Muslim refusal to send girls to a co-educational secondary school.[1]

In this connection it is important to consider article 9 of the Convention on Human Rights of which Great Britain is a signatory:[2]

(1) Everyone has the right to freedom of thought, conscience and religion; this right includes freedom to change his religion or belief, and freedom, either alone or in community with others and in public or private, to manifest his religion or belief, in worship, teaching, practice and observance.

(2) Freedom to manifest one's religion or beliefs shall be subject only to such limitations as are prescribed by law and are necessary in a democratic society in the interests of public safety, for the protection of public order, health or morals, for the protection of the rights and freedoms of others.

2 History

The early schools in this country were chiefly church foundations and the state did not concern itself with education until the nineteenth century. Since that time there have been many struggles over religion in schools, opinions varying from belief in a fully Christian education at one extreme to a demand for a completely secular system at the other.

The compromise expressed in the 1944 Act seems to have brought a measure of peace, at least for a time.

The early elementary schools were established chiefly by two societies. The National Society for Promoting the Education of the Poor in the Principles of the Established Church throughout England and Wales was founded in 1811, and still plays an active part in Anglican education although with a less florid title – it is now generally known simply as 'The National Society'. Some schools and colleges of education are still closely associated with it,

[1] See page 50.
[2] See pages 69–71.

it makes money available in the dioceses, and it has established a register of teachers.

The British and Foreign School Society was founded about the same time by a Quaker, Joseph Lancaster, and is also in existence today. It provides schools and colleges of education, and administers a number of educational charities.

For some years the two societies worked on similar lines in establishing 'National' and 'British' schools, the former teaching according to the tenets of the Church of England, the latter being unsectarian but with a strong nonconformist bias. The first of the government grants for education were given to these two societies in 1833.

In 1870 school boards were set up to provide schools in areas not covered by the societies and the dual system of provided ('Board' or 'Council') and non-provided ('National' or 'British') schools came into being. With variations in nomenclature the dual system remains to this day, the present distinction being between 'county' and 'voluntary' schools.

A recent development must be noted here since it is indicative of the changing climate of opinion about religious education. In 1959 the Church of England Board of Education, the Church in Wales Council for Education and the Free Church Federal Council established a Central Joint Education Policy Committee. This followed a suggestion made by the Minister of Education during the discussions on the Education Act 1959, which gave increased grants to voluntary-aided schools. The Minister's advice to the Churches was that they should get together in order to discuss their problems and their differences, and to try to solve them in a friendly spirit. The Central Joint Education Policy Committee meets this need.

In March 1963 the Central Joint Policy Committee issued a statement, *Christian Teaching in Schools – A Common Basis*, which is indicative of the more positive approach to religious education which is characteristic of the mid-twentieth century.

Similar local joint education policy committees have been established throughout England and Wales, using the Anglican dioceses as the basis.

Discussions continued through the sixties. In 1970 a commission under the chairmanship of the then Bishop of Durham produced a report advocating a non-proselytizing approach to the subject.[1] In the same year the Social Morality Council said: 'One of the results of religious education should be to create in boys and girls a more sensitive understanding of their own beliefs and of the different beliefs by which others govern their lives.' The DES supported a working party set up by the British Council to investigate and report on the shortage of specialist teachers,[2] and the Schools Council produced two working papers on the subject.[3]

At the time of writing (October 1974) there are signs that many people are becoming increasingly concerned by the secularization of religious education and the campaign to replace it by moral education. The Order of Christian Unity, including among its members a wide spectrum of the Christian Church, carried out a survey amongst heads which produced evidence of a very considerable desire to retain religious education as an essential part of education. Indeed, there is clear evidence that the Churches have taken to heart the advice given by the Minister in 1959, and are working closely together in a spirit undreamt of in 1944.

3 The 1944 Act

The Act lays down that there must be religious education in all schools within the statutory system.[4] This is the only subject so specified by statute. Apparently, a head could dispense with English and arithmetic in his school, so long as he could persuade HMIs that the children were receiving efficient full-time education suitable to their respective ages, abilities and aptitudes, but he may not omit religious education from the timetable.

No local education authority may issue any instruction relating to secular education which would interfere with the provision of

[1] *The Fourth R* (SPCK).

[2] *The Recruitment Employment and Training of Teachers of Religious Education* (British Council of Churches).

[3] *Religious Education in Secondary Schools* (Schools Council Working Paper 36); *Religious Education in Primary Schools* (Schools Council Paper 44).

[4] Education Act, 1944, s. 25 (1).

reasonable facilities for religious education during school hours, or with the opportunity of any pupil to receive religious education unless an alternative time is provided.[1]

4 The daily act of worship

The school day must begin with a collective act of worship attended by all the pupils, subject of course to withdrawal on conscientious grounds, provided that there is suitable accommodation for assembling the whole school.[2] In county schools the worship must be undenominational in character;[3] the form to be used in voluntary schools is not stipulated in the Act, but it is generally held that, like denominational instruction in such schools, it may be in accordance with the trust deed, or, where there is no such provision, in accordance with the practice in the school before it became a voluntary school.

The worship should take place on the school premises both in county and voluntary schools. The managers or governors of an aided or special agreement school may, on a special day, make arrangements for the worship to take place elsewhere, but this must be an exception and not the rule.[4]

When it is proposed to take the school to church, due notice must be given to the parents so that they may, under the conscience clause, have an opportunity of requesting the withdrawal of their children from such worship. An announcement to the school, coupled with a written notice on the school notice board could be sufficient. It is important that this should be done, as many parents who have no objection to their children attending religious instruction in school will prefer them not to attend church.

Occasionally clergy and ministers visit a school on special occasions, e.g. for Founder's Day or for leavers' services. On such occasions a similar opportunity for withdrawal should be given.

In voluntary schools the regular daily act of worship may be

[1] Education Act 1944, s. 25 (6).
[2] Education Act 1944, s. 25 (1).
[3] Education Act 1944, s. 26.
[4] Education Act 1946, s. 7.

led by a clergyman or minister. If this is done in controlled schools the fact should be noted in the school annals.

5 The agreed syllabus

In county schools it has long been the law that religious education shall be 'without any catechism or formulary distinctive of any particular religious denomination'.[1] This is the famous Cowper-Temple clause named after Mr William Cowper Temple who first introduced it as an amendment to the 1870 Act. It has been re-enacted in all succeeding legislation. The law officers of the Crown have decided that the ten commandments, the Lord's Prayer, and the Apostles' Creed are not distinctive and their use is not a violation of this clause. On the other hand, that section of the catechism known as the 'Duties' is distinctive in this sense, and may not be taught in county schools.

Soon after the first world war a number of local education authorities, of which Cambridgeshire became the best-known, produced syllabuses of religious instruction which had been agreed between representatives of the protestant denominations as suitable for use in county schools.

Each education authority must now adopt such a syllabus[2] in accordance with the decision of a conference representative of the religious denominations, the authority and the teachers' organizations. Such conferences were given power either to adopt a syllabus prepared by another authority, or to appoint a committee to draft a special syllabus for use in the authority's area.

Agreed syllabuses are drawn up in general terms, and the re-responsibility of adapting them to the needs of a particular school is left to the staff of the school. HMIs are required to ascertain that the religious education in county schools is in accordance with the syllabus adopted by the authority. Provision is also made for the reconsideration of the syllabus from time to time. An authority may appoint a standing advisory council on religious education

[1] Education Act 1944, s. 26.
[2] Education Act 1944, s. 29 (1) and Schedule V.

to report to the authority on matters concerning the agreed syllabus, to recommend books and to sponsor courses.[1]

In 1944 many fears were expressed about the effectiveness of agreed syllabus instruction, especially by those who thought that the Act weakened the whole position of Church schools. They felt that religious education was of little value unless it brought children into close contact with, and active membership of, the Church. Time has done much to allay these fears, for the religious education in county schools is frequently in the hands of sincere and capable teachers who, whilst honouring the limitations placed upon them by the Act, have gone far towards achieving the aim of religious education as defined by a former Bishop of Bristol[2] whilst the 1944 Act was still in the making. He said, 'The aim of religious education is to give every child a chance to understand what the Christian faith is and what the Christian way of life in Christ involves so that, if he ultimately accepts or rejects it, he will at least know what it is that he is accepting or rejecting.'

6 Voluntary schools

In aided schools, religious education is under the control of the managers or governors and must be in accordance with the provisions of the trust deed or, where there is no provision of this nature in the deed, in accordance with the practice in the school before it became a voluntary school. The position in special agreement schools is precisely the same. In both kinds of school agreed syllabus instruction must be provided for the children whose parents request it and who cannot conveniently be educated elsewhere. If the managers or governors fail to make such arrangements, the local education authority must do so.[3]

In controlled schools the agreed syllabus must be used, but the school may, at the request of parents, give further teaching for not more than two periods a week on denominational lines. Such additional teaching may be given by clergy or ministers.[4]

[1] Education Act 1944, s. 29.
[2] Dr F. A. Cockin, then Canon of St Paul's Cathedral, at a course for teachers organized by the Colchester Religion and Life Council, 4 and 5 March 1944.
[3] Education Act 1944, s. 28.   [4] Education Act 1944, s. 27.

In voluntary schools, regular religious instruction may be given elsewhere than on the premises. The fact must be entered on the timetable, opportunity for withdrawal given, and care exercised to see that the children return to school in time to be able to complete the minimum period of secular instruction required by the Schools Regulations. It should be particularly noted that this applies to regular instruction and not to the regular daily act of worship. The latter should normally be held on the school premises.

A proportion of the staff of controlled and special agreement schools may be appointed as reserved teachers, especially qualified for their ability to give trust-deed religious instruction.[1]

7 Inspection

HMIs and the inspectorate of a local education authority may inspect and report upon all religious instruction, whether in county or voluntary schools, where such instruction is given in accordance with an agreed syllabus. They may also inspect the undenominational form of worship in county schools. In aided or special agreement schools, the function of the inspector would be limited to the agreed syllabus instruction provided for the children whose parents request it. Although many such schools use parts of an agreed syllabus for their normal religious instruction, such portions are really taken over and incorporated in the syllabus approved by the managers or governors.

In voluntary schools, denominational instruction may be inspected, on not more than two days a year, by the managers or governors or by inspectors acting on their behalf. Fourteen days' notice of such visit must be given to the local education authority so that arrangements can be made to see that the authority's officials do not visit the school on such days. No child whose parents have withdrawn him from denominational instruction can be compelled to attend school on the day of such an inspection.

In controlled schools the agreed syllabus instruction would be inspected by the secular, the denominational instruction by the denominational, inspector.

[1] See pages 110–11.

8 Timetable

The requirement that religious instruction should be given only at the beginning or end of the school day no longer applies, and the abolition of this rule has opened the door to specialization in religious education. If children are withdrawn, however, for denominational instruction elsewhere than on the school premises, this must be done at the beginning or end of a session.

9 Withdrawal from religious instruction

A parent may withdraw his child from any part of the religious instruction or worship of the school or from the whole of it.[1] This is the conscience clause, and once such a request has been made it must be strictly honoured unless and until it is withdrawn. It is desirable that such a request should be in writing but it is probable that an oral intimation is legally sufficient.

In 1971 the secretary of the Humanist Teachers Association complained that a boy who asked to be allowed to withdraw from religious education was first refused permission, and later permitted to withdraw by sitting at the back of the room whilst taking no part in the lesson. It must be recognized that it is often difficult to make special supervision arrangements for individual pupils, but it would seem that such an arrangement is contrary to the spirit, if not the letter, of the law.

A parent is not required to give a reason for requesting withdrawal, and it is doubtful whether school authorities should inquire into a parent's motives. If the request is made by the child himself, however, it is probably as well to verify that it represents the parent's, and not just the child's, wish, since section 25 gives the right to the parent.

When a child cannot with convenience be educated in a school providing such instruction, he may be withdrawn by the parent for religious instruction in accordance with the parent's wishes. A pupil in a county school may thus be withdrawn for denominational instruction, or a pupil in a voluntary school for instruction of a denominational kind which is not provided by that school. Adequate arrangements must be made for the withdrawal instruc-

[1] Education Act 1944, s. 25 (3).

tion, which must be given at the beginning or end of a session. It need not coincide with the provision for religious instruction in the timetable.

If a county secondary school is so situated that arrangements cannot conveniently be made for withdrawal, the authority may provide facilities in the school for such instruction if it is satisfied that the parents desire such instruction to be given, and that adequate arrangements have been made. No cost for this provision may fall on the authority.[1]

10 Days of obligation

Parents may withdraw their children from attendance at school for all or part of a day which it is the practice of their religious persuasion to set apart exclusively for religious observance,[2] e.g. Ascension Day (for Anglicans and Roman Catholics) or the Day of Atonement (for Jews). It is not certain how many such days are recognized by the Church of England; an Act of 5 & 6 Edward VI mentions seventy-nine, including Sundays, which are 'separated from profane uses'.[3]

It was decided in the 'Darfield Case'[4] that a parent still has this right, even though the child does not attend any form of worship on that day. To avoid misunderstanding, it is desirable that the parent should give notice to the head, and some religious bodies provide printed forms for this purpose.[5]

Teachers may also withdraw their services on such days. It is usual for leave to be granted with pay, subject to the right of the

[1] Education Act 1944, ss. 25 (5) and 26.

[2] Education Act 1944, s. 39 (2) (b).

[3] The relevant passage in the Act is quoted in the author's *Legal Cases for Teachers* (Methuen, 1970), page 184.

[4] *Marshall* v *Graham; Bell* v *Graham* [1907] 2 KB 112; LCT 178.

[5] One such form reads as follows:

To the Head Teacher.............................School.
Dear Sir or Madam,

I am writing to give notice that as next Thursday is Ascension Day – a day set apart for religious observance by the Church of England, of which I am a member – I shall not be sending my children to school on that day.

..........................Parent
....Address

authority to use the teacher in another school on an equivalent number of days when his own is closed.

11 The Jewish Sabbath

The Jewish Sabbath begins at sunset on Friday, and Jewish children attending a school which does not cater exclusively for that faith should be allowed to leave school in time to reach home before sunset on Fridays during the winter. Some authorities issue a list of the times at which Jews may be allowed to go home on different Fridays during the shorter days.

12 Staffing

The question of reserved teachers, and the safeguarding clause dealing with the religious opinions of teachers, have already been considered.[1]

Until 1 April 1959 clergy and ministers of any religious denomination were ineligible for appointment to the staffs of maintained schools, except as occasional teachers, unless there were exceptional circumstances. On that date the Schools Regulations 1959, came into force. The new regulations omitted no. 19 of the Schools Grant Regulations, and it is now possible for clergy and ministers to hold any appointment on the staff of a maintained school.

This does not affect the nature of religious instruction and worship in a county school. A clergyman or minister on the staff of such a school must observe the provisions of the Cowper-Temple clause, except in a voluntary-aided school or when giving denominational religious instruction in a controlled or special agreement school.

13 Visits of clergy to schools

Clergy and ministers sometimes visit schools as speaker when, for example, pupils' conferences are organized through the medium of the Christian Education Movement or similar bodies. Though these lie outside the normal religious education of the school it is as well to make the denominational allegiance of the

[1] See pages 110-11 and 215-16 for these items respectively.

speaker known beforehand. Attendance at such meetings must be purely voluntary.[1]

14 Boarders

Parents of pupils who are boarders may request that their children attend worship conforming to the tenets of the religious body to which they belong.[2] Similarly they may request that their children receive denominational instruction out of school hours. Such requests must be complied with, but no expense in this connection can be met by the local education authority.

These facilities may be provided on the school premises so long as they do not entail the meeting of any expense in connection therewith from public funds.

15 Special schools

Provision must be made, so far as is possible, for every pupil to attend religious worship and receive religious instruction in accordance with the wishes of his parent. No pupil may be required to attend such worship, or receive such instruction, contrary to the wishes of his parent. These regulations apply both to boarders and day-pupils in special schools.[3]

[1] Conditions have changed vastly since the passage of the 1944 Act, and practice has moved ahead of the law. Clergy and ministers frequently visit schools to speak on purely secular subjects, and there is no need to make such occasions voluntary.

[2] Education Act 1944, s. 25 (7).

[3] Handicapped Pupils and Special Schools Regulations 1959, no. 8.

XI

ACCIDENTS AND NEGLIGENCE

---

1 Negligence

Circumstances vary so widely that it is impossible to secure a short definition of negligence which will cover every possible situation. The court applies the law to the facts of the case so far as it has been able to ascertain them from the evidence placed before it. It must be remembered that in civil actions the decision of the court is based in the 'balance of probabilities', and not on proof 'beyond all reasonable doubt' which is the standard required in a criminal trial. No superior knowledge or skill is required of the defendant unless he has failed in a duty of which he may be presumed to have special knowledge: thus, when an accident occurs to a child whilst he is under school discipline, the court would take into account the fact that a teacher may be presumed to have a special knowledge of children and their behaviour, and to act accordingly.

If an action for negligence is to succeed, three factors must be present. In the first place, the defendant must have owed a duty of care to the plaintiff. Secondly, he must have failed, either by what he has done or by what he has left undone, to perform that duty. Finally, the plaintiff must have suffered damage through that act or omission. These tests are applied by the courts in all cases where negligence is alleged.

It follows from this that no claim for damages will succeed in respect of what is strictly an accident, i.e. an event which cannot be prevented, or which could not reasonably have been foreseen so that steps should have been taken to guard against it. In 1921 a seven-year-old blind boy was playing with other children, some of whom had full sight, in a hostel for blind children. He was injured when, without warning, another boy jumped suddenly on his back. Lord Justice-Clerk Scott Dickson said: 'What actually occurred was an unexpected, an unforeseen, and, I think, an almost unforeseeable misfortune, and even if there had been a matron or some other servant in the room where the children were playing, I do not see how that would have prevented the accident. The occurrence is described as one boy jumping unexpectedly on the back of the boy who was injured. It was the thing of a moment. . . . I think the case fails because the obligation which was sought to be imposed on the education authority was higher than the law imposes upon it.'[1] Although this was a Scottish case, English law is identical at this point.

Special circumstances may put a plaintiff outside the duty of a defendant's care. Such a case might occur when a boy is compelled to play games which, because of a hidden physical defect, cause him harm. If the defect were known to the teacher he would, of course, be required to exercise a sufficient degree of care to prevent injury to the pupil.

It is important that articles which might harm children, or with which they might harm each other, should not be left lying about. The case of *Williams* v *Eady*[2] arose because some phosphorus was left in a conservatory. Lord Justice Kay asked, 'Was it not evidence of negligence to have left the bottle of phosphorus lying about in a place to which boys had access, knowing what boys are?'

A contractor left a mixture of sand and lime in the corner of a school playground, and a boy's eye was injured when another lad threw a lump of the mixture at him. The headmaster was found to be negligent although he had telephoned the contractor and asked him to remove the materials, and the contractor was also found to be negligent in failing to remove the 'rough stuff' within a reasonable time of the request to do so.[3]

On the other hand it was found that it was not necessary to have

---

[1] *Gow* v *Glasgow Education Authority* [1922] SC 260; LCT 295.

[2] *Williams* v *Eady* (1893) 10 TLR 41; LCT 240. See also pages 27–8.

[3] *Jackson* v *London County Council* and *Chappell* (1912) 28 TLR 359; LCT 293.

a protective cover, over which boys could not climb, round a heap of coke in a playground. One boy injured another by throwing a piece of coke at him. There was proper supervision. The trial judge found for the plaintiff, but his decision was reversed on appeal.[1]

Much publicity is often given to cases where there is an allegation of negligence towards children and a good deal of sympathy – sometimes false sympathy – is aroused thereby. Mr Justice Hilbery referred to this whilst summing up in an action resulting from an accident in which a small boy lost an eye whilst a patient in a convalescent home.[2] He said, 'Our law reports show how fatally attractive children's cases have been to those who have to try them. Judges are human beings and their feelings are easily aroused in favour of the child, especially children of tender years. When they meet with an accident, any court is liable to strain the law in favour of the child, but an infant plaintiff has exactly the same burden of proving his case as any other plaintiff.'

Lord Atkin once summed up the question of negligence in words which echo the parable of the Good Samaritan.[3] He said, 'You must take reasonable care to avoid acts or omissions which you can reasonably foresee would be likely to injure your neighbour. Who then, in law, is my neighbour? The answer seems to be, persons who are so closely and directly affected by my act that I ought reasonably to have them in contemplation as being so affected when I am directing my mind to the acts or omissions which are called in question.'

2 The duty of a schoolmaster

Many school accidents occur during the course of a year and most of them have no repercussions, but sometimes parents consider that the school authorities have been negligent in some way, and an action is brought in the courts. It is therefore vitally important that teachers should understand their responsibilities, and that

[1] *Rich* v *London County Council* [1953] 2 All ER 376; LCT 308.
[2] *Marston* v *St George's Hospital, Hyde Park Corner* (1956) *Daily Mail*, 1 May.
[3] In *Donoghue* v *Stevenson* [1932] AC 562.

they should take all reasonable steps to prevent their pupils from coming to harm.

The courts have always taken a realistic view of these cases and have recognized that it is quite impossible, even if it were desirable, to watch every child during every minute of the school day. On the other hand, they expect that teachers should exercise supervision strictly enough to prevent unnecessary accidents. Mr Justice McNair, for instance, said,[1] 'A balance must be struck between the meticulous supervision of children every moment at school and the desirable object of encouraging sturdy independence as they grow up.'[2]

In this case, a child of five had climbed on to the glass roof of a lavatory after his class had been dismissed at four o'clock. He fell through and received injuries from which he died. The child's father maintained that an adult should have been present until the children had left the premises. The judge continued, 'In the case of children under five attending the nursery department of this school it was thought right to have some person in actual supervision of them until they were collected by their mothers. That was not thought necessary in the case of the five-year-olds and that was a decision taken by a responsible person. I should require strong evidence to convince me that it is wrong.' The case was dismissed.

Towards the end of the nineteenth century Mr Justice Cave defined a schoolmaster's duty in the following words:[3] 'The schoolmaster is bound to take such care of his boys as a careful father would take of his boys.' This definition was quoted by Lord Esher, then Master of the Rolls, who added that there could not be a better definition of a schoolmaster. Mr Justice Cave's statement is still the leading definition of a teacher's duty and is usually cited in cases where teachers are accused of neglect.

The doctrine of the careful parent has been followed quite

[1] *Jeffery* v *London County Council* (1954) 119 JP 43; LCT 242.

[2] The danger of crushing initiative and independence was also noted by Mr Justice Vaisey in another case when he said, 'It is better that a boy should break his neck than allow other people to break his spirit': *Suckling* v *Essex County Council* (1955) *The Times*, 27 January.

[3] In *Williams* v *Eady* (1893) 9 TLR 637; 10 TLR 41; LCT 240.

literally in nearly every case since *Williams* v *Eady*, but there is a general tendency in the courts to raise the standard of the duty of care, and educational cases have followed this trend. Two examples will serve to show the way in which the rising standard of care is being applied, but it must be remembered that these were settled at a lower level, and do not override the rule in *Williams* v *Eady* which was decided in the Court of Appeal.

In the autumn of 1962 damages were awarded against the Middlesex County Council in an action following injuries to a boy who put his hand through a pane of glass. It was held that the glass was too thin. Mr Justice Edmund Davies said, 'The test of the reasonably prudent parent must be applied not to the parent in the home, but the parent applying his mind to school life. . . . It may be that the consequences of the decision I have arrived at may be widespread. If this widespread nature leads to greater safety in the care of the young, then no consummation can be more devoutly desired.'[1]

In 1968 the Surrey County Council was sued for damages for negligence following injury to a boy's eye during morning break. The case[2] is considered in more detail in a later section; here it is sufficient to note that Mr Justice Geoffrey Lane considered the duty of care *in loco parentis* in the following terms: 'The duty of a headmaster towards his pupils is said to be to take such care of them as a reasonable careful and prudent father would take of his own children. That standard is a helpful one when considering, for example, individual instructions to individual children in a school. It would be very unwise to allow a six-year-old child to carry a kettle of boiling water – that type of instruction. But that standard when applied to an incident of horse-play in a school of nine hundred pupils is somewhat unrealistic, if not unhelpful.

'In the context of the present action it appears to me to be easier and preferable to use the ordinary language of the law of negligence. That is, it is a headmaster's duty, bearing in mind the known propensities of boys and indeed girls between the ages of

[1] *Lyes* v *Middlesex County Council* (1963) 61 LGR 443; LCT 198.
[2] *Beaumont* v *Surrey County Council* (1968) 66 LGR 580; LCT 246.
See also pages 28–9.

eleven and seventeen or eighteen, to take all reasonable and proper steps to prevent any of the pupils under his care from suffering injury from inanimate objects, from the actions of their fellow pupils, or from a combination of the two. That is a high standard. . . . They, the defendants, in the manner which I have described, regrettably fall short of the standards which the law demands of them.'

Proceedings may be brought against the managers or governors, against the local education authority, or against teachers acting as their servants. Only one sum, however, may be awarded in damages. Where, in an action against a teacher, the employer is made a joint defendant, the court may find against both and, under the Law Reform Act, 1935, apportion the amount of damages to be paid by each. In general, the employer would be liable for accidents arising from defective premises or equipment unless the accident is directly caused by the negligence of the servant.

It is in a teacher's own interest to report immediately any defect in buildings or equipment which may give rise to an accident and, pending action by the responsible authority, to take reasonable steps to prevent any use which might lead to a mishap. Failure to take these steps might raise the question of the teacher's negligence.

3 'The System'

When damages for injury arising from negligence are claimed before the courts the onus is on the plaintiff, as has already been said, to prove negligence on the defendant's part. In reaching its decision the court must judge whether the plaintiff has made out his case; or whether the injuries were due to some other cause, for example an accident which could not have been prevented, or which could not reasonably have been foreseen.

In different contexts the local education authority, the managers or governors, the headmaster and the assistant staff (including, sometimes, ancillary workers and caretakers) have a duty of care to the pupils of a school in the management of which they have a share. In the case of the teaching staff and, perhaps, to a greater or lesser extent the other groups as well, there is a common law duty of care based on the rule in *Williams* v *Eady*.[1]

The matter, however, extends more widely than that. The owners of the school, be they the proprietors of an independent school, the managers or governors of direct grant or voluntary schools, or the local education authority in the case of county schools, have a duty of care for all persons on school premises whether by statute (e.g. the Occupiers Liability Act 1957[2]), by regulation (e.g. the Schools Regulations), and some would say that it is the local education authority which stands *in loco parentis*.[3]

Be that as it may, the rules of management or articles of government prescribe that the head shall control 'the internal organization, management and discipline of the school'. This requirement postulates that he must create and maintain a system which, amongst other things, will be the machinery for discharging his duty of care for the safety of his pupils. It further postulates that this system will include a suitable code of rules, known to all members of the school; and, since the head cannot be everywhere at once, he will be assisted in the observance of these rules of the system by his assistant staff. He will himself from time to time ensure in one way or another that the system is being maintained at a fully efficient level.

This burden of responsibility is laid upon the head because he is the principal servant of his employers in the school, and it is not unreasonable to assume that his professional experience is such that he is the person who will most clearly understand his pupils, their needs and the special circumstances of the school. Conditions vary so widely, even between similar neighbouring establishments, that it would not be practicable to impose the same system throughout an authority's schools. In framing a scheme to meet the needs of his school a head must take into account such matters as the number and age-range of the pupils, any handicaps from which they may suffer, any special problems posed by the

---

[1] See pages 27–8, 228.

[2] See pages 274–5.

[3] E.g. Mr Ashley Bramall, Leader of the Inner London Education Authority, writing in *The Head Teacher's Review*, June 1971, p. 8.

building, traffic and other conditions in the neighbourhood, and such other matters as may seem to him to be relevant.

One issue which must be determined as a fact by any court hearing an action for damages for negligence is whether a system existed which, so far as could reasonably be foreseen, was adequately designed to prevent such mishaps as that which gave rise to the claim. In the light of the argument which has been outlined in this section it is clear that, if such a system has not been provided, there has been negligence. The only exception would be a genuine accident which could not have been prevented if such a system had been enforced; or which was so unforeseeable that no reasonable person, having regard to all the circumstances, would have judged it necessary to guard against it.

If, however, the court is satisfied that an adequate system existed, it must then examine another matter: whether at the time of the event giving rise to the action the system was being maintained at a peak of full efficiency. If not the court is likely to hold that there had been negligence to the extent that the system was not being observed. Three recent cases illustrate this point:

Martin v *Middlesbrough Corporation* – An eleven-year-old girl slipped on an icy playground, severing the flexor tendons of the middle and ring fingers of her right hand, and injuring the little finger on a broken piece of milk bottle lying on a drain cover. In court the headmistress gave detailed evidence of the way in which the free milk was distributed to various parts of the school, including the fact that the empty bottles were not brought downstairs until the midday break, and then under the supervision of two mistresses. The plaintiff said that they were in the playground before the end of the mid-morning break. In the Court of Appeal, Lord Justice Willmer said: 'The evidence of the headmistress (whom the judge said he found an impressive witness) was rather different from that of the plaintiff. . . . This conflict of evidence was never in terms resolved by the judge. But there was evidence from the school's caretaker, which corroborated that of the plaintiff, evidence to show that quite often there were loose bottles standing on the ground alongside the crates in the playground, and this he regarded as dangerous.

'I am quite sure that the headmistress was correctly describing what was supposed to be the routine, but notwithstanding that I am left with the impression that the plaintiff probably knew more about what usually happened in practice. . . .

'The headmistress said that when the empties were carried down by the girls and stacked outside, there were always two mistresses on duty, and they would see that the girls did it. This answer at least recognized the need for supervision if and when the bottles were brought downstairs and stacked outside. I have no doubt that there ought to be such supervision. But the evidence given by the plaintiff as to the prevailing routine for bringing the bottles down seems to show that in actual practice there was in fact no such supervision. Moreover, as I have said, the defendants did not see fit to call any mistress to prove that such supervision was in fact exercised. . . .

'In my judgment, on the evidence, the risk of an accident such as this occurring was a reasonably foreseeable risk against which the defendants could and should have guarded by making better arrangements for the disposal of empty milk bottles. I do not think that the arrangements which they in fact made were such as would commend themselves to any reasonably prudent parent.'[1]

Beaumont v *Surrey County Council* – At a boys' secondary school in Surrey, morning break lasted for eighteen minutes, and was supervised by two masters, four prefects, four sub-prefects and four monitors. Before going into the playground the masters were responsible for clearing the school; on the day in question this operation took some time, and break had continued for ten minutes before they reached the playground. During that time some boys had found a discarded piece of trampette elastic which they used as a catapult for the purpose of projecting their school-mates across the loggia. The elastic either broke, or flew out of the hand of one of the boys who were holding it, and one end struck another pupil in the eye, the sight of which was to all intents and purposes destroyed.

After defining the headmaster's duty of care towards his pupils

[1] *Martin* v *Middlesbrough Corporation* (1965) 63 LGR 385; LCT 316.

in the terms already quoted,[1] Mr Justice Geoffrey Lane found that the presence of the elastic in an open waste-paper basket amounted to a failure in the standard of care required: 'It is sufficient as far as the law is concerned for the possibility to be there – for the possibility to be foreseen that some physical injury might be caused by the extension or use of, or horseplay with that piece of elastic. If such, even slight, injury is foreseeable, then the defendants must foot the bill if unforeseen and major injury occurred.'

The learned judge also found that the standard of supervision did not measure up to the high standard of care required: 'It may be that this was a particularly difficult day as Mr Clerke has indicated, it may be that the system of prefects, sub-prefects and monitors was not quite up to standard. It may be that on the one day when pupils were possibly reluctant to get out on to the playground insufficient staff were available to clear out the class-rooms which meant that insufficient staff were available on the loggia to supervise. Suffice it to say that had the system been working properly I have no doubt that either a prefect, sub-prefect, monitor or one of the staff would have seen or would have been summoned to see what was going on. . . .

'A whistle would have been blown and the forces of law and order would have moved into action. The offenders would either have been put into what I am told is the supervising master's detention or into the school detention or would have been reported to the headmaster, according to the view which the master took of the gravity of the offence. At all events it would have been stopped immediately, and had it been stopped immediately, or even within two or three minutes of this inception by the eleven-year-olds, then this tragic matter would never have happened.'[2]

Barnes v *Hampshire County Council* – At an infants' school at Chandlers Ford in Hampshire, nearly 200 yards from the A30 trunk road, it was the system that those pupils who were met by their parents at half-past three were escorted to the gate by a teacher. If a parent was not there, the child concerned was in-

[1] See page 230.
[2] *Beaumont* v *Surrey County Council* (1968) 66 LGR 580; LCT 246.

structed to return to his teacher. The children were given kerb drill, and a traffic warden was on duty on the main road.

One afternoon in 1962 a five-year-old girl began to make her way home whilst her mother was still on her way to meet her. Attempting to cross the main road at a point 250 yards from the schoolgate, she was knocked down and sustained partial paralysis of the left arm and foot. A man working in his nearby garden heard the accident, walked down his drive, saw that a girl had been hurt, and ran back to his house to telephone for an ambulance. The call was recorded in the telephone exchange at 3.30 p.m.

The plaintiff's claim for damages for negligence was rejected at Winchester Assizes. This judgment was affirmed by a majority of the Court of Appeal, Lord Justice Dipluck observing that the school system was reasonable: 'Ordinary people in ordinary life do not carry a chronometer; and I do not think that the three to five minutes in the present case constituted a breach of duty.' The Master of the Rolls, Lord Denning, dissented. He maintained that 'the school's system depended on the parents being there to meet the children at half-past three, and the school not letting them out until that time: to let them out before the mothers were due to arrive was to release them into a situation of potential danger and, in my view, a breach of duty'.

The House of Lords reversed the decision and awarded damages amounting to £10,000. Lord Pearson said: 'I agree with the Master of the Rolls. The system proved by the evidence was as he stated it. It was the duty of the school authorities not to release the children before the closing time. Although a premature release would very seldom cause an accident, it foreseeably could, and in this case it did cause the accident to the plaintiff.'[1]

4 Contributory negligence

At one time an action for negligence could be defeated if it were proved that the plaintiff himself contributed to the damage he sustained. In such a case the question of duty did not arise if it

[1]*Barnes* v *Hampshire County Council* (1969) 67 LGR 605, LCT 403

could be proved that the plaintiff acted without due care. The courts, however, took into account the fact that children are reckless and that it is to be expected that teachers will know this. The standard of care demanded from teachers is, however, that of the reasonably careful parent.

The law of contributory negligence has been amended by the Law Reform (Contributory Negligence) Act 1948. Under this Act, a claim in respect of damages can no longer be defeated purely because the injured person contributed to his own harm. The amount of any damages, however, must be reduced to such an extent as the court thinks just and equitable, having regard to the claimant's share of responsibility. The new Act does not operate against any defence arising under a contract.

In 1841, some boys clambered on to an unattended cart and another moved it away by leading the horse. As a result, one boy fell and injured his leg. Had he been an adult, his action in climbing on the cart would probably have been held to have contributed to his injury, and would have invalidated his case. As the plaintiff was an infant, however, the case was decided differently and the court accepted the submission of Serjeant Shee that it is impossible to say what is want of ordinary caution in a child seven years old.[1]

5 Higher duty of care

A defendant who, through training or experience, may have grounds to visualize more clearly the results of his acts in a particular sphere than would be expected of the proverbial man in the street, owes what is known as a higher duty of care. Obviously a doctor would be expected to render first aid more effectively than a person who is completely untrained, and it has been noted above that teachers are expected to know more of the vagaries of children than most people do.

A case which contained this element[2] arose out of an accident which occurred when a chemistry master sent two boys across a school cloister with a bottle of sulphuric acid. Contrary to the

[1] *Lynch* v *Nurdin* [1841] 1 QB 29.
[2] *Baxter* v *Barker* and *others*, (1903), *The Times*, 24 April.

school rules some other pupils were playing cap touch in the vicinity after the end of school. One of the players backed into the boys who were carrying the flask of vitriol with the result that it was shattered, and the plaintiff was permanently scarred. Actions were brought against the managers and the headmaster.

For the defendants it was urged that the chemistry master was competent and qualified, and that the boys carrying the jar were monitors who were well aware of the properties of sulphuric acid. The plaintiff should have left the school premises before the accident occurred. The monitors had called out in warning when they saw him running backwards towards them.

The managers were dismissed from the case, but the special jury[1] found for the plaintiff against the headmaster, who was ordered to pay £50 in damages. It was held that no steps had been taken on this occasion to ensure that boys left the premises at the end of school, and the chemistry master – with his special knowledge of the nature of the liquid – should have made sure that the cloister was clear before he sent the monitors on their errand. The school rules were sufficient, but they were not carried out. There was no contributory negligence by the plaintiff.

6 Scope of employment

An employer is liable for the acts of his servants so long as they are acting within the scope of their employment. It is difficult to say where the scope of a teacher's employment begins and ends today, for there is a multitude of out-of-school activities which would once have been considered beyond his province. It is clear that the scope of employment is not to be construed in any narrow sense. An unauthorized teacher inflicting corporal punishment in defiance of the local education authority's rules would obviously be acting outside the scope of his employment and would have to take full personal responsibility for any mischance arising therefrom. The same would apply in the case of a teacher who sent a child across the road on a purely personal errand.

[1] Special juries consisting of persons of a certain status, e.g. esquires or persons of higher degree, bankers or merchants, have now been abolished except in the City of London.

Some years ago, a teacher sent a fourteen-year-old girl to the staffroom to poke the fire and draw the damper. Whilst she was doing this her pinafore caught fire and she was burned. An action[1] was brought against both the teacher and the local education authority. The judge held that the order was given by the teacher for her personal convenience, that she was therefore acting outside the scope of her employment, and the authority had no liability in the matter. He dismissed the authority from the suit, and awarded £300 damages against the teacher.

Two appeals followed. That by the teacher against the parent failed, but the latter appealed successfully against the dismissal of the authority from the case. Lord Justice Farwell held that the teacher was acting within the scope of her employment, and said, 'In my opinion the Education Acts are designed to provide for education in its truest and widest sense. Such education includes the inculcation of habits of order, obedience and courtesy; such habits are taught by giving orders and, if such orders are reasonable and proper under the circumstances of the case, they are within the scope of the teacher's authority even though they are not confined to bidding the child to read or write, to sit down or to stand up in school, or the like. It would be extravagant to say that a teacher has no business to ask a child to perform small acts of courtesy for herself or for others, such as to fetch her pocket handkerchief from upstairs, to open a door for a visitor, or the like.

'It is said that these are for the teacher's own benefit, but I do not agree. Not only is it good for the child to be taught to be unselfish and obliging, but the opportunity of running upstairs may often avoid punishment. The wise teacher who sees a child becoming fidgety may well make the excuse of an errand for herself an outlet for the child's exuberance of spirits very much to the benefit of the child. Teachers must use their common sense, and it would be disastrous to hold that they can do nothing but teach.'

The question of scope of employment can also affect claims for industrial injuries benefit. Some years ago the author's caretaker,

[1] *Smith* v *Martin* and *Kingston-upon-Hull Corporation* [1911] 2 KB 775.

out of sheer good will, used to play cricket with the boys and staff during the lunch break. One day he was hit on the knee by a ball bowled by a master, and claimed for industrial injuries. The author had, somewhat regretfully, to say in answer to an official inquiry that playing cricket was not part of his duties as a caretaker.

A favourite topic for staffroom discussions is the legality o using pupils for various duties which are for the benefit of the staff. In many schools senior pupils prepare the cup of tea which is enjoyed by the staff at break time, and a case arising out of this practice was heard by the Court of Appeal in 1959.[1]

A fourteen-year-old girl was carrying a pot containing half a gallon of tea to the staffroom, and was scalded when she collided with a small boy who charged out of a room. In the county court she was awarded £275 damages against the Corporation. For the plaintiff it was claimed that the girl was engaged in a dangerous operation, and that if the school desired free labour a greater burden of care was placed on it. She had to walk twenty-five yards along a narrow corridor, which gave on to a number of rooms from which anyone might properly emerge, and round three blind corners.

On appeal it was maintained that this was not a dangerous operation. The older girls had lessons in domestic science and carried out certain duties, partly in furtherance of their training and partly for the convenience of the staff. The county court judge possibly rather disapproved, but it was part of their general training for life. The girl was required to take the tea to the staffroom before the beginning of break, and was doing so on this occasion, but the county court judge had believed that children were thronging the corridors at this time. If children of fourteen were to be guarded against the least physical injury, cricket would be played with soft balls, gymnastics would be abandoned, and cookery classes would cease.

In allowing the appeal, Mr Justice Hodson said that a great many domestic operations carried danger with them. There was no evidence of crowds of children thronging the corridor, and it

[1] *Cooper* v *Manchester Corporation* (1959) *The Times*, 13 February.

had not been contended that it was the case. There was no reason to see that a single boy would be outside a classroom at that time. On the facts of the case there was nothing to justify a finding of negligence.

7 Damages

The assessment of damages where a plaintiff succeeds in an action is not a matter of caprice, and potential defendants should be aware of the fact that, like everything else, they are following current inflationary trends. This must be so, for example, in considering the future loss of earnings, due to someone else's negligence, of a young person whose career had shown promise of considerable success for a further period of thirty years or more. *Povey* v *Rydal School* – In 1969 a young man confined to a wheel-chair after dislocating his neck in a school gynmasium was awarded £78,398 in damages. It was said that he had been forced to give up his ambition to become a doctor, that he would never be able to stand up or walk again and that he was constantly reliant on others for all physical need except for propelling his wheel-chair. The award consisted of £14,920 for loss of earnings, £19,400 for nursing costs, £7,000 for miscellaneous costs, £25,000 for general damages, £400 for loss of expectancy of life, and £3,278 agreed special damages. Special damages are disburse-ments actually and necessarily made before the trial including, for example medical and nursing attention not provided by the National Health Service. They do not include the legal costs of the action.[1]

Hamp v *St Joseph's Hospital, Alderley Edge* – Three years later the damages awarded against the proprietors of a convent school were so far in excess of the insurance cover taken out by the owners that a special appeal had to be launched to save the school. The award stemmed from an incident in 1965, when an eleven-year-old girl was grinding chemicals for a teacher and an explosion virtually destroyed her sight. For the next six years she underwent almost continuous medical attention, including eighteen months

[1] *Povey* v *Governors of Rydal School, Colwyn Bay* (1969) *The Times*, 13 March.

in a hospital in Barcelona where she had an average of an operation each month, and a corneal transplant in Houston, Texas. For long periods she had to lie in total darkness. She was awarded £76,878 in damages to include £36,000 for pain, suffering and loss of amenities, £11,000 for loss of future earnings and £5,500 for future medical expenses. Special damages were agreed at £24,378. In addition, interest of between 6 and 7½ per cent was due on the general damages from the issue of the writ until the date of judgment nearly four years later, and at half that rate on the special damages from the date of the accident seven years previously. The father was also awarded £4,471 for his expenses in travelling with his daughter to Spain and the United States. When the costs were added the school was faced with a bill in the region of £95,000. At the time of the accident the school's insurance policy for contingencies of this kind provided cover for £25,000.

Loss of marriage prospects formed an element in the assessment of damages in this case, and when the school's appeal was heard in July 1973 it was known that she was about to marry an American electronics engineer. By this time interest had raised the damages, apart from costs, to more than £88,000, and counsel for the school submitted that the impending marriage should go to the reduction of damages. The Court of Appeal did not agree. The Master of the Rolls, Lord Denning, said that if she had children she would probably have to have paid help, and he thought the pecuniary loss would be more in a way when she is married than if she is unmarried. Lord Justice Lawton thought that, if anything, the award was 'a little on the low side'.[1]

Although an employer is liable for the torts of his servants committed in the execution of his duty, there is nothing to prevent a head or assistant being joined with the employer in an action for negligence and, as has already been stated,[2] he may be ordered to pay a proportion of the damages if there has been gross personal negligence on his part. In any case, if he is a joint

[1] *Hamp* v *Saint Joseph's Hospital, Alderley Edge* (1972) *Daily Telegraph*, 19, 23 and 24 October; (1973) 26 and 27 July.
[2] See pages 239–42.

defendant, he may find himself faced with costs or, at least, considerable out-of-pocket expenses when he is not condemned in damages.

To believe that actions of this kind happen only to other people is to live in a fool's paradise. If for no other reason than this, a teacher should belong to a professional association which will not only undertake his defence and pay for it, but will also insure him in respect of any damages which may be awarded against him. The only reasonable alternative is to take out an equivalent insurance policy privately, and there are underwriters prepared to do business in this field. The snag in this case is that general insurers may not have the specialized knowledge of educational law which has been built up by the professional associations.

Teachers in voluntary-aided, direct grant and independent schools are not the servants of the local education authority, but of the governors or proprietor. They are in a particularly vulnerable position. Some local education authorities are unwilling to extend the same degree of protection to the staffs of voluntary-aided schools as to those in county schools; they can do nothing for teachers in direct grant or independent schools. Unfortunately, these schools do not always carry sufficient cover, and it is even more essential that teachers in these establishments should take steps to protect themselves.[1]

8 General and approved practice

A common defence to an action for negligence is that the act causing harm was in accordance with general and approved

---

[1] Although, strictly speaking, it is outside the scope of this book, teachers should be aware that they can find themselves defending a claim for damages for negligence in respect of something they have done (or failed to do) as private citizens, e.g. if they have neglected to keep their garden wall in good repair, and it falls on a passer-by and injures him. Damages and costs in such a case can be equally heavy, and it is not widely enough known that for a premium of about £2 a year it is possible to take out what is usually known as a 'public liability policy' which covers damages and costs up to a sum of £100,000 in respect of any one incident. The negligence of members of the policyholder's household is also covered, but this cover does not extend to negligence in the course of a profession, vocation or trade; nor to negligence which must, in law, be protected by insurance such as the use of a motor vehicle.

practice (sometimes called 'the custom of the trade') in the circumstances. A selection of examples will show how this defence has
been used in cases arising from accidents in school.

In the first,[1] some children were playing when one fell on the
lance of a toy soldier with which another was amusing himself.
The lance pierced the child's eye. It was held in this case that
children are commonly allowed to play with these toys, and it
cannot therefore be considered negligent for them to be permitted
to do so in school.

In another case[2] the plaintiff was a girl of seven who was
injured in an exercise which consisted of running across the floor
and jumping over an inverted waste-paper basket. The head,
an assistant and a student were present. An action for damages
was based on the grounds that the basket was an unsuitable
obstacle, the child was not physically fitted for the exercise, no
landing mat was provided and there was no stand-by. In the
defence, which was based on a plea of general and approved
practice, it was pointed out that the Board of Education's suggestions included running and jumping for children of this age, that
the head had been at the school for two and a half years during
which the exercise had been performed regularly without accident,
and that there had been no accident arising from this exercise at
the head's previous school. Moreover, it was contended that the
rope which the plaintiff suggested as a more suitable obstacle was,
in fact, more dangerous. The suit was dismissed.

During the slump in the early 'thirties an unemployed lad of
seventeen was ordered to attend a juvenile instruction centre, as
a condition of receiving unemployment benefit. Whilst engaged
in physical training at the centre, he fell and injured his arm
during a game of Horses and Riders. He sued the local education
authority[3] and was awarded £1,000 in damages in the county
court. This decision was reversed by the divisional court, whereupon Jones took the case to the Court of Appeal. Giving judg-

[1] *Chilvers* v *London County Council* (1916) 80 JP 246; LCT 259.

[2] Reported in the *School Government Chronicle* (1925) 19 February.

[3] *Jones* and *another* v *London County Council* (1932) 30 LGR 455;
LCT 277.

ment for the Council, Lord Justice Scrutton asked whether it could be negligence to play a game which had been played for twenty years. He added that there were few physical exercises without the possibility of an accident.

9 The effect of age

It has already been mentioned that what amounts to negligence in one case may not be so in another because the age of the plaintiff must be taken into account. This may be further illustrated by a case[1] arising from an accident to a lad of nineteen who was using an unguarded circular saw. It was alleged that the education authority was negligent in failing to provide a guard. In an appeal from the decision of the county court, it was said that the plaintiff knew the use of the saw, and voluntarily took the risk. Observing that there was no evidence of a general practice to protect saws, Mr Justice Lush added, 'If he had been a child, the case might have been different but, so far from being a child, he was a lad of nineteen years of age and had been in the habit of using the saw for two years.'

The circumstances outlined in the last paragraph might amount to a breach of statutory duty if any regulations had been ignored. In *Lyes* v *Middlesex County Council* the plaintiff grounded his case both in negligence and in breach of duty.[2]

It has been held that a college of further education is not a factory, and the provisions of the Factory Acts do not apply. A sixteen-year-old trainee printer at the Camberwell School of Arts and Crafts caught his hand in a Thomson-British auto platen machine, which he was using for the first time. Three of his fingers were broken, one being permanently shortened by a quarter of an inch.

The Court of Appeal dismissed the local education authority's appeal against the award of £150 in damages. Lord Justice Danckwerts found that the Factories Act 1961, s. 14, required such machinery to be fenced, in spite of evidence that it was not usual for automatic machines to be guarded. The Act, however,

[1] *Smerkinich* v *Newport Corporation* (1912) 76 JP 454; LCT 265.
[2] See pages 28 and 31.

did not apply in the circumstances of the case, which therefore fell to be considered in terms of common law negligence: 'It is said, of course that if no guard was provided in factories, a school of this kind could not be expected to go to the trouble, and the expense, I suppose, of obtaining a guard, which would have to be made specially for the purpose, from the manufacturers. It seems to me, however, that it is the duty of the school to provide for the safety of their pupils.'[1]

More than a century ago it was held by Lord Ellenborough that it was negligent to allow children of tender years to play with fireworks unsupervised.[2] In *Williams* v *Eady*,[3] Mr Justice Cave said, 'To leave a knife about where a child of four could get at it would amount to negligence, but it would not if boys of eighteen had access to it.' *Charlesworth on Negligence* defines this test by asking the question, 'Is the thing one of a class which children of that age are, in the ordinary course of things, not allowed without supervision?'

In July 1964 an experienced teacher was taking a class of nine- and ten-year-old girls, who were given pointed scissors to cut out illustrations during a geography lesson. Whilst the teacher was attending to one girl, another pupil waved her scissors about so that the point destroyed the sight of the plaintiff's eye. There were thirty-seven children in the class. At first instance the plaintiff was awarded £3,350 damages, Mr Justice Mocatta holding that it was incumbent on the education authority to ensure that the waving about of scissors was rendered impossible by proper supervision. If personal attention was to be given to one child, it must be given either out of class, or after the class had been told to put down the scissors.

This judgment was unanimously reversed in the Court of Appeal. 'If every little child got into a difficulty', asked Lord Denning, the Master of the Rolls, 'was she to be told to come back afterwards? That did not seem practical. Nor was it practical

---

[1] *Butt* v *Inner London Education Authority* (1968) 66 LGR 379; LCT 268.

[2] *King* v *Ford* (1816) 1 Stark NP 421; LCT 256.

[3] See pages 27–8, 228, 230 and 231.

to make sure that the rest of the class put the scissors down. Was the whole class to stop still if one little girl needed supervision? It was a large class, but that was inevitable in conditions today. The teacher conducted the class in a good and efficient way. It was a very unfortunate accident, but there was no justification for finding either the education authority or the teacher at fault. The judge had the evidence of experienced teachers that there was no fault in the system of using pointed scissors.'[1]

The question of allowing children of different ages to leave the school premises with or without an escort is dealt with in other sections.[2]

10 Warning of danger
A teacher who can prove that he has warned a pupil of the dangerous consequences which may follow from a particular act is in a much stronger position when sued for negligence.

A teacher told an eleven-year-old girl to take a pair of pincers from a drawer to remove a broken, rusty nib from a penholder. The nib broke and the child's eye was damaged by splinters. A case[3] was brought, claiming damages for personal injuries resulting from the negligence of the teacher, it being claimed that such an order should not have been given to a child. Directing the jury, Mr Justice Avory said that it was not contended that the pincers were dangerous, and the case rested on a direct order to take the pincers from the drawer in order to pull out the nib without any warning of the possible danger. Even at arm's length, the accident might have happened. The jury awarded £100 and special damages.

It will be noted that the judge stressed the fact that the girl was not warned of the danger.

Crouch v *Essex County Council* – The most important case on this issue was heard in 1966 before Mr Justice Widgery.[4] Four years

---

[1] *Butt* v *Cambridgeshire and Isle of Ely County Council* (1970) 68 LGR 81.

[2] See pages 236–7, 260–62 and 266–8.

[3] *Foster* v *London County Council* (1927) *The Times*, 2 March; LCT 255.

[4] Now Lord Chief Justice Widgery: *Crouch* and *another* v *Essex County Council* and *another* (1966).

previously a young science master had given a lesson on the reaction of the oxides of zinc, aluminium and tin to caustic soda. The first twenty or thirty minutes of the lesson were taken up with an account of the experiment, after which the pupils worked in pairs at sinks, each couple being provided with the necessary apparatus and, subject to one exception, a normal solution of caustic soda. On the master's bench was an unlabelled beaker of a much stronger solution from which a group of pupils at the back of the laboratory, who were working with the tin oxide, were required to draw a supply.

The witnesses on whom his Lordship relied principally said that Mr Ford had constantly warned his pupils of the danger of playing about with chemicals, and he certainly did so on this occasion. One quoted him: 'If you put your hand into this solution, it will turn it into a bar of soap.' It was said semi-seriously and, commented the learned judge, no doubt had a two-fold purpose: partly to convey a warning, and partly to drive home the chemical lesson that the reaction between caustic soda and animal fat is the creation of soap. The witness admitted that some of the class may not have heard the warning, but she had no difficulty whatever in doing so.

The plaintiff, who was at that time aged fifteen, said that there was talking and squirting of water with pipettes during the lesson. He did not really know what was being taught and that, soon after the practical part of the lesson started, he took some test-tubes to the front of the room to clean them, and to ask as to the nature of the experiment. 'In particular, I was going to ask a couple of girls at the teacher's desk who seemed to know exactly what they were doing.' As he reached them one girl squirted a liquid into his ear; he thought it was water. Immediately afterwards the other girl squirted the concentrated caustic soda into his eyes. Through his father, as next friend, he claimed damages for negligence on the master's part for which the local education authority were vicariously liable.

The master said that he liked a free and easy atmosphere and, as far as he could, he tried not to be the strict Victorian discip-linarian. The class was a fairly well-behaved group, although there were isolated acts of horse-play, such as connecting bunsen burners to the water taps and squirting water through the burners. He often had to repeat himself because of talking. He taught that all chemicals were potentially dangerous, he had warned them that alkalis are as dangerous as acids, and he remembered the reference to the bar of soap mentioned by a former pupil. He was walking about among the pupils when he heard the plaintiff scream.

Having analysed the evidence, his Lordship said: 'I accept the evidence of Mr Ford so far as the facts of the matter are concerned. I am quite satisfied that for students as advanced as these students were in March 1962, there was no danger or impropriety in allowing them to help themselves to this stronger solution of caustic soda once an adequate warning as to the nature of the solution and its properties had been given. I am quite satisfied that one cannot say, as a general rule, that fifteen-year-olds with this background in the study of chemistry should not be allowed to draw supplies of caustic soda of this strength without direct supervision, provided that they have had an adequate warning and are supplied with adequate materials.

'Further, I am quite satisfied that no criticism can be attached to the failure to label the beaker in the circumstances of this case because the nature of the contents had to be put over to the class by oral instruction, and, if oral instruction given by Mr Ford was inadequate for this purpose, I find it difficult to believe that a label on the beaker would have had any other effect. I am impressed by the evidence that the labelling of the beaker would primarily be a means of avoiding confusion with other liquids; and as it seems there was no other liquid available at that time, labelling seems to me to be a matter of no relevance.

'The case, therefore, really turns on whether in the circumstances of this class and these pupils it was right for Mr Ford to allow the pupils from the back bench to come up and draw this liquid in the manner which I have described. That it would have been proper for him to do so in regard to pupils generally of the status of these I have no doubt at all.

'The plaintiff's case, in brief, is that there was such lack of discipline in this class, such lack of control and such lack of responsibility, that it was a dangerous act for Mr Ford to leave the caustic soda in the position in which it was left, and to allow these irresponsible girls and boys in the back row to approach it with the tempting pipettes which they were likely to use as weapons. I have considered this aspect of the case with care overnight, and I am quite satisfied that the plaintiff's case is not made out.

'That there was some horse-play in this class I do not question. Chemistry classes seem given to that kind of activity, and possibly the teacher's position is not made easier when the class is a mixed one. I think all the witnesses who spoke in this case have been honest and have done their best, but nineteen-year-olds, looking back on their schooldays, will naturally remember the entertaining features rather than the dull ones, and can quite easily look back on Mr Ford's lectures after four years as an unbroken orgy of distilled water and squirting, which I am quite satisfied they were not. If that had been the kind of atmosphere which one found in this class, I have no doubt whatever that Mr Smith and Miss Veall would have disclosed it to me.

'Having listened in particular to them, I am quite satisfied that Mr Ford maintained a standard of discipline which, at any rate, was adequate from a safety point of view. It is not for me to express an opinion as to whether that type of discipline is satisfactory from an educational point of view. That is not my concern.

'Furthermore, I am satisfied that there was no particular incident on this morning which would suggest any unusual outbreak of indiscipline. Indeed, Miss Veall's account of the general hum of conversation is indicative of the fact that the class as a whole were perfectly normally well-behaved. So really, in the last analysis, one has to ask oneself whether it was reasonably foreseeable to Mr Ford, approaching his duties as being equivalent to those of a careful and prudent parent, that on this occasion not only should Miss Crispin and Miss Jackson and the plaintiff have studiously ignored everything which was said to them in the earlier part of the period, but should also have proceeded to his desk, and then proceeded to squirt a wholly unidentified liquid at the plaintiff's face.

'This conduct was a little short of lunatic, and it was utterly irresponsible, and I am quite sure on the evidence which I have heard that the general atmosphere and standard of Mr Ford's class was not such as to make that kind of conduct foreseeable. He gave an adequate warning on this occasion of the nature and properties of the caustic soda. He was not to foresee that Miss Jackson should, first of all, fail to listen; and then – which is the important point – should have proceeded to pick up this pipette and, with complete and utter irresponsibility, to have squirted it into the plaintiff's face.

'In those circumstances the allegations of negligence against Mr Ford fail; and with them, of course, any allegations against the county council as well.'

This case has been quoted in some detail not only because of its importance as an illustration of the need to give adequate warning of potential dangers, but also because it is an outstanding example of the care with which the courts examine the details of a system in applying the common sense of the common law.

11 Special dangers

Special dangers exist in some subjects because of the nature of the tools or materials employed. So far as the law is concerned, the tests applied by the courts are the same. The important point to watch is that all reasonable care is used by teachers in charge of such subjects.

The risk in science laboratories is highlighted in *Crouch* v *Essex County Council* in the preceding section. It should be noted also that a scientist could be expected to ensure a higher standard of care in a science laboratory than would be the case if a person not highly trained in his subject were in charge. It will be remembered that this was an element in *Baxter* v *Barker*.[1]

Other places where there is a high degree of risk include workshops where edged tools and an increasing amount of machinery are installed. A special risk today is to be found in the modern

[1] See pages 238–9.

fashion for long hair adopted by many boys, with the attendant risk that this may get caught in quickly revolving plants. Handicraft masters should take care to see that such hair is fastened back or covered adequately. Accidents of this nature not infrequently lead to the victim being scalped.

Handicraft's sister subject, Housecraft, also has a comparatively high risk rate. In the leading case[1] Salford Corporation was condemned in damages arising from serious injuries to an eleven-year-old girl when her apron caught fire. The particular kind of accident on that occasion is less likely to arise today, but modern equipment, such as washing machines, drying cabinets and electric food mixers, can be used in an unsafe way. Again, it is important that long hair should be kept well away from naked flames and quickly moving machinery, and that on no account should girls be allowed to wear aprons made of flammable material.

Needlework is also a subject in which injuries are relatively common. In particular danger can arise from horse-play with scissors – which, of course, are often used in other subjects, as well. This question was discussed in *Butt* v *Cambridgeshire and Isle of Ely County Council*.[2] Electric machines and irons can also be a source of danger.

The dangers of Physical Education require a separate section.

12 Physical education

Gymnasia and playing fields are, perhaps, the most common scenes of school accidents and there have been many cases arising from such mishaps. So far as the gymnasium is concerned, authorities are careful to prohibit the use of apparatus, as far as possible, by those who are not qualified. Disregard of such a requirement may place the teacher, and the head if he has knowledge of the infraction, outside the scope of his employment. The tests which are most likely to be applied by the courts will concern the adequacy of supervision, and the following of general and approved practice. For this reason it is important in games

---

[1] *Fryer* v *Salford Corporation* [1937] 1 All ER 617; LCT 271.
[2] See pages 246–7.

periods that the rules of the game be adhered to strictly, and dangerous play penalized.

In 1968 the DES drew attention to the danger of using apparatus giving a high rebound, especially in primary schools.[1] A more recent pamphlet by the DES[2] advises against the use of the Fosbury flop technique of high jumping, where the athlete leaps backwards over the bar and lands on his back. This can result in serious permanent injury in school sandpits, which are not designed for such a purpose. The pamphlet also questions boxing as a school activity, pointing out that the Royal College of Physicians warned in 1968 that permanent brain damage can result from the cumulative effect of injuries. To allow boys to lift weights to the limit of their capacity is another dangerous practice, which can lead to permanent injury of the spine.

There is, says the DES, no such thing as a safe fire-arm, and there are risks inherent in the use of large-bore starting pistols, which can be drilled to convert them into firearms (even though not actually drilled). The pamphlet advises that all starting guns should be marked with the school's name. A case[3] followed an accident when a boy fell whilst jumping from an agility stool in 1951. The boy was then aged five and it was claimed that he was required to jump from a stool which was almost his own height, the nearest adult being twelve to fourteen feet away. For the defence it was said that there was no permanent damage to the boy's elbow, and the headmistress maintained that the whole point of the apparatus was to give the children confidence. Mr Justice Devlin said that the apparatus itself, and the way in which it was designed to be used, were safe. It was clear that the headmistress was not negligent, neither was the teacher, and he did not see what they could have done if they had seen the boy jump. There was nothing to show that it was anything but an accident.

The importance of having a 'stand-by' during vaulting cannot be too strongly emphasized. During a physical education lesson

[1] Administrative Memorandum no. 2/68: *Physical Education Apparatus Schools and Colleges.*

[2] *Safety in Physical Education* (HMSO, 1973).

[3] *Webb* v *Essex County Council* (1954) *Times Educational Supplement*, 12 November, LCT 290.

a boy fell whilst vaulting over a horse. It was held that reasonable care to prevent a fall had not been taken, and the master did not seem 'to have acted with the promptitude which the law requires'. The Court found for the plaintiff.[1] In another case there were four classes in the gymnasium when a boy fell whilst vaulting over the buck at a time when the master was dealing with another class. It was held that the supervision was in accordance with normal practice, had been safely practised for years, and that it was not negligent.[2]

Some years ago an accident in a comprehensive school pin-pointed another risk arising from the diversification of activities. On that occasion some boys were practising golf strokes indoors when one pupil was killed by a blow on the head from the club being used by another boy. This emphasizes the need for care when outdoor activities are being coached in a confined space and on a hard surface.

Professional players are often used for training in the specific skills at which they are expert. It is important that they should be warned about any pupils who may indulge in dangerous behaviour; alternatively, such pupils may be removed from the group.

Bathing and boating are considered in another chapter.[3]

A boy of fourteen put his arm through a glass partition during a relay race at a play centre. The children had been told to touch the supervisor, and had not been told to touch the partition, as they turned at the end of the hall. There was no negligence.[4]

Allowing pupils to do gym in stockinged feet has been held to be negligent. This was held in an unreported case where a master, not having a spare pair of plimsolls of the right size, allowed a boy who had forgotten his own to wear his socks. The boy slipped and hurt himself badly. It was held that the risk of falling was greater when wearing socks than when wearing plimsolls or doing gym in bare feet.

---

[1] *Gibbs* v *Barking Corporation* (1936) 1 All ER 115; LCT 279.
[2] *Wright* v *Cheshire County Council* (1952) 2 All ER 789; LCT 284.
[3] See pages 315–16.
[4] *Cahill* v *West Ham Corporation* (1937) 81 SJ 630; LCT 280.

13 Before and after school

Many teachers are concerned about their responsibility for pupils
on the school premises before the beginning, and after the end,
of the school day. This section does not deal with supervision
during the midday break which is included in the chapter in
extraneous duties.[1]

Before school – Children arrive at school early for a variety of
reasons; sometimes as much as an hour before the beginning
of the morning session. Some are 'latch-key' children sent out
by their parents when the adult members of the family leave for
work; in rural areas public transport may be infrequent, so
that a child must be very early, or late; sometimes the local
education authority arranges a shuttle service of privately hired
coaches, the vehicles depositing their load at the school on their
first journey long before opening time.

The generally accepted practice, which has no legal sanction
unless it is provided for by the authority's regulations or the
head's requirements as to supervision made in pursuance of his
duty under the rules of management or articles of government, is
for the teaching staff to accept responsibility for pupils for ten or
fifteen minutes before morning school.

The local education authority, however, has a duty of care as
soon as they arrive on the premises, at any rate with the authority's consent. If the authority insists on permitting, or by its
transport arrangements causes, children to arrive before it is
reasonable to expect the teaching staff to accept responsibility, it
is the authority's responsibility to make suitable arrangements for
supervision. The ILEA laid down the principle in its *School-
keepers' Handbook* that the schoolkeeper was entirely responsible
for the premises until fifteen minutes before the beginning of
morning school, at which time a member of the teaching staff
must be on the school premises. Until that time this arrangement
ensured that the schoolkeeper could admit, or refuse admission to,
any person; but once he had given permission for entry he was
responsible for any consequences which might ensue. At the
time of writing the handbook is in the course of revision, and it is

[1] See pages 370–74.

understood that this laudable arrangement may not be renewed.

One thing which a prudent head will not do is to take a unilateral decision to lock the playground or playing field gates
against children. If, as a result, a child should be knocked down
and injured it is doubtful if he would be held to have acted as
a careful parent when he had refused the victim admission to a
place of safety. It would go to mitigation if he had advised parents
well in advance of his intention to do so, but every other avenue
should first be explored to achieve the co-operation of the local
education authority.

If a head is concerned about the safety of children who arrive
early, for whatever reason, he should ask the local education
authority to take appropriate action to safeguard their own
position. It would also be prudent, if the cause is within the
parents' control, to write to parents asking them not to send their
children to school before a certain time, and pointing out the
unreasonableness of expecting teaching staff to accept responsibility for an excessive period before the beginning of school.

Ward v *Hertfordshire County Council* – Unfortunately, the only
case dealing with the matter of supervision before morning school
is not very helpful.[1] In a Hertfordshire primary school, where the
playground was surrounded by an unrendered flint wall, the
children were allowed into the playground from 8.15 a.m. and
played there unsupervised until they were called into school at
8.55. One day an eight-year-old boy was racing across the playground when he stumbled and crashed into the wall about five
minutes before the beginning of school. A steel plate had to be
inserted in his skull but, although he made a good recovery he
was not able to join in pursuits such as boxing and rugby football.

At first instance Mr Justice Hinchcliffe awarded the plaintiff
£950 damages, holding that the wall was inherently dangerous
and that the authority were in breach of their duty under the
Occupiers Liability Act 1957, and their common law duty to take
reasonable care for the safety of the children.

[1] *Ward* v *Hertfordshire County Council* (1969) 67 LGR 418; (1970
68 LGR 151.

On the question of supervision, the learned judge said: 'In my judgment a prudent parent of a large family would have realized that this playground, with its flint walls and sharp and jagged flints protruding was inherently dangerous. In my judgment reasonable supervision was required, not only during the working day, but also when the children were collected together in the playground before the school starts. I do not suggest that there should necessarily be a continuous supervision from 8.15 onwards, but there should have been supervision from time to time controlling any risky activity of the children having regard to the proximity of this dangerous wall: and really it is not too much to ask that there should be supervision between 8.30 or 8.45 and 8.55 when the supervision might well have been continuous.'

The Court of Appeal unanimously reversed this decision. The Master of the Rolls, Lord Denning, did not think that the wall was dangerous. A third of the village had similar walls, so had sixteen schools in the county 'and goodness knows how many in the country at large. . . . But this does not mean that they are dangerous. We have lived with them long enough to know.' About supervision he added: 'The headmaster said that the teachers took charge of the children from the time they were due to be in school at five minutes to nine until the time when they were let out. Before the school began, the staff were indoors preparing the day's work. They cannot be expected to be in the playgrounds too. He said that even if he had been in the playground, he would not have stopped the children playing. It often happens that children run from one side of the playground to the other. It is impossible so to supervise them that they never fall down and hurt themselves. I cannot think that this accident shows any lack of supervision by the school authorities.'

In a concurring judgment, Lord Justice Salmon said: 'The judge said that a master, if he had been present in the playground, should have prevented this racing. I am afraid I cannot agree with him. We know from the headmaster that racing between the walls had continually gone on during all the time he was there and no harm has come of it. I dare say a small boy has occasionally fallen and scraped his knees or hands or elbows on the ground, or perhaps on the wall, and hurt himself to some extent. But this is the sort of thing that happens to children in playgrounds. It would in my view be wrong to try to protect them against minor injuries of that kind by forbidding them the ordinary pleasures which school children so much enjoy. I appreciate the point that during the breaks during the day, children playing in the playground are supervised but are not supervised in the morning before 8.55. Some of the children arrive at 8.15 in the morning, and the school does not start until 8.55. For reasons which have been explained to us, there is no master in the playground before 8.55 a.m., although they are in school getting ready for the day's work and would hear what is going on outside. If this accident had been caused by the children fighting or indulging in some particularly dangerous game which a master should have stopped if he had been there, the fact that there was no supervision at the time might have afforded anyone who was injured in that way a good cause of action. *It is not necessary to express any concluded view on that point. To my mind the fact that there was no master in the playground on this occasion is irrelevant*, because even if there had been a master there I can see no reason why he should have prevented the children racing or playing as Timothy was doing at the time when he met with this most unfortunate accident.'

Although the Court of Appeal clearly thought that the trial judge had set the requirement of supervision too high, it must be observed that the court limited itself strictly to the facts of this particular case where the headmaster had said that he would not have stopped the game if he had been present. In this case, therefore, the higher court found the supervision issue irrelevant. The words in Lord Justice Salmon's judgment, italicized by the author, indicate that the question of supervision before school is not closed and any future judgments will be based on the merit of the precise facts at that time before the court.

After school – It is general and approved practice for the majority of pupils to be expected to leave the premises within ten or fifteen minutes of the close of school. It is also common practice for a member of the staff to see that this is done. Failure to do so resulted in adverse judgment in *Baxter* v *Barker*.[1] With young children, who are commonly met by parents or other adults, it is necessary to have, and maintain an adequate system which is properly maintained, as is shown by *Barnes* v *Hampshire County Council*.[2] On the other hand, if the system breaks down because of a failure by the adult meeting the child, the school will not be held negligent if it has maintained its own part of the system efficiently: *Jeffery* v *London County Council*.[3]

If there is to be any change in the system, e.g. the time of release, whether this be permanent or temporary, it is important that parents, especially those of very young children and those who normally meet their children from school, should be given adequate warning.

The question of supervising children crossing roads at the end of school is dealt with elsewhere.[4]

Where pupils are kept in school, whether as part of a formal or informal detention class or for any out-of-school activities, it should be the recognized practice in the school that the teacher in whose charge they are should be responsible for supervising their departure and for ensuring that they have all left the premises.

In general – Beyond recognizing the fact that children are in the care of the school authorities, which for this purpose includes the staff, *in loco parentis* so long as they are on the school premises, the law remains somewhat nebulous. In many ways this is unfortunate, because it is a matter which causes the gravest concern to teachers throughout the country, particularly in primary schools. What, for example, is to be done about the neglectful parent who habitually fails to collect her child, trusting that a teacher or somebody else will look after him for an indeterminate period?

The answer in such a case is that the parent, provided she has been properly instructed, has broken the part of the system for which she is responsible, and if this can be proved there is little likelihood that the courts will find against the school, even if a very young child has been released at the proper time into a potentially dangerous situation. Few caring teachers would take

---

[1] See pages 238–9.   [2] See pages 236–7.   [3] See page 230.
[4] See pages 374–6.

this risk though more from a moral and professional, rather than a legal, standpoint. Should the child be taken home? What then happens if there is no one there, or if the child has an accident whilst being escorted? Again, everything would turn on the precise facts in each case.

Some authorities have an arrangement by which the educational welfare service or the police may be telephoned and asked to deal with this situation on individual occasions. Frequently, however, there is no officer available when needed; even if there is, he may be unwilling to accept this responsibility.

The essential point is that each school must have its own system especially tailored to suit its own needs. That system must be rigorously enforced so far as the school's part is concerned, and every reasonable effort should be made to encourage the parents to shoulder their share of the responsibility. The local education authority for Cornwall supplies a letter for schools to send to parents stating the limits between which the authority will accept responsibility; blanks being left for the head to insert the appropriate times for his school. This is a worthwhile attempt by a local education authority to remove a burden of worry from its teaching staff; and would be valuable evidence in a lawsuit provided, of course, that it can be proved that the parent concerned received the notice, and that the school had kept its part of the bargain on the occasion in question.

14 The straying child

The House of Lords gave judgment, in 1955, in a case which had been before the Cardiff Assizes and the Court of Appeal.[1] In all three courts the decision was for the plaintiff who was awarded more than £3,000 damages in respect of the death of her husband.[2]

The accident occurred in 1951, when the plaintiff's husband

[1] *Lewis* v *Carmarthenshire County Council* [1955] 2 All ER 1403; LCT (as *Carmarthenshire County Council* v *Lewis*), 326.

[2] The reason for taking the case to the House of Lords was the dissatisfaction of the National Union of Teachers with the imputation of negligence which the Assizes and the Court of Appeal has sustained against the teacher. It is a good example of the extent to which a professional association is prepared to go in vindicating one of its members. The whole of the teacher's legal costs were borne by the Union.

was driving a lorry along a road leading past one of the Council's schools. A four-year-old pupil ran in front of the lorry, which swerved into a telegraph pole to avoid him. The driver was killed. His widow alleged that the child would not have been in the road if the children had been properly supervised.

It was the habit of the teacher-in-charge of the school to take two nursery children for a walk and, on the day in question, she had prepared them for this. She had left them in a classroom whilst she went to the lavatory, but her absence was protracted by the fact that on the way back she met an injured child and stopped to dress his wound. In all, she was away for about ten minutes, during which time the children disappeared.

The youngsters made their way to the road, and the accident occurred when one of them tried to cross it in the path of the oncoming lorry.

In the House of Lords, Lord Chief Justice Goddard said that the question of general importance was whether the occupiers of premises adjoining the highway had a duty to prevent young children from escaping so as to endanger other persons lawfully passing upon it. By young children, he meant those whom a prudent parent would not allow to go into a street unaccompanied. He could not hold that an inference of negligence on the teacher's part should be sustained, but that did not conclude the matter. If it was possible for children at that age, when a teacher's back might be turned for a moment, to go out into a busy street, that did seem to indicate some lack of care or precautions that might reasonably be required. No satisfactory explanation had been given. The appeal was dismissed.

The interesting feature of this case is that both the Assizes and the Court of Appeal held that the teacher had been negligent. The House of Lords fixed the responsibility on the local education authority, maintaining that the gates must either have been open, or so easy to open, that a child of three or four could escape.

15 Duty of supervision

It is the duty of a schoolmaster to exercise reasonable supervision over his pupils in all parts of the school premises. What is reasonable depends on the age of the children,[1] and the activity in which they are taking part.[2]

A higher degree of supervision is required during instruction than during play. A tipping lorry delivering coke to a school was standing in the playground when some pupils jumped on it and set the tipping mechanism in motion. The headmaster did not know of the lorry's arrival. It was held that there was no negligence on the part of the school, as it is not necessary to provide continuous supervision in the playground for normally healthy children of school age. The Gas Company was also exonerated as the driver could not have foreseen that the boys would jump on the lorry.[3] Similarly, when a girl of six was injured by a ten-year-old boy using a bow and arrow during the teacher's absence from the playground, it was held that there was no negligence in supervision.[4]

The best supervision in the world cannot prevent every possibility of accident, for a mishap may occur three feet behind the back of a teacher on duty. When a girl was about to jump from the springboard into a swimming pool, another girl who had been holding on to the board let go without warning. It was held that this was a sudden accident which could neither be foreseen nor prevented.[5] An accident which could not be prevented by supervision is not attributable to negligence, even if there has been a breach of duty, as in the case of *Gow* v *Glasgow Education Authority*.[6]

Pettican v *London Borough of Enfield* – At Enfield Lower Grammar School it was the practice, on wet days, for pupils who stayed for lunch to go into classrooms for the remainder of the midday break. During a frolic on such an occasion a fourteen-year-old boy was hit in the eye by a piece of chalk, and lost the sight of that eye. In an action for damages counsel for the plaintiff complained that there was no games room, no library and no prefects;

[1] See *Jeffery* v *London County Council*, page 230.
[2] See also *Camkin* v *Bishop*, page 307.
[3] *Rawsthorne* v *Ottley* [1937] 3 All ER 902; LCT 300.
[4] *Ricketts* v *Erith Borough Council* [1943] 2 All ER 629; LCT 301.
[5] *Clarke* v *Bethnal Green Borough Council* (1939) 55 TLR 519; LCT 281.
[6] See pages 227–8.

and only one master to control two hundred and forty boys. The school was negligent in not giving the boys an outlet for their high spirits, and for not providing enough supervision.

Mr Justice Kilner-Brown did not accept the evidence of the master on duty that he paid twelve visits on a patrol system during the lunch break. Neither did he accept the evidence of the boys that no master appeared at all. The boys had agreed that they might not have seen a master appear in the doorway to make a cursory glance. He held that a system of supervision was in operation on this day, and that it was being exercised: 'It has recently been said that what used to be known as the "prudent parent" test is not applicable to a large school.[1] I adopt the suggestion that the duty is to take such care as is reasonable in the circumstances of the case. It was said by the plaintiff that a reasonable system would involve a master on duty in each classroom for a period of one hour. This is not right and, even given three or four masters on duty with three or four prefects, schoolboys of fifteen are perfectly able, as soon as the master's back is turned, to start fooling about. This high standard suggested by the plaintiff puts an intolerable burden on schoolmasters. They are not policemen or security guards or prison officers. The case of *Beaumont* v *Surrey County Council*[2] is not analogous: that case involved injury to an eye by a piece of elastic which had been carelessly discarded. The risk of injury in those circumstances was foreseeable. It was argued by the plaintiff that the risk of injury from the blackboard and chalk was likely as a foreseeable consequence arising from a frolic. In my view, this sort of suggestion was getting very near to placing on a local authority an absolute liability.

'The phrase used by one of the schoolboys who gave evidence, "I knew that there was authority about", summed up the position exactly. The boys knew perfectly well that there was a master about, and that is what supervision is all about. I have looked at

[1] See *Lyes* v *Middlesex County Council*, pages 28 and 231.
[2] See pages 28–9 and 235–6.

the case broadly, and common sense says that supervision is the implanting of the feeling that there is authority about, that is, that there is some control and sanction.'[1]

Apart from the definition of supervision at the end, this judgment is interesting in that it shows the way in which the courts distinguish one case from another, the distinction turning on the precise facts. In *Beaumont* v *Surrey County Council* there was a much more comprehensive system of supervision as a system but it was not fully enforced, and the fact that the trampette elastic had been discarded in a place to which pupils had access, created a foreseeable risk. In *Pettican* v *Enfield* the system itself was less rigid, but was held to be adequate to protect against foreseeable risks in all the circumstances of the case.

16 Criminal negligence

The cases which have been considered are civil matters where an action has been brought by a person who has suffered damage and seeks redress for himself. These are cases of the kind most likely to affect teachers. If, however, it is maintained that conduct has been so reckless as to amount to a crime, the action would be brought before the criminal courts. It is necessary to prove a much greater degree of negligence to establish criminal liability.

Few teachers are likely to act so recklessly, but it is possible to imagine a hypothetical case which might be held to constitute a crime. A teacher brings a party of junior children to London for the day from the heart of the country. On arrival, he tells them to amuse themselves until six o'clock, and goes off alone to watch a test match. During the afternoon one of his pupils is knocked down and killed. It is probable that in such circumstances – admittedly so extreme that it is difficult to imagine any teacher being so rash – a criminal charge might be brought.

Failure to observe the law relating to the risk of burning may

---

[1] *Pettican* v *London Borough of Enfield* (1970) *The Times*, 22 October and other reports.

well result in a criminal action. The section[1] is worth quoting in full:

> If any person who has attained the age of sixteen years, having the custody, charge or care of any child under the age of twelve years, allows the child to be in any room containing an open fire grate or any heating appliance liable to cause injury to a person by contact therewith, not sufficiently protected to guard against the risk of his being burnt or scalded without taking reasonable precautions against that risk, and by reason thereof the child is killed or suffers serious injury, he shall on summary conviction be liable to a fine not exceeding ten pounds ;
>
> Provided that neither this section, nor any proceedings taken thereunder, shall affect any liability of any such person to be proceeded against by indictment for any indictable offence.

The warning of the last paragraph is perfectly plain: if a child is killed in this way, the law may hold the negligence to be gross enough to sustain a charge of manslaughter.

It is not generally realized that a child or young person who is a member of a household in which this offence has been committed may be brought before a juvenile court as being in need of care, protection or control.

17 Accidents away from school

Between school and home – When a pupil meets with an accident on his way to or from school there is no liability on the part either of the teacher or of the authority. It would be quite impossible to care for each child's safety from the time he shuts his front door behind him in the morning until he arrives back in the afternoon, so far as the journey is concerned. This does not mean that the school is unable to deal with indiscipline on the way to or from school.[2] The supervision of pupils on public transport is the concern of the transport authority. If the local education authority

[1] Children and Young Persons Act 1933, s. 11, as amended by the Children and Young Persons (Amendment) Act 1952, s. 8.

[2] *Cleary* v *Booth*, page 283; and *R.* v *Newport (Salop) Justices* ex parte *Wright*, pages 25–6 and 283–4.

hires coaches for this purpose under contract, responsibility is a matter for negotiation between the authority and the operator. In one case a boy was injured by a pellet on a bus hired in this way. The local education authority provided an adult supervisor on buses for very young children and on those used by sub-normal children. In this particular case supervision was in the hands of prefects. Finding that the behaviour was not 'abnormally boisterous or undisciplined', Mr Justice Waller applied the test laid down in *Lyes* v *Middlesex County Council*[1] of the careful parent of a large family applying his mind to school life where there is a greater risk of skylarking. He found the system adequate, and dismissed a claim for damages.[2]

Occasionally a local education authority allows teachers, as a matter of convenience, to travel free on contract coaches; expecting, in return, some supervision on the journey. A teacher considering such an offer should obtain its precise terms in writing from the local education authority and, if it seems desirable, consult his professional association before accepting.

Visits to clinics, etc. – If a child visits a clinic on his way to or from school at either end of a session there is no liability on the school authorities. If a child is sent from school during the course of a session, the teacher should make arrangements for an escort if he considers it necessary, having regard to the age of the pupil and the nature of the route. In any case no child under the age of eight should be allowed to undertake such a journey on his own. Even in secondary schools it may be desirable to provide an escort (who may be a prefect) in suitable cases, when, say, a first-year child is leaving the school officially. The position is similar with regard to practical subjects centres, swimming baths and the like.

Errands – Children should not be sent away from the school premises on personal errands for teachers. A teacher who takes this responsibility is acting outside the scope of his employment and would probably be liable personally in the event of an accident.

[1] See page 28.
[2] *Jacques* v *Oxfordshire County Council* and *another* (1968) LGR 440; LCT 330.

Games and educational visits – The teacher in charge is *in loco parentis* and this responsibility continues even though the normal school time has ended. The Wembley case[1] occurred during the dinner-hour. Sometimes teachers who take children on visits which extend beyond the normal school hours dismiss the pupils from the place visited. Probably this would not render the teacher liable for negligence in the case of older pupils who might reasonably be expected to reach home safely, but much depends on the facts of the case. If, for example, it is proposed to dismiss a party from a railway station, the parents should be asked to agree to this in advance. If any objects, that parent's child must be brought back to the school, or some agreed nearby point.[2]

School journeys – Teachers in charge are *in loco parentis* twenty-four hours a day and seven days a week.[3]

18 Commencement of proceedings

Actions for damages for negligence, nuisance or breach of duty, which include a claim for damages in respect of personal injuries, must generally be commenced within a period of three years. It is immaterial whether the duty is contractual or statutory, or whether it is independent of such provisions.[3]

In general, it is a defence to plead that an action has been commenced 'out of time'; that is, after the expiry of this period. The law has now been amended to provide that if material facts of a decisive nature were unknown to the plaintiff until at least two years after the cause of action arose *and* he brings the action within twelve months of learning these facts *and* the court gives leave (before or after the commencement of the action), an extension may be granted in respect of actions including damages claimed for personal injury to the plaintiff or anyone else. This relaxation is strictly limited.[4]

Briden v *Ashby* – The Court of Appeal held in December 1973

[1] See pages 30–32.
[2] See Chapter XIII.
[3] Law Reform (Limitation of Actions) Act 1954, s. 2.
[4] Limitation Act 1963.

that there had been inexcusable delay on the part of a plaintiff's solicitors after a Registrar had dismissed an action for want of prosecution in the previous March. The plaintiff alleged negligence by the local education authority in appointing as a prefect a boy known to be of a bullying disposition. He alleged that in June 1965 the prefect treated him in such a way that he was concussed, and had to have stitches in his head. The plaintiff's father had admitted that his son had been cheeky to the prefect when requested to leave a room. The Master of the Rolls, Lord Denning, said it was a most serious delay: 'Memories grow dimmer all the time, especially when the witnesses were small boys. One witness is in Canada. There must be a risk that a fair trial is no longer possible. The last year's delay was inexcusable: it was far more than marginally prejudicial to every one.'[1]

19 Delegation of duty

It is sometimes necessary for a person on whom a duty is laid to delegate all or part of that duty to someone else. Indeed, it is the function of the assistant staff of a school to accept reasonable delegation of responsibility from the head: as the rules of management and articles of government are structured at present, he is responsible for the entire internal organization, management and discipline of the school. Manifestly, he cannot personally undertake all these duties in detail, but it is through him that the staff receive their authority.

The question then arises as to how far, having delegated duties to the teaching staff or to ancillary workers, he is liable if a person to whom a duty has been delegated fails to perform it properly.

Again, much must depend on the facts in each case, but it is possible to lay down certain guidelines to be taken into consideration at the moment of delegation.

In the first place he must be satisfied that the person to whom the responsibility is being given is capable of discharging it. Secondly, he must ensure that that person understands fully what is required

[1] *Briden* v *Ashby* and *West Sussex County Council* (1973) *The Times*, 6 December.

of him. Thirdly he must be reasonably certain that the person is not only able to carry out the delegated duty, but also that he can do so for the period required. Finally he should, by one means or another, satisfy himself from time to time that the duty is actually being undertaken efficiently.

Similar considerations apply in delegating responsibilities to prefects, their ages and dispositions being matters to take into account. Assistant teachers will also do well to give some thought to these matters when delegating responsibility to junior colleagues, ancillary helpers and pupils.

Wright v *Cheshire County Council* – If all these things are taken into account in choosing the duties to be delegated to another there is little to fear although, once again, everything will depend on the precise facts. During group activities in a gymnasium, one exercise consisted of vaulting over a buck. As the master moved round from group to group, and the pupils were trained and experienced, he delegated his duty to see that boys made a safe landing after the vault to the pupils in the group itself. Whilst the master was at the other end of the gymnasium, the bell went for the end of the lesson and the 'stand-by' ran off to the changing room. A boy in mid-vault landed badly and sustained serious injuries. The defendants pleaded general and approved practice.

The Court of Appeal rejected the plaintiff's claim. Lord Justice Singleton said: 'The bell was an indication of a break for play-time. In the ordinary course the boys, on the sound of the bell, would receive an order to go to the corner at which their squad paraded before being dismissed. Why should the defendants apprehend that on this or any other occasion the boy would run away when the plaintiff was in the act of vaulting? So far as we know, that sort of thing had never happened before. The boys all had experience, seven months, in this school, and the plaintiff (and no doubt the other boys) had been in a junior school before and had taken part in physical exercise and drill.' Earlier in his judgment, he had pointed out: 'There may well be some risk in everything one does or in every step one takes, but in ordinary everyday affairs the test of what is reasonable care may well be answered by experience from which arises over the years a practice adopted generally, and followed successfully over the years so far as the evidence in this case goes.'

Lord Justice Birkett added: 'For my own part, if I were asked what a reasonable and prudent man would do, I think, first of all, he would have regard to the nature of the exercise; and the nature of the exercise, as I see it, requires care, but it is not in itself a dangerous operation, and I think further that, if there had been a system in vogue, as there was here, whereby a boy waited to support the boy vaulting, a reasonable and prudent man would say: "If the boy has been made proficient by his training, there is no negligence in not having an adult there." It is, I think, impossible to avoid the conclusion that it was a most unfortunate, unforeseeable, and quite unpredictable thing which occasioned the accident on this day. . . . It appears that this was the first time such a thing had happened. In those circumstances I find it is impossible to say on the facts that any negligence was shown on the part of the defendants.'[1]

20 When an accident occurs

Circumstances vary greatly and it is impossible to give advice except in very general terms, but it is as well to remember that not only may emergencies be caused through negligence, but also that it is possible to be negligent in the treatment of such situations.

The teacher's first duty is to the children in his charge. If there is still danger to pupils who are uninjured, as when dangerous gas is escaping in a laboratory, they must be removed from the possibility of harm at once.

Suitable action must be taken in the case of children who are hurt. First aid should be rendered, remembering that it is *first* aid and that detailed treatment in a serious case is a matter for the doctor. Whenever it appears prudent to do so, a doctor must be called and, if necessary, an ambulance summoned. If the child's own doctor attends, the local education authority will not pay a fee in respect of the visit; in any case, the teacher calling the doctor should state that he is acting as the agent of the child's

[1] *Wright* v *Cheshire County Council* [1952] 2 All ER 789.

parents and that he is not personally responsible for the payment of fees.

A teacher should use his own judgment as to the need for summoning further assistance. If possible, another teacher should be asked to look after the children who are not hurt, and the head should be notified at once.

Unless the incident is manifestly trivial – and a teacher should err on the side of caution – the first opportunity should be taken of notifying the child's parents. If the child is removed to hospital, or has to be taken home or to a doctor, he should be accompanied by a teacher, or other responsible person, who will remain until a parent arrives or the doctor says that the child may go home. This may sound over-meticulous but, should there be a charge of negligence later, evidence of attention to detail of this kind would greatly strengthen the teacher's case. Even more important, in a border-line case where a parent is perhaps likely to sue, a teacher is more likely to gain his good-will and so, possibly, avoid action altogether if the parent is assured that everything possible is being done for his child.

The local education authority will require a report on the accident which will be passed to their solicitor so that he is briefed should action be contemplated at a later date. The head should also be fully acquainted with the facts, and a note made of any details for future reference. Memories are often short.

In the event of a serious accident, or one which, though trifling, looks as though it may lead to legal difficulties, a teacher should consult his professional association before forwarding any report, even to his local education authority. If the police are called in, he may also deem it wise to consult his association before making any statement. In speaking to the professional association's legal advisers, the teacher must give a full and frank account of the facts so far as they are within his knowledge. A similar precaution should be taken if the local education authority appears to be making any moves towards disciplinary action against the teacher.

In the event of a complaint by a parent about an accident, the teacher should take care not to admit liability in any way. The safest course is to express regret, and to say that the accident occurred whilst the teacher was acting in accordance with general and approved practice.

21 Religious convictions and medical treatment

From time to time a teacher is faced with the problem where, in his opinion, skilled medical treatment is essential, but where it is known that the child belongs to a religious body to which such treatment is repugnant. Normally, of course, it is possible to get in touch with the parent who will take appropriate action in accordance with his conscience and, where possible, this should be done. Sometimes, however, the matter may appear extremely urgent and the parent is not available. This applies *a fortiori* to school journeys abroad.

How is the teacher to deal with this *in loco parentis*? It is not generally permissible to probe into a family's religious beliefs, but in such cases they are usually known. If a child is being taken on a school journey, and it is reasonable to apprehend that medical treatment may – under normal circumstances – become necessary, it is as well to discuss the matter quite frankly with the parents, and to point out that apparent medical neglect might well cast a reflection on the teacher's care for the child as a careful parent. Unless the parent is prepared to give written instructions, and an indemnity, the teacher might well consider whether the child should be taken away.

Nevertheless, such drastic action would be repugnant to most teachers, and certainly gives an aura of religious prejudice. The position with regard to Christian Scientists and Jehovah's Witnesses is not nearly as difficult as popular misunderstanding suggests. For this reason it is dealt with fully in another chapter.[1]

As the United Kindgom becomes increasingly multicultural, teachers will have to deal with a wider variety of practices rooted in religious belief. It must be admitted that this is a thorny problem, and the best advice which can be given is that the teacher should use his judgment to find a solution which will, as far as possible, avoid violence to another's conscience without a breach

[1] See pages 329–32.

of his duty to act as a prudent parent or, at the same time, causing disadvantage to a pupil.

22 Accidents to visitors

Until 1958 the duty of care owed to a visitor depended upon the relationship between a guest and the occupier of the property, a distinction being drawn between *invitees* (who visited the occupier in pursuance of some common material interest) and *licensees* (who were permitted to visit the premises, but were not there for material interest). It has been held that pupils at a school are invitees,[1] as are parents who visit the school for an exhibition of pupils' work.[2] The ruling relating to parents was given in a case which arose out of an exhibition of work during which the floor collapsed. On the other hand a guest who is invited to a private house is a licensee.

Whilst these distinctions remain for certain purposes, a new Act has substituted a 'common duty of care' which an occupier owes to all visitors other than trespassers, unless he has extended, modified, or excluded it in any case, whether by agreement or otherwise.[3] This duty requires him to see that his visitors will be reasonably safe in using the premises for the purpose for which they are invited, or permitted, to be there.

The Act provides that an occupier must be prepared for children to be less careful than adults, and also that a visitor in the exercise of his calling will appreciate and guard against any special risks incidental to that occupation. Thus, an electrician would be expected to take necessary precautions in dealing with defective wiring.

In deciding whether an occupier has discharged his duty, all the circumstances must be considered. A warning of danger, by itself, may not be sufficient unless, in all the circumstances, it is enough to enable the visitor to be reasonably safe. In the case of accidents due to faulty construction the extent of the occupier's liability is fixed by his good faith in assuring himself

[1] *Woodward* v *Hastings Corporation* [1945] KB 174; LCT 65.
[2] *Griffiths* v *Smith* [1941] AC 170; LCT 63.
[3] Occupiers Liability Act 1957, s. 2.

that the contractor was competent, and the work properly done.

An occupier is not liable in respect of risks willingly accepted by a visitor.

Trespassers are those who enter the property of another with no legal right or justification. They have no redress for any damage they may suffer from the defective state of the premises, but the occupier must not create a new danger whilst they are there, neither may he deliberately harm them. Unauthorized persons who have no business on the premises, licencees whose leave to remain has been withdrawn, and children who have broken bounds by going to a forbidden part of the premises, are trespassers.[1]

A person entering premises under a statutory right is regarded as having the occupier's permission whether, in fact, he has received it or not.

In the event of a visitor suffering damage through the defective state of a school or its equipment, the local education authority may be responsible or, in certain cases, the managers or governors of a voluntary school. The owner who is also an employer will be liable for damage arising through the negligence of his servants in the course of their employment. Where danger is known to exist, liability may to some extent be avoided by suitable warning notices and guards.

23 In loco parentis

This chapter must end where it began by reminding the reader that he is *in loco parentis* to the children in his charge, and that the law asks merely that he should act reasonably in this capacity. Provided that his actions are in accordance with general and approved educational practice, and provided that he takes such care of his children as a careful father would take, he has little to fear from the mischances of school life.

A year or two before the war, some grammar school pupils were playing, contrary to the school rules, with a cricket-pitch roller which ran over one of them. The parents sued the governors

[1] See Section 23.

and the master in charge, claiming damages for negligence.[1] The case was heard at Leeds Assizes in March 1938, and Mr Justice Hilbery's summing up, which was a masterly exposition of the doctrine of the careful father, will form a fitting conclusion to this chapter.

The judge said, 'It was not suggested for the plaintiff that anybody could reasonably say that a master must watch boys, not merely in classes, but throughout every moment of their school lives.

'What has a reasonably careful parent to do? Supposing a boy of yours has some other little boys, who are friends of his, coming to tea on a Saturday afternoon and you see them all playing in the garden. Suppose your garden roller happened to be there. Would you consider you had been neglectful of your duty to the parents of those other boys because, for five minutes, you had gone into the house and two of them had managed to pull the roller over the third?

'Would you think that, in those circumstances you had failed to exercise reasonable supervision as a parent? These things have got to be treated as matters of common sense, not to put on Mr Johnson any higher standard of care than that of a reasonably careful parent.

'If the boys were kept in cotton-wool, some of them would choke themselves with it. They would manage to have accidents: we always did, members of the jury – we did not always have actions at law afterwards.

'You have to consider whether or not you would expect a headmaster to exercise such a degree of care that boys could never get into mischief. Has any reasonable parent yet succeeded in exercising such care as to prevent a boy getting into mischief and – if he did – what sort of boys should we produce?'

[1] *Hudson* v *Governors of Rotherham Grammar School* and *Selby Johnson* (1938) *Yorkshire Post*, 24 & 25 March 1938; LCT 303.

XII

PUNISHMENT

1 The teacher's authority

When appointing a tutor for himself, the infant Henry VI gave him licence 'reasonably to chastise us from time to time', and the law has always recognized the right of the teacher to inflict such reasonable punishment on his pupils. In a leading case,[1] Mr Justice Phillimore laid down the principles by which the law judges a teacher's punishment in these words: 'My brother, Mr Justice Walton, and I have considered the matter carefully and I will read a sentence which he has been good enough to compose: "The ordinary authority extends not to the head teacher only but to the responsible teachers who have charge of classes." In other words, if I may add anything to what he has written, a teacher of a class has the ordinary means of preserving discipline and, as between the parent of the child and the teacher, it is enough for the teacher to be able to say, "The punishment which I administered was moderate, it was not dictated by any bad motives, it was such as is usual in the school and such as the parent of the child might expect that it would receive if it did wrong".'

The teacher's powers in this matter stem from the fact that he is *in loco parentis* to the children in his charge and thereby he assumes some of the rights – and duties – of the natural parent. The latter's duty in this matter was defined by Mr Justice Field,[2] who said, 'It is his duty, if the child will not do what he advises it to do, to take whatever steps he considers necessary for its correction. But he must act honestly in this course; there must be

[1] *Mansell* v *Griffin* [1908] 1 KB 947; LCT 216.
[2] In *Hutt* v *Governors of Haileybury College* (1888) 4 TLR 623; LCT 226.

277

a cause which a reasonable father believes justifies punishment.'

Parliament has endorsed the views of the judges in this matter by a clause in the Prevention of Cruelty to Children Act 1904, which was re-enacted in a later statute:[1] 'Nothing in this section shall be construed as affecting the right of any parent, teacher or other person having the lawful charge of a child or young person to administer punishment to him.'

2 The canons of punishment

There are three standards by which punishment, generally, must be judged. In the first place it is retributive – an expression of the displeasure of society at the offence for which a person is punished. Secondly it is deterrent – an example to prevent others from committing the offence for which punishment is meted out. Finally, it should be reformative – an attempt to turn the offender into an acceptable member of the community. Modern practice has tended to place the greatest emphasis on the last of these principles.

The exact forms of punishment to be used in schools are not laid down by Parliament. Teachers are left largely to their own discretion and they would do well to bear a double criterion in mind. Not only should their punishments come within the scope both of Mr Justice Phillimore's summing up in *Mansell* v *Griffin* quoted above and the local education authority regulations, but they should also apply the test of the canons cited in the last paragraph in order to assure themselves that their motives are right.

3 Local education authority regulations

All local education authorities have some regulations dealing with punishment. These are usually concerned chiefly with the more severe forms such as corporal punishment, suspension and expulsion. Minor punishment, as a rule, is left largely to the discretion of the teacher, although some guidance may be given on certain points such as the length of time for which it is reasonable to detain a child. Teachers must know the rules of their own authority and be careful to observe them.

[1] Children and Young Persons Act 1933, s. 1 (7).

Two forms of action against the teacher may follow the use of punishment and, as they are quite independent, a particular case may lead to either or both. A case may be brought in the courts, either as a civil action claiming damages,[1] or as a criminal charge of assault. The second course is for the local education authority to take disciplinary measures against the teacher for breach of its regulations.

In the latter case, the authority is concerned merely with the fact that its rules have been broken and the teacher's contract, which includes a requirement that he shall serve in accordance with the rules of the local education authority from time to time in force, thereby breached. This may be so, even where there has been no offence of which the courts can take cognizance; indeed, legal action against the teacher may have failed.[2] In accepting appointment the teacher has undertaken to obey the authority's code and, if he fails to do so, he has broken the terms of his agreement. It is for this reason that a newly appointed teacher cannot be urged too strongly to acquaint himself with his authority's rules.

The fact that a teacher has broken the authority's regulations does not, however, necessarily deprive him of a defence in the courts, though it may weaken his case. In *Mansell* v *Griffin*, Mr Justice Phillimore said, 'It did not, in our view, necessarily follow because, as a matter of internal government, the teacher was prohibited from administering corporal punishment herself that she was necessarily without defence when it came to a question of an action brought by the pupil against her for trespass to the person or of an indictment for assault. It seems to us that the question must be deeper and must rest on more general considerations. It was admitted that the question depended on the delegation of parental authority to administer moderate corporal punishment to a child, but it was contended for the plaintiff that a parent could only be considered as delegating his or her authority to a headmaster or headmistress. . . . The fact that the teacher herself did not know of the restrictive regulation is probably

[1] See pages 242–4.
[2] This was so in *Gill* v *Leyton Corporation*. See pages 118–19.

immaterial, although it does have a bearing on the teacher's good faith.'

It is very possible that, before long, a test case will come before the courts in the area of an authority which has prohibited the use of corporal punishment. Parents sometimes authorize a teacher to use corporal punishment when his authority has forbidden him to do so. It will be interesting to see how the courts react in such circumstances when, in all other respects, the punishment in question was reasonable.

In another case a teacher used an unorthodox instrument – a blackboard pointer – to cane all but one of her class of thirty-eight children. Eight parents took out summonses against the teacher, of which seven were adjourned when the teacher decided to appeal against a fine of £1, with 5 guineas costs, on the first case. Allowing the appeal,[1] the Recorder said, 'I think it was most regrettable that this prosecution was launched. . . . The only point I was concerned with has not given any difficulty. I have concluded that what she did to the child did not amount to excessive punishment.'

Nevertheless, the use of an unorthodox or forbidden method of punishment is bound to imperil the teacher's position, and it can afford no defence against disciplinary action by the local education authority.

In December 1971, a young probationary teacher, said to be 'of above average ability' was fined £25 by the West Ham magistrates for gagging and binding an eleven-year-old boy with adhesive tape. The boy was said to be a disruptive influence about whom parents, as well as other teachers, had complained. The teacher pleaded guilty, although prosecuting counsel said: 'I am not suggesting that the sellotape hurt him. After speaking to the boy twice about his behaviour, with no success, the teacher stuck some tape across his mouth and stood him in a corner. When he fidgeted with the tape she fastened his hands to his sides, later slapping him and sending him home. She had previously tried to control the boy by giving him lines and detention.[2]

[1] *Hazell* v *Jeffs* (1955) *The Times*, 11 January.
[2] *Times Educational Supplement* (1971) 24 December.

4 Unreasonable punishment

It has already been mentioned that any punishment inflicted in school must be reasonable. If it is so, a teacher is not liable for accidental injury to a pupil.[1] The consequences of a mischance during excessive or illegal punishment were clearly pointed out by Lord Chief Justice Cockburn in a case[2] concerning a boy who died after being beaten by a schoolmaster with a thick stick and a skipping rope, 'secretly in the night' for two and a half hours. The Lord Chief Justice said, 'If it [corporal punishment] be administered for the gratification of passion or rage, or if it be immoderate or excessive in its nature or degree, or if it be protracted beyond the child's power of endurance, or with an instrument unsuited to the purpose and calculated to produce danger to life or limb: in all such cases, and if evil consequences ensue, the person inflicting it is answerable to the law and – if death ensue – it will be manslaughter.' In this case the jury did convict of manslaughter. The fact that the father had authorized punishment was irrelevant as he did not, and no one can, authorize excessive punishment.

Happily, cases of excessive punishment are now rare. In 1964 the headmaster of a grammar school and the senior mistress pleaded guilty to assaulting two girl pupils aged seventeen and eighteen, and were fined £50 and £30 respectively. The punishments were administered after the girls had been caught kissing and cuddling a sixth form boy and another youth in the school's green room. The two members of the staff spanked the girls on their bare buttocks with a hairbrush. Two days later one girl had seventy-two, the other thirty-three square inches of bruising. In her defence the senior mistress pleaded that she had to take orders from the headmaster, otherwise she would undermine his authority.[3]

In the nature of things excessive punishment takes place from time to time, but the subject has become highly charged with emotion during the last few years, and the mass media have given

[1] *Scorgie* v *Lawrie* (1883) 10 R Ct of Sess 610.
[2] *R.* v *Hopley* (1860) 2 F and F 202; LCT 220.
[3] *Daily Telegraph* (1964) 3 July.

considerable prominence to isolated excesses. In an outstanding article on a positive approach to school discipline the Devonshire County Inspector for Special Education and Treatment, Mr Peter C. Love, pleaded for more facts and less emotion in discussing this subject: 'On occasion,' he wrote, 'corporal punishment is given in anger. Individual adults differ in their tolerance of stress, and there are some of us who are likely to lose our tempers on relatively slight provocation. All of us vary from day to day in our degree of self-control according to the variation in physical and emotional stresses placed upon us. There is certainly a danger to pupils in the use of corporal punishment by adults who are liable to uncontrolled bursts of temper. Teaching is a particularly stressful vocation. . . . My own experience and observation lead me to the belief that when teachers use corporal punishment, it is not in a mood of sadism, nor in a mood of anger, but more in a mood of despair.'[1] Sadly, it is in this mood of despair that any form of punishment is most likely to become excessive and unreasonable.

5 Authority out of school

Some cases concerning punishment are brought by parents who maintain that the schoolmaster's writ does not run beyond the school's walls. The courts have laid it down clearly that the authority is not so limited, but the precise bounds of that power have never been defined. In general, it may be said that the teacher may exercise such control over the pupil as is necessary to maintain the implied contract between parent and teacher. If this is so, the teacher's jurisdiction extends to all matters which may affect the welfare of the school.

It is important to distinguish between matters where the child is the offender and those where the parent has exercised control over the child to prevent him from acting in accordance with the school rules. In cases falling in the latter category the child must not be punished, although it is possible to consider suspending him with a view to expulsion if it appears that the parent's action is so subversive of school discipline as to break the contract to educate.

[1] *Education* (1968) 12 July.

A boy threw some putty at a fellow-pupil on the way to school. The latter complained to the headmaster who caned the assailant. The justices convicted the headmaster of assault, but the divisional court quashed the verdict.[1] Mr Justice Collins said, 'It is clear that a father has the right to inflict reasonable personal punishment on his son. It is equally the law, and is in accordance with very ancient practice, that he may delegate this right to the schoolmaster. Such a right has always commended itself to the common sense of mankind. It is clear that the relation of master and pupil carries with it the right of reasonable corporal punishment. As a matter of common sense, how far is this power delegated to the schoolmaster? Is it limited to the time during which the boy is within the four walls of the school, or does it extend beyond that limit?

'In my opinion, the purpose with which the parental authority is delegated to the schoolmaster, who is entrusted with the bringing-up and discipline of the child must, to some extent, include an authority over the child while he is without the four walls.

'It may be a matter of fact in each case whether the conduct of the master in inflicting corporal punishment is right. Very grave consequences would result if it were held that a parent's authority was exclusive right up to the door of the school and then, and then only, the master's authority commenced. It would be a most anomalous result to hold that, in such a case as the present, the boy who had been assaulted had no remedy by complaint to his master who could punish the assailant by thrashing. . . . It is obvious that the desired impression is best brought home by a summary and immediate punishment. . . . In my opinion, parents do contemplate such an exercise of authority by the schoolmaster. I should feel very sorry if I felt myself driven to come to the opposite conclusion, and am glad to say that the principle shows that the authority delegated to the schoolmaster is not limited to the four walls of the school.'

In another case[2] a headmaster caned a boy for smoking in the

[1] *Cleary* v *Booth* [1893] 1 QB 465; LCT 235.
[2] *R.* v *Newport (Salop) Justices*, ex parte *Wright* [1929] 2 KB 416; LCT 237.

street and the father brought an action on the grounds that the boy had parental permission to smoke. The case was dismissed by the magistrates and the father was ordered to pay 5 guineas costs. He asked for a case to be stated, but the magistrates certified the application as frivolous. A rule *nisi* was then obtained to allow a hearing in the High Court on the grounds that the magistrates were wrong in allowing that the defendant had authority to inflict corporal punishment on the boy, that the boy was at the material time under the authority of his father and that, since the father had given the boy permission to smoke, the headmaster had no power to inflict punishment on him for so doing.

Lord Hewart held that the rule forbidding pupils to smoke during term time, whether within the school precincts or elsewhere in public, was a reasonable rule. The boy knew of the rule and deliberately broke it; the punishment administered was a reasonable and proper punishment for the breach of the rule. By sending the boy to school the father had authorized the schoolmaster to administer reasonable punishment to the boy for the breach of a reasonable rule.

In a more recent case,[1] a boy ran across the road on the way to school, just in front of a teacher's car. The headmaster, who had frequently spoken to the children about road safety, caned the lad and the parents brought a case against him for assault. The magistrates dismissed the case and ordered the plaintiff to pay 5 guineas costs.

As Mr Justice Collins said in *Cleary* v *Booth*, it is a matter of fact in each case as to whether the schoolmaster's authority extends far enough to justify his interference. It is probable that it would be held not only that it was within his power but that it was his duty to deal, for example, with any of his scholars engaged in street feuds with pupils from a neighbouring school. It is most unlikely that he would be thought to be controlling the internal organization, management and discipline of his school if, seeing one of his pupils not wearing the school uniform on a private holiday in Ibiza, he waited until the beginning of term and then punished the boy for that breach of the school rules.

[1] *Cook* v *Attock* (1955) *Evening Standard*, 13 January.

6 Trespass against the person

The two forms of punishment which give rise to the greatest number of legal problems are detention and corporal punishment. Both of them lie within that field of the law in which they would, were it not for the special status of the teacher, constitute trespasses against the person. Either may, in general, be punished as a crime or be the root of a civil action as a tort.

In common speech the word 'trespass' is usually employed today to refer to trespass to land, and it is often forgotten that there may also be trespass to goods and trespass against the person. Trespass is an ancient legal concept to describe a 'direct and forcible' entry or injury, and, so far as trespass against the person is concerned, includes assault, battery and false imprisonment.

The criminal aspect of these matters was largely, though not entirely, removed from the realm of common law to that of state by the Offences against the Person Act 1861. Civil law retains the element that a plaintiff in an action for trespass does not have to prove that he has suffered damage: he can recover compensation, often purely nominal, merely by proving the act of trespass.

The total restraint of another person's liberty, whether by force or show of authority, is false imprisonment. This act usually involves assault and battery in addition, but this is not true in all cases: if a person walks willingly into a room, and is then forced to remain there because the door is locked behind him, that would be false imprisonment. In an Australian case it was held to be false imprisonment to detain a passenger against his will in a car by driving too fast for him to be able to alight.

The essential element in false imprisonment is that the restraint must be entire. No degree of permanence is involved and complete temporary restraint, even for a few moments, is false imprisonment. The restraint need not be the personal act of the defendant, nor need he personally know of it at the time. Once the restraint has been proved, the onus is on the defendant to show that it was lawful, e.g. that he had a reasonable and honest belief that the detention was justified. Such a defence may be grounded on the duty of every citizen to arrest a person provoking a breach of the peace, about to commit a crime, reasonably suspected of committing a crime or escaping from legal authority. In all such cases the person detained must be taken to a magistrate or the police with all reasonable despatch.

An assault is an unlawful attempt, offer or threat to do violence to another in such a manner as to cause him reasonably to believe himself to be in immediate danger. Thus to wave a cudgel threateningly at someone whilst within arm's length is an assault ; it would not be so if the parties were a hundred yards apart. It is an assault to threaten another by pointing an unloaded gun at him unless at the time the complainant did not know that it was unloaded.

Immediately a threat is translated into action, battery is added to assault. The least touch is sufficient.

There are several general defences. One is *volenti non fit injuria* (no one suffers injury from that to which he has consented): thus, a person using a public highway is presumed to have consented to people brushing past him. One may also take reasonable steps to defend oneself, one's family, one's property and possibly anyone else. What is reasonable is a question of fact in each case, having regard to the gravity of the circumstances. Similarly a citizen may use such force as is reasonably necessary in all the circumstances in exercising his duty of arrest. Alternatively it is possible to plead that a battery was an 'inevitable accident'.

A civil action for assault or battery cannot be brought against a person who has been summarily convicted of that particular commission of either act.

A defence to false imprisonment or assault and battery may be set up on the ground of lawful parental discipline. The success of the defence will depend on the facts of the case; what, for example, is reasonable in the case of a seven-year-old child might be held to be unreasonable when he is ten years older. Nevertheless, a parent has a legal duty to exercise proper custody and control over his children, and he will be supported by the courts if he reasonably forces them to remain under his roof or uses corporal punishment.

By analogy these powers are transferred to the schoolmaster *in loco parentis*. 'This power is not limited to corporal punishment, but extends to detention and restraint.'[1] The power may, on occasion, include trespass to goods as, for example, a master took away a boy's note-book containing the names of the ringleaders in a plot to disturb order.[2] It used to be said that the schoolmaster's powers were derived from the parent by delegation, but it is doubtful in days, when a parent is by law required to provide efficient full-time education for those of his children who are of statutory school age, whether this is the soundest basis, in spite of the precedents. The matter is considered further in another section,[3] in the meantime it is sufficient to note that the courts have so far accepted reasonable punishment by a teacher *in loco parentis* as a defence both in cases of detention and of corporal punishment.

It is necessary to remember that both these forms of punishment are grounded in trespass at a time when what are sometimes called 'the custodial functions of the teacher' are under criticism. Much of the opposition to corporal punishment has come from a body known as the Sociey of Teachers Opposed to Physical Punishment. So far its activities have been confined to attacking corporal punishment but, in a sense, detention is physical restraint, and has the same basis in law. It is not unlikely, therefore, that this body may at some time decide to include both trespasses against the person in its campaign.[4]

7 Detention

As has been said above, the total restraint of another's liberty by force or show of authority is false imprisonment and actionable before the courts. Of this, Mr Justice Phillimore said, in *Mansell* v *Griffin*, 'It is, I suppose, false imprisonment to keep a child locked up in a classroom, or even to order it to stop under penalties in a room for a longer period than the ordinary school time without lawful authority. Could it be said that a teacher who kept a child back during play hours to learn over and say a lesson, or

---

[1] *Hutt* v *Governors of Haileybury College* (1888) 4 TLR 623; LCT 226.
[2] *Fitzgerald* v *Northcote* (1865) 4 F and F 656; LCT 148.
[3] See pages 295–9.
[4] See pages 297–8.

who put upon him a dunce's cap – could it be said that such a person would be liable in an action for trespass to the person? The cases I have instanced are not cases of the infliction of blows, but they are cases of interference with the liberty of the subject and it seems to me that the principle must be the same for all these cases.'

The right of a teacher to detain a child was also referred to by Mr Justice Field,[1] when he said, 'The law, therefore, does justify a parent[2] in a case where he honestly considers correction necessary, in administering blows in a reasonable and proper manner. This power is not limited to corporal punishment but extends to detention and restraint.'

Teachers should be aware of any regulations of their employing authority which may limit the period for which a child may be detained, and should ensure that they comply with them. In any case the tests applied in *Mansell* v *Griffin*[3] are equally appropriate in dealing with all punishments. The variable criterion is that the punishment should be moderate and reasonable: this is a matter of fact in each case, and includes such factors as the offence which is being punished, the age of the child, the distance and quality of the travel facilities between the school and the home, traffic and other dangers, and the child's ability to cope with the journey in question alone and at an unusual hour.

The use of detention in a school should be included in the school rules, and made known to parents when their children are admitted. In areas where there is particular danger much parental worry can be avoided, and parental support may often be secured, if the performance of a detention is not required on the day it is awarded. A note of advice that a child will be late on the following day, incorporating a space for the parent to sign, may be helpful. It must be stressed, however, that such a note does not seek the parent's consent to the detention. This is not required in view of

[1] *Hutt* v *Governors of Haileybury College* (1888) 4 TLR 623; LCT 226.

[2] And hence, by delegation of parental authority, a teacher. See *Cleary* v *Booth*, page 283.

[3] See page 277.

the teacher's legal right to detain his pupils, and parents should be clearly aware of this fact.

8 Corporal punishment

By far the greatest number of cases concerning discipline arise from the use of corporal punishment. Much has already been said to show that the courts have consistently upheld the teacher's right to administer reasonable physical chastisement, but perhaps the best summary is to be found in the words of Lord Chief Justice Cockburn.[1] He said, 'By the law of England, a parent or schoolmaster (who for this purpose represents the parent, and has the parental authority delegated to him) may, for the purpose of correcting what is evil in the child, inflict moderate and reasonable corporal punishment – always, however, with this condition: that it is moderate and reasonable.'

Mass corporal punishment is to be deprecated, but on professional rather than legal grounds. In the case of *Hazell* v *Jeffs*, already quoted,[2] the punishment of a large number of children was involved and, in a similar case, where a master had caned a whole class four times because particular offenders failed to own up, the magistrates dismissed the case, commenting that the teacher had acted reasonably in the interests of discipline.[3]

Opinions vary widely on the question of the most suitable part of the body for the infliction of corporal punishment, and teachers with authority to use the cane should make certain of any directions by their own local education authority. Some years ago, a bench convicted a schoolmaster who had caned a pupil on the hands, because the justices felt that the risk of injury was grave, even though none had resulted in that particular instance. Quashing the conviction,[4] Mr Justice Charles said, 'When Parliament lays down a chart showing the particular region of the body to which corporal punishment in schools shall be confined, the court will take care that those limits are not overstepped. At present there is no such chart.'

---

[1] In *R* v *Hopley* (1860) 2 F and F 202; LCT 226.   [2] See page 280.
[3] *R* v *Dennis* (1954) *The Times*, 19 November.
[4] *Gardner* v *Bygrave* (1889) 53 JP 743; LCT 224.

In the former approved schools the Home Office laid down strict regulations regarding corporal punishment[1] and, although these have never bound other schools, they are of interest as the only statement ever published showing to some extent what may be officially regarded as reasonable. The following is a summary:

Boys

(*a*) Only a cane or tawse of an approved pattern may be used;

(*b*) Only a cane may be used on the hands, and the number of strokes must not exceed three on each hand. No boy over fifteen may be caned on the hands;

(*c*) When applied on the posterior, either a cane or a tawse may be used over the boy's ordinary cloth trousers, and the number of strokes must not exceed six for boys under fifteen or eight for boys of fifteen and over, with the proviso that the managers may authorize up to twelve strokes for a boy in the higher age-group;

(*d*) In the case of boys with any physical or mental disability the prior approval of the medical officer must be obtained;

(*e*) It must not be inflicted in the presence of other boys.

Girls

(*a*) Only a cane of an approved pattern may be used;

(*b*) Only girls under fifteen may be caned, and the number of strokes may not exceed three on each hand;

(*c*) In the case of girls with any physical or mental disability the prior approval of the medical officer must be obtained;

(*d*) It must not be inflicted in the presence of other girls.

Legally, there is no difference between boys and girls in this matter, so far as ordinary schools are concerned. Most authorities have their own rules which normally lay down that it may be inflicted on girls only by a woman. In general, it is confined to the hands.

Local authority regulations normally forbid the use of corporal punishment by probationary, supply or temporary teachers, and some require several years' experience before they will authorize a teacher to use the cane. All irregular forms of punishment,

[1] The Approved School Rules 1933, nos. 35 and 36.

such as boxing the ears and shaking, are strictly forbidden. Some authorities forbid the caning of children under eight.

The rules of management and articles of government of voluntary-aided schools do not, in general, require the school to be conducted in accordance with the regulations of the local education authority, except insofar as there may be special requirements dealing with finance and other matters. In such cases a head would be wise, in his own interests, to ask his managers or governors to adopt rules on corporal punishment.

9 Punishment by prefects

The law regards prefects as part of the disciplinary system of a school. Punishment which is otherwise legal does not become unlawful merely because it has been administered by a duly authorized prefect. There is, however, a duty to ensure that the penalties enforced by prefects are reasonable and moderate.

10 Suspension and expulsion

The technical procedure for dealing with cases where suspension or expulsion has become necessary is contained in the rules of management or articles of government for each school, and has already been noticed.[1] Since these penalties are the ultimate sanctions which can be employed by a school, it is important that they should not be used lightly or unadvisedly. Even if the rules of management or articles of government give the head the power to expel, it is desirable that he should suspend in the first instance in order to give the pupil and his parents the opportunity of a constitutional hearing.

On this subject, Lord Chief Justice Cockburn said,[2] 'It is incidental to the authority of a headmaster to expel from the school over which he presides any scholar or student whose conduct is such that he could not any longer be permitted to remain without damage to the school. This is, however, not be exercised arbitrarily. It may be questioned and, although no doubt a large

[1] See pages 176–80.
[2] In *Fitzgerald* v *Northcote* (1865) 4 F & F 656; LCT 148.

discretion must be allowed, it must not be exercised wantonly or capriciously.'

11 Civil actions concerning punishment

It is, of course, open to a plaintiff to bring a civil action for damages arising out of punishment. In 1965, Judge Duveen held at Slough County Court that a parent's claim must be rejected. The father had said that the corporal punishment administered to his son was excessive and sadistic, and the mother gave evidence that her son suffered from nightmares and bed-wetting afterwards. The judge said, 'There is no doubt in my mind that the punishment was made to fit the crime.'[1]

12 Violent pupils

'Teacher raped at knife point' was the headline under which a journal reported two cases of sexual assault on New York teachers in a period of eight hours.[2] The report continued with an account of a Safe Schools Act with which Congress was proposing to make federal funds available for school security programmes. One Representative had told Congress: 'The problem of crime in the schools has grown to such proportions that it now threatens the very viability of our educational system. You can't have good education when children are afraid to walk in the halls or go to the bathroom.' He added that in four years the number of assaults on teachers had increased from twenty-five to more than 2,000 in 110 school districts.

Since that time there has been considerable discussion in this country of a similar increase of violence among pupils, although no one has claimed that it has reached proportions of the kind outlined in the last paragraph. Before proceeding to a discussion in the next section on the effect of some current thinking on the practice and development of deterrents in schools, an account of several cases will indicate the general approach when the prob-

[1] *Daly* v *Buckinghamshire County Council, Marchant,* and *Buckland* (1965) *Daily Telegraph,* 22 December 1964, and *Evening News,* 5 January 1965.

[2] *Times Educational Supplement* (1971) 26 March.

lem of violence reaches proportions which remove it from the school's disciplinary procedures to the Queen's courts.

In December 1971 a fifteen-year-old pupil smoked during morning break, made rude gestures at the head of the physical education department, swore at him, kicked him in the stomach, and then ran away. The master gave him a light blow, which broke his jaw. The boy was later found to have taken half a tablet of the drug LSD before morning school. The master was charged with assault and causing grievous bodily harm, the more serious charge being dropped during the trial at Birmingham Crown Court. He was also suspended from duty. Summing up to the jury, Mr Justice Ackner said: 'Have we really reached the stage in this country when an insolent and bolshie pupil has to be treated with all the courtesies of visiting royalty? You may think we live in very strange times. Whatever may be the view of our most advanced, way-out theoreticians, the law does not require a teacher to have the patience of a saint. You may think that is a good thing, too. You may think that a superabundance of tolerance fails to produce a proper degree of self-discipline in any pupil.

'Nothing has happened to the boy concerned, although he could be brought before a juvenile court and receive a wide range of penalties. Yet a schoolmaster, "a man of exemplary character and an able, efficient and conscientious teacher" has been brought before the court. That is why I say we live in very strange times. The issue before you is not whether we suffer nowadays from an excess of sentimentality or sloppy thinking with regard to the criminal responsibility of the young. It is whether the prosecution has proved the master guilty.'

The master was acquitted.[1]

During the same week a master in the south of England was cleared of assault by a bench of magistrates. The court was told that the class had been in an uncontrollable uproar for thirty-five minutes. 'It was like trying to stop a riot,' said the master. He added that when he told a boy to stop fighting, the complainant made a very provocative remark which was the last straw. 'I meant to cuff him,' he said, 'but not with the board rubber.'

[1] *The Times*, 17 March 1972.

He was sorry that he had cut the boy's forehead, but thought that his actions were justified in the circumstances.[1]

Five months later the Bristol Juvenile Court heard the story of two sixteen-year-old boys who admitted causing grievous bodily harm to a master in a comprehensive school by punching his head. They also spat on him, emptied the contents of a wastepaper basket over him, and wrecked science apparatus. The master's skull was fractured, and he would have died if surgery to remove a blood clot near the brain had not been performed immediately. Because he was a Quaker the master did not retaliate. At the time of the trial his speech was still impaired, and it was not certain whether there was brain damage which would render him permanently unfit to teach. The boys said they believed the master had prevented them from being entered for their advanced level examinations.

The chairman said: 'In this court we believe that mercy is part of justice. We have to consider the possibility of you being taken away from society and the community for a considerable time. Maybe we are wrong in deciding otherwise. Your behaviour has been offensive and arrogant; the school had done everything possible for you, and no one had tried to stop you taking your A levels.'

The boys were sent to a detention centre for three months, followed by a year's after-care order.[2]

In December 1973 a boy was acquitted at the Old Bailey both of the murder and manslaughter of an older and much larger boy in a classroom. The boy who died was said to be 'hot-tempered, quick to take offence, and a bit of a bully'. He often kicked the defendant unnecessarily during football matches, and referred to him as a 'yellow bastard' and a 'mongol'. On the day following a serious scuffle on the football field, the younger boy, who had come to this country from Hong Kong some three years previously, took a knife to school to frighten his tormentor. The older boy picked a quarrel and raised a chair above his head as though to throw it at the immigrant lad. However, he flung the chair to the

---

[1] *Daily Mail*, 16 March 1972.
[2] *Daily Telegraph*, 8 and 22 August 1972.

floor and lunged forward on to the knife which was being held towards him. The defendant tried to pull the knife back but, before he could do so, it penetrated his assailant's heart.[1]

The cases cited above may be isolated incidents, but three salient points emerge. It is certain that a new form of aggravated violence, reckless of life or limb is, at least occasionally, manifesting itself in the schools of this country, and that the ordinary means of controlling discipline are inadequate to prevent this on some occasions. It is also clear that the courts are prepared to take a strong line with the perpetrators of this violence when they appear before them. Finally there must be considerable concern among headmasters, charged with a legal duty to control the internal discipline of their schools and a common law duty *in loco parentis* to take all reasonable steps to prevent any of their pupils from suffering unavoidable harm, that it is becoming increasingly difficult to discharge their responsibilities at a time when their authority to do so is subject to constant challenge.

13 The disciplinary future

The post-war years have witnessed a shift of emphasis in dealing with recalcitrant children from punishment to treatment, a movement which has gained considerable impetus since 1967. In society at large the age of criminal responsibility was raised from eight to ten, and there are some who think that twelve, or even fourteen, would be more appropriate. The Children and Young Persons Act 1969 made it virtually impossible to bring a child before the courts charged with an offence other than homicide, unless it was also possible to allege that he was also in need of care or control.

In the schools the battle has been waged largely over the issue of corporal punishment. In 1967 the Plowden report on primary education recommended that the Schools Regulations be amended 'to provide that the infliction of physical pain as a method of punishment should not be allowed'. The committee also suggested that legislation should deny registration to any independent school in which 'the infliction of physical pain is a recognized form of punishment'. Although the committee's terms of reference

[1] *Education*, 14 December 1973.

restricted its deliberations to the primary sector of education, these recommendations gave the appearance of being applicable to the secondary schools as well.

The Secretary of State at that time, Mr Patrick Gordon Walker, expressed similar views, and in the following year the Cardiff education authority decided to ban corporal punishment in its schools for an experimental period of twelve months. Opposition from the teaching profession, notably the National Union of Teachers and the National Association of Head Teachers, led to the lifting of the prohibition after two months. A survey revealed that only four out of sixty-four primary schools were in favour of abolition in the conditions prevailing at that time, although forty-four were in favour of phasing out.

The year 1968 also saw the formation of the Society of Teachers Opposed to Physical Punishment. The Society is dedicated to the abolition of corporal punishment, pointing out that of the European countries only the United Kingdom, the Republic of Ireland and parts of Switzerland and West Germany have retained its use. Within the Commonwealth it is still employed in Canada, Australia and New Zealand. It is also used in the Union of South Africa and parts of the United States of America.

The argument for abolition is based on a number of grounds. It is said to be degrading both for the teacher and the pupil. It is psychologically dangerous, and leads to disturbance later in life. The frequency with which some names appear in the punishment book is proof that it is ineffective. It produces school phobia. It is used too frequently on the recidivist (on whom it has no effect) and the maladjusted (who should never be caned). It gives an opportunity to a sadistic teacher to gratify his perversion. Above all, violence begets violence, and destroys the possibility of a satisfactory relationship between teacher and taught.

The first effective step towards abolition was taken by the ILEA which announced in 1971 that it proposed to ban the use of all corporal punishment in its primary schools from the beginning of 1973. Since they are not subject to the Authority's regulations, the prohibition does not apply to voluntary-aided schools in which the position varies considerably. In October 1972 the Shropshire authority forbade the use of the cane in infants' schools, but did not go so far as the ILEA in that as it decided to allow slapping to continue in certain restricted circumstances.

Peter Newell, at that time the education officer of the National Council for Civil Liberties, published *A Last Resort*,[1] a compilation prepared from the files of the Society of Teachers Opposed to Physical Punishment by 'people who dislike the concept of physical punishment'. 'It is unrepentantly an abolitionist book' and, therefore, tendentious in its choice of words and its general tone.

Two legal questions of considerable interest to teachers may be considered at this point. In *Mansell* v *Griffin*[2] the last of the four tests applied was that punishment should be 'such as the parent of the child might expect it would receive if it did wrong'. Does this mean that an individual parent can order the headmaster of a school where corporal punishment is still customary not to use it on his child?

The Society of Teachers Opposed to Physical Punishment think this is possible, and in 1972 they produced a form for this purpose. It seems quite certain that such requests cannot bind the head-master provided he is acting within the law, that is, the general principles laid down in *Mansell* v *Griffin*; and within the regula-tions of his local education authority or, in the case of a volun-tary-aided school, those of his managers or governors. Being *in loco parentis*, he must act as a wise and prudent parent in using the authority delegated to him.[3] By sending his child to the school the father authorizes the schoolmaster to administer reasonable punishment for the breach of a reasonable rule.[4] If the parent of every pupil in a school required a headmaster to exercise his authority *in loco parentis* to suit his particular whims an impossibly contradictory situation could result, making it quite impossible to organize the school to suit the wishes of all. This, however, is not the end of the matter. By the rules of management or articles of

[1] *Penguin* (1972).
[2] See page 277.
[3] See Lord Chief Justice Cockburn's statement in *R* v *Hopley*, page 289.
[4] *Per* Lord Chief Justice Hewart *R* v *Newport* (*Salop*) *Justices*, page 284.

government the internal discipline of the school is a duty laid on the headmaster. In pursuance of that duty he must make rules and enforce them; if those rules and punishments are reasonable, they will be upheld by the courts.[1] It is for the courts to decide, as a matter of fact in each case, what is reasonable, and an unusual request by a single parent is a single factor to be balanced against all the other relevant considerations.

The second question concerns the power of a local education authority to remove a teacher's common law right *in loco parentis* to administer corporal punishment. There seems to be no doubt that this power exists. An employer has the right to exercise a legitimate control over the way in which a servant performs his duties. For many years there have been restrictions of various kinds, such as prohibition of the use of corporal punishment by probationary teachers, or a ban on the caning of girls by masters. These controls are matters of local education authority regulations imported into the teacher's contract of service, and not part of the common law. Since the contract requires the teacher to serve in accordance with the authority's regulations from time to time in force, it follows that any change in the regulations also becomes part of the contract of service. If, therefore, a local education authority decides to prohibit corporal punishment it would be a breach of contract for any member of its teaching staff to continue to use it. It is also possible that a court would not regard corporal punishment as 'legitimate punishment' in the prosecution for assault of a teacher who had been instructed by his employer to desist from such action.

It must be remembered that there is a clear distinction between legal rights and duties. The former can be restricted by mutual consent, the latter cannot be abrogated. By the rules of management or articles of government the headmaster is placed under a duty to control the discipline of a school, and the assistant staff are required, reasonably, to assist him in so doing. The employing authority cannot remove this duty, except in those cases where it has the power to vary the rules or articles. On the other hand the power to administer corporal punishment is a common law right,

[1] See pages 25–7.

and not a duty. In accepting appointment the teacher has agreed to obey regulations in the full knowledge that changes made from time to time will be binding on him, including those which place lawful limitations upon his rights. He cannot, therefore, complain if his employer says, in effect: 'You must continue to carry out your duty to preserve discipline, but you must do so by some method other than the use of corporal punishment.'

In November 1973 Baroness Wootton of Abinger introduced the Protection of Minors Bill 1973 in the House of Lords. The bill sought to end corporal punishment by all persons having the custody, care or control of a child, including all teachers, through the creation of a statutory offence to be known as wilful assault on a minor; that is, any person under the age of eighteen. The bill proposed to exempt natural, adoptive and foster parents, and legal guardians and their spouses in each case, but not the employees of a local authority in charge of a child committed to the care of that authority. The bill proposed the abolition of the defence of reasonable corporal punishment. The proposed penalties were a fine of £50 or four months' imprisonment, or both, on summary conviction; or on indictment a fine of £250 or one year's imprisonment, or both. The motion for the second reading was debated on 10 December, and was rejected by sixty-seven votes to fifty-one.

On all sides it is being said that discipline in schools is more difficult than ever before, and problems which were once peculiar to secondary schools are now appearing in the primary sector. Some would retain, even increase, the sanctions already available; others wish to see them diminished and replaced by suitable treatment. The supportive social services are labouring under increasingly heavy case loads, and are not yet adequately staffed with experienced workers to take over the treatment of all pupils who have become problems in school. Indeed, in spite of promises, the problems appear to be increasing in number and severity faster than the services created to deal with them. The debate continues.

XIII

SCHOOL JOURNEYS AND
EDUCATIONAL VISITS

1 General

The widening of young peoples' experience by 'opening windows' so that their educational vision is not confined to the school precincts is a practice which has grown far beyond expectation since the war. The scope of these activities has been considerably extended to include visits to museums, art galleries and concerts; visits to factories either as part of environmental studies or in connection with work experience; day excursions, sometimes extending to the Continent; field studies, for which purpose many schools now have their own centres; Outward Bound and adventure courses, including ski-ing holidays; school journeys at home and abroad; and educational cruises.

As the number and variety of these activities have increased, improved means of travel and a general decrease of formality in the requirements of international travel have encouraged schools to visit more and more distant lands. The first educational cruises were organized in the early 'thirties by a group of Southampton and Portsmouth schoolmasters who seized the opportunity of making some use of the merchant shipping laid up in Southampton Water during the economic recession.[1] In more recent years this particular form of journey has been largely developed as a commercial organization. Visits to the Soviet Union, unthinkable before 1960, are now commonplace, as are school journeys to the Holy Land, North Africa and the United States.

[1] This group eventually became the English Secondary Schools Travel Trust, a body still in existence, but which has concentrated its attention on journeys to Switzerland since 1945.

Schools planning journeys now have three basic methods of organization available to them. One is to make use of one of the commercial travel agents who specialize in school journey work. Many of these undertake the full responsibility of organizing travel, hotels, visits, and other necessary details. If a school intends to plan a journey in this way it must, of course, accept the necessity of verifying the experience and quality of the organizers in this field. Those who are members of the Association of British Travel Agents are governed by that Association's code of conduct.

The second possibility is to use the services of one of the reputable voluntary bodies established for the promotion of school journeys. The School Journey Association of London[1] was one of the earliest, and organizes a large number of visits to centres at home and overseas. Some may find the international services of the Youth Hostels Association more appropriate to their needs; and there are specialist organizations dealing with working holidays abroad, vacation study, cultural holidays and other activities.

Thirdly, a school may decide to 'go it alone'; a course not recommended unless the party leader is experienced in school journey organization, with particular reference to the kind of visit planned. Schools who decide to follow this practice may still obtain advice from the School Journey Association of London, if they are in membership, and this country has the only national organization in the world established to foster overseas journeys: the Central Bureau for Educational Visits and Exchanges[2] which was set up by HM Government in 1948, and is financed entirely from public funds. The Bureau has linked more than 2,500 schools in this country with counterparts in Europe, and works with more than ninety countries throughout the world.

Teachers undertaking responsibility for educational visits and school journeys are responsible for the pupils in their care throughout the whole period; in the case of a journey for twenty-furo

[1] Those planning school journeys for the first time will find invaluable advice in the three pamphlets issued by the School Journey Association of London which are noted on page 470. Free to members, they are obtainable by others at a small charge. Membership of the Association is not confined to schools in London.
[2] 43 Dorset Street, London, W1H 3FN.

hours a day and seven days a week. It is therefore essential to have an adequate staff competent to deal with any emergencies which may arise. If there are both boys and girls in the party, the staff must also be mixed. To attempt a visit or journey with insufficient teachers is the most ardent way to court disaster.

2 Educational visits

All local education authorities have regulations dealing with educational visits, and these should be thoroughly understood and observed by any teacher undertaking such a visit. It is particularly important to observe any requirements as to the pupil – teacher ratio. Some years ago a headmistress organized a visit which took place during the spring half-term holiday. Not wishing to spoil the holiday of any of her colleagues, she took the twenty-one pupils herself; the authority's regulations permitted a maximum of twenty pupils to one teacher. On the way a boy was knocked down by a car which failed to stop at a zebra crossing. Fortunately the lad was not seriously hurt; but the headmistress, in the kindness of her heart, had laid herself open to discipline by her authority. Had the accident been more serious, she could have been in grave difficulties.

The responsibility of a teacher for the welfare of his pupils is not lessened by the fact that he has undertaken the duty voluntarily whether he is on, or away from, the school precincts. Neither is such liability affected by the end of the normal school hours. In all cases where he has accepted the care of children, he must take reasonable precautions for their safety.

The East Ham Corporation was sued in 1926 following an incident at the British Empire Exhibition at Wembley. During the dinner-hour, the master in charge of a school party gave the boys permission to amuse themselves for a while. One boy caught his foot between the platform and the train on the Never-Stop Railway, and was so badly injured that he spent nineteen weeks in hospital. Despite a contention that a reasonable father would have allowed a fourteen-year-old boy to go on the railway, the jury found that negligence had been proved and awarded £60 agreed damages against the Corporation.

In cases where a teacher voluntarily takes charge of children out of school hours in an unofficial capacity, i.e. an activity which is not organized by the school, it should be made clear by the head to the parents in advance that such an arrangement is purely between themselves and the teacher as an individual. In such cases the school authorities can accept no responsibility.[1]

Teachers taking parties of children to concerts, sports meetings and similar events where there are large gatherings of children from many schools should be especially watchful of their charges. On such occasions there is normally a corps of experienced stewards who are concerned with the general oversight and marshalling of parties, but the discipline of each group is the responsibility of the teachers escorting it. Quite apart from the fact that it creates a thoroughly bad impression if teachers settle down to enjoy themselves and allow their pupils to do as they please, it should be remembered that with large crowds there is always the risk that small children may be lost and, furthermore, in the event of a mischance, panic spreads rapidly. Rigid supervision is especially necessary on staircases.

General guidance on educational visits has been given by the DES,[2] and an administrative memorandum, *Liability for Pupils and Students visiting Industry*[3] deals with liability arising from accidents or damage to property taking place during visits to industrial firms. Local education authorities are advised to take out appropriate insurance to cover this kind of risk. It is also recommended that parental consent should be obtained in the case of minors, though this might not be necessary on every occasion unless special risks are involved. If a firm asks for indemnity against accidents or damage caused by visitors not in their employment, this may be given provided it does not relieve the firm of liability arising from its own negligence or that of its employees.

Visits falling within the scope of the Education (Work Experience) Act 1973 have been dealt with in a previous chapter.[4]

---

[1] As a matter of pastoral care towards the teacher concerned, rather than as a legal duty, the head should warn the teacher concerned of the risks involved, and advise him to secure adequate insurance cover.

[2] Circular 8/72.

[3] Administrative Memorandum no. 22/67.   [4] See pages 197–8.

Schools, particularly those in the south-east of England, sometimes arrange day visits to the accessible parts of the Continent, usually Calais or Boulogne. The general provisions relating to school journeys must be observed, as must the appropriate parts of the requirements relating to overseas school journeys. It should be remembered that there are no Customs concessions for travellers who have been out of the country for less than twenty-four hours. It is also important to ensure rigid compliance with the conditions set out in the travel documents. On one occasion a school visited Calais on a day excursion which allowed three and a half hours between the time of landing and the time of the return sailing: the ticket specified that passengers should be at the quay an hour before the sailing time. Feeling that the time ashore was somewhat inadequate, the party arrived on the quay a quarter of an hour before the ship was due to leave, only to find that it had already sailed. In order to get the party home at a reasonable time the staff had to book a crossing with another line but, as the conditions had been broken, British Rail refused a refund on the unused return tickets.

3 Standard of care

On both educational visits and school journeys, the ordinary standard of care *in loco parentis* applies. Teachers may, however, be concerned about accidents arising as a result of defective premises or equipment which are outside their control. In 1961 a pupil at an approved school took part in a confidence course established by the Outward Bound organization at Reigate. Whilst using an aerial ropeway, the wire cable snapped, and he fell to the ground. He was disabled until his death (which was not connected with the accident) five years later. The cable was found to be rusted internally, but the defect could not have been discovered without dismantling. The warden who, without the knowledge of the owner of the site or the school, was no longer employed by the Croydon Outward Bound Group, was ordered to pay £1,760 in damages for failure in his duty under the Occupiers Liability Act 1957 and at common law. The owner and the school were dismissed from the suit.

Mr Justice Nield said: '. . . where a school must take their pupils to other premises, they discharge their duty of care if they know the premises and if the premises are apparently safe, and if they know that the premises are staffed by competent and careful persons. They further discharge their duty if they permit their pupils there to use equipment which is apparently safe, and is under the control of competent and careful persons who supervise the use of such equipment. They do not in such circumstances have an obligation themselves to make an inspection.'[1]

4 Parental permission

Although, as has already been said, it is not essential to have parental permission for every short educational visit not involving special risk, many teachers feel it advisable. If, on a perfectly legitimate educational visit, an accident happens to a child whose parent believed him to be safely on the school premises the situation can, to say the least, be embarrassing. If children are undertaking a series of visits in connection with a particular course, a general permission given at the beginning would be sufficient. Everything depends on the nature of the visit, and the age and capability of the pupils.

It is essential, and many authorities have a regulation to this effect, to obtain permission in writing before taking children on a school journey. In the case of overseas school journeys the Passport Office may require to see the written parental permissions.

When taking children abroad it is desirable, also, to obtain the parent's consent to any necessary medical treatment.[2] This is essential in the case of a pupil known, for example, to have a grumbling appendix. As a matter of good personal relationships it should be explained to the parent that the teacher is *in loco parentis* and must be free in a pupil's interest to take such decisions as a prudent parent would take in connection with his own child. It is also wise to say that the natural parent's consent will be ob-

[1] *Brown* v *Nelson* and *others* (1971) 69 LGR 20.
[2] For the special circumstances which arise in the case of Christian Scientists and Jehovah's Witnesses, see pages 329–32.

tained if possible,[1] but that, in a sudden emergency there may be insufficient time to do so. A suitable form of words to be added to the parental consent would be:

> I authorize the leader of the party, or any other member of the school staff who may be present, to consent to such medical treatment (including inoculations, blood transfusion or surgery) which in the opinion of a qualified medical practitioner may be necessary during the course of the journey.

A pupil who has attained the age of sixteen may, himself give consent to medical treatment.[2]

A child who is the subject of a court order may not be taken out of the country without permission of the court. This applies to school journeys, and if it is proposed to include any such pupils in a party, it is necessary to make an application to the court in good time.

5 Letters of indemnity

Before taking children on an outing or school journey, it is desirable to obtain a letter of indemnity from the parent of each child. Such letters do not have sufficient legal force to prevent a parent issuing a writ claiming damages for negligence if he believes that someone responsible for the journey has not acted as a wise and prudent parent in taking care of his pupil and that, as a result, his child has suffered damage. A parent cannot be asked to sign away his common law right. Nevertheless, in the event of a claim arising from alleged negligence, the fact that the parent's attention had been drawn to possible risks would weigh in the teacher's favour.

The real protection is insurance, and no teacher should consider taking a school journey party away without adequate third party cover. Some insurance companies specialize in this particular cover, and can give sound advice on the subject. It is not so

---

[1] The party leader should compile a list of emergency contact addresses, with telephone numbers if possible. It is sometimes practicable to make arrangements with the school caretaker to pass on urgent messages, and the police are always willing to assist in such circumstances.

[2] See pages 192–3.

essential to arrange for personal accident insurance for the children. If this is not to be covered, it is worthwhile mentioning this to the parents, and offering to put them in touch with the company which is insuring the journey.

Some years ago a party of twenty-two boys spent a half-holiday working for a farmer. No master was present. During the course of the afternoon one of the boys made an offensive remark which annoyed another, who promptly threw a clod at him. The missile hit a third boy on the temple, injuring his eye which had to be enucleated the following day. In the action which followed £800 were awarded in damages.

The verdict was reversed in the Court of Appeal, the judges maintaining that no supervision was needed on such an occasion. 'I must ask myself,' said Lord Justice Goddard, 'whether any ordinary parent would think for a moment that he was exposing his boy to risk in allowing him to go into a field with others to weed beet, and lift potatoes – occupations far safer than bicycling about on the roads in these days. . . . For one boy to throw something at another is an ordinary part of school life.'[1]

It is possible that the original decision was influenced by the fact that no letters of indemnity had been signed before the outing. A suitable form is as follows:

> I agree to allow my child...............to take part in a school...............on...............19.... and I hereby indemnify all responsible in any way for the organization of the activity named against all claims arising through illness accident or any other cause.
>
> (Signed)........................
...............19....

6 School journeys
Whatever form school journeys take, whether they be field studies weeks, travel experience, archaeological expeditions, or simply holidays, there are certain basic principles which apply to them all.

---

[1] *Camkin* v *Bishop* [1941] 2 All ER 713; LCT 334.

The duty of care *in loco parentis* has already been mentioned, and the regulations of the local education authority on staffing, as on all other matters, must be rigidly followed. In order that a due succession of qualified leaders may be retained in a school, it is a valuable practice to give subordinate leadership experience to a number of younger members of the staff. The leader, however, must have some experience, and it is important to remember that the standard of care imposed is that of a reasonably careful parent. The standard of conduct which should be exacted is similar and, although these standards may be modified over the years, it must be remembered that the great majority of parents do not expect their children to be encouraged to develop behaviour patterns which are lower than those of their homes merely because they appeal to a teacher who may not be much older than the pupils, and who has no personal experience of bringing up children in a family. Relationships between pupils and staff are usually more relaxed than they are in school, and it is good that they should be so, but the journey location is essentially an extra-mural extension of the school, and the rules of the school may still be applied. Some of the laws of England, e.g. those concerned with currency control, also extend beyond the British Isles to United Kingdom citizens, and of course in any country aliens are subject to the domestic law of their hosts.

The numerical adequacy of the school journey staff is also important. The benefit and enjoyment of the journey may well be lost if the programme has to be seriously reduced because staff sickness has reduced the ratio below the permitted limit for any particular activity. It is always useful to have a reserve member of the staff standing by, willing to travel at short notice in the event of serious illness which reduces the school journey staff to a level which would vitiate the success of the journey.

Overseas journeys require particularly careful planning. In recent years exchange rates have fluctuated wildly, and the general trend has been against sterling. In addition, most European countries have suffered from internal inflation, and what appeared to be a reasonable costing when the journey was planned may turn out to be completely unrealistic when the journey takes place six or twelve months later. Most countries now have a national tourist office in London, and the staffs of these bureaux are always willing to give considerable help in the planning of overseas visits. Further assistance can be obtained by joining one of the cultural exchange organizations which exist, such as the Anglo-Austrian Society.[1]

In planning overseas journeys it is essential to take the length and means of travel into account in relation to the age of the children and the facilities available on the way. During the past decade large numbers of primary schools have extended their activities to the Continent. Setting on one side the problem that, if their experience is widened too rapidly, these children may, when they reach their secondary schools, sit down like Alexander and weep because there are no more worlds to conquer, there is a problem of stress. As improved means of transport have made the Continent more accessible, it would be churlish to suggest that primary schools should not undertake overseas travel. It would seem wiser, however, to restrict their activities to those parts of Europe nearest to the British Isles, so that the overland journey following the crossing is reasonably short. The author remembers seeing an exhausted party of nine-year-olds from Scotland sleeping on the platform at Basel. They were on their way to Rome, no couchettes had been arranged, their only food consisted of the sandwiches they had brought with them, they still had some hundreds of miles to go and, as they waited for their connecting train, they were utterly exhausted. This hardly seems the standard of care of a prudent parent, and the first two days after arriving at their destination must have been wasted whilst they recovered from travel fatigue.

Couchettes are well worth the extra cost for any journey involving all-night train travel on the Continent, and arrangements for adequate meals should be made in advance.

It is not good practice for staff to carry travel-sickness pills for indiscriminate distribution, as some children suffer from side-effects as a result of taking such drugs. At least one authority forbids teaching staff to dispense these unless they have been

[1] 139 Kensington High Street, London, W8 6SX.

obtained by a parent on the advice of the family doctor. In making arrangements with the parents, it is wise to ask whether there are any medical points which should be watched so far as individual children are concerned. Parents should be encouraged to hand over any drugs, together with the appropriate instructions, to the party leader to ensure that they are taken at the correct intervals without risk either of under- or over-dosage.

If an all-night train journey is involved, it is essential to know if there are any sleep-walkers in the party, otherwise there is a risk of such a pupil walking on to the track instead of finding the toilet door. In any case the staff should arrange for a supervision rota by which a sufficient number of teachers is on duty at all times during the night to deal with any emergency.

7 Mountaineering

In 1971–2 three fatal accidents overtook school parties, one in the Cairngorms, one in Snowdonia and one in the Lake District. After the Cairngorms incident, in which five children died, the inquest returned a verdict that the children died of cold and exposure, but ascribed no blame. The jury made, however, a number of recommendations:

(a) More care should be exercised in fitness and training;

(b) Parents should be more fully informed about, and asked to acknowledge, such activities;

(c) Qualified teachers should accompany the parties, and the actual expeditions should be led by qualified and long-experienced instructors;

(d) Certain areas should be designated as suitable for summer or winter expeditions by children;

(e) The removal, or otherwise, of high-level bothies should be left to experts;

(f) Mountain rescue work should be furthered, financially and otherwise;

(e) The education authority should maintain closer liaison with parents in the event of disaster.

Following these tragedies, local education authorities reviewed their regulations, and teachers who are considering such activities should observe the requirements of their own authority.

A summary of the new regulations of the ILEA for hill walking and mountaineering provides a general guide. By reason of altitude, terrain, remoteness and climate, the Authority has defined the following areas as subject to these rules:

Dartmoor	Peak District
Exmoor	Pennines
Bodmin Moor	North Yorkshire Moors
Black Mountains	Lake District
Brecon Beacons	Cheviots
Central Welsh Mountains	Southern Uplands
Snowdonia	Highlands and Islands.

In these areas any departure from metalled roads is defined as hill walking, and only instructors holding the Mountain Leadership Certificate and approved by the ILEA may lead expeditions involving these activities. Leaders who have passed the introductory course may act under the general supervision of a MLC leader. Parties using centres run by the Field Studies Council are exempt if the Warden is satisfied that the programme conforms to his safety precautions. Similar conditions apply to areas of potential hazard outside the United Kingdom.

There must be at least one teacher for every eight pupils; and at least two teachers (normally one at the front and one at the rear) must accompany all expeditions into high or remote areas.

Equipment must be of a kind approved by the ILEA. All parties walking or camping in mountains must take 120 feet of No. 3 rope with them, and all pupils must wear suitably soled *boots* and suitable protective clothing which must be examined by a teacher before setting out. All pupils must carry a whistle, spare clothing, food for an emergency and a polythene bag measuring eight by four feet. At least two members of the party must each carry a torch, map, compass, first-aid kit, knife and watch.

All pupils must be instructed in basic emergency procedures and signals. A reliable local weather forecast should be obtained before setting out on any expedition.

8 Transport

Many schools now have their own mini-buses or coaches. It is obviously important that such vehicles are kept in a serviceable condition and comply with all the regulations, whether those of HM Government or the local education authority.

Adequate comprehensive insurance must be arranged, including injury or damage to other road users and their vehicles as a result of the actions of passengers.

If fares are charged, and the vehicle is above a certain size, it becomes a public service vehicle. This means that it must comply with the more stringent requirements relating to such vehicles, and the driver must have a public service vehicle licence. These requirements apply whether the passengers are charged directly or indirectly for their travel. Local education authorities have drawn up rules or memoranda of guidance for schools which have their own vehicles, and any school planning to purchase one should study these carefully. There are many snags, some of which do not appear until misfortune strikes unless one has taken the trouble to be forewarned.

To save expense, school parties are sometimes transported by lorry. No charge may be made by the owner of the lorry for this service but he may, if his vehicle is properly licensed and insured, charge for the carriage of luggage and equipment. The lorry must be correctly insured for the purpose for which it is used, and the tax paid must be adequate for the conveyance of the children. The owner is not, however, obliged to insure against accidents to passengers travelling free of charge and, if he has not adequate cover, teachers are strongly advised to take out a policy in respect of such risks.

One of the advantages of joining the EEC is that the insurance 'green card' is no longer necessary for travel within the Common Market by cars registered in a member state. If, however, a vehicle is equipped to carry ten or more persons, including the driver, special requirements apply, and these include journeys to Eire.

Under Regulation No. 117/66, school journeys undertaken in a mini-bus or coach owned by the school would normally be classified as 'occasional closed door tours', i.e. services where the

vehicle makes a round trip back to its starting point, carrying the
same group of passengers throughout. The destination of such a
tour is regarded as the member state where the point of departure
lies: for a school journey, the destination will be the school!

The control document for these journeys is a book of fifty
waybills in duplicate, valid for five years in respect of any vehicle
operated by the person to whom the book is issued. A duplicate
waybill must be completed by the person responsible for the tour
before its commencement, and the top copy must be carried on
the vehicle throughout the journey. This exempts the vehicle
from domestic licensing in member states, and must be produced
on demand. The duplicate remains in the book. The penalty for
non-compliance is, in this country, a fine of up to £20.

Provided the vehicle is registered in a member state, and its
destination is a state within the Common Market (which, as has
been said above is normally the case with school journeys) the
waybill is valid for crossing Austria, Greece, Norway, Portugal,
Spain, Sweden, Switzerland, Turkey and Yugoslavia. It should be
observed, however, that if the vehicle takes a party to a country
outside the EEC and returns empty, the destination is not held
to be within the Common Market and advice should be sought
from the school's Traffic Area Office. Books of waybills can be
obtained free of charge from the Traffic Area Office or, in
Northern Ireland from the Ministry of Development.

On completion of the journey the top copy of the waybill must
be sent to the Department of the Environment or, in Northern
Ireland, to the Ministry of Development. Failure to do so can entail a fine of up to £20. The duplicate waybills must be retained
in the book throughout the period of its validity.

EEC Regulation No. 543/69 deals with the drivers of vehicles
equipped to carry ten or more persons, including the driver. It
applies to international journeys within the EEC, including those
to Eire. On such a journey the driver must be at least twenty-one
years of age, hold a valid British driving licence, and have had at
least one year's driving experience. Before setting out the driver
must send the appropriate form and his driving licence to a Traffic
Area Office to obtain a certificate of age and experience. This is

not needed by holders of a public service vehicle or heavy goods vehicle driver's licence. The requirements apply to that part of an international journey which lies within the country of origin, and contravention will lead to prosecution. For offences within the United Kingdom the maximum fine is £50, together with endorsement and possible disqualification.

The driver must carry an individual control book in which to enter his driving record during the journey. Except in cases of emergency, provided that road safety is not endangered and to the extent which it is necessary to reach a suitable stopping place at the end of the journey and ensure the safety of the passengers or vehicle, driving hours are rigidly controlled. A driver must not drive for more than eight hours a day (with an extension of one hour twice in any period of seven consecutive days), nor for more than forty-eight hours in any consecutive period of seven days, subject to a maximum of ninety-two hours in a fortnight. He may not drive for more than four hours without a break of at least half an hour (or two breaks of twenty minutes, or three breaks of fifteen minutes). At any moment he must have had a break of at least ten consecutive hours during the preceding twenty-four hours. He must have a period of twenty-four consecutive hours' rest during each period of seven days, and this must be immediately preceded or followed by a daily rest period: in other words, he must not be at the wheel for a continuous period of thirty-four hours each week. Between March and October the weekly rest may be replaced by a single rest period of sixty hours immediately preceded or followed by a daily break in any consecutive fourteen days, i.e. a break of seventy hours.

Failure to comply with these regulations can lead to prosecution; in this country the maximum fine is £200.

The school's insurers should be consulted about the latest requirements relating to insurance.

There are special requirements relating to the drivers of public service vehicles, but as most school transport is not so registered, they are not dealt with here.

The United Kingdom representatives in Brussels are seeking to have privately owned vehicles with up to sixteen seats exempted from the regulations. At the time of writing (October 1974) it is not known whether these proposals will be accepted nor, if they are, when they will take effect.

It must be emphasized that that part of an international journey which lies within the home country is treated as international, and the requirements outlined above apply.[1]

A valid United Kingdom driving licence is sufficient for most countries in western Europe. Teachers planning journeys which involve driving in more exotic countries should ascertain whether an international driving permit is required. The permit costs £1, and is valid for a year in every country except that in which it is issued. International driving permits may be obtained from the Automobile Association.[2] A passport-type photograph must be enclosed with the application.

9 Bathing and boating

When bathing or boating form part of the activities of a school excursion, it is desirable to seek – and follow – local advice regarding currents, tides and general safety. In bathing it is a good rule to have two strong swimmers as pickets. The pickets should be changed and ready for any emergency, but they should not enter the water, unless an emergency arises, until all the other bathers have left. This is the rule of the Scout movement and is based on long experience. In the case of school Scout camps it must be observed.

It is also useful to obtain specific permission for swimming from the parents of each child. Those with any defect which may be aggravated by bathing should in no circumstances be allowed to enter the water.

10 The law of waterways

Canoeing and boating are becoming increasingly popular with

[1] Fuller details may be found in the following leaflets issued by the Department of the Environment, 2 Marsham Street, London, SW1 3EB: *Journeys to Europe by Coach or Mini-bus* (Int. P. 39, June 1973), *Driving to Europe after 31 March 1973* (Int. P. 1.) and *International Rules* (*Public Service Vehicles*) (PSV. 149, April 1973).

[2] Fanum House, 7 High Street, London, TW11 8EQ.

school parties, and it is necessary, if trespass is to be avoided, to know something of the law of waterways.

Tidal waters are public highways and their ownership is vested in the Crown. They may be used freely by anyone who does not interfere with the similar rights of others.

Non-tidal waters are vested in the owners of the adjacent land and there is no right of passage across them unless, in specific cases, it has been granted by Act of Parliament or has become customary through immemorial use. Such a right is similar to the usage of a public footpath across a field and is primarily for passage from one place to another; it confers no right to recreation, to fishing or to landing on the banks. Where no right of way exists, entry to non-tidal waters is trespass.

Canals are the property of the authority to which they belong, and passage along them may be granted on payment of the appropriate dues, subject to observance of the regulations.

11 Treasure trove

The development of field studies, sometimes with active participation in archaeological excavation, makes it possible that from time to time school parties may discover hoards of valuable items. In general, gold or silver, whether in plate, coin or bullion, which has been hidden in the ground or a building, and of which the owner cannot reasonably be traced, is regarded as treasure trove and is the property of the Crown.

It is important, therefore, that any such finds should be reported to the police, as HM Coroner has a duty to hold an inquest to determine whether the find is treasure trove. He may find that the goods have been abandoned by their owner, in which case they belong to anyone who cares to claim them; they may have been lost, in which case it would be theft not to return them to their rightful owner. Treasure openly buried, like the Sutton Hoo burial hoard, belongs to the owner of the ground.

The test applied by the coroner is whether, so far as can be discovered, the treasure was hidden by its owner with the intention of recovering it at some future time. It is this category which is treasure trove and, if its find is reported immediately to the police, the finder is allowed its full market value. Concealment is an offence. In Scotland all finds are treasure trove, and the intention of the owner to recover his property does not have to be proved.

12 Ancient monuments

Schools taking part in field studies or archaeological excavations should be aware that the Ancient Monuments Acts 1913 and 1931 have made the Ministry of Works responsible for preparing a list of ancient monuments whose preservation is a matter of national importance.

The list includes not only a large variety of buildings and structures, but also barrows, forts, earthworks and other remains from ancient times. No scheduled monument may be destroyed, altered, or added to without the Ministry's consent. Unauthorized excavation is also forbidden. To injure or deface an ancient monument renders the offender liable to a fine of £5 or a month's imprisonment, together with compensation for the damage.

Schools undertaking work in this field should enlist the help of the local archaeological society who will always support serious research. Advice can also be obtained from the Chief Inspector of Ancient Monuments at the Ministry of Works.

13 Medical requirements

Many local education authorities require that all pupils should undergo a medical examination by a medical officer whose services are made available to the authority by the Secretary of State for Health and Social Services. Alternatively, they may produce a medical certificate of fitness for the journey from their own doctor.

The Department of Health and Social Services recommends everyone travelling abroad to be vaccinated against smallpox, and to have other inoculations appropriate to the countries being visited. From time to time countries enforce protection against certain diseases if there has been an epidemic in their own country, or in any place where an immigrant has recently lived or visited. At the time of vaccination against smallpox it is possible to obtain an International Vaccination Certificate from the doctor,

whose signature must be verified by the local health authority's
official stamp. The certificates are normally valid for three
years.

It is not considered good medical practice, except as an emergency, to give a smallpox vaccination to anyone suffering from
eczema, or who is being treated with steroids, or to a pregnant
woman. In such cases the doctor will provide a certificate stating
the reason for the traveller's failure to be vaccinated.

14 Insurance

When taking children away for educational visits, school
journeys or camps, inquiry should be made to ascertain whether
the local education authority or the organization sponsoring
the visit has an adequate policy to cover possible claims. If
not, a special policy should be arranged with an insurance
company, the premiums being chargeable to the cost of the
journey.

Some authorities which do not carry bulk insurance for such
activities require evidence that the organizers of the journey have
taken out adequate cover. Where the authority does provide its
own insurance, teachers should ensure that their own interests
are covered as well as those of the authority and the pupils and,
if in doubt, they should consult their professional association.

For some educational visits and school journeys where special
risks are involved, e.g. canoeing or mountaineering, an additional
premium may be payable, and such proposed activities should be
disclosed when effecting the insurance.

If a journey is arranged through a commercial travel agent or
a school journey organization, the promotion booklet may refer
to the fact that 'full insurance' is included in the cost of the tour.
This is not good enough: the organizer should require the agent
to disclose the full terms of the policy to see whether it complies
with the local education authority's minimum requirements, or
whether it will need to be supplemented by additional insurance
arranged by the school. The minimum cover required is set out in
the following list which represents the standard terms of insurers

experienced in the school journey field, although some, obviously, apply only to overseas journeys:

(*a*) the death or disablement by accident of any member of the party;

(*b*) loss of or damage to personal luggage and loss of money;

(*c*) expenses incurred due to the unforeseen extension of the visit or to any forced change in the planned route of the journey;

(*d*) additional expenses incurred in connection with the return home of any person in the party due to the death, serious injury or illness of a member of the family;

(*e*) medical, surgical, nursing and other similar expenses which might have to be met;

(*f*) expenses incurred as a direct result of remaining with a sick or injured person;

(*g*) additional expenses incurred in transporting home on medical advice any sick or injured person or, in the event or death, the body or ashes of the deceased;

(*h*) expenses necessarily incurred by the parent or guardian of any sick or injured person travelling on medical advice to visit such person.

It will be noted that personal accident insurance of the kind which provides, for example, £5,000 in the case of death, £1,000 for the loss of one limb, and so forth, is not included in the suggestions listed above. There is no reason why a school should not take out a personal accident policy, and add the premium to the cost of the journey. Many schools, however, prefer to advise parents that insurance of this nature is their responsibility and that, if they wish for this cover, they should make their arrangements privately.

15 Passports
All persons taking part in visits to countries outside the United Kingdom of Great Britain and Northern Ireland must be protected by valid passport documentation without which both admission

to a country overseas will be refused, and re-admission to the United Kingdom will be difficult.

Day visits – For 'no-passport' day visits to the Continent a simple identity card is sufficient. If the journeys are organized by British Rail, the railway authorities will arrange for the issue of these cards, and will include the cost in the charge for the excursion.

Party leader – If a collective passport, formerly called a collective certificate, is used, the party leader must be the holder of a valid full British passport. These are issued to British subjects who are also citizens of the United Kingdom and Colonies, although in certain circumstances they may be obtained by British subjects without citizenship and by British protected persons. They are valid for ten years, and cost £5. Regular travellers to countries requiring a visa may now obtain a 'jumbo-passport' containing ninety pages instead of the usual thirty. These cost £10, and are heavy and bulky. A wife may be included in her husband's passport provided that, if the marriage took place before 1 January 1949, she was a British subject at the time of the marriage, or has become a British subject by registration. A wife who is a citizen of another Commonwealth country cannot be included unless she is also a citizen of the United Kingdom and Colonies. Children under the age of sixteen may also be included on their father's passport; an individual passport is issued to a child under five only in exceptional circumstances.

Although it is more economical for a husband and wife to have a joint passport, a problem can arise in the case of illness as, although the husband can travel alone on such a document, his wife cannot; and should they have to travel separately in such circumstances, special arrangements will have to be made through the nearest British Consulate. The deputy leader of the party must also hold a full passport.

Other adults – Other adults travelling in the party may hold a full British passport as described above; alternatively, they may travel on a British Visitor's passport which is valid for one year, and costs £1.50. British Visitor's passports are valid for visits of up to three months to the following countries, but may not be used for taking up employment or for gainful activity:

Andorra	Liechtenstein
Austria	Luxembourg
Belgium	Malta
Canada[1]	Monaco
Denmark[2, 3]	Netherlands[3]
Federal Republic of Germany[4]	Norway[3]
Finland[3,]	Portugal[5]
France[6]	San Marino
Gibraltar	Spain[7]
Greece[8]	Sweden[7]
Iceland[3]	Switzerland
Italy[9]	Turkey

A British Visitor's passport can be issued only to a British subject who is a citizen of the United Kingdom and Colonies, and who is resident in the United Kingdom, the Isle of Man or the Channel Islands.

Pupils travelling on individual passports – Pupils holding valid individual full or visitor's passports may travel under the protection of these documents, subject to the restrictions on the use of British Visitor's passports noted above. When a full passport is issued to a child under the age of sixteen, it has an initial validity for five years. It can then be renewed for a further period of five years on production of a new photograph if the holder is

[1] A British Visitor's passport must be valid for three months beyond the last day the visitor is in Canada, and is not valid for travel to the United States of America.

[2] Including the Faroe Islands and Greenland.

[3] Visits to this group of countries as a whole must not exceed three months in any period of nine months.

[4] And, for travellers by air only, the Western Sector of Berlin.

[5] Including Madeira and the Azores.

[6] Including Corsica.

[7] Including the Balearic and Canary Islands.

[8] Including the Greek Islands, but not available for the overland routes through Yugoslavia.

[9] Including Sicily, Sardinia and Elba.

still under twenty-one years of age. No fee is charged for this renewal.

Collective passports – Collective passports are issued for approved parties of students and members of the Scout and Guide movements. Not less than five, nor more than fifty, persons may be included in a collective passport, which is not acceptable in some countries where the members of the party are staying in separate households.[1] The leader and deputy leader must be at least twenty-one years of age, and must hold valid full British passports.

Any child born in the United Kingdom or a place which is still a colony, or whose father was so born, and who is under the age of eighteen on the date of departure may be included. If the birth qualifications are not satisfied, the Passport Office must be consulted at an early stage so that, if the child is not eligible to travel on a collective passport on some other ground, there is time to apply for an individual passport to the appropriate High Commission, the Irish Embassy or the appropriate Consulate. Nationality is the one test which is applied, and only those who would be entitled to hold a United Kingdom passport in their own right will be included. Citizens of independent Commonwealth countries, Irish citizens and foreign nationals will not be accepted.

Every person included in a collective passport who will be sixteen years of age on the date of re-entry must carry a personal identity card bearing his photograph. These cards, signed by the headmaster or headmistress, must be submitted, with the photograph attached, for authorization with the application for the collective passport.

The application must be accompanied by a supporting letter from the governors or the head of the school. Maintained schools should obtain the support of their local education authority; independent schools must state that they are registered, provisionally registered or deemed to be registered by the Registrar of Independent Schools at the DES. The Passport Office may also require written evidence of the consent of the pupils' parents or legal guardians.

[1] See pages 324–5.

The fee for a collective passport is £5; there is no charge for the supporting identity cards.

Whilst it is a general rule that no person may hold, or be included in, more than one United Kingdom passport, there is no objection to the inclusion of an individual passport holder on a collective passport. Individual passports can cause delay at frontier controls, and there is always a risk that they may be lost. Each has to be collected in advance of the journey for currency control entries to be made. In general it is preferable to include all eligible pupils on the collective passport, and to persuade them to leave their individual documents at home.

All persons named in a collective passport must travel and remain together. If a member of the party becomes separated, or is unable to return with the party, the leader must inform the local authorities, and must report the fact to frontier passport controls. The nearest British Consul must also be informed so that he can make arrangements for the issue of individual travel documents.

The application for the collective passport must name all countries to be visited, even if only for a day excursion. It is also a useful practice to include countries through which a diversion may be necessary. If, for example, a journey to Italy is planned by rail through France and Switzerland, and is disrupted at the last moment by, say, a railway strike in France, it might be possible to re-route the party through Belgium, Holland and West Germany if these countries are named in the collective passport.

For some countries visas or more than one copy of the collective passport may be required. In some countries every pupil must carry an identity card. The current details are set out in the next section.

Teachers from independent countries of the Commonwealth, or who are citizens of Eire or foreign nationals, should ensure that their papers are in order to permit re-entry before leaving the country with a school journey party. They can receive advice on the appropriate action to be taken from their High Commission, Embassy or Consulate.

Issue of passports – Arrangements for the issue of passports by local offices of the Department of Employment were withdrawn at the beginning of 1974, and there is now no Central Passport

Office which can deal wih applications from any part of the country. Clive House has now become the local Passport Office for Greater London, Kent, Surrey and Sussex, and applications can be dealt with only by the local office for the applicant's home address. The Passport Offices are:

London: Clive House, 70 Petty France, London, SW1H 9HD.

Liverpool: 5th Floor, India Buildings, Water Street, Liverpool, L2 0QZ.

Newport: Olympia House, Upper Dock Street, Newport (Mon.), NPT 1XA.

Peterborough: Westwood, Peterborough, PE3 6TG.

Glasgow: 1st Floor, Empire House, 131 West Nile Street Glasgow, G1 2RY.

Applications should be forwarded at least three weeks before the passport is required. A duty officer is available for very limited periods on Saturdays to deal with passports required for an emergency such as death or serious illness. The applicant must produce documentary proof of the emergency.

16 Visas, etc.

No visas or additional copies of the collective passport are required in the following countries:

Austria[1]	Luxembourg
Belgium[2]	Malta
France[3]	Monaco
German Federal Republic[1,4]	Netherlands
Greece	Portugal
Iceland	Spain
Liechtenstein	Switzerland[3]
Turkey	

[1] Each child, including those under sixteen, must carry an identity card with a photograph.

[2] If the children are staying in individual households, each child, including those under sixteen, must carry an identity card with a photograph.

[3] If the children are staying in individual households, a collective passport is not acceptable.

[4] These arrangements also apply to parties travelling *by air* to the Western Sectors of Berlin.

Copies of the collective passport must be produced at the points of entry and departure in the following countries, but no visa is required:

Denmark[1]   Finland[1, 2]

Norway[3]

Visas are required by the following countries:

Italy[1, 4]   Yugoslavia[1, 5]

An endorsement is required if Sweden[1,2] is the first Nordic country to be visited.[6] The application for endorsement, enclosing the collective passport and one copy for each point of entry and departure, should be sent to the Swedish Consulate-General, 23 North Row, London, N.1.

Schools taking part in cruises should consult the shipping company responsible for the organization.

In the case of visits planned to countries other than those listed above, schools should ask the Consulates concerned whether collective passports are accepted, and what requirements must be met concerning visas.

17 HM Customs

Smuggling is a crime, and the penalties are heavy. Teachers travelling with school journey parties should make it a point of honour to observe the Customs regulations, and to do their best to ensure that the pupils follow their example.

Before the journey begins, teachers should advise children not to bring home with them large quantities of goods which attract Customs duty or value added tax. The pupils should be instructed

[1] Each child, including those under 16, must carry an identity card with a photograph.

[2] The minimum number of persons to be included in a collective passport is ten.

[3] A copy of the collective passport is required at the point of entry only.

[4] The application, enclosing the collective passport and one copy for each point of entry, should be made to the Italian Consulate-General, 38 Eaton Place, London, S.W.1.

[5] Enquiries shold be made of the Yugoslav Consulate, 19 Upper Phillimore Gardens, London W.8.

[6] The Nordic countries are Sweden, Norway, Denmark and Finland.

to make a complete list of all items which they have obtained abroad, with their approximate value, so that this can be handed to the Customs officer should the traveller be stopped. Receipts or guarantees should be carried if valuable items such as foreign cameras and watches are being taken abroad, to establish proof either that they were purchased in this country, or that duty has been paid on them previously.

Counterfeit coins, dangerous drugs, firearms and ammunition, flick-knives, plants and bulbs, radio transmitters (including walkie-talkies), meat and poultry not fully cooked, and live animals are prohibited or restricted.

Travellers from a country in membership of the EEC[1] may bring items into the United Kingdom without paying duty:

   (a) 300 cigarettes, or 150 cigarillos, or 75 cigars, or 400 grammes of tobacco;[2]

   (b) 3 litres of still table wine and 1½ litres of alcoholic drink over 38·8° proof,[3] or 3 litres not over 38·8° proof or fortified or sparkling wine;[2]

   (c) 75 grammes (3 fluid ounces) of perfume;

   (d) ⅜ litre of toilet water; and

   (e) other goods not exceeding £50 in value.

Travellers from a country outside the European Economic Community may bring the following items into the United Kingdom free of duty:

   (a) 200 cigarettes, or 100 cigarillos, or 50 cigars, or 250 grammes of tobacco;[2]

   (b) 2 litres of still table wine and 1 litre of alcoholic drink over 38·8° proof,[3] or 2 litres not over 38·8° proof or fortified or sparkling wine;[2]

   (c) 50 grammes (2 fluid ounces) of perfume;

   (d) ¼ litre of toilet water; and

   (e) other goods not exceeding £10 in value.

[1] Belgium, Denmark, France, West Germany, Eire, Italy, Luxembourg, the Netherlands and the United Kingdom, but not the Channel Islands.
[2] Persons under seventeen may not import tobacco or alcoholic drinks free of duty.   [3] 22° Gay-Lussac.

Goods bought in a duty and tax-free shop in the Common Market, or under similar conditions of sale on a ship or aircraft, are treated as though they were purchased outside the EEC; and the lower level of allowances applies.

Any traveller entering Britain with goods acquired abroad (whether by purchase or gift) in excess of the allowances quoted above must pass through the red channel at the Customs control in order to declare the excess. Those bringing back items entirely within the duty-free allowances may go through the green channel, but they may be stopped by a Customs officer in the course of a spot check.

18 Exchange visits

Schools often arrange exchanges by which a pupil from overseas spends some time staying with an English family in this country in return for a visit on a reciprocal basis. Every endeavour should be made to ensure that the exchange is well matched, and that the British home has the facilities necessary for a successful visit to this country. It is also wise to make some inquiries about the visitor from overseas.

It should be pointed out to the parents that such arrangements, by their very nature, are of the order of 'blind dates', and the school can accept no responsibility for any mischances which may arise.

19 Finance

School journey accounts – All monies received must be paid promptly into a separate bank account, and a careful record must be made. Most local education authorities include school journey accounts in their routine audits. If this is not done, it is desirable that the accounts should be audited by at least two persons not connected with the organization of the journey. Under no circumstances should such funds be placed, even temporarily, in a private account.

Pocket money – In the case of foreign journeys it is often possible to get a better rate of exchange by collecting pocket money with the school journey subscriptions, and changing in bulk. It is useful to have a regular time each day for the issue of pocket money, and to warn pupils who appear to be overspending early in the journey so that they are not out of funds before the visit ends.

Currency control – The law relating to exchange control varies from time to time in accordance with the economic climate. Those responsible for the organization of school journeys abroad should consult their bankers at an early date so that arrangements for the transfer of currency can be made in good time. Penalties for breaking the law in this respect are heavy.

Emergency float – The organizer of a school journey abroad must have sufficient funds available to meet any emergency which might reasonably be expected to arise. Although the United Kingdom now has reciprocal agreements in the social security field with a large number of countries,[1] these are intended to apply to British nationals living in those states and, in any case, they do not cover such matters as medical attention or hospital fees. It is by no means unusual for these fees to be demanded in advance in continental countries. It is no good assuring the medical authorities that the members of the party are adequately insured: payment has to be made on the spot, and the insurance issue settled later. A teacher, one of whose pupils has acute appendicitis which needs immediate surgery, is in an impossible position if he cannot find perhaps £100 or more to get the boy admitted to hospital.

Occasionally the British consulate may be able to help, but the diplomatic service, as many stranded Britons have found, is not in business as a moneylender. People travelling abroad are expected to exercise reasonable prudence in planning for all contingencies.

On Good Friday 1967 the author was in charge, in Switzerland, of a party of about two hundred and fifty pupils and staff from ten different schools. One of the masters died after a heart attack during the early hours of the morning, and the necessary arrangements had to be undertaken in a Roman Catholic canton which had, effectively, closed down for business until the following Tuesday. The doctor would not even type out the certificate of the cause of death until he received his fee of fifty francs. By

[1] See pages 130–31.

the end of the day, the funeral director's account, the air charges for a flight from Zürich to London, the cost of a hearse to the airport, a number of telephone calls to England, and various other items had run up a bill of £130. Ultimately, everything except the telephone charges was recovered from the insurers, but the ready cash had to be found immediately.

Eurocheques – Holders of British cheque cards can cash cheques at banks in Europe which display the Eurocheque symbol. Cheques are drawn in sterling to a maximum of £30, payment being made in any currency desired and available, subject to the bank's deduction of commission. Money drawn in this way may be used only for travel purposes, and any balance of foreign currency remaining unused at the end of the journey must be surrendered to a bank in the United Kingdom within one month of return. This facility is a valuable additional safeguard for a teacher, who can obtain full details from his bank.

20 The law abroad

Many teachers with long experience of taking school parties abroad have also had some experience of dealing with the forces of law and order at sometime or another.

Pupils must be reminded that so long as they are guests in another country they are amenable to its law, without being released entirely from their obligations under the law of their homeland.

Not only do continental legal systems differ widely from our own; police methods are also different, and the language barrier may make problems seem even more intractable.

In the event of serious difficulty a teacher should get in touch with the nearest British consulate. This is especially important if an arrest is threatened.

21 Christian Scientists

Teachers are sometimes concerned about the legal risks involved when pupils who are Christian Scientists are included in the party. Party leaders feel that, should such a pupil need medical attention of a kind which they would provide for their own children, they are fettered in their discretion to act *in loco parentis* by the conscientious rejection of usual medical treatment. If they call in a doctor they have offended the religious conviction of the pupil and his parent; if they fail to do so, and the child dies, will they be held legally responsible?

These fears are completely groundless. Christian Scientists rely on the practice of their religion for healing because they find it efficacious; they do not neglect conditions which others would treat medically and, since most European countries have a number of Christian Science practitioners, parents would expect teachers in charge of school journey parties to seek the assistance of such a practitioner with the same urgency with which they would consult a doctor in the case of a pupil who is not a Christian Scientist.

The Christian Science Committee on Publication for Great Britain and Ireland have produced a form of request for exemption from medical treatment which indemnifies both the teaching staff and the local education authority. The form gives the name and address of the nearest Christian Science practitioner to the school journey base, and is so clearly worded that it is worth reproducing in full:

> I wish my son/daughter................, on religious grounds, to be exempted from emergency operations, from all medical treatment, vaccination and/or immunization (except where legally required for entry into a foreign country) in connection with the proposed school journey to ....
> To the best of my knowledge and belief he/she is and has been in normal good health and is free from all communicable diseases.
>
> In consideration of these exemptions, it is understood that I accept complete responsibility for the health of this minor, and I hereby release the Local Education Committee and those in charge of the school journey from any liability for unforeseen circumstances which might arise during the approved journey, by virtue of these exemptions. I request that, should an emergency arise, the person in charge of the school party shall first try to contact me by telephone or the Christian Science practitioner named below. In the event that neither the undersigned nor the practitioner can be immediately located, the school

authorities may take such measures as on medical advice appear to them to be absolutely necessary for the protection of life, having regard to my wishes as expressed above.

This form should remove any qualms. In the first place the party leader is asked to act strictly in accordance with the dictates of the parent's conscience, a procedure which is strictly in accordance with the spirit of the 1944 Act. Secondly, both he and the local authority are indemnified for so doing. This is different from the kind of indemnity issued by the school for the parent to sign,[1] because in this case the indemnity is offered by the parent, and not requested by the school. Thirdly, if the channels of healing desired by the parent are not available, it is recognized that the teacher must make a responsible and conscientious decision *in loco parentis* which may involve recourse to ordinary medical treatment.

So far as immunization is concerned, Article 83 of the International Health Regulations enables those with conscientious objections to claim exemption, even in unusual circumstances.

Nor need a head, or the parents of children who are not Christian Scientists, have any fears about allowing a teacher, who is a Christian Scientist to take charge of a school journey party. If a member of the party were taken ill such a teacher would not allow his religious convictions to intrude, and he would arrange for medical treatment such as the child's natural parent would wish.[2]

22 Jehovah's Witnesses

Some teachers are also concerned about including Jehovah's Witnesses in a school journey party because of a fear of complications should a child need medical treatment.

Jehovah's Witnesses have no code of rules, each individual being

[1] See pages 306–7.
[2] If there is any difficulty in obtaining the indemnity form locally when it is known that a Christian Science pupil is taking part in a school journey, a copy can be supplied from the office of the Christian Science Committee on Publication, Ingersoll House, 9 Kingsway, London, WC2B 6XF. I am greatly indebted to the District Manager, Mr Bryan G. Pope, for his kindness and help in preparing this section.

guided by his own understanding and application of Biblical principles. They accept any form of treatment which does not involve the introduction of blood or blood fractions into the body. The Houston Texas heart transplant team now rarely use blood transfusions, having found substitutes more effective, and Jehovah's Witnesses freely accept blood substitutes. All forms of immunization are acceptable.

It is for parents who are Jehovah's Witnesses to make their wishes clear to leaders of school journey parties in advance. No such parent would authorize a teacher to override his religious convictions, and it would be most unwise for a party leader *in loco parentis* to do so. Since the only problem is one of blood transfusion, and there are now several substitutes which are acceptable both to the medical profession and to Jehovah's Witnesses, the problem should not arise in any reasonably foreseeable circumstances.

Jehovah's Witnesses do not eat food which has not been bled, such as some poultry, or which is partly made of blood, such as black pudding. A Jehovah's witness who is in doubt about food which is set before him will merely leave it.

In general, a teacher who is a Jehovah's Witness in charge of a school journey party will follow the wishes of a pupil's parent with regard to medical treatment. It is possible, however, that he might not feel able to authorize treatment which he believes to be contrary to the law of God. Again, since this is confined to one area where medically acceptable substitutes are available, this should cause no worries.

XIV

CONCERTS AND PLAYS

1 Licensing of hall

Stage plays – Before a hall is used for the public presentation of stage plays, a licence must be granted by the licensing authority[1] to the owner or licensee of the premises. In the case of a school, the licence is normally taken out by the head. The procedure for dealing with applications for licences varies somewhat from county to county, and some authorities grant only an occasional licence for halls which are used by amateurs. In such cases a fresh application must be made for every production. Others also grant what is called a restricted licence which authorizes the use of the hall for drama-tic presentations on not more than a specified number of nights during its currency, normally a year. In some cases an authority issues the licence through its administrative machinery; others require an application to be made through a magistrates' court.

In Greater London the Greater London Council is the licensing authority; elsewhere in England and Wales the district council has been given the responsibility of issuing such licences.[2]

An applicant for the grant or transfer of a licence must give at least twenty-one days' notice to the licensing authority and to the chief officer of police of his intention to apply, and must provide such particulars as are required. In the case of an application for renewal not less than twenty-eight days' notice of the intention to apply must be given.

If the application is for one or more specified occasions only, the period required for notice of intention to apply (whether an

[1] Theatres Act 1968, s. 12 (1).
[2] Theatres Act 1968, s. 18 (1) (*a*); and (*b*) as amended by the Local Government Act 1972, s. 204 (6).

original application, or one for transfer or renewal) is reduced to fourteen days, and the chief officer of police need not be informed.[1]

The Secretary of State (in this case, the Home Secretary) prescribes the scale of fees to be charged for licences; except that no fee is payable if the licensing authority are satisfied that the play or plays to be performed are of an educational or other like purpose.[2]

Before a licence is granted, the hall is inspected to ensure that the safety of the public is adequately secured by the provision of sufficient exists, gangways and fire extinguishers. The licence is granted subject to such conditions as may be endorsed upon it, and these must be rigidly observed. The police, the fire and the licensing authorities may enter the hall at any time during a performance to satisfy themselves that the conditions are being observed.

Such an inspection may be very thorough. One fire officer refused to accept an assurance that the scenery had been fire-proofed in accordance with the regulations, and tried the effect of his cigarette lighter on some flimsy and combustible-looking flies. They stood up to the test but, with only forty minutes to go before the curtain rang up on the first performance, it is not difficult to imagine what the effect would have been if they had not been treated.

On the death of the licensee the licence continues in the name of his personal representatives for three months unless it is transferred, cancelled or revoked in the meantime. It then expires, unless the licensing authority is satisfied that an extension is necessary for winding up the deceased's estate. This last contingency might conceivably occur in an independent school: in a maintained or direct-grant school steps should be taken to transfer the licence within the period.[3]

The licence may be cancelled on the holder's application. In the case of premises which are being constructed, extended or altered, the licensing authority may grant a provisional licence. This does

[1] Theatres Act 1968, Schedule 1. 2.
[2] Theatres Act 1968, Schedule 1. 3 (1).
[3] Theatres Act 1968, Schedule 1. 4.

not become effective until it has been confirmed on completion of the building operations.[1] The licensing authority may impose any restrictions they consider necessary in the interests of physical safety or health, or in connection with an exhibition, demonstration or performance of hypnotism within the meaning of the Hypnotism Act 1952.[2] On the licensee's application the authority may vary the terms of the licence, subject to any conditions or restrictions within the terms of the Act, as they see fit to impose.[3]

'Any person concerned in the organization or management of a public performance of a play, or any other person knowing or having reasonable cause to suspect that such a performance will be given who allows, lets or otherwise makes available unlicensed premises for that purpose is guilty of an offence.' So is the holder of a licence or any other person who knowingly allows any of the terms of the licence to be broken. The licensee is not guilty if he can prove that the breach took place without his consent or connivance, and that he used all due diligence to avoid it. The penalty on summary conviction of these offences is a fine of up to £200, or a maximum of three months' imprisonment, or both. If the licensee is convicted, the licensing authority may revoke the licence.[4]

If an offence is committed by a body corporate, and is proved to have been committed with the consent or connivance of, or attributable to the neglect of any director, manager, secretary or similar officer, or any person purporting to act in such a capacity, that individual is guilty, as well as the body corporate, and he may be prosecuted and punished accordingly.[5]

Music and dancing – The stage play licence does not cover the use of the building for music and dancing, for which a separate licence is required. Similarly, a music and dancing licence does not authorize the public presentation of stage plays.

Where annual licences are obtained for these purposes, it is advisable to apply for them as a matter of routine at the same time

[1] Theatres Act 1968, Schedule 1. 5 and 6.
[2] Theatres Act 1968, proviso to s. 1 (2).
[3] Theatres Act 1968, Schedule 1. 7.
[4] Theatres Act 1968, s. 13.
[5] Theatres Act 1968, s. 16.

each year. This avoids the possibility of the application being overlooked immediately before a performance.

2 Public performance of plays and their direction

A play is:

(*a*) any dramatic piece, whether involving improvisation or not, which is given wholly or in part by one or more persons actually present and performing; and in which the whole, or a major proportion of what is done by the person or persons performing, whether by way of speech, singing or action, involves the playing of a role; and

(*b*) any ballet given wholly or in part by one or more persons actually present and performing, whether or not it falls within paragraph (*a*) of this definition.[1]

'A public performance includes any performance in a public place within the meaning of the Public Order Act 1936[2] and any performance which the public or any section thereof are permitted to attend, whether on payment or otherwise.[3]

For the purposes of the Act the word 'premises' includes any place,[4] and it is explicitly stated that no other licence is necessary for any premises merely because plays are presented there. In this context any occasional music played at a performance of a play is treated as part of that performance provided the time taken by the music on any day is less than one quarter of the time taken by the performances on that day.[5] This of course applies to incidental music, and not to music which forms an integral part of a performance such as the accompaniment to a ballet. Provided that

[1] Theatres Act 1968, s. 18 (1).

[2] A public place is defined as 'any highway, public park or garden, any sea beach, and any public bridge, road, lane, footway, square, court, alley or passage, whether a thoroughfare or not; and includes any open space to which, for the time being, the public have, or are permitted to have, access, whether on payment or otherwise'. Public Order Act 1936, s. 9 (1).

[3] Theatres Act 1968, s. 18 (1).

[4] Theatres Act 1968, s. 18 (1).

[5] Theatres Act 1968, s. 12 (2) and (3).

the incidental music is confined within the specified limits, a music and dancing licence is not required for the performance of a stage play.

A person is not treated as presenting a play merely because he takes part as a performer; but if, as a performer in a play directed by someone else, he performs without excuse otherwise than in accordance with that person's direction, he will be treated as a person directing the performance. The director of a play shall be held to have directed a performance notwithstanding the fact that he was absent from that particular performance. This definition is necessary for precision in connection with sections 2 (obscene performances), 5 (incitement to racial hatred) and 6 (provocation of a breach of the peace). A person who is merely a performer shall not be held to have aided or abetted an offence under one of these sections merely by reason of being a performer.[1]

3 Censorship of plays

Prior to the operation of the Theatres Act 1968 no stage play could be produced publicly until it had been licensed by the Lord Chamberlain, in accordance with the Theatres Act 1843, which was completely repealed by the new statute. In granting a licence, a licensing authority may not impose any term, condition or restriction as to the nature of the plays to be presented or as to the manner of their performance. This prohibition is subject to the proviso already mentioned dealing with physical health, safety and hypnotism.[2]

Nevertheless, certain restrictions remain. Within one month of the first performance of a play based on a script, a free copy of the script must be delivered to the British Museum, in default of which the person presenting the performance may be fined a sum of up to £5. This requirement applies only to plays which have not been publicly performed.[3]

The removal of the Lord Chamberlain's powers of censorship has not produced a state of affairs which allows complete licence

[1] Theatres Act 1968, s. 18 (2).
[2] Theatres Act 1968, s. 1; see also page 335.
[3] Theatres Act 1968, s. 11; see also s. 7 (2) (a) and (b).

to those who present plays. The 1968 Act has substituted a number of statutory offences in a number of fields:

Obscene performances – A performance is obscene if, taken as a whole, its effect would be such as to tend to deprave and corrupt persons likely to attend. So far as teachers are concerned, an important circumstance which the courts would consider would, of course, be the age of any members of the audience. Under this section no person may be prosecuted for a common law offence alleging that the performance was obscene, indecent, offensive or injurious to morality; nor for the common law offence of conspiring to corrupt public morals. A person cannot be convicted under this head if it is proved that the performance was justified as being for the public good in the interests of drama, opera, ballet or any other art, or of literature or learning. Expert evidence as to the artistic, literary or other merits of the production may be called by the prosecution and defence. On summary conviction the maximum penalty is a fine of £400 or a term of six months' imprisonment. On indictment (which must be commenced within two years of the offence), the penalty may be a fine, the upper limit of which is not specified, or imprisonment for up to three years, or both.[1]

Defamation – Defamatory words spoken during the performance of a play, although impermanent in form, are now statutory libel both for civil and criminal purposes.[2] So, in similar circumstances, are pictures, visual images, gestures and other methods of signifying meaning.[3] The crime remains a common law offence.

Incitement to racial hatred – It is an offence if a play performed in public involves threatening, abusive or insulting words intended to stir up hatred against any section of the public in Great Britain distinguished by colour, race, or ethnic national origins. It is also an offence if the tendency of the performance as a whole is likely to stir up hatred against such groups. It should be noted that for the first of these offences it is necessary to prove intention, whereas for the second the mere likelihood of fomenting racial hatred is

[1] Theatres Act 1968, ss. 2 and 3.
[2] The law of defamation is dealt with in Chapter XVIII, pages 394–402.
[3] Theatres Act 1968, s. 4.

sufficient. In either case the person responsible is the person who presents or directs the play, whether for gain or not. The amateur producer is as vulnerable as the professional. The maximum penalty on summary conviction is a fine of £200 or six months imprisonment, or both; on indictment a fine of up to £1,000, a maximum of two years' imprisonment, or both.[1]

Provocation of breach of peace – It is an offence if a play produced in public involves threatening, abusive or insulting words or behaviour and either the person (whether for gain or not) who presented or directed the performance intended to provoke a breach of the peace; or the performance, taken as a whole, was likely to occasion a breach of the peace. The person presenting or directing the performance is liable in either case. On summary conviction he can be fined up to £100 or imprisoned for a maximum of three months, or both. On indictment the maxima rise to £500 or twelve months imprisonment, or both.[2]

Institution of proceedings – Prosecutions for the statutory offences set out in the Act or for the common law offence of libel in the course of the performance of a play may be commenced only by, or with the consent of, the Attorney-General.[3] This does not, of course, affect the right of anyone believing himself to have been libelled to commence a civil action. In the case of a play based on a written script, which for this purpose includes the music and stage or other directions, that script is admissible in evidence and the performance is held to have been in accordance with it unless the contrary be proved. If a police officer of above the rank of superintendent believes that one of the statutory offences has been, or is likely to be, committed he may make an order requiring the script to be produced and the opportunity to make a copy. A copy so made will be accepted by the court as the script on which the performance was based. Failure, without reasonable excuse, to comply with such a requirement can lead to a fine of up to £100 on summary conviction.[4]

---

[1] Theatres Act 1968, s. 5.
[2] Theatres Act 1968, s. 6.
[3] Theatres Act 1968, s. 8.
[4] Theatres Act 1968, ss. 9 and 10.

4 Infringement of copyright

The law of copyright is dealt with generally in a later chapter.[1]
In connection with plays and concerts it should be noted that
whilst it is not an infringement to write a short extract on the
blackboard, or an overhead projector transparency, for teaching
purposes, it is illegal to duplicate copyright material or to reproduce substantial portions, e.g. parts for plays, so that the purchase
of copies becomes unnecessary.

5 Royalties on stage plays

It is a condition of the performance of most stage plays in which
copyright still subsists, that a fee known as a royalty should be
paid to the author. This is usually done through his agents.

Royalties must be paid in advance, and a licence is then issued
for the performance. Authors are sometimes asked to waive the
fees due to them for the production of their plays, particularly
when they are being presented on behalf of charity. Unless there
is a note in the printed copies to the effect that the playwright is
prepared to do this in particular circumstances, such requests are
grossly unfair. No author wishes to appear ungenerous, but royalties are the due reward which a writer receives for his work, and
at least he should be allowed to choose for himself the charities to
which he wishes to subscribe.

In some cases, even when royalties are paid, it may be a condition that an announcement appears in all printed matter stating
that the play is produced by arrangement with a particular agent.
Failure to observe the conditions of presentation may result in
action being taken against the school.

Some copyright plays carry a statement that they may be freely
produced by amateurs provided that the ownership of the copyright is acknowledged. This may be taken as a general licence,
subject to any conditions stated.

6 The Performing Right Society

Under the Copyright Acts, the performance of copyright musical
matter is subject to a fee similar in nature to the stage play

[1] See Chapter XV, pages 344–69.

royalty. Most composers and music publishers belong to the Performing Right Society which acts as their agent to collect and distribute their fees. Through its links with similar organizations in more than thirty countries, for which it is the agent in Great Britain, it is able to license performance of the works of nearly 200,000 composers, authors and music publishers of many nationalities.

Schools affiliated to the Music Masters' Association of the Incorporated Society of Musicians may take out an annual licence covering all performances for a very low fee. In other cases the form should be obtained from the Society,[1] and when this has been completed the performer will be notified of the fee to be paid. Failure to ensure that these formalities have been completed, at least a week before the performance, will result in action by the Society.

Individual application is not necessary if the proprietor of the hall has an annual licence, or the local education authority has a similar arrangement. In such cases, a return should be made on the appropriate form to the licensee, who will forward it to the Society which then makes arrangements for the composer and publisher to receive their fees.

The Performing Right Society does not make a charge for performances in churches during religious worship, or at competitive musical festivals. Fees are, however, payable in respect of winners' or other concerts at the end of such festivals.

7 Gramophone records and pre-recorded tapes

The copyright in gramophone records and pre-recorded tapes is vested in the manufacturer, and the agent for the collection of fees is Phonographic Performance, Ltd, from whom licences can be obtained.[2] Such licences may be annual or occasional, but they are granted only to individuals or societies, and not to the owner of a hall to cover all users.

This licence covers merely the mechanical reproduction of the

[1] The Performing Right Society Ltd, 29–33 Berners Street, London, WiP 4AA.

[2] Phonographic Performance, Ltd, 62 Oxford Street, London, WiN 0AN.

music, and does not extend to the music itself. A separate fee in respect of the music may be payable to the Performing Right Society under the conditions noted in the preceding section.

8 Broadcast music

It is an offence under the Copyright Act 1956 and the Performers' Protection Acts 1958 and 1963 to make records of broadcasts, or video-tapes or records of telecasts, other than for private purposes, without the prior approval of the broadcasting authority. Neither may a telecast be shown in public to a paying audience. If, for some particular reason, it is wished to do this, it is essential to obtain permission in advance from the broadcasting authority, the owners of any copyright material and the performers taking part. Both the British Broadcasting Corporation and the Independent Television Authority are protected by the Acts.

9 Private performances

The private performance of a copyright play by a school company to an audience composed *entirely* of members of the school is not an infringement of copyright.[1] The admission of one member of the public however, and for this purpose parents, unless they are directly connected with the school organization, are treated as members of the public, would render the school liable in damages. The point at issue here is that the author's rights might be injured if such a person, because he had seen the play at the school, failed to go to a performance at a theatre where royalties are paid.

In all cases of doubt about the nature of a private performance, it is advisable to consult the author or his agents in advance.

10 Use of schools by outside bodies

Some heads have encountered difficulties because their local education authorities have held them responsible for ensuring that outside individuals and bodies using the school have complied with the law.

In 1972 Sir William Alexander,[2] the Secretary of the Association of Education Committees, wrote to all chief education officers,

[1] See page 360.   [2] Now Lord Alexander.

pointing out that a distinction should be made between domestic use by the school where the head has a clearly defined responsibility as part of his duty to control the internal organization, management and discipline; and the use of the school by outsiders for the presentation of stage plays and the like.

Sir William advised that in cases falling within the latter category it is the local education authority's responsibility, not the head's, to ensure that the necessary licences have been obtained under the Provision of the Theatres Act 1968, and that their conditions are observed.

This would presumably apply to all other legal requirements in connection with entertainments organized by outside bodies.

By analogy, in a voluntary school this responsibility falls on the managers or governors, and not the head.

Heads are strongly advised, when approached for the use of a school for entertainments by outside bodies, to pass such requests to the local education authority, managers or governors as may be appropriate, and to do nothing which might be construed as suggesting that they had taken part in the organization of the entertainment or that they had purported to act on behalf of the owners of the school.

It is for the authority, managers or governors to require the hirer to provide such assurances, indemnities and evidence of adequate insurance as may seem necessary.

11 Performances by children

The law relating to professional public performances by children has already been dealt with in connection with the employment of children and young persons.[1] These restrictions do not, of course, apply to children taking part as amateurs in school productions.

[1] See pages 199–200.

XV

COPYRIGHT

1 Copyright and schools

In 1970 Mr Ronald Barker, the secretary of the Publishers Association, complained that many educational establishments were unintentionally breaking copyright law by the use they were making of photocopying apparatus: 'If the practice is allowed to an unlimited degree,' he said, 'the time will quickly come when no one can afford to publish anything.' In his book,[1] published in the same year, Mr Barker added: 'The fact that it is cheaper to steal someone else's property rather than buy it does not make it right to steal.'

In the last edition of this book the law of copyright was dealt with in less than two pages. The past nine years, however, have witnessed a remarkable escalation in the amount of copying undertaken in schools, much of it undoubtedly illegal. Teachers may claim that they are acting only in the interests of their children, but this defence availed little to a father who pleaded in the nineteenth century that he had stolen bread for his starving offspring. In the light of recent development and the on-going discussions designed to control and regularize modern practice, it is now necessary to devote a whole chapter to this subject.

The intensification of dishonest copying practices in educational institutions in recent years is due to a number of factors. Inflation has had a marked effect on the price of books and other copyright learning materials. Capitation allowances have not kept pace with rising costs and as the chairman and director of the Educational Publishers Council pointed out in a letter to *The*

[1] R. E. Barker: *Photocopying Practices in the United Kingdom* (Faber 1970).

344

Times[1] the increased amounts spent by schools represent a cutting back in the actual number of copies bought. A second factor is the development of educational techniques which postulate greatly increased flexibility, and the use of a vast amount of instant topical source material obtained much more quickly by copying than by waiting for the supplies department to deal with a requisition. Thirdly, there has suddenly become available a large range of relatively cheap and versatile reproductive hardware such as photocopiers and tape recorders. Finally, the growth of teachers' centres, often lavishly equipped and staffed to prepare material of this kind, and the appointment of media resource officers in many schools and colleges, have increased the facility with which material may be reproduced.

2 History of copyright

The concept of copyright dates back to the invention of printing, when it first became possible, on a large scale, to make multiple copies of the actual form in which an author had put his thoughts on paper. From time to time the common law right was reinforced by statute, and extended to include engravings (1734), sculpture (1814), performing rights in plays (1833), similar rights in musical works (1842), paintings, drawings and photographs (1862) and gramophone records (1911).

The need for the reciprocal international recognition of copyright holders' rights led to the Berne Convention of 1885, effect being given to its decisions in English law by the International Copyright Act 1886. A further convention was held in Berlin in 1905, after which the Copyright Act 1911 consolidated the law and expressly put an end to common law copyright. The Berne Convention was reversed in Rome in 1928 and in Brussels in 1948, the latter meeting paving the way for the present statute, the Copyright Act 1956, which repealed the whole of the 1911 Act with the exception of three sections, one of which is that dealing with the delivery of copies of works to the British Museum.

The United Kingdom is also a signatory of the 1952 Geneva (Universal) Copyright Convention, commonly called the UCC.

[1] 24 October 1970.

The rights of performers are protected by the Dramatic and Musical Performers' Protection Act 1958 and the Performers' Protection Act 1963. The latter Act gives effect in the United Kingdom to the International Convention for the Protection of Performers, Producers of Phonograms and Broadcasting Organizations agreed in Rome in 1961.

3 The nature of copyright

The law of copyright is based on the assumption that the creator of intellectual material is entitled, just as much as any other craftsman, to control the use of what he has produced and to benefit from its use by others. Copyright is therefore a valuable property, and the law gives its owner an exclusive power to do, or to authorize others to do, certain acts in respect of the protected material.

If there were no law of copyright, publishing, in all its forms, would quickly come to an end; for, as soon as a particular and valuable piece of work came into existence, anyone would be free to reproduce it without let or hindrance. The author or originator would not receive the due reward accruing from such acts of piracy; neither would publishers be prepared to undertake the financial risks inherent in their work if the author could not assign to them a right sufficiently wide to protect their interests.

As has been said above, copyright may be owned not only by writers, but also by painters, artists, sculptors and composers. For the sake of brevity the word 'author' when used in this chapter without qualification may be taken to include all originators of material in which copyright subsists.

Also protected by the Copyright Act 1956 are the makers of sound recordings, films and video-tapes[1] to safeguard their rights in these forms. As has already been mentioned, performers are protected by the Dramatic and Musical Performers' Protection Act 1958 and the Performers' Protection Act 1963.

There is no copyright in ideas; but immediately an author

[1] Video-tapes are not specifically mentioned in the Act because the process had not been developed at the time the legislation was passed: presumably, however there is an analogy between them and films.

commits his ideas to some material form, that expression of his ideas becomes copyright without further formality. Publication is not necessary, indeed it has been held that an author dictating work to his secretary who takes it down in shorthand has already established his copyright. The essential element is that the ideas must be established in a material form.

There is no copyright in titles.

By United Kingdom law copyright may be acquired only by 'qualified persons'. A qualified person is an individual who is of British nationality, or who is domiciled or resident in the United Kingdom or in any country to which the Berne and Universal Copyright Conventions extend. Similar rights extend to corporate bodies in these countries, and the domestic law of these states gives similar protection to the owners of copyright in all the subscribing states.

Generally speaking, the original copyright is the property of the author who has the exclusive power to deal in and assign any of rights given to him by law. If, however, the original work is produced in the course of the author's employment, the copyright, subject to any specific terms in the contract of employment, is vested in the employer. This proviso is clearly of some importance to teachers, and is dealt with in a later section.[1]

The rights reserved to the author of a literary, dramatic or musical work are:

    (a) reproduction in any material form;

    (b) publication;

    (c) performance in public;

    (d) broadcasting;

    (e) transmission through a diffusion service;

    (f) adaptation;

    (g) any act in relation to adaptation falling within any of the categories (a) to (e).[2]

Adaptation includes any conversion of a non-dramatic into a dramatic work (or vice versa), whether in the original language or another; translation; or a version wholly or mainly in pictures

---

[1] See pages 351-3.   [2] Copyright Act 1956, s. 2 (5).

suitable for publication in a book, newspapers, magazine or similar periodical. In the case of musical works it includes an arrangement or transcription.[1]

For copyright purposes an artistic work is (irrespective of artistic merit) a painting, sculpture, drawing, engraving, photograph, work of architecture (whether a building or a model for a building) or any other work of artistic craftsmanship not included in these categories.[2]

The rights reserved to the copyright owner are:

(a) reproduction in any material form;

(b) publication;

(c) inclusion in a television broadcast;

(d) transmission of a television broadcast including the work through a diffusion service.[3]

The maker of a sound recording, film or video-tape owns a separate copyright in the recording itself which is additional to the rights of the author. Video-tape recording is a new invention since the passage of the 1956 Act but 'the majority opinion is that a video-tape recording must be treated legally as though it were a film'.[4]

For copyright to subsist, the maker must be a qualified person at the time the recording or film is made. In the case of a sound recording it is the person who owns the recording at the time of making, in the case of films and video-tapes the person or corporate body arranging for it to be made.[5]

In the case of sound recordings the rights reserved are:

(a) making a record embodying the recording;

(b) performing the recording in public;

(c) broadcasting the recording.[6]

[1] Copyright Act 1956, s. 2 (6).

[2] Copyright Act 1956, s. 3 (1). Works of architecture and of artistic craftsmanship must have artistic merit.

[3] Copyright Act 1956, s. 3 (5).

[4] *Copyright and Education* (NCET, 1972), page 6. The National Council for Educational Technology has, since October 1973, become the Council for Educational Technology for the United Kingdom.

[5] Copyright Act 1956, ss. 12 (1) and (4) and 13 (1).

[6] Copyright Act 1956, s. 12 (5).

The restricted acts in the case of films (and, by analogy, video-tapes) are:

(*a*) making a copy;
(*b*) causing it to be seen or heard in public;
(*c*) broadcasting;
(*d*) transmission through a diffusion service.[1]

Similarly, an additional copyright subsists in every published edition of a work where the publisher is a qualified person. It is a breach of copyright to make 'by any photographic or similar process . . . a reproduction of the typographical arrangement of the edition'. This applies only to editions published since 1 June 1957, and is the domestic law in the United Kingdom and Australia; it does not form part of the Berne or Universal Copyright Conventions.[2]

Transfer of copyright

Any person in whom copyright is vested may sell, give away, or otherwise dispose of his rights, e.g. by will. In the case of intestacy copyright forms part of the estate and is dealt with according to the law in such cases.

There have been many cases where authors in urgent need of ready cash have parted with their property in this way, and the publisher has made profits vastly exceeding the amount he has paid for the rights. Once he has sold the copyright, however, the author has no further financial interest in his work. Regrettably, in the past, some publishers put pressure on authors to part with their rights in work which was obviously going to be a money-spinner; but this has never been the practice of reputable houses, and has become much more rare as a result of the vigilance of the Society of Authors.[3]

[1] Copyright Act 1956, s. 13 (5).
[2] Copyright Act 1956, s. 15; and Australian Copyright Act 1968. Thus, to photocopy an edition of *David Copperfield* would not infringe Charles Dickens 'copyright' in the work, since this has expired. If the edition were published after 1 June 1957, however, the publisher's permission would be needed to avoid an infringement of his right in the edition.
[3] 84 Drayton Gardens, London, SW10 9SD.

The more usual practice is for the copyright owner to issue a licence granting those rights which he wishes to transfer. The licensee is then responsible for acting strictly within the terms of the licence.

Authors need to exercise particular care in submitting articles to journals. If they make it clear that they are offering only 'first serial rights', the journal concerned may publish the article, but the copyright remains with the writer, and he may have it republished elsewhere in any form. There are journals, however, including some of high repute, who take the copyright of all freelance material submitted. The contributor may know nothing of this until his cheque arrives with a form of receipt on the back assigning the copyright to the publishers. If he has specified that he is offering only 'first serial rights', he should refuse to sign this; the periodical should not have proceeded to publication on a basis not offered by the author. This matter is dealt with further in the section on school magazines.[1]

Artists taking part in a recorded, filmed or video-taped performance are protected by the rights granted to them under the Performers' Protection Acts 1958 and 1963.

Lectures, addresses, speeches and sermons are defined as 'performances',[2] but copyright in these can subsist only if it is expressed in literary form, i.e. in print or writing,[3] and there is no copyright in an extempore speech. If the speech is made from notes, publication of the speech might infringe the copyright of the notes. The delivery of a lecture does not amount to publication, and a lecturer would probably be held to have licensed publication if he delivered a lecture knowing that reporters were present.

A letter is an original literary work. No matter how poor its literary quality, it is protected by copyright.[4] The writer of a letter can restrain publication unless the circumstances imply a licence to publish. Unless specific limitations are imposed the

[1] See pages 356–7 and 429.

[2] Copyright Act 1956, s. 48 (1).

[3] *University of London Press Ltd* v *University Tutorial Press Ltd* [1916] 2 Ch 601.

[4] *Walter* v *Lane* [1900] AC 539; *British Oxygen Co Ltd* v *Liquid Air Ltd* [1925] Ch 383.

receiver of a letter has an unqualified title to the physical document, which he may keep, destroy or sell for waste-paper or the value of the signature. Whilst the signature is not a literary work, its reproduction might in some cases be protected as an artistic work. A long series of precedents going back for more than two hundred years[1] has settled the law that the one thing the receiver cannot do is to publish the ideas in their particular verbal expressions.

5 'In the course of employment'

'Where a literary, dramatic or artistic work is made by the author in the course of his employment by the proprietor of a newspaper, magazine or similar periodical under a contract of service or apprenticeship, and is made for the purpose of publication in a newspaper, magazine or similar periodical, the said proprietor shall be entitled to the copyright in the work insofar as the copyright relates to publication of the work in any newspaper, magazine or similar periodical, or to reproduction of the work for the purpose of its being so published; but in all other respects the author shall be entitled to any copyright subsisting in the work by virtue of this Part of this Act.'[2]

'Subject to the last preceding subsection, where a person commissions the taking of a photograph, or the painting or drawing of a portrait, or the making of an engraving, and pays or agrees to pay for it in money or money's worth, and the work is made in pursuance of that commission, the person who so commissioned the work shall be entitled to any copyright subsisting there in by virtue of this Part of this Act.'[3]

'Where in a case not falling within either of the last two preceding subsections, a work is made in the course of the author's employment by another person under a contract of service or apprenticeship, that other person shall be entitled to any copyright subsisting in the work by virtue of this part of this Act.'[4]

[1] *Pope* v *Curl* (1741) 2 Ark. 341 to *Philip* v *Pennell* [1907] 2 Ch. 577.
[2] Copyright Act 1956, s. 4 (2).
[3] Copyright Act 1956, s. 4 (3).
[4] Copyright Act 1956, s. 4 (4).

'Each of the three last preceding subsections shall have effect subject, in any particular case, to any agreement excluding the operation thereof in that case.'[1]

The four subsections quoted above are clearly of great importance to teachers, not only in schools but also in universities where research and its publication form an integral part of the work of the academic staff. Subsection (5) clearly permits the exclusion of the employer's right to copyright whether by operation of the general terms of the contract of service or by a special agreement referring to a specific piece of work.

It is an essential feature of a contract of service that the master has a right 'in some reasonable sense to control the method of doing the work'.[2] If a man employs another, and leaves it to the servant to decide how the work should be done, the contract is not one of service, but for services: 'In each case the question to be asked is, what was the man employed to do? Was he employed upon the terms that he should, within the scope of his employment, obey his master's orders, or was he employed to exercise his skill and achieve an indicated result in such manner as, in his judgment, was most likely to ensure success?'[3] As far as is known, the courts have not been called upon to consider whether a teacher's contract is a contract of service or for services. Generally, most people would probably regard it as the former as the requirement to comply with the reasonable instructions of the head suggests a measure of control. In very recent years, however, some teachers have claimed that neither the governors nor the head have any right to interfere with the way in which they carry out their professional duties. This may one day be a matter for the courts to decide; it is certainly not, in the present climate, a matter on which the author of this book or individual teachers can pronounce authoritatively.

The work must be made in the course of the employment under a contract of service. A translation by a member of a newspaper

[1] Copyright Act 1956, s. 4 (5).
[2] *Per* Lord Thankerton in *Short* v *J. and W. Henderson Ltd* (1946) 39 BWCC 62.
[3] *Per* Buckley, L. J. in *Simmons* v *Heath Laundry Co* [1910] 1 KB 543.

staff[1] or lectures prepared by an accountant employed under a contract of service,[2] in each case in their spare time, were held not to have been carried out in the course of their employment.

The problem has shown up in its most acute form in educational circles in the preparation of material for closed circuit television programmes produced by local education authorities. In at least one case the authority has seconded members of its teaching staff to work as members of production teams. It is clearly envisaged that work produced during such periods of secondment should fall within the scope of the teacher's employment, but members of the teams have complained that much of their work, particularly the writing of scripts, has to be done outside normal working hours.

The authority claims that it is impossible to distinguish between the contributions of different members of a team and that, in the course of preparation, original scripts are so altered by the co-operative thinking of the team that the original is no more than an idea in which, of course, there is no copyright. Following this line of argument, it is held that the copyright of the material is vested in the employing authority.

The teachers' professional associations have contested this point of view. There is, certainly, one important issue which, at the least, should be the subject of a special exclusion agreement under section 4 (5) quoted above. It may be that a teacher is preparing, in his own time, a book or teaching pack including diagrams or other material suitable for inclusion in a programme, and allows the local education authority to make use of them. It would be obnoxious if he were, by such an act of grace, to lose control of the copyright. If material of this kind taken from a work already published is to be included, the teacher's contract with his publishers will probably have given them a sufficiently exclusive licence to control this use. The authority will then have to negotiate with the author's publishers who will watch his interests as well as their own.

[1] *Byrne* v *Statist Co* [1914] 1 KB 622.
[2] *Stevenson, Jordan & Harrison Ltd* v *Macdonald & Evans* (1952) 1 TLR 101.

6 Duration of copyright

Literary, dramatic, musical and artistic works – Fifty years from the end of the calendar year in which the author dies in the case of works published during his lifetime; in the case of post-humously published works, fifty years from the end of the calendar year it was first published, performed in public or offered for sale as a recording.[1]

Photographs – Fifty years from the end of the calendar year of first publication:[2] copyright is therefore perpetual until publication, which consists of the issue of reproductions to the public (not necessarily for value) but does not include the exhibition of an artistic work.[3]

Sound recordings – Fifty years from the end of the calendar year of first publication.[4]

Cinematograph films – Fifty years from the end of the calendar year of registration in the case of films registrable under Part II of the Films Act 1960; in other cases for fifty years from the end of the calendar year of first publication. In the case of newsreels copyright is not infringed by performance after fifty years from the end of the calendar year in which the principal events depicted occurred, though it might still be an infringement to reproduce them.[5]

Published editions – Twenty-five years from the end of the calendar year of the first publication of the edition.[6]

Television and sound broadcasts – Fifty years from the end of the year in which any broadcast is made by the British Broadcasting Corporation, the Independent Television Authority, in any

[1] Copyright Act 1956, ss. 2 (3) and 3 (4).

[2] Copyright Act 1956, s. 3 (4) (*b*).

[3] Copyright Act 1956, s. 49 (2) (*a*). Photographs taken before the 1956 Act came into force are protected for fifty years from the date they were taken.

[4] Copyright Act 1956, s. 12 (3). Sound recordings made before the 1956 Act came into force are protected for fifty years from the date they were made.

[5] Copyright Act 1956, s. 13 (3) and (8). Films made before the 1956 Act came into force are protected as dramatic works (if fiction) or photographs (if non-fiction).

[6] Copyright Act 1956, s. 15 (2).

country to which section 14 of the 1956 Act has been extended by the European Agreement on the Protection of Television Broadcasts 1964 (France, Sweden and Denmark), and by Orders in Council made in 1961 and 1964.[1] The term of copyright is not extended by the repetition of a broadcast, although any new material included would presumably acquire its own copyright. As broadcasts made before 1 June 1957 are specifically excluded, the first repeat after that date of a broadcast originally made before the commencement of the Act would count as a new broadcast, and copyright would run from the date of that repetition.[2]

Crown copyright – Perpetual until publication and then for fifty years from the end of the calendar year of first publication in the case of literary, dramatic or musical works, engravings or photographs made by or under the direction of the Crown or a government department. Fifty years from the making of other artistic works, or photographs taken before 1 June 1956. Crown copyright in sound recordings and cinematograph films is the same as for other holders of these rights.[3]

Perpetual copyright – By the Copyright Act 1775 the Universities of Oxford and Cambridge, the four universities in Scotland, and the colleges of Eton, Westminster (to which, by a later Act, Trinity College, Dublin, was added) were given perpetual copyright in books given or bequeathed to them for the advancement of useful learning and other purposes of education. Such books had to be printed by the universities and colleges on their own presses and for their own benefit. Perpetual copyrights still in existence at the commencement of the 1956 Act continue, but all proceedings in respect of them must be in accordance with the terms of the 1956 Act. No new perpetual copyrights may be acquired.[4]

Joint works – Fifty years from the end of the calendar year in which the last surviving author dies; except in the case of any literary, dramatic and musical work or engraving which has not

---

[1] 1961, no. 2460 and 1964, no. 690.
[2] Copyright Act 1956, s. 14 (2) and (3).
[3] Copyright Act 1956, s. 39 (1), (2) and 3.
[4] Copyright Act 1956, s. 46 (1).

been published, performed in public, offered for sale as records or broadcast during the lifetime of the last surviving author: in such cases copyright continues for fifty years from the end of the calendar year in which one of these acts is first done.[1] Joint authorship involves a collaboration in which the work of each author is not separate from that of the other author or authors.[2]

Anonymous and pseudonymous works – Fifty years from the end of the calendar year of first publication (except in the case of a photograph. If before the expiry of this period it is possible for a person without previous knowledge of the facts to ascertain the identity of the author by reasonable inquiry, copyright will run in the usual way from the date of the author's death. A work published under two or more names is not pseudonymous unless all those names are pseudonyms.[3]

7 Minors

Minors, that is persons under the age of eighteen, are not specifically mentioned in the Copyright Act 1956. Nevertheless, since copyright is a valuable property, they must be able to own this right, though they may not sell, deal in, or otherwise dispose of it except through their parent or legal guardian.

In default of any decided cases it must be assumed that the copyright of any original work produced by pupils in the course of instruction is vested in the author. A child is not employed by a school under a contract of service, and the school authorities can hardly be regarded as the child's employer. Neither do they, in the ordinary course of school work, commission work for money or money's worth.[4] It seems most unlikely that the school authorities can lay any claim to copyright in such material: it is quite certain that no such right can pass to any individual teacher.

It is the 'custom of the trade' for schools to solicit and accept original work for publication in school magazines. No payment is usually, if ever, made for such publication. The practice is so

---

[1] Copyright Act 1956, Schedule II, 1, 2 and 3; Schedule III. 3.
[2] Copyright Act 1956, s. 11 (3).
[3] Copyright Act 1956, Schedule II.
[4] See page 351.

long-established that it is doubtful if it would be considered a breach of copyright, and it could, in any case, be regularized by a simple form of consent signed by the parent or guardian. Whether or not this is done, the acceptance by the school should not be regarded as more than acquiring 'first serial rights',[1] and the copyright must remain with the pupil.[2]

8 General exceptions

The 1956 Act provides a number of exceptions to the general prohibition of infringement of copyright. Those which are purely concerned with educational use are dealt with in later sections. The principal reliefs from infringement in the ordinary affairs of life are considered here.

Fair dealing – 'No fair dealing with a literary, dramatic or musical work for purposes of research or private study shall constitute an infringement.'[3] A further section extends this to artistic works.[4] 'No fair dealing with a literary, dramatic or musical work shall constitute an infringement of the copyright in the work if it is for purposes of criticism or review, whether of that work or of another work, and is accompanied by a sufficient acknowledgement.'[5] Similar provisions extend to artistic works.[6]

'Sufficient acknowledgement' is 'an acknowledgement identifying the work in question by its title or other description and, unless the work is anonymous or the author has previously agreed or required that no acknowledgement of his name should be made, also identifying the author'.[7]

The Act, however, is silent on the meaning of fair dealing, since this is a matter of fact for the courts to determine in each case, and depends on a number of elements. A guideline was given in a statement issued jointly by the Society of Authors and the Publishers Association in 1958. This stated that objection could

[1] See page 350.
[2] See also 'School Magazines', page 429.
[3] Copyright Act 1956, s. 6 (1).
[4] Copyright Act 1956, s. 9 (1).
[5] Copyright Act 1956, s. 6 (2).
[6] Copyright Act 1956, s. 9 (2).
[7] Copyright Act 1956, s. 6 (10).

not normally be taken to a quotation in a book, criticism or review of a single extract up to four hundred words, or a series of extracts (none of which exceeds three hundred words) totalling up to eight hundred words. In the case of poetry, an extract or extracts up to forty lines would be acceptable, but in no case exceeding one quarter of any poem.[1]

Substantiality – 'Any reference in this Act to the doing of an act in relation to a work or other subject matter shall be taken to include a reference to the doing of that act in relation to a substantial part thereof. . . .'[2] The Act does not define the term 'substantial part' which is, again, a matter of fact in each case. Much will depend upon whether an alleged infringement would compete with the original, or make the purchase of copies of it unnecessary. The test is: 'Is the act one which will damage the copyright owner?' The reproduction *in toto* of a diagram summarizing the argument of a book will almost certainly do so.

Libraries – In 1957 the Board of Trade issued the Copyright (Libraries) Regulations[3] empowering the library of any school, university, college or other establishment of further education, any public library, any parliamentary library or that of any department of government, or any library conducted for . . . facilitating or encouraging the study of religion, philosophy, science (including any natural or social science), technology, medicine, history, literature, languages, education, bibliography, fine arts, music or law to make for their readers a copy of a single article from any one periodical or a 'reasonable proportion' of any other copyright work. Before this is supplied the applicant must *personally sign* the following declaration:

I, ... of ....
hereby request you to make and supply to me a copy of
....
which I require for the purposes of research or private study.

---

[1] See also the reference to a further statement on photocopying (1965), pages 365–6.

[2] Copyright Act 1956, s. 49 (1).

[3] Under the Copyright Act 1956, ss. 7 (1), (3) and (7); 15 (4) from which they derive their statutory force.

I have not previously been supplied with a copy of the said article/the said part of the said work by any librarian.

I undertake that if a copy is supplied to me in compliance with the request made above, I will not use it except for the purposes of research or private study.

If a librarian (including a school librarian) is asked for multiple copies of copyright work, he must, by law, seek the approval of the owner of the copyright. The exception provided by the regulations does not extend to libraries conducted for profit.[1] The library must make a charge for this service and, even for a single copy, the owner of the copyright must be approached if his whereabouts can be reasonably ascertained.

Collections for schools – It is not an infringement of copyright to include a 'short passage' of a copyright work in a collection intended for school use. The collection must be described as intended for this purpose, but the extract must not itself have been published for this purpose. 'Sufficient acknowledgement'[2] must be made, and the bulk of the collection must consist of material which is out of copyright. Not more than two extracts may be included from one author's copyright works.[3]

The Act does not define the meaning of 'short extract' but the Society of Authors and the Publishers Association stated in 1958 that they would regard this as not more than 750 words from a prose work or seventy-five lines from a poem, provided that the extract did not exceed one-third of the whole poem, essay, story or other literary or dramatic work.

9 Educational exceptions

It is not an infringement to reproduce a copyright literary, artistic, dramatic or musical work in the course of instruction so long as this is not done by a duplicating process. Apparently a teacher

[1] This subject is dealt with fully in R. E. Barker: *Photocopying Practices in the United Kingdom* (Faber, 1970), pages 23–7, and *Copyright and Education* (NCET, 1972), pages 42–9, which reproduces the relevant section of the British Copyright Council's statement *Photocopying and the Law* (1970).

[2] See page 357.

[3] Copyright Act 1956, s. 6 (6).

may write copyright material on a blackboard, and his pupils may copy it individually, but he may not hand out multi-copies prepared in an unauthorized manner. Neither is it an infringement of copyright to include, and reproduce in multiple form, such material in an examination question or answer. It would be breach of copyright, say, to copy out the parts of a copyright play so as to deprive the copyright owner of his livelihood by making it unnecessary to purchase or hire copies.[1]

It is not an infringement to perform a copyright literary, dramatic or musical work in class or otherwise in the course of the activities of a school, provided that both performers and audience are members of the school. Any other members of the audience must be directly connected with the activities of the school, and a person is not held to be so merely because he is the parent or guardian of a pupil.[2] The same exemption extends to sound recordings, cinematograph films and television broadcasts.[3]

Public performances of copyright literary, dramatic and musical works, including the use of recorded material, are dealt with in Chapter XIV: *Concerts and Plays*.[4]

10 Broadcasting and television

Reference has already been made[5] to the duration of copyright in broadcasts and telecasts by the British Broadcasting Corporation, the Independent Television Authority and in countries to which section 14 of the 1956 Act has been extended, but it has been felt wiser to leave a review of the nature of this particular form of copyright to a separate section in which it is possible also to discuss its effect on educational use. It must be remembered that this right is independent of, and additional to, any other rights vested in authors, makers of recordings and performers.

It is a breach of copyright to make a cinematograph film (or a

---

[1] Copyright Act 1956, s. 41 (1). The use of the term 'or elsewhere' in s. 41 makes it uncertain whether its provisions are restricted to schools, to the exclusion of further and higher education.

[2] Copyright Act 1956, s. 41 (3) and (4).

[3] Copyright Act 1956, s. 41 (5).

[4] See pages 333–43.

[5] See pages 354–5.

copy of such a film) of a telecast insofar as it consists of visual images or, in the case either of a sound or television broadcast insofar as it consists of sounds, to make a sound recording or a record including such a recording. It is not a breach of copyright to do any of these acts for private purposes. It is also a breach of copyright to cause a telecast to be seen or heard in public by a paying audience; or to rebroadcast it on a sound broadcast.[1]

The restrictions apply to breaches by the reception of the broadcast or telecast itself, or the use of any record, print, negative or tape on which the broadcast or telecast has been recorded.[2] In the case of telecasts any sequence of images sufficient to be seen as a moving picture is sufficient to breach copyright.[3]

A recording is not made for private purposes if it is made for the sale or hire of any copy of the film or record embodying the recording; broadcasting the film; broadcasting the film or recording; or causing the film or recording to be seen in public.[4]

A television broadcast has been heard or seen by a 'paying public' if they have been admitted for payment to the place where it is to be seen or heard, or to a place of which that auditorium forms a part; or who have been admitted to a place in circumstances where goods or services are supplied at a higher price than is usual there, such enhancement being attributable to the facilities for hearing or seeing the broadcast or telecast. The first part of this definition does not apply to residents or inmates of the place in question, or if persons are admitted as members of a club or society where the only payment they make is the membership subscription, and the broadcasting and telecasting facilities are only incidental to the main purposes of the club or society.[5]

In order to facilitate the use of broadcasts and telecasts *transmitted for educational purposes*, the British Broadcasting Corporation and the Independent Television Authority have made arrangements with the British Record Producers Association and with certain performers' unions to enable teachers and pupils in

[1] Copyright Act 1956, s. 14 (4).
[2] Copyright Act 1956, s. 14 (5).
[3] Copyright Act 1956, s. 14 (6).
[4] Copyright Act 1956, s. 14 (7).
[5] Copyright Act 1956, s. 14 (8).

the course of instruction to record these programmes off the air. Such recordings may be used only for instructional purposes in classes in the school or other educational institution in which they are made. The recordings cannot, therefore, be made, for example, in a teachers' centre and syndicated among the schools served by that centre. The recording must be erased within one year of being made or, in the case of BBC radio vision programmes, by the end of the third school year.

The British Broadcasting Corporation requires no formalities in connection with this facility, but the Independent Television Authority issues an annual licence to local education authorities and other appropriate bodies, such as universities, for a fee of £5. The local education authority may determine which schools within its area may make use of the facilities afforded by the licence, and this may include independent schools within its boundaries.

It must be clearly understood that this facility applies only to educational programmes advertised as such, and confers no right to record any other material put out by the broadcasting authorities. Open University broadcasts are not regarded as educational programmes for this purpose; and the consent of the University, as owner of the copyright, must be obtained before a re-recording is made.

Not all local education authorities have taken out Independent Television Authority licences, and schools should ensure that they do not record programmes put out under the aegis of that body unless the licence has been obtained.

11 Records and pre-recorded tapes

With the limited exception of recorded material included in broadcasts and telecasts referred to in the last section, it is an offence to re-record, without licence, any record or pre-recorded tape for public, educational or private use.

The leading recording companies have formed a company, Phonographic Performance Ltd, to control the use of their recordings by the issue of licences and to distribute the fees received from public performances among the various owners of the rights. The use of recordings at public performances given by schools has been discussed in the previous chapter,[1] and this section is concerned with the use of recordings and with re-recording in schools.

Phonographic Performance Ltd is concerned only with the rights of recording companies. Those of composers, authors and publishers are the concern of the Performing Right Society which licenses the public performance, broadcasting and diffusion of copyright music, and collects and distributes royalties on behalf of its members. The Society is not concerned with non-musical plays or sketches, ballets, operas, musical plays or other dramatico-musical works performed in full by living persons on the stage. Again, the function of the Society in connection with public performances by schools is dealt with in the previous chapter.[2]

Neither Phonographic Performance Ltd nor the Performing Right Society make any charge in respect of the use in accordance with the educational exemptions granted under section 41 of the Copyright Act 1956.[3] In the case of recordings, however, it has until recently been illegal to make copies without obtaining all the necessary consents, even for private use in the home.

In this country the necessary negotiations for permission to re-record (as distinct from playing the actual record by arrangement with Phonographic Performance Ltd) are conducted on behalf of copyright holders by the Mechanical Rights Society Ltd, and the collection and distribution of the fees arising from negotiated licences is undertaken by an associated company, the Mechanical Copyright Protection Society Ltd.[4]

---

[1] See pages 341–2.   [2] See pages 340–41.   [3] See pages 359–60.
[4] Elgar House, 380 Streatham High Road, London, SW16 6HR. Teachers who wish to make recordings for use in their own homes, in amateur tape recording clubs or for amateur recording competitions may not be aware that the MCPS will issue to anyone an amateur recording licence. The present annual fee is 55p including VAT. The licence authorizes recording of musical works owned by members of the Society which have previously been released on gramophone records. Since 1974 it has covered re-recording on sound tape, from records issued under labels and/or trademarks owned or controlled by members of the British Photographic Industries Copyright Association.

In August 1973 the Council for Educational Technology announced a proposed form of licensing for re-recording records and pre-recorded tapes for curricular purposes. These licences will be issued by the Mechanical Copyright Protection Society on behalf of the British Phonographic Industries Copyright Association and the British Copyright Protection Association. The licences will permit the use of re-recorded material in an establishment used for the curricular purposes of the institution where it is made, e.g. during teaching practice in schools.

The licences will be of two kinds. The first form will be available to local education authorities to enable re-recordings to be made in their maintained institutions for use in the institution in which the recording is made. The licence waives the restriction that the re-recording shall be made in the course of instruction as required by section 41 of the 1956 Act. Now that many secondary schools and further education establishments have their own media resource officers, the new licence will enable re-recordings to be made for curricular purposes in the institution's resource centre; a course of action not previously possible as this could hardly be considered as falling within the restriction. Local education authorities pay a fee which consists of a basic sum together with an addition for every fifty institutions to be covered. No addition is charged for institutions in excess of one thousand. The licence also permits the recording of the live performance of copyright music, provided that the consent of the performers has been obtained in writing.

The same form of licence may be obtained by direct-grant schools, independent schools and universities.

The second kind of licence is designed to waive the restriction that re-recordings must be used only by the copying institution. It provides that teachers' centres and resource centres, maintained by the licensee to augment the resources and facilities of a group of educational institutions, may copy recordings as parts of a composite sound programme of short extracts from commercially published records and pre-recorded tapes. A single extract must not exceed four minutes in duration, and the licence does not cover re-recording on the sound track of a cine film or video tape, for which special arrangements must be negotiated with the owners of the copyright. Any visual images included in the programme must be stills, and physically separate from the re-recording. The original record or tape from which the copy is made must be the property of the licensee at the time of copying.

Not more than twelve copies may be made of any programme, they must be labelled as the property of the centre, and they may be used only in institutions served by the centre. The label must state that re-recorded extracts have been included by permission of the owners of the copyright in the recording and in the work recorded, and that further copying is prohibited. A register, which may be inspected by the licensors, must contain in respect of each programme the distinguishing label mark, number and title of each original from which an extract has been copied, the length of each extract, the title of the works copied and the number of programmes prepared.

VAT is payable on the licences. The Mechanical Rights Protection Society Ltd[1] and the British Copyright Protection Association[2] grant the necessary rights on behalf of the copyright holders of the recorded works, and the Phonographic Industry Copyright Association[3] are the representatives for the copyright owners of the originals. The Society is endeavouring to negotiate terms for the extension of similar facilities to individual domestic licensees.

12 Photocopying

The accessibility and convenience of photocopying and other facilities for making multiple copies of printed material has undoubtedly led to a great deal of illegal copying of books, magazines, music and diagrams for which the permission of the copyright owner should have been sought.

In 1965 the Society of Authors and the Publishers Association issued a joint statement setting out what they considered as 'fair

[1] 380 Streatham High Road, London, SW16 6HR.
[2] 29–33 Berners Street, London, W1P 4AA.
[3] 33 Thurloe Place, London, SW7.

dealing' in the case of single copies made for research or private study. Under the terms of this statement it is not unfair to make a single photo-copy from a copyright work of a single extract not exceeding four thousand words, or a series of extracts (none of which exceeds three thousand words) to a total of not more than eight thousand words. In neither case may the total exceed 10 per cent of the whole work. Poems, essays and other short literary works are whole works in themselves and not 'parts' of the volumes in which they appear. An unlimited number of copies may be made by hand.

It is probable that the making of a single photocopy of a diagram for use in transparency form on an overhead projector is an extension of the former practice of projecting such diagrams by means of an episcope. The episcope did not involve any physical reproduction, and therefore could not infringe copyright. The Society of Authors and the Publishers Association have indicated that they would not regard the making of single copies for projection transparencies within the terms of section 41 of the 1956 Act (solely for instruction in a school or other educational establishment) as an infringement of copyright.

The making of multiple copies is an infringement unless the permission of the owner of the copyright has been obtained. It is clearly difficult, however, to avoid constant breaches of copyright of this kind, and in the autumn of 1973 the Council for Educational Technology and the Publishers Association conducted an experiment to discover whether a licensing scheme might be necessary or desirable to legalize the practices which had developed.

Those responsible for the experiment recognized that there was no reliable assessment of the extent of multiple copying in breach of copyright. Obtaining consent in each case is a cumbersome procedure, and the terms on which permission is granted by different copyright owners are by no means identical. Some, for example, may give permission freely, others may charge a fee. Information was required about the extent to which multiple copying would be used if the copyright owners granted bulk licences to local education authorities enabling all their schools to reproduce material on specific terms and conditions, without the need to seek individual permission on each occasion.

For the purpose of the experiment the Publishers Association gave the Council for Educational Technology permission to select a number of schools which, for a limited period, were 'licensed' to copy for curricular purposes all the published printed material which they needed, British or foreign, text-books, work cards, examination papers, sheet music, newspapers and periodicals. The schools were asked to complete a simple return giving details of the title and form of the work copied, the proportion of the work used, the number of copies made and the method used.

It is hoped that the results will provide sufficient information to form the basis of negotiations which will put an end to much illegal infringement, remove obstacles from the path of those who do try to comply with the law by seeking individual permissions, and safeguard the rights of copyright owners.

13 Language laboratories
It is the essential nature of work in a language laboratory that a master tape is repeatedly copied on the students' tapes. In order to safeguard the copyright in such tapes the publishers charge a higher price for the master tapes than would normally be applicable to a similar commercial tape. This 'levy' is distributed among the owners of the various rights, and in consideration of this the purchaser is licensed to make copies in such numbers, and as frequently as may be necessary, within the laboratory.

14 Closed circuit television
Some local education authorities and many educational establishments now have closed circuit television systems. The exposure of work by a television camera does not amount to reproduction, and does not infringe copyright. If, however, the work is reproduced in material form the consent of the owner of the copyright must be obtained. Few closed circuit television programmes are 'live', the majority being transmitted on video-tape, and in all such cases consent must be obtained.

15 Juke boxes

Juke boxes installed for entertainment are not exempt.

16 The future of copyright

The law of copyright is complex, and is not made simpler by the necessary international conventions to protect rights not only in the country of origin, but also throughout as wide a part of the earth's surface as possible. It is also constantly changing. During the 'sixties problems arose in the developing countries because of their need for ready access to educational material. The Paris Revisions of 1971, which are in the process of ratification, provide that such countries will be able to apply compulsory licensing for educational use after specified periods which vary between one and five years. Royalties must be paid on such licences.

In this country, and particularly within our educational system, the biggest problems posed at present are those arising from the sudden development of facilities for copying print, sound and vision. In its pamphlet *Copyright and Education* the National Council for Educational Technology[1] examined several possible changes.

One was a proposal that the exemptions granted to schools by the 1956 Act should be extended to other educational institutions. The difficulty about this solution is that it would conflict with the international conventions to which the United Kingdom is a party. Another idea was the imposition of a levy on copying hardware (photocopiers, tape-recorders, etc.), or on software (such as copying paper or tapes), the purchaser being authorized by payment of the levy to copy copyright works, and the levy being distributed among copyright owners. In Western Germany a levy of 5 per cent has been placed on tape recorders for domestic purposes and, as has been said earlier, this is already the practice in this country in the case of language laboratory tapes.[2] The Council's objection to this scheme is that it would bear hardly on the many purchasers of tape-recorders and blank tapes who have

[1] Now the Council for Educational Technology for the United Kingdom.
[2] See page 367.

no intention of using them for recording copyright material.

Possibly the most acceptable solution is the further development of 'blanket' agreements within the framework of the 1956 Act, such as those concluded in 1973 for re-recording in educational establishments and centres,[1] and those which it is hoped may grow from the multiple copying experiment carried out in the autumn of the same year.[2] The Council admits, however, that printed matter presents more intractable problems than other copyright material because there is no central licensing body to speak for the owners of all the rights in this medium.

The Government has set up a committee under the chairmanship of Mr Justice Whitford to examine the law of copyright, and to make proposals for any changes which may seem necessary. The Council for Educational Technology has submitted evidence on behalf of educational interests.

17 Caveat praeceptor

In the meantime let the teacher beware. If he wishes to reproduce material which he may have reasonable grounds to believe to be subject to copyright, he should make careful inquiries before doing so. Ignorance is no excuse for breaking the law and, in the case of published material, an inquiry to the publishers is the best way of discovering whether the work concerned is still protected and, if so, the name of the owner of the copyright from whom it will be possible to secure details of the terms and conditions upon which he will allow his work to be used. This is not, of course, necessary when working within the educational exemptions permitted by section 41 of the 1956 Act or under a blanket agreement.

[1] See pages 364–5.
[2] See pages 366–7.

XVI

EXTRANEOUS DUTIES

1 General

It has long been accepted that the work of a teacher is not merely to instruct, but also to educate his pupils in the fullest sense of the word. Teachers have themselves recognized this fact and they have undertaken a wide range of voluntary duties, including those connected with games, school societies, visits and ourneys.

Legally, these duties remain voluntary, except supervisory duties necessary for the good conduct of the school, and it should be remembered that in maintained schools a teacher may not be compelled to perform any duties except such as are connected with the work of a school. It must be admitted that this definition leaves plenty of scope for discussion. In any case, most schools now have a more or less highly developed social life and there are few teachers who would not wish to take some active part in this.

It should be remembered, however, that once a person undertakes a voluntary duty he accepts a legal obligation to carry it out to the best of his ability for as long as he has undertaken to perform it. The standard of care which is exacted by the court in these circumstances is that which would be applied by a reasonable and prudent man in the conduct of his own affairs.

2 Meals and midday supervision

The positive power to require teachers to supervise school meals was removed in 1968, but the Act still provides that duties in connection with school meals 'shall not impose upon teachers at any school or college duties upon days on which the school or college is not open for instruction, or duties in respect of meals other than the supervision of pupils'.[1]

All duties in connection with meals are now voluntary. In 1956, a case concerned with the collection of dinner money decided the point as far as all duties, other than supervision, are concerned.

Early that year members of the National Association of Schoolmasters, after giving reasonable notice to the local education authority, had stopped collecting dinner-money in Sunderland schools as a protest against the Teachers (Superannuation) Bill, then before Parliament. They were given notices of dismissal by the authority, but the notices were subsequently withdrawn, except in the case of six teachers. These teachers sought an injunction in the High Court to restrain the authority from acting on the notices on the ground that they were *ultra vires*, and a declaration that the Council was not entitled to impose on its teachers any duties in respect of meals other than the supervision of pupils.[2]

Mr Justice Barry said that he was unable to accept the authority's contention that, because the 1921 Act specifically stated that teachers need not collect dinner-money and the 1944 Act had no such reference, Parliament had intended to change the law because teachers in many places were collecting such money. He held that the collection of dinner-money was a duty in respect of meals within the meaning of section 49 of the Act, and that the service which had been given by the teachers for this purpose was voluntary service. The Council had, therefore, acted *ultra vires* in dismissing the teachers for refusing a service which the local education authority had no right to impose as a condition of appointment.

It should be noted in this case that the teachers were not opposed to the actual collection of dinner-money, indeed they had stopped doing so as a protest against something quite unconnected with school meals. Their lawsuit was based on an attempt by the local education authority to compel them, under threat of

[1] Education Act 1944, s. 49.
[2] *Price* and *others* v *Sunderland County Borough Council* [1956] 1 WLR 1253, 3 All ER 153; LCT 377.

dismissal, to perform a service which was purely voluntary and which, therefore, they could withhold at will.

The withdrawal of the requirement to supervise school meals followed the report of a working party on school meals and midday supervision which had been established by the Secretary of State. The report recommended the abolition of the compulsive element, suggested that free meals might be allowed in return for the performance of duties during the midday break other than meals supervision, e.g. playground supervision, coaching for games and the organization of clubs; and paved the way for an improved scale of ancillary assistance. It stated categorically that the head retained an overall responsibility for the conduct of meals as he 'does for everything else which goes on in and about his school'.

Unfortunately, the result has been a considerable degree of confusion. One professional association maintained in the meetings of the working party that its aim was to end all compulsory duties during the midday break on the ground that a teacher is entitled to his dinner hour as much as anyone else. After the working party reported, and before any change in the regulations was made, the association advised its members that all duties during the midday break would, henceforth, be voluntary. Other associations have given contrary advice.

So far, no case has come before the court for decision on this issue: *Pettican* v *Enfield*[1] arose from an incident which occurred before the regulations were changed. The difficulties appear to have arisen from an attempt to join together two duties which have quite distinct foundations in law.

The supervision of school meals was a statutory duty bound on teachers by regulations[2] made by the Secretary of State following the provisions of section 49 of the 1944 Act which has already been quoted. This requirement could be, and was, repealed by order of the Secretary of State.[3] At no time did this duty comprise anything more than the supervision of school meals; and

[1] See pages 263–5.
[2] Provision of Milk and Meals Regulations 1945, nos. 13 and 14.
[3] Provision of Milk and Meals (Amendment) Regulations 1968.

it would give altogether too wide a meaning to the words 'school meals' to make them include playground supervision, chess clubs and the many other activities which go on in a school during the midday break.

Supervision of the school, the meal apart, during the period stems from a completely different root. It is the duty of the schoolmaster *in loco parentis* to take care of his pupils. It is the duty of the head to control the internal organization, management and discipline of the school. In certain circumstances, other duties arise from the Occupiers Liability Act 1957. As has been shown in the chapter on accidents and negligence,[1] it is necessary to have an adequate and fully maintained system to ensure that these duties are performed. Assistant staff are appointed to assist the head in discharging his legal obligations, and he can, as the law stands at present, require them reasonably to do so.

The common law duty of care is an ancient precedent, and is binding so long as there are pupils on the school premises. It may develop as a result of distinguishing cases in the courts; it can be changed only by Act of Parliament, not by statutory instrument, and certainly not by a professional association. No steps have been taken to vary this duty by statute. Neither have the rules of management nor the articles of government been varied. The duty under the Occupiers Liability Act also remains.

This seems to lead to the conclusion that the view taken by some, that the abolition of the compulsive element in meals supervision extends to the whole of the midday break, is based on a confusion of statutory and common law, and a failure to distinguish between achievement and aspiration. The association concerned sought to remove both compulsory meals supervision and obligatory midday supervision elsewhere. The first leg of this policy was achieved when the 1968 regulations were issued, but the amending regulations did not, and could not, affect a change in the common law. The second law remains, for that association, an aim for the future.

This is not to deny the right of the association to continue to campaign for the necessary changes to outlaw midday supervision.

[1] See particularly pages 232–7.

In the meantime teachers would be well advised to differentiate clearly between policy and law.

3 Playground duty

It is generally agreed that when a large number of children are gathered together in a playground during a break in the school session it is desirable that they should be under some form of supervision. In principle this need not be as rigid as the supervision which is exercised in the classroom.[1] This is a matter of the internal organization and discipline of the school and, in accordance with the rules of management or articles of government, is under the control of the head. Whilst the presence of a teacher in a playground will not prevent every accident from happening, the teacher can ensure that dangerous play is, as far as possible, avoided and he will be there to give assistance should an accident occur.

In planning supervision, including the deployment of ancillary staff, the head will have regard to the general principle that he must have an adequate system which is efficiently maintained.[2] If there is a duty rota and a teacher has failed to perform a duty to which he has been allocated, the question of negligence might be raised in the case of an accident.

4 Road crossing

At one time it was quite usual for teachers to supervise children leaving school premises which opened onto a busy road. They have no authority over the traffic, and local authorities have been given powers[3] to make arrangements for the patrolling of places where children cross roads on their way to or from school by persons other than police constables. Between eight o'clock in the morning and half-past five in the afternoon, such patrols have power to control traffic on exhibiting a sign of a size, colour and type prescribed by the Minister of Transport's regulations. Patrols must wear a uniform approved by the Secretary of State.

[1] See also page 263.   [2] See also pages 232–7.
[3] Road Traffic Regulation Act 1967, s. 25, which incorporates the general provisions of the School Crossing Patrols Act 1953.

It is an offence for traffic to continue so long as the crossing patrol is properly exhibiting the sign. The Queen's Bench Divisional Court allowed an appeal by the police against the acquittal of a driver who passed behind a party of women and children who had reached the centre of the road. The magistrates had based their finding on the words 'so as not to impede their crossing'.[1] The last pedestrian had quickened his steps to avoid the car. The court held unanimously that, in the words of the Lord Chief Justice, 'if the sign was still exhibited, there was an obligation to stop which could not be released until section 25 (2) (b) had been satisfied – until the sign was no longer exhibited'. The case was sent back to the justices with directions to convict.[2]

Newport (Monmouthshire) Corporation was ordered to pay £8,000 in agreed damages following an accident where a crossing patrol was employed to provide additional security on a zebra crossing. To ease the flow of traffic, classes were dismissed at two-minute intervals and taken to the crossing by their teachers. The driver of a furniture van saw the elderly patrol but, as he was at the roadside, he accelerated to a speed of thirty miles an hour. A six-year-old boy 'shot out like a pea from a pea-shooter', and collided with the van. His claim for damages against the owners of the van was dismissed at Monmouthshire Assizes, Mr Justice Browne finding it reasonable for the driver to assume that the crossing was clear because the patrol had gone back to the pavement. An alternative claim against the Corporation was successful: the system was not as good as it should be, the teacher had not done all she should and the patrol was negligent.

Dismissing an appeal by the Corporation, the Master of the Rolls, Lord Denning, said: 'Mr Hubbard's action or inaction was decisive. Though he was well liked by the children, there was no doubt that the mothers were very nervous. The police thought that if he had really been exercising control over them and keeping them back as he should have done, it should have been possible so to handle them that there would not be the sudden dart into

[1] Road Traffic Regulation Act 1967, s. 25 (2) (a).
[2] *Franklin* v *Langdown* (1971) *The Times*, 27 July.

the road. There was ample evidence on which the judge could find Mr Hubbard negligent, and the Corporation liable for his negligence.'[1]

When children are being taken through the streets for school purposes, the teacher in charge is *in loco parentis* and therefore responsible for the safety of the pupils. It is important that any ratio of staff to pupils laid down by the local education authority is observed. If children in the party suffer from any disability, it is desirable to increase the number of accompanying teachers.

5 Games

It is important that teachers supervising games should ensure that they are played in accordance with the accepted rules, and that unfair play is penalized. It is, therefore, highly desirable that staff should be acquainted with changes in the rules – and should know the difference between what is permitted, and what is sometimes seen on television! If parents assist with games on a voluntary basis, it is essential that they are made aware of the need to keep to the rules and to penalize rough play. If they are not properly briefed, the duty has not been delegated with the care which is necessary.[2] Only if games are strictly supervised can a defence of 'general and approved practice'[3] be raised in the event of a court action following an accident.

6 Uniformed youth organizations

School units of national youth organizations, such as the cadet forces and the Scout movement, must observe the rules of the responsible national body insofar as they apply to school groups. It is quite wrong for a school unit to feel free to indulge in idiosyncrasies in such matters; indeed it should set an example. This is particularly important in the case of uniformed organizations where parades may sometimes be held jointly with units which are not attached to schools.

[1] *Toole (An Infant)* v *Sherbourne Pouffes Ltd* and *another* (1971) *The Times*, 29 July.

[2] See pages 269–71.

[3] See pages 244–6.

It should also be remembered that, in most cases, such organizations have indemnity policies covering their officers against claims arising from accidents during approved activities. Such policies may be void in respect of incidents where the organization's rules have been broken in a material point.

7 Dereliction of duty

Once a teacher has undertaken a duty, whether it be obligatory or voluntary, it is incumbent upon him to perform it conscientiously. There are few heads who would burden their staffs with a multitude of unnecessary tasks, but a certain amount of supervision is necessary for the good order and discipline of a school.

The fact that duties were normally performed with care in a school influenced a judgment by Lord Justice Scrutton.[1] A boy had hit a golf ball through an open door from a playground and struck another boy in the eye, with the result that the sight of that eye was lost. The governors of the school were dismissed from the case by Mr Justice Horridge, who awarded £250 damages and £45 special costs against the headmaster.

Allowing the headmaster's appeal, Lord Justice Scrutton said that there was no evidence of lack of supervision, or that lack of supervision contributed to the accident. A golf ball is not in itself dangerous, and it was not habitual to hit them about the playground.

As was said in this case, no schoolmaster in the world can prevent a naughty boy doing naughty things on some occasions. However carefully duties are performed, it is quite impossible to ensure that accidents will not occur. Where, however, a plaintiff can show that there has been dereliction of duty on the part of a teacher, the defendant's case is seriously weakened.

By the rules of management or articles of government, the whole internal organization, management and discipline of a school are under the control of the head. If, therefore, a teacher fails to perform a duty which the head has prescribed as necessary, he may be condemned for negligence should an accident occur.

[1] *Langham* v *Wellingborough School Governors* and *Fryer* (1932) 147 LTR 91; LCT 297.

XVII

CHILDREN IN TROUBLE

1 The Juvenile courts

Since 1909 a special system of juvenile courts has existed to deal with children (under the age of fourteen) and with young persons (over fourteen and under seventeen). Originally conducted in much the same way as adult petty sessions, the juvenile courts have in the course of time become much more concerned with reform and rehabilitation than with punishment, in pursuance of the statutory duty laid on them in the following terms: 'Every court in dealing with a child or young person who is brought before it, either as an offender or otherwise, shall have regard to the welfare of the child or young person.'[1]

Juvenile courts are less formal than their adult counterparts, and must not be held in a room used for any court, other than a juvenile court, less than an hour before or after an adult court sitting.[2] Only members and officers of the court, the parties to the case being heard, with their advocates and witnesses, *bona fide* reporters and other persons specially authorized by the court may be present. Press reports are restricted and nothing may be printed which might lead to the identification of the juvenile or of his school, except by direction of the Secretary of State in cases where it appears to him to be in the interests of justice to dispense with secrecy.[3]

---

[1] Children and Young Persons Act 1933, s. 44 (1), as amended by the Children and Young Persons Act 1969, Schedule 6. In this chapter the word 'juvenile' is used to describe features of the system common both to children and to young persons as defined in this paragraph.

[2] Children and Young Persons Act 1933, s. 47 (2) as amended by the Children and Young Persons Act 1963, s. 17 (2).

[3] Children and Young Persons Act 1933, s. 49.

Outside the metropolitan area the court consists of two or three justices selected from a panel of juvenile court magistrates, specially chosen for their suitability to sit in juvenile courts. Any stipendiary magistrate with jurisdiction in the area is *ex-officio* a member of the panel and may, in special circumstances, sit alone. Unless there is a specific direction by the Lord Chancellor, lay justices must retire from the panel on reaching the age of sixty-five. At any hearing the bench should include both a man and a woman unless this is impossible because of unforeseen circumstances. The chair is normally taken by the chairman or deputy chairman of the panel.[1]

In the metropolitan stipendiary court area and the City of London the court consists of three justices selected from a panel of juvenile court magistrates appointed by the Lord Chancellor. The chairman is a metropolitan stipendiary magistrate, or a justice of the peace for the county of London who is a member of the panel. There must be a man and a woman on the bench at each sitting. If, however, on any occasion the bench is not fully constituted, the chairman may sit with one magistrate of the same sex if this is necessary to prevent an adjournment. A metropolitan stipendiary magistrate may sit alone.[2]

2 Definitions

Different Acts of Parliament, and even different sections of the same Act may assign different definitions to particular words. This is particularly confusing in the various meanings given to the terms 'child' and 'young person'. Some definitions essential to an understanding of the law relating to children and young persons are given below.

Child

    (*a*) *a person under the age of fourteen*: Children and Young Persons Acts 1933 to 1969 (generally) except as below;

    (*b*) *a person under the age of ten*: Children and Young Persons

[1] Children and Young Persons Act 1963, Schedule 2, Part I.
[2] Children and Young Persons Act 1963, Schedule 3, Part II. The City of London is included in this area by the Justices of the Peace Act 1949, s. 11 (5).

Act 1969, ss. 5 (8) (notification of offences to the local authority), 7 (7) (orders of the court on a finding of guilt), 7 (8) (remission to the juvenile court of young persons found guilty of an offence by an adult court), 9 (1) (investigations by local authorities), 23 (1) (remand of juveniles convicted of homicide), 28 (4) and (5) (special arrangements for detention and release of children arrested), and 29 (1) (further detention or release of juveniles);

(c) *a person under the age of twelve:* Children and Young Persons Act 1969, s. 13 (2) (designation of a child's probation officer by the court only if the local authority so requests, and a probation officer is or has been, in touch with the family), s. 34 (2) and (3) (passage of responsibility to make pre-hearing inquiries from local authority to probation officer):

(d) *a person under the age of sixteen:* Education Act 1944 (a person who is not over compulsory school age);

(e) *a person under the age of eighteen, or who has attained that age and is the subject of a care order:* Children Act 1948 (orphans, lost or abandoned children, children living away from their parents, children with parents unfit or unable to take care of them), Children and Young Persons Act 1969, ss. 27 (children in care), 63 (functions of children's committees), 64 (financial liability for Secretary of States's expenses in providing homes with special facilities), and 65 (grants to voluntary bodies).

Young Person

(a) *a person who has attained the age of fourteen and is under seventeen:* Children and Young Persons Acts 1933–69 (generally) except as below;

(b) *a person who has attained the age of ten and is under seventeen:* Children and Young Person's Act 1969, ss. 5 (8) (notification of offences to the local authority), s. 7 (7) (orders of the court on a finding of guilt), 7 (8) (remission to the juvenile court of young persons found guilty of an offence by an adult court), 9 (1) (investigations by local authorities), 23 (1) (remand of juveniles convicted of homicide), 28 (4) and (5) (special arrangements for detention and release of children arrested), and 29 (1) (further detention or release of juveniles);

(*c*) *a person who has attained the age of twelve and is under seventeen:* Children and Young Persons Act 1969, s. 13 (2) (designation of a child's probation officer by the court only if the local authority so requests, and a probation officer is, or has been, in touch with the family), s. 34 (2) and (3) (passage of responsibility to make pre-hearing inquiries from local authority to probation officer);

(*d*) *a person who has attained the age of sixteen and is under eighteen:* Education Act 1944, s. 114, by reference to the upper limit of compulsory education;

(*e*) *a person who attains the age of seventeen whilst court proceedings are pending or taking place:* In such cases the juvenile retains its jurisdiction until the end of the proceedings: Children and Young Persons Acts 1963, s. 29; and 1969 ss. 7 (8) and 16 (11).

Protected child – A protected child is one below the upper age limit of compulsory education who is in the care and possession of a person (other than his parent, guardian or other relative) who proposes to adopt him, and someone else (not being his parent or guardian) takes part in the adoption arrangements; or alternatively in the care and possession of a person who has given notice of intention to apply for an adoption order under the Adoption Act 1958, s. 3 (2).

Guardian – Any person who has, for the time being, the actual charge of, or control over, a juvenile.

Legal guardian – A person appointed to be a juvenile's guardian by deed or will, or by an order of the court. A local authority may exercise legal guardianship.

Local authorities

(*a*) *Employment of juveniles:* Local education authorities.[1]

(*b*) *Local authorities functions and powers under the Adoption Act* 1958, Parts II and IV are exercised by a Social Services Committee.[2] The authorities for this purpose are the Common

[1] See pages 36–41.   [2] Local Authority Social Services Act 1970, s. 2(a).

Council of the City of London, the London boroughs, the non-metropolitan counties and the metropolitan districts.

Place of safety – A place of safety includes a community home[1] provided or controlled by a local authority, a police station, a hospital or surgery, or any other suitable place whose occupier is willing to receive a juvenile temporarily.

3 Offences by juveniles

The Children and Young Persons Act 1933 provided: 'It shall be conclusively presumed that no child under the age of eight can be guilty of an offence.'[2] Thirty years later Parliament substituted ten as the age below which criminal proceedings could not be brought.[3] Considerable pressure was then brought to raise the age of fourteen, sixteen or even eighteen, and the current Act states: 'A person shall not be charged with an offence, except homicide, by reason of anything done or omitted while he was a child.'[4] This section, however, has not been brought into force, and children can still be prosecuted from the age of ten. The common law doctrine *doli incapax* presumes that a child under fourteen has not reached years of discretion, and is therefore incapable of forming a guilty intention. In the face of strong evidence, however, the common law doctrine does not necessarily avail a defence. In 1971 a twelve-year-old boy was said to have plotted the murder of a Southwark octogenarian, and to have goaded his mother's lover into committing the crime whilst he watched. The man was sentenced to life imprisonment for murder; the boy was acquitted of homicide but found guilty of conspiracy. Sentencing him to six years' detention, Mr Justice Ackner commented: 'What the law says is that there is a presumption that between the ages of ten and fourteen the child is incapable of criminal intention. It is a presumption that weakens as the child moves up in years towards fourteen. It is a presumption that can be rebutted – eliminated.'[5]

[1] See page 384.   [2] Children and Young Persons Act 1933, s. 50.
[3] Children and Young Persons Act 1963, s. 16 (1).
[4] Children and Young Persons Act 1969, s. 4.
[5] Reported in *The Times*, 30 October 1971.

On being arrested, a juvenile must be bailed unless he is brought immediately before the court. He can be detained however if he is charged with homicide or some other grave crime, or if it is in his own interest to remain in custody, or if his release would defeat the ends of justice or if, having been arrested without a warrant, he is unlikely to appear to answer any charge.[1]

The court may require the juvenile's parent to attend, and must do so if it thinks it desirable. The father may be compelled to attend as well as the mother, and at least one person who may be needed in court should be informed immediately a juvenile is arrested. The parent's attendance may be ordered by summons or warrant, or he may be included in the juvenile's summons.[2]

Unless charged with homicide a juvenile must be tried summarily unless he is charged jointly with an adult, and it is in the interests of justice to commit them both. Similarly, he may be committed for trial if he has attained the age of fourteen, is charged with an offence for which an adult could be sentenced to fourteen years' imprisonment or more, and the court believes that, if found guilty, he should be considered for a period of detention which does not exceed the maximum for which an adult might be liable.

The procedure of the court is kept as simple as possible; the nature of the charge must be explained in simple terms, the parent or guardian must be allowed to represent the juvenile, and the court must do everything in its power to assist any unrepresented juvenile. Reports are received on the juvenile's conduct, home, school work and so forth, and the court must tell the child or parent of any relevant matter contained in these reports which would help in avoiding further trouble.

The terms 'conviction' and 'sentence' are not used, being replaced by 'finding of guilt' and 'order made upon a finding of guilt'.[3]

A child or young person may only be brought before the court

[1] Children and Young Persons Act 1969, s. 29.
[2] Children and Young Persons Act 1969, s. 34.
[3] Children and Young Persons Act 1933, s. 59.

for an offence other than homicide, if it is also submitted that he is 'in need of care or control which he is unlikely to receive unless the court makes an order'.[1] No order can be made unless this condition is satisfied.

It is the duty of the court to have regard to the welfare of the juvenile brought before it.[2]

4 Orders of the court (offences)

On a finding of guilt the court may make one of the following orders:

Care order – A care order can be made only for an offence for which an adult could be imprisoned. It replaces the former fit person and approved school orders, and commits the juvenile to the care of the local authority, which then assumes the powers of the parent or guardian. It was, perhaps, unfortunate that at the time this change was made there was an administrative upheaval of the local authority welfare services.[3]

The Children and Young Persons Act 1969 was designed to remove much of the penal element by transferring children in care to the children's departments of local authorities but, by the time it was implemented, these departments had been swallowed up in the new Departments of Social Services.

The powers of guardianship transferred to a local authority by a care order do not permit the authority to bring up a child in any religion other than that in which he would have been brought up if the order had not been made.

A juvenile who is the subject of a care order may be placed in a community home, boarded out or, in some cases, allowed to remain at home. The local authority (which in this case is the authority in whose area the child lives) must exercise due guardianship, but, as has been said above, the service is badly under-staffed. It is reported that a fourteen-year-old boy who was the subject of a court order committed fifty-two offences during the

[1] Children and Young Persons Act 1969, s. 1.
[2] Children and Young Persons Act 1933, s. 44 (1).
[3] Local Authority Social Services Act 1970.

week-end after his court appearance, whilst another managed a hundred burglaries whilst an absconder.[1]

A care order lasts until the juvenile reaches the age of eighteen if the order is made before he is sixteen, otherwise it continues until he is nineteen. They can, however, be varied or rescinded.

Detention centres – A young person found guilty of an offence which, if he were an adult might involve imprisonment, may be sent to a detention centre for a period of not more than three months. Detention centres are establishments where the inmates are subjected to extremely rigid discipline. The number of such centres is very restricted.

Attendance centres – A juvenile found guilty of an offence punishable for an adult with imprisonment may be sent to an attendance centre for a number of periods, totalling not less than twelve hours (unless he is under fourteen), not more than twenty-four hours. The centre provides suitable employment or instruction. In the case of failure to attend, or a serious breach of the rules, the juvenile may be brought back to court and dealt with as though the attendance centre order had not been made. Those who have previously been to prison, borstal, a detention centre or an approved school cannot be sent to an attendance centre. The centre must be reasonably accessible.

Supervision order – An offender may be placed under the supervision of a local authority or, if he has attained the age of twelve, of a probation officer. If the offender is aged fourteen or more, the order cannot be made without his consent. Requirements as to mental treatment and residence with a named person may be inserted. The courts may no longer make a probation order in the case of a juvenile. The court names the local authority and petty sessions area of the juvenile's residence, and if residence with a named person is inserted, that person's residence will determine these conditions. The court has a discretion, if a child is aged at least twelve, to decide whether the supervising officer shall be a probation officer or social worker. There are circumstances in which a probation officer may be responsible for the supervision of a child under twelve.

[1] *The Times*, 8 November 1972.

The maximum period for a supervision order is three years, but it may be discharged earlier on application, and cannot extend beyond the offender's eighteenth birthday.

The Act charged twelve regional planning committees with the responsibility for developing 'intermediate treatment', which can be attached as a condition of a supervision order. Such a condition can specify that a child must live at a particular centre for not more than ninety days (if for a single period) or from time to time for a period not exceeding thirty days during each year of the order's currency. Intermediate treatment includes a requirement that a child shall take part in approved activities, which may include open youth clubs and evening classes, physical, cultural and recreational activities, and outdoor pursuits. Sir Keith Joseph, the Secretary of State for Social Services, announced that the first scheme had started in Yorkshire during the summer of 1973, and he hoped that a number of others would follow shortly.

Provisions exist for dealing with those who fail to comply with the requirements of a supervision order.

Hospital or Guardianship Orders – Where a juvenile is convicted of an offence for which an adult could be imprisoned on summary conviction, and two doctors certify that he is suffering from a mental illness, psychopathic disorder, sub-normality or severe subnormality, the court may make an order for detention in hospital if the offender can be admitted within twenty-eight days. Mental disorder in this sense is defined by the Mental Health Act 1959, s.4.

Alternatively, the court can commit such a person to the guardianship of the local authority, or any person willing to receive him.

If the court, in the interests of the public, deems that a hospital order should restrict the offender's discharge, he must be committed to the Crown Court[1] which may then make a hospital order with or without restriction.

Absolute discharge – After a finding of guilt the court may order the offender to be discharged absolutely. No further action may then be taken in respect of this offence, but it should be noted that

[1] Formerly the Assizes and Quarter Sessions.

an absolute discharge is to be distinguished from a discharge after acquittal. The court may order an absolute discharge if it feels that it is not desirable to inflict punishment and that a probation order is not appropriate.

Conditional discharge – The court may order the offender to be discharged on condition that he commits no further offence during such period as it may order which does not exceed twelve months. The offender must be told that, should he commit another offence during that period, he will be liable to punishment both for that and for the offence in respect of which he is now being discharged. The court may allow a consenting person to enter into a security for the child's good behaviour during the period of the discharge.

Fine – If an indictable offence is tried summarily,[1] the court may impose a fine, as it may for an offence for which an adult could be fined. A child may not be fined more than £10; a young person not more than £50,[2] but the parent or guardian may be ordered to pay the fine, and this must be done in the case of a child unless the court is satisfied that the parent has not neglected to exercise due care and control.

If a child is the subject of a care order, the local authority, acting *in loco parentis*, may be ordered to pay the fine. In July 1971 a thirteen-year-old boy was placed under a supervision order, and ten months later he was committed to the care of the Croydon local authority. In September 1972 he was again before the court charged with six motoring offences, burglary and wilful damage to a telephone box. The justices ordered the local authority to pay the fines amounting to £20, and this was upheld in the Queen's Bench Divisional Court.[3]

Compensation – An aggrieved person may ask for compensation for personal injury, loss or damage arising from an offence. This is limited to £400 for each offence, and the order is suspended until the time limit for an appeal has expired. A compensation order may be additional to any other order imposed, but juveniles may not be imprisoned for failure to pay a fine or compensation.

[1] Children and Young Persons Act 1969, s. 6.
[2] Magistrates' Courts Act 1952, s. 32; s. 6 and s. 34 (5).
[3] *The Times*, 9 December 1972.

Binding-over – The court may require the parent or guardian to enter into a recognizance to take proper care and exercise proper control in a sum not exceeding £50.

Borstal – Juveniles over the age of fifteen may be sent to the Crown Court for a borstal sentence, subject to certain conditions.[1] A person of similar age committed to the care of the local authority, and accommodated in a community home, may be brought before a juvenile court, with the consent of the Secretary of State, and committed to borstal if the court is satisfied that his behaviour in the community home is detrimental to others there. The Act provides power to raise this age if it is ultimately deemed appropriate.

Deferred sentence – With the offender's consent, the court may defer sentence after a finding of guilt for not more than six months. This will give the court an opportunity to test the offender's conduct (including the making of reparation where appropriate).

5 Remission to the juvenile court

If found guilty of an offence by another court, a juvenile may be committed to the juvenile court. This must occur if the court which has tried the case is a magistrates court other than a juvenile court unless the adult court has discharged him absolutely or made one of a number of specified orders. There is no right of appeal against remission, but the juvenile may, after the decision of the juvenile court, appeal to the Crown Court which may vary or rescind the order, or direct that the case be heard by different justices.

6 Appeals

A juvenile may appeal to the Crown Court against a finding of guilt, or against sentence, or both. If he pleaded guilty he may appeal only against sentence, but even then he may not do so if the order was a conditional discharge. A parent or guardian may also appeal to the Crown Court against a fine or other order for payment.

[1] Magistrates' Courts Act 1952, s. 28.

7 Care proceedings

A local authority, a constable, or other authorized person (such as an officer of the NSPCC) may bring a juvenile before the court if he is reasonably satisfied that the juvenile is in need of care (including protection and guidance) or control (including discipline). He must be further satisfied that this care or control cannot be achieved without an order of the court, and also that one of the following conditions applies:[1]

(a) his proper development is being avoidably prevented or neglected, or his health is being avoidably impaired or neglected, or he is being ill-treated;

(b) he is a member of the same household as a person found by the juvenile court to be suffering as in (a), and, having regard to this, he is likely to suffer similarly;

(c) he is exposed to moral danger;

(d) he is beyond the control of his parent or guardian;

(e) he is of compulsory school age, and is not receiving efficient full-time education;

(f) he is guilty of an offence other than homicide.

A summons or warrant may be issued, but if an arrested juvenile cannot be brought to court immediately he may be detained in a 'place of safety'[2] for not more than seventy-two hours, during which period he must be brought before a justice who may make an interim order. If a constable believes one of the first four conditions outlined above is applicable, he may be held in a place of safety for up to eight days, subject to a right by the juvenile or his parent or guardian to apply for release.

A justice may order detention in a place of safety for up to twenty-eight days if he is satisfied that one of the first five conditions mentioned above is fulfilled.

Proceedings for failure to receive full-time efficient and suitable education may be brought only by the local *education* authority.

A parent may no longer bring a juvenile before a court as being beyond control, but he may request the local authority to do so.

[1] Children and Young Persons Act 1969, s. 1.
[2] See page 382.

If the authority does not act within twenty-eight days the parent may ask the court to direct them to do so.

If reasonable, the parent or guardian's attendance may be required and enforced. The juvenile must be told the purpose of the hearing, but he may be excluded from the court whilst certain evidence is given, other than that relating to character or conduct. The parent or guardian, however, has a right to remain, but may in certain circumstances be excluded whilst the juvenile is giving evidence. Reports are received, as in the case of juveniles alleged to have committed an offence.

In attendance cases the head's certificate is admissible evidence.[1] When a parent appears before an adult court charged with failure to cause his child to receive efficient full-time education, the child or young person may be remitted to the juvenile court even though the parent is acquitted. The former provisions of the Education Act 1944, s. 40 have been repealed, and truancy *per se* without the need for care or control is no longer sufficient for prosecution of a juvenile. A child may be brought to court under the care procedure in such cases, provided he has reached the age of criminal responsibility, and even though he is old enough to be prosecuted. The standard of proof and the rules of evidence are the same as in a criminal case. If the offence be proved, the need for care or control must then be established on the basis of the civil burden of proof.[2]

In general, any juvenile court may hear care proceedings but, unless the case is dismissed, the juvenile must be sent to the court in whose area he lives for an order to be made.

8 Orders of the court (care or control)

The orders which can be made in case proceedings are similar to those in the case of offences outlined in section 4, above,[3] and the details in such kinds of orders are not repeated.

Case order – (page 384).

[1] Education Act 1944, s. 95 (2) (c).

[2] In a criminal trial the case must be proved beyond all reasonable doubt; in a civil action the court will proceed on the balance of probabilities.

[3] See pages 384–8.

Supervision order – (page 385).

Hospital or guardianship order – (page 386).

Binding over – Parents may be bound, provided they consent, to enter into a recognizance to exercise proper care and control. Where a young person is found guilty of an offence he may be bound over to keep the peace and to be of good behaviour for one year in a sum of up to £25. There is no appeal against this order.

Compensation – Compensation of up to £100 may be ordered if there is a finding of guilt arising from an indictable offence. This may be in addition to a case, supervision, hospital or guardianship order. The parent of a young person may be ordered to pay the compensation, and the parent or guardian of a child must be so ordered unless he has not conduced to the offence by neglect to exercise proper care or control.

Interim order – A court may commit a juvenile in case proceedings to the care of the local authority for not more than twenty-eight days if it has not decided how to deal with the case. Further interim orders may be made, and an unruly young person may be sent to a remand centre if one is available. The High Court may discharge an interim order and there is a right of appeal against it to the Crown Court.

9 Educational reports

Heads may be asked to provide a local authority with information to assist in making a decision whether to bring a child before the Court. The National Association of Head Teachers has advised its members that any written report for this purpose should be clearly marked as not intended for use as a report for the Court. When there has been a finding of guilt, or the justices have found proved a case in which there is no offence by the juvenile, the court is provided with reports on the child's general conduct and home surroundings, his school record and his medical history. The provision of the school report is the duty of the local authority but it is prepared, in the first instance, in the child's school. If the report is not immediately available, the court may remand the juvenile, either in custody or on bail, until it is received.

The purpose of these reports is to put the court in possession of the child's whole background so that it may deal effectively with the case and have regard to its duty to consider the welfare of the youngster before it. It is therefore important that the reports should be both factual and full. They are marked *Confidential* but the parent has a right to be told the substance of any part which reflects upon the home surroundings, and the child must be told of anything which deals with his conduct. This is not a breach of confidence: neither the parent nor the child can be expected to correct things which are wrong unless they are told what those things are.

In some cases a juvenile is remanded in custody for a special report which can be made only whilst he is under the supervision of a remand home for some time.

It cannot be too strongly emphasized that reports emanating from the school should be strictly factual, and confined to the juvenile's school career and matters which have a direct bearing on school life. Heads may be required to justify their statements in court, and should avoid subjective opinions.

10 Children at risk

The fact that English law has for many years been subject to the general principles of the European Convention on Human Rights has already been mentioned.[1] A conference of European ministers responsible for family affairs in fifteen countries was held in Nice in September 1973. The ministers felt that maladjustment attracts more attention today than in the past, but it has always existed in more or less acute forms. The community has a role to play which is preventive, rather than remedial, by helping the family to fulfil its tasks in an improved social environment.

The ministers noted that many countries are 'depenalizing' certain forms of behaviour, and relying more on the social services than the judicial authorities. It was felt that the cost of a preventive policy was offset by a sizeable decrease in the financing of remedial activities. Preventive action must begin before school age is reached. The first duty of governments is to improve the

[1] See pages 69–71.

quality of life: in town planning, day-care arrangements, and leisure facilities.

In all European countries there is an increasing tendency to keep the child in its family environment whilst, at the same time, providing necessary help. Any alternative environment should recreate, as far as possible, the family unit. Institutional treatment should be reserved for exceptional cases, and the services concerned with rehabilitation and prevention must have adequate and qualified personnel.[1]

Whatever the problems raised by the Children and Young Persons Act 1969, and however valid the criticisms made of its effectiveness in practice, it is interesting to note from the report of this conference that it is clearly in line generally with the practice of the remainder of Europe.

[1] Council of Europe Press Communiqué: Social News B (73) 67, 18 September 1973.

XVIII

IN CONFIDENCE

1 General

In the course of their duties, teachers collect a mass of confidential information of a widely varied character. On professional as well as on legal grounds it is vital that they should not abuse the confidence thus reposed in them.

Some of these items concern the work of their employers, as it is often necessary for a local education authority to take the advice of the schools, and particularly of the heads. Not infrequently this consultation is for the benefit of the profession and the inevitable result of a breach of confidence would be a tendency to withdraw similar confidences in the future.

Most confidential information, however, relates to pupils, and through it teachers learn a great deal about the history, character and homes of the children. It is grossly unfair to the children that such knowledge should be revealed, except where there is a duty laid upon the teacher to do so. There may, also, be occasions when information concerning colleagues should not be given, except under necessity of duty. The law relating to defamation of character is involved, and it is desirable that teachers should know something of this subject.

2 Libel and slander

Defamation of character is the publication of matter which may bring a person into the hatred, contempt or ridicule of other reasonable individuals, or which may cause him to be shunned by such people. It may take two forms, according to the permanence of its nature, spoken defamation being generally known as slander, whilst the more permanent forms, as, for example, written words, are known as libel. Defamation by broadcasting, although the words are spoken, is now statutorily libel,[1] as are words spoken, pictures, visual images, gestures and other methods of conveying meaning during the performance of a play.[2]

Where the defamation is transient in nature, as in spoken words or by gesture, it is slanderous and is always a civil, as distinct from a criminal, matter. To bring a successful action, the person defamed must prove 'special damages', that is, some actual pecuniary loss which is capable of valuation. It is not sufficient for the plaintiff to establish a risk of loss, or loss of a kind which cannot be valued, such as the loss of friends or health. There are, however, four classes of slander which are exceptions to this general rule, and which are actionable without proof of special damage:

(*a*) an implication that a woman is unchaste;

(*b*) an assertion that a person has committed a crime for which he could be imprisoned;

(*c*) a statement that a person is suffering from an infectious or contagious disease which would make him unfit for decent society;

(*d*) words which would disparage a person in his trade, business, profession or calling, even though the words do not refer directly to his conduct in that capacity.

Defamation of a more permanent character, as in writing, picture, effigy, cinematograph film or gramophone record, is known as libel and may be either a civil or, in certain circumstances, a criminal matter. The offender may be sued for damages by the person affronted, prosecuted by the Crown, or both. Libel becomes criminal if it is gross, often repeated, or likely to lead to a breach of the peace.

It is not a sufficient defence to maintain that there was no intention to defame, or even that the defendant had no knowledge of the plaintiff's existence. If the words might be considered by reasonable persons to refer to the plaintiff, they may be held by the courts to be defamatory. Since 1952, however, some relief has

[1] Defamation Act 1952, s. 1.
[2] Theatres Act 1968, s. 4.

been given to a defendant who has defamed someone innocently, and it is now possible to make an offer of amends. This may include an apology and, perhaps, a notification of the falsity of the statement to anyone to whom it has been made. Even if such an offer is not accepted, it will stand a defendant in good stead provided that he makes it as promptly as possible. This course is only open in the case of innocent, as distinct from careless, defamation.

Some years ago, a newspaper published a fanciful article about a motor rally at Dieppe, in which were described the amorous continental adventures of an imaginary Peckham churchwarden named Artemus Jones, 'the life and soul of the party that haunts the casino and turns night into day'. The writer probably thought that he had chosen a sufficiently unusual combination of names to avoid any real person but, unfortunately for him and the publishers, the article came to the attention of a barrister of the same name, who sued for libel. Both the jury and the House of Lords[1] found for the plaintiff. Under the Defamation Act 1952, it is probable that this would now be a set of circumstances in which an offer of amends would be accepted.

In May 1970 an anti-authoritarian publication called *Schoolkids' Oz* appeared. It included a letter, signed by a pupil at Owen's School, Islington, in which it was claimed that one of the masters at the school liked caning people, and that the writer had been caned by him. The letter was headed 'School Atrocities', and a large picture beside it contained unpleasant insinuations. The master issued a writ for damages for libel against the publishers, editor, distributors and eight other persons concerned with the publication. After the defendants had withdrawn any imputations, apologized for the embarrassment and humiliation caused, and agreed to pay substantial damages, the court gave leave for the record to be withdrawn.[2]

Defamation becomes actionable immediately the offending matter has been published, that is, the words spoken or the document shown to some person other than the complainant, or the

[1] *E. Hulton & Co.* v *Jones* [1910] AC 20.
[2] *Butler* v *Oz Publications (UK) Ltd* and *others* (1972) *The Times*, 30 June.

spouse of the defamer, but not before. The posting of a libellous postcard is actionable because, even though it is addressed to the person defamed, it may be read by someone else in the course of the post. Several years ago, a schoolmaster took a boy into his private room and spoke to him about his character. The boy told his father, who threatened to sue for slander. Such an action could not succeed, because the words complained of were not overheard by a third party.

No action for defamation can lie when the subject of the matter complained of has consented to its publication.

The truth of the matter complained of is a complete answer to an action for defamation, provided that the truth is complete and an answer to the whole defamation. A further defence is that the matter complained of is fair comment on a matter of public interest. A third line of defence is privilege and, since this might well be a teacher's answer should he be sued for defamation, the question must be considered in some detail.

3 Privilege

The law recognizes that, on certain occasions, it is so necessary to be able to speak or write freely, that statements made in these circumstances are privileged and not actionable for defamation.

Privilege is of two kinds, absolute and qualified. Absolute privilege is restricted to a limited class of speeches and documents and, within that class, the speaker or writer is protected even if the statements were made maliciously. It applies only to speeches in Parliament, reports published by order of either House, statements made during proceedings in courts and other tribunals recognized by law (whether by judges, parties, witnesses, counsel, solicitors and jurors), fair and accurate contemporaneous newspaper accounts of court proceedings,[1] and communications between officers of state in the course of their duty.

Qualified privilege covers reports made, whether written or

[1] The Judicial Proceedings (Regulation of Reports) Act 1926, has removed certain details of matrimonial causes and indecent matters arising in court proceedings from the protection of privilege, and they may not be published.

spoken, in the execution of a public or private duty, provided that they are made without malice, that is, absence of right motive. This defence may be used, therefore, in the case of testimonials and references, reports on children to parents, and reports made by teachers to the courts or youth employment officers. In the example quoted above, where a schoolmaster rebuked a boy,[1] he might have reported his conversation with the boy to the head-master. Had the boy's father then taken action on the ground of publication, the defence could have maintained that it is a school-master's duty to acquaint his head with certain facts about the boys in his care and that the occasion was privileged, since the schoolmaster had the boy's welfare at heart and the report could not, therefore, be construed as malicious.

In order to claim privilege, it is necessary for the person making the statement to believe, at the time he makes it, that the sub-stance of what he says is true. To make a defamatory statement knowing it to be false, is patently malicious and unworthy of the protection of such a defence.

Hume v *Marshall* – This is illustrated by a case in which the second master of a school reported a colleague's drunkenness to the headmaster. Lord Chief Justice Cockburn[2] held that the occasion was privileged but, since the report was exaggerated, he remitted the case to the jury for consideration of damages. The plaintiff was awarded forty shillings.

M'Carogher v *Franck* – In another case it was held that there may be circumstances in which the secretary of an Old Boys Association has a duty to speak to pupils of the school about a member of the teaching staff, in which case malice must be proved if an action for defamation is to succeed. It was alleged that the defendant, a magistrate, churchwarden, former city councillor and founder of the association had said of a member of the staff to six thirteen-year-old pupils: 'She is abnormal. She has been like that for three years. Women of that age are often like that. She is a rotten teacher.' Mr Justice Paull instructed the jury: 'There are occasions when a person ought to speak out about what he really

---

[1] See page 397.
[2] *Hume* v *Marshall* (1877) 42 JP 136; LCT 338.

thinks, and I have held that this is a proper case for Mr Franks to say what he really believed, provided that what he said was reasonable. If you find that Miss M'Carogher has not proved that Mr Franks acted maliciously . . . unless you think that Mr Franks was speaking because, for some reason, he had a down on her, he is entitled to the verdict.' The jury found for the defendant.[1]

4 Teachers and defamation

The law of defamation may affect teachers in two ways. From time to time, slanderous statements are made about teachers; most of these issue from parents in the heat of anger but, where professional damage could follow, a teacher may consider taking action in the courts. He cannot be too strongly urged to consult his professional association before doing so – and to abide by its advice. An ill-considered and hasty legal action may well do him more harm in the long run, professionally as well as financially, than he would suffer if he swallowed his pride and left the matter alone. If the circumstances warrant it, the association's solicitor will send a warning letter or, in some cases, the local education authority may be prepared to do this.

Barraclough v *Bellamy* – Letters about teachers written by parents to the local education authority are probably privileged, unless malice is proved. A successful action[2] was brought by the headmaster and headmistress of a school, following a 'round robin' sent to the authority by a number of people, some of them neither ratepayers nor parents of pupils in the school. The letter complained of the school's treatment of Empire Day, and the fact that the children had not saluted the flag on that occasion. The petition, described by Mr Justice Swift as 'a highly dangerous, cruel document, highly defamatory of the headmaster and headmistress', was held to be malicious, and damages amounting to £50 were awarded.

Ripper v *Rate* – In another case,[3] a subscriber to a school complained to the local education authority that the headmaster's

---

[1] *M'Carogher* v *Franks* (1964) *The Times*, 25 November; LCT 349.
[2] *Barraclough* v *Bellamy and others* (1928) *The Times*, 18 July; LCT 350.
[3] *Ripper* v *Rate* (1919) *The Times*, 17 January; LCT 342.

corporal punishment was excessive and amounted to cruelty. The court held that the occasion was privileged and that the letter was actuated, not by malice, but by a sincere desire to help towards the truth. The question of whether there had, or had not, been excessive corporal punishment was immaterial.

Hardwick v *Daily Express* – The courts are frequently very ready to uphold a professional reputation which has been maligned, but if the harm is not serious the damages awarded may seem a small return for the strain and time accompanying a High Court action. In December 1970 the *Daily Express* published the story of a small girl who was sent home to change when she appeared in a trouser suit at the infants' Christmas party at a Lincolnshire primary school. When she did not return, the headmaster suggested that she should come to the juniors' party on the following day, an invitation which was taken up.

The girl's mother complained to the press, and an article was published under the headline: 'NO TROUSERS – THE HEAD BANS JULIE, 6, FROM SCHOOL CHRISTMAS PARTY.' An apology was refused on the ground that the story represented the truth, the story was repeated in a feature article a month later, and the headmaster had to have his telephone disconnected because of the abusive calls he received.

In court it was said that the articles painted the headmaster as 'an unreasonable and unfeeling man which was a complete antithesis of the truth'. He tried to maintain a happy atmosphere, encouraging conventional dress without requiring school uniform, and he did not like children to feel deprived when others wore 'way-out fashionable gear'. The pupils had been warned beforehand that trouser suits would not be allowed. Awarding damages of £1,000, Mr Justice Bean said: 'It was a trivial, unimportant, insignificant incident, capable of so many quiet solutions; but it was blown up by the national press into a *cause célèbre* with specially posed photographs of the girl.' There had, however, been no serious aggravation of libel.[1]

Waldron v *Archer* – The warning at the beginning of this section

[1] *Hardwick* v *Daily Express* (1972) *Daily Telegraph*, 19 and 21 December.

not to rush headlong into a libel action is illustrated by a case in which the teacher plaintiff was successful. Nine parents wrote to the local education committee complaining that a teacher in a Kidderminster school had slapped her pupils, poked them with pencils, called them liars, and had sworn at them. The teacher had been forced to resign her appointment following a disciplinary inquiry based on the complaint. Mr Commissioner Gibbens found that there had been intense antagonism between the plaintiff and her headmaster who had told the education authority of complaints about her nagging and bullying. She was 'more of a strict disciplinarian than usual', but the parents complained that she ruled by 'sheer terrorism'. They had based their allegations on complaints by their children, but a child of seven or eight is an unreliable informant. 'With every day memory fades and imagination grows. The parents dredged every recess of memory and imagination for every pebble they could sling at the plaintiff. She was sometimes moody and sharp, but was popular.'

As has been said above, letters written about teachers by parents to their local education authority are privileged: but, as in this case, the defence of privilege is destroyed by malice on the part of the writer. The Commissioner found that the parents had acted recklessly out of 'anger, prejudice and ill-will', and the teacher was awarded £500 in damages with costs estimated at £5,000 to £10,000.

The sequel, however, was less happy for the teacher. Her new post was eighteen miles away from her home, involving her in extra expenditure of £20 a month in fares and £10 for a dog-sitter. Five months after the hearing the damages had been paid into court, but some of the mothers were saying they could not afford their share of the costs; and that their husbands, who were not signatories to the libellous petition, were not liable. In the meantime the successful plaintiff had found it necessary to borrow money to meet her additional expenses.[1]

At times teachers may have, in the course of their duties, to make comments on the work or character of other persons. When,

[1] *Waldron* v *Archer* and *others* (1971) *Guardian*, 16 February; (1971) *Education*, 26 February and 16 July.

in the nature of things, such reports must be adverse, it is possible that the issue of defamation may arise in some degree. If the reports are made in the execution of a duty, whether it be public, private, legal or moral, they are protected by qualified privilege, provided that they are not actuated by malice. In such cases, no action can succeed against the teacher. More than a century ago, Mr Justice Wightman, speaking of the importance of letters of character, said,[1] 'It is of importance to the public that characters should be readily given. The servant who applies for the character and the person who is to take him are equally benefited. Indeed, there is no class to whom it is of so much importance that characters should be freely given as honest servants. It is for that reason that the communications are protected.'

So far as teachers are concerned, such reports fall into five main categories: testimonials, references, school reports, reports on teachers, and reports to the juvenile courts. The last group has already been considered in the chapter on 'Children in Trouble';[2] the others must be treated in some detail here.

5 Testimonials
A testimonial is an open letter of recommendation which becomes the property of the person to whom it refers immediately it is given to him. There is no obligation on a teacher to give a testimonial to a pupil, nor on a head to write one for an assistant. If he does so, however, it must be a fair report. There is no need to assign any reason for refusal and, indeed, it is unwise to do so, but it is advisable to point out that this does not necessarily mean that the testimonial, if given, would therefore be adverse. When a testimonial is refused, it is reasonable to give a certificate of service which states the period and capacity in which the writer has known the applicant.

It should be remembered that actions arising from testimonials may be initiated from either of two directions. The recipient may claim that the document is malicious, and sue for libel. If, on the other hand, it is over-generous and the new employer suffers thereby, he may bring an action for damages.

[1] In *Gardener* v *Slade* [1849] 13 QB 796.   [2] See pages 391–2.

Testimonials may be withdrawn if, at any time subsequent to their issue, the writer learns of any fact which would materially affect his opinion. This course should be taken only in extreme cases, and after the writer has consulted his professional association, since withdrawal may lead to the threat of an action for defamation.

The practice of giving testimonials to pupils by assistant teachers varies from school to school. In some, the head prefers that the official school testimonial, over his signature, should stand alone because of the embarrassment which may arise when there are marked differences between the head's and an assistant's opinion of a pupil. In such cases it would be unprofessional for an assistant to act contrary to the head's wishes. This is particularly the case when there are certain categories of pupils who are debarred from receiving testimonials. Some heads of grammar schools refuse testimonials to 'premature leavers' who have not completed the course for the Ordinary level of the General Certificate of Education, merely giving a statement to the effect that the person named was a pupil of the school between certain dates. It would be disloyal for an assistant to grant a testimonial in such cases.

Testimonials for pupils are less common than was once the case, having been replaced to a large extent by the *proforma* required by the careers service. Nevertheless, it is still not uncommon for a school-leaver to ask for an open testimonial. More often such a request comes from a former pupil who may have left a decade or more earlier, so that few of the staff can remember his achievements clearly if, indeed, they ever knew him. It is therefore important in secondary schools to retain indefinitely an adequate record about every pupil who has passed through the school in order that verification can be provided at any time.[1]

[1] When civil servants and others employed in work involving national security are being screened intensively, it is by no means unusual for the authorities to investigate their school lives, even when they have reached the middle of their careers. On such occasions it is greatly to the benefit, not only of the nation but also of the ex-pupil, to be able to retrieve the necessary information.

An open testimonial for a pupil or former pupil should include the following points:

(a) Clear evidence to identify the subject (e.g. if there has been a change of name by marriage or otherwise), including date of birth and the dates of admission to, and leaving, the school;

(b) an outline account of the pupil's record, with an indication as to whether he stayed beyond the age of compulsory education; application to and quality of work; external examination results;

(c) a note on the pupil's general development throughout his school career, including any factors beyond the pupil's control which may have accounted for erratic progress, e.g. a protracted period of ill-health;

(d) a summary of the pupil's contribution to the school in out-of-school activities, on the sports field, or in special responsibilities undertaken or offices held;

(e) a positive comment on character and conduct: this is especially important in the case of pupils who have struggled to achieve even moderate results against overwhelming odds.

In large secondary schools it is now usual for the official school testimonials to be written (and even signed) by the house staff.[1] There is no reason why pupils should not be asked to provide a list of any achievements which they wish to have included. When there is doubt as to whether a particular point should be included it is wise for the writer to consult as many appropriate staff as possible, especially if there is a risk that the resulting comment might be held to be derogatory.

In selecting those who will be asked to write testimonials for them, teachers should remember that appointing bodies expect to see an up-to-date recommendation from the head under whom they are serving at the time of the application. Local education

---

[1] In the author's school this is the practice for pupils until the time when they actually leave school; after which individual records are sent to the Director of Studies who is thereafter responsible for both open testimonials and confidential references.

authorities will often write for a confidential statement if there is
no testimonial, even though the head may not be named among
the referees. Those who feel diffident about their head's reaction
to a request for a testimonial should remember that it is likely to
be far less favourable if the first news he has that one of his staff
is on the wing comes through an inquiry from another school.

It is always useful to include testimonials from people whose
names or positions carry weight, *if the candidate is really well-
known to them,* but a sound testimonial from someone relatively
unknown will do the candidate far more good than a vague statement by some eminent individual who has manifestly met the
applicant casually and infrequently.

It is an increasingly common practice, especially in large
secondary schools, for heads to ask teachers for a note of any
points which they may wish to have included and, particularly,
for a list of their special contributions to the life and work of the
school beyond the ordinary calls of duty. It is also now not unusual for a head to show a draft to the teacher concerned or, at
least, to give him a specific opportunity to discuss it if he feels
there might be any relevant omissions. This does not mean that
teachers are asked to write their own testimonials. It is very easy,
particularly when a teacher has served in a school for a number of
years, to forget at the moment of writing some signal contribution
which the teacher feels with every justification to merit inclusion.
It is often those who have rendered most meritorious service in
this way who would be most diffident about appearing to criticize
an appraisal of their work. Yet they are bound to feel hurt that
something which they believe to have been worthwhile has been
overlooked.

A testimonial given to a serving teacher should contain some
reference to such of the following points as are applicable:

(*a*) the professional relationship between the writer and the
subject, and the period for which they have been known to each
other;

(*b*) the work done by the teacher in the school including the
subjects and the age-range of the pupils taught, details of

external examination work, and posts of responsibility held (including, with dates, any internal promotions).

(c) courses attended, additional qualifications gained during service in the school, and a note of additional relevant experience, e.g. evening work in a local college of further education;

(d) an assessment of the quality of this work, of the teacher's relationships with children, colleagues and parents, including a reference to the teacher's discipline;

(e) a note on any out-of-school activities connected with the school and, if of some importance, in the neighbourhood generally;

(f) an assessment of the teacher's character and general suitability for the profession;

(g) an expression of regret (if this is so!) that the teacher is seeking another appointment, and an offer to answer any specific questions.

It is sometimes thought that this final offer is designed by an unscrupulous head to give him an opportunity of 'playing down' what is written in the testimonial, but this is not so and, indeed, the reverse is often the case. It should be remembered that a testimonial may be used for a considerable number of applications; further inquiries may enable the head to make a particularly strong recommendation in view of the specific requirements of a particular appointment.

A testimonial often speaks most clearly through what is omitted, rather than through what is actually written. For this reason it is important to ensure that no material details are missed. The absence of a reference to discipline in a teacher's testimonial is a case in point, and may – though by no means necessarily – mean that the holder is a poor disciplinarian. Since testimonials are open documents, they tend to refer to the strengths of those on whose behalf they are written, and to make no mention of weaknesses. It is open to a teacher who has received a testimonial which does not cover such a detail to ask for its inclusion, but he can hardly then complain if the reference is uncomplimentary provided, of course, that it is not malicious.

Testimonials, whether for staff or pupils, should be as factual as possible. Anything which might be regarded as a slur should be omitted. It is wiser to refuse a testimonial if, when honestly given, it is likely to be more of a hindrance than a help to the subject. In short, an open testimonial should 'accentuate the positive'.

The owner should not part with the original of a testimonial, as some authorities do not return documents enclosed with applications; in any case there is always a risk of loss in the post. A type-written, duplicated or photo copy should be forwarded, and this must be an exact copy, without addition or omission. The original should be taken to any interview in order that it may be compared with the copy if the appointing body wishes to do so.

Under the Servants Characters Act 1792, a candidate 'offering himself as a servant with a false certificate of character' is liable to a fine of £20 for each offence.

6 References

Whereas testimonials are general appraisals of an individual either in a professional or personal capacity, references are confidential letters of recommendation. They constitute an attempt, within the honest judgment of the writer, to assess the suitability of the subject for a particular appointment for which he has applied. They remain the property of the person to whom they are addressed. In the nature of things they may be much more frank and detailed than testimonials, but they also must be fair and without malice. When the writer of a testimonial is also asked for a reference, he should take care that the two are not inconsistent; a brilliant testimonial followed by a mediocre reference reflects more clearly on the character of the writer and his inability to judge that of others, than on the capabilities of the person about whom he is writing.

On the other hand the writer of a reference should not feel completely inhibited by this warning. Situations arise where someone who is, in general terms, a most acceptable person, uses a testimonial to apply for a post for which he is not a suitable candidate or for which he is not yet, perhaps, sufficiently experienced. In such cases the referee must be utterly frank, whatever his general approval of the candidate's qualities which he has praised sincerely in an open testimonial.

The contents of a confidential reference should never, in the author's view, be divulged to the person about whom it has been written. In recent years there has been a growth of opinion amongst certain persons concerned with education that a teacher is entitled to see everything which is written about him. It is argued that this course would avoid the malicious reference, or one by which a head seeks to retain a valuable member of his staff by preventing his success in applications elsewhere. It is argued that, if what is written in the reference is true, no one will be harmed by disclosure; and at least one governing body makes a practice of revealing the full contents of all confidential references to every candidate called for interview.

There are several objections to this practice. Human nature being what it is, there is always a risk that a referee may be malicious or prejudiced; but such cases are extremely rare. The generality of the statement is an unjustified slur on the great majority of educational referees, most of whom go to a great deal of trouble to write honest reports in the belief that their confidence will be respected. If a referee believes that a candidate has overreached himself in an application he must remember that he has a duty not only to the applicant, but also to the prospective employer.[1] If, however, the contents of a reference given in such circumstances are revealed to the teacher who is the subject they may, quite unnecessarily, destroy his self-confidence, inhibit his professional development, damage his relationship with the referee, lead to unjustified accusations of bias and make continuation in his existing post difficult, if not impossible. The NUT, in a footnote to its Code of Professional Conduct, recognizes this need for confidentiality and exempts such documents from its general rule that it is unprofessional for one teacher to make a report upon another without at the time acquainting him with its nature.[2]

[1] The reader is referred back to Mr Justice Wightman's statement in *Gardener* v *Slade* [1849] 13 QB 796, quoted on page 402.
[2] See footnote on page 99.

Some employers ask for a reference when they have made an offer of employment to a candidate. If the referee knows this to be so, he should send a courteous note explaining that it is not his practice to give references in such circumstances, since an adverse report might lead to a withdrawal of the offer (or to dismissal, if the employee has started work) and a consequent action for defamation of character. He may add a certificate of attendance (in the case of pupils) or of service (in the case of staff) and, if able to do so, a statement that the candidate's conduct was satisfactory. He should express no view as to the suitability of the candidate for the post which has been offered. Employees who follow this practice have been roundly condemned by the Head Masters Association and the National Association of Head Teachers, but in spite of this there are still some who continue to make such inquiries.

When a head is called upon to reply to categorical questions about a pupil and the answer must be adverse, it is often worthwhile to see the child's parent before doing so, in order to explain the circumstances. Presumably, now that the age of majority has been lowered, it would be more correct to hold this discussion with the pupil himself if he has reached the age of eighteen.

References should be addressed personally to the inquirer, and the envelope should be marked 'Private and Confidential'.

As a general rule, references should follow the broad lines of a testimonial, but, as has been indicated above, they are structured to show to the best advantage the candidate's suitability for the post in question. Unlike testimonials, it is practically impossible to withdraw them for, whereas a testimonial may be used for successive applications over a period of some years, a reference is usually acted upon finally within a matter of weeks, or even days, from the time of writing.

Inquiries are sometimes made by telephone. Exceptional care should be taken in answering questions in this way, particularly if there is a chance that the call may be intercepted. Adverse answers should not be given over the telephone, the inquirer being advised that a reply will be sent in writing.

When it is the practice to return copy testimonials to unsuccessful candidates, care should be taken to see that references are not inadvertently enclosed. The author once received a request from a candidate for the return of references on the ground that she did not wish to trouble her referees again. To have returned the documents under such circumstances would have been a sheer breach of confidence.

Teachers proposing to use a person's name for reference purposes should remember that it is exceedingly discourteous to do so without previous inquiry as to the willingness of that person so to act. When entering the particulars of a reference on the application form, it is important to spell the sponsor's name correctly and to add his status for the guidance of the employer. It is surprising how careless teachers are about details of this kind. The author has received applications from avowed churchmen who have made complete havoc of the niceties of ecclesiastical nomenclature and, on one occasion, having taken up a reference he received an acid comment on the spelling of the referee's name which was, apparently, not that adopted by the candidate. Carelessness in an important document such as an application is not indicative of the kind of attitude which heads are looking for amongst members of their staff.

7 School terminal reports

Some firms make a practice of writing to schools to ask for copies of the recent terminal reports on a pupil who has applied to them for a post, or asking a candidate to take them to the interview.

Such reports are confidential as between the head of the school and the parent of the pupil. The nature of the comments and the standards employed are such that they are not readily comparable between schools, or even between different classes in the same school. They are thus likely to present a misleading picture to an employer who does not really understand their true purpose. A note explaining this will sometimes be sufficient, but if the firm is pressing the head should consult his professional association.

It has to be remembered that terminal reports are written in bulk at times of the year when teachers are subject to great pressure. Their function is to keep open a formal channel of communication between the school and the parent for the benefit of a particular pupil. As a rule every teacher who has a hand in a child's education at any given time will have his other hand in the preparation of the report. To some extent, therefore, these documents consist of a number of subjective statements which the form-master, house-master or head tries to draw into a coherent whole in a short comment at the end.

Sometimes an able pupil, who is going through a period when he is not giving of his best, may have a poor report which is intended as a spur to greater effort. If, as a result, he reforms and thereafter produces work of a standard commensurate with his ability, it is both unfair and embarrassing that his lapse in, say, the third form should be subjected to the scrutiny of a prospective employer several years later. *Per contra* a pupil of limited ability may receive a glowing report for a massive effort which has taken him near the top of a remedial form. It is rare, moreover, for terminal reports to reveal some underlying causes of bad patches in a pupil's career such as personal illness, the death of a parent or, perhaps, staffing difficulties in school.

On one occasion the author received a visit from the father of a pupil who had just left school. On the following Monday she was due to start work as a junior clerk in one of the best-known corporations in the country, and had been asked to take her school reports, not to the interview, but on her first day of employment! The school report card was issued annually and in this particular case there were two poor reports: one, unhappily, for her last year at school. The purpose of the father's visit was to put a request for a modified and more satisfactory replacement. 'Let's face it,' he said, 'would you employ anyone with a report like that?' He clearly foresaw his daughter's first post lasting one day. Even had it been possible to comply with his wish (some of the staff who had signed the card were scattered to the four corners of the earth), it would have been thoroughly dishonest to do so. A telephone call to the staff controller of the organization safeguarded that particular girl's career and, after a lengthy correspondence, the corporation agreed to drop the practice.

Enough has been said to indicate that terminal (or yearly, or half-yearly) reports are inadequate and unreliable predictions of a pupil's likelihood of success or failure in any given career. It is the testimonial, reference or careers service report which is designed, and most likely, to provide a balanced assessment of the pupil in his future working life.

If, in the end, the only chance of a successful candidature is the production of the report, this is the responsibility of the parent. Under no circumstances should the head forward the document, and he should advise any parent who proposes to do so of its limited purpose.

8 Reports on teachers

It is part of the National Union of Teachers' Code of Professional Conduct that it is unprofessional for a teacher to make a report on another teacher without first acquainting him with the nature of the report and, if it be written, allowing him to read it before transmission. In the case of a written report, the teacher should be asked to sign a statement that he has read the report and noted its contents. Although this practice is binding only on members of the Union in making reports, it is widely accepted as good practice throughout the profession.

This does not apply to confidential references concerned with appointments, but it does include reports on teachers on probation, whether such reports be satisfactory or not. Some local education authorities include on their probation report forms a space for the teacher to sign an acknowledgement that he has noted the character of the report, and such authorities will not accept these reports without the probationer's signature save in the most exceptional circumstances. Teachers who discover that such a report has been made without their knowledge may consider it desirable to approach their professional associations.

Teachers have no right to see reports which are made on them by inspectors either of the local education authority or of HM Inspectorate. It is, however, now the practice of inspectors to discuss with teachers any adverse comments which they propose to include in a report.

The strictly legal position may be somewhat different from the professional ethic. A headmistress wrote to the local education authority, requesting the transfer of one of her staff for the benefit of the school. The judge held[1] that the occasion was privileged, provided that the letter had been written without malice.

9 Addresses of staff and pupils

The addresses and telephone numbers of staff and pupils should not be divulged to any outside person by a teacher. If asked by a police officer, in the course of his duty, for the address of a child, the head should consult his local education authority before giving it. If the officer objects, he should give the information, note the objection in the school annals, and inform the authority.

When persons unconnected with the school organization request the addresses of members or former members of the staff, they should be instructed to write to the teacher at the school so that the letter may be forwarded.

10 Press, radio and television

Some local education authorities have a clause in their staff code which restricts the activity of their employees in making public statements on any work which is the concern of the authority. When such a clause exists, it is implied in the teacher's agreement.[2]

Quite apart from this rule, it is inadvisable for teachers to give to the press any information which they may have acquired through their employment, whenever such information may cause embarrassment or distress to anyone, whether employer, pupil, parent or colleague. Most authorities allow certain non-controversial news items to be disseminated by the schools. It is, for example, usually permitted to release the news that the mayor will present the prizes at the annual speech day, but it is extremely risky to admit to the press, even when the editorial staff have wind of the fact, that a pupil has absconded from home, or that Such-

[1] In *Reeve* v *Widderton* (1927) *Daily Telegraph*, 16 June.
[2] This does not apply to the staffs of voluntary aided schools unless the code is imported into their agreements.

and-Such Primary School is the only one in the town to have secured grammar school places in the eleven-plus examination.

If an authority requires its staff to dissociate their books or articles from the views of the authority, and to make it clear that the work is purely individual, care should be taken to see that this is done.

This is an area where practice has tended to leave precept far behind. For many years teachers complained that the mass media took no interest in what went on in schools; today the complaint is often heard that education has become too much a subject of discussion of the wrong kind. Those authorities which restrict public pronouncements by their teachers do not always enforce their regulations, even when statements are damaging to the authority, its schools, its teachers and the children whose education is in their care.

Unfortunately bad news is often more acceptable than good news; and there is a tendency to emphasize what is wrong, and to ignore what is right in the public services. The mass media also give considerable opportunity to those who seek to promote themselves by denigrating others. Furthermore, as everyone who has made statements knows only too well, the most carefully considered comment can be transformed to suit editorial policy by blue pencil or scissors.

Strictly speaking, teachers are bound by any regulations which apply to them. If, because regulations do not exist (or are not applied), they find themselves free to express their views and to reveal information acquired in the course of their duties, it is to be hoped that they will use their discretion to avoid damaging others with whom they are professionally concerned.

XIX

MISCELLANEOUS

1 Official visitors

All schools today receive a large number of official visitors. Many of them are concerned only with the head; others will also wish to meet the assistant staff.

Managers or governors may visit the school from time to time in order to see for themselves what is happening in the establishment for which they are responsible. The periodic visits of HMIs (and the penalties for obstructing them) have already been noticed,[1] and there are also callers who are concerned with such matters as audit, buildings and equipment.

In most cases there is no doubt about the identity of the visitor, but it is not unknown for unauthorized persons to attempt to gain access to schools by pretending to have official business there. There is no discourtesy in asking an unknown person to produce evidence of his authority in case of doubt. This is particularly important if the visitor seeks any contact with the pupils.

From time to time, specially invited guests may come to a school to give lectures to children, as the principal speaker at a prizegiving or on other similar occasions. Such visitors must be treated with due honour, and it is a good practice to keep a visitors' book to be signed on such occasions.

The increase in the number of ancillary services has produced a corresponding rise in the number of people who call at the schools from time to time. The medical staff, meals staff, youth organizer, welfare officer and careers officer all pay more or less frequent visits. If children are subject to court orders, it is not uncommon for the supervising officers to look in from time to time

[1] See page 35.

for an up-to-date progress report on the children in whom they are interested.

2 Publishers' representatives and others

Some heads and, to a lesser extent, some assistants are concerned about their position in dealing with representatives who visit schools to promote, or sell, the products of a commercial undertaking. Their fear may be based on an unfortunate personal experience or on reports which they have heard of colleagues who have suffered at the hands of unscrupulous salesmen.

Like every other area of life, the commercial world has its bad eggs. Unfortunately the reputation of honest, straightforward businessmen, who form by far the great majority, is tarnished by the activities of the few. Local education authorities vary in their attitude to representatives' visits to schools, and heads should be aware of the rules and practice of their own authority.

There are, however, certain general guidelines, and in discussing this subject it is convenient to distinguish between those who operate on a free-lance basis and the accredited representatives of the principal educational publishing houses.

Schools are sometimes approached by representatives who employ what are known as 'hard sell' tactics. The author knows of a young schoolmaster who was persuaded into buying, on hire-purchase, an admittedly good set of educational reference works by being told that it was his duty to his pupils to spend money on keeping himself abreast of modern practice. This happened many years ago.

There are various other practices which are dubious from an ethical point of view. Some years ago a very small number of photographers gave schools a good deal of trouble, either by failing to produce promised discounts for the school fund, or by insisting that the school paid for any copies not returned or paid for by pupils. Vigilance on the part of the professional associations seems to have solved this problem and, in recent years, schools have suffered more from the purveyors of plastic labelling tape.

In this trade a representative may visit the school or, and this is more usual, a telephone call may be made offering a free embossing machine or some additional piece of equipment which is attractive to a school struggling to cope on a limited capitation budget. Some time after the order is delivered and paid for, another telephone call advises the head that 'the next part of your order is now ready for delivery' and, if he protests, he is told that he has ordered a considerable quantity, sometimes running into some hundreds of pounds in value. In a large school the head should verify at this point that no other authorized person has placed the order.

Occasionally, if the protests continue, the head is told that unless he accepts the order the local education authority will be informed. It is most unlikely that this would be done, and the person who should do so (the head concerned) often refrains through fear of appearing incompetent, naïve or downright foolish. Unless he does advise either the authority or his professional association, the next consignment will undoubtedly arrive, and the next. . . .

Sometimes, in reply to an inquiry about goods which are attractive to a particular school, a firm will send additional products which have not been ordered. In one case the head's protest brought a photocopy of the order form she had sent. The tick inserted by the description of the unwanted item was, even on a photostat, plainly made by another hand with another pen.

A person who receives unsolicited goods may, after six months, treat them as an unconditional gift. This is contingent on the proviso that he has not agreed to acquire or return them, that the sender did not take possession within that period, and that the recipient did not refuse the sender reasonable permission to take his goods back. Furthermore the recipient must, at least thirty days before the end of the six months, advise the sender of his name and address, the address from which the goods may be collected, and that the goods were unsolicited. The notice may be sent by post. It is an offence to demand payment or to threaten (or take steps towards) any process to recover the value of unsolicited goods. Unsolicited goods are defined as goods received by a person who has not requested them, or on whose behalf no request has been made.[1]

Without implying that all of the others are rogues (indeed, most are honest and helpful) there is one body of representatives about whom schools need have no qualms. The representatives of the leading educational publishers may belong to their own professional body, the Association of Publishers' Educational Representatives. Most of them do belong, and are bound by the strict code of conduct laid down by an organization which is jealous of the reputation of its members, their profession and their employers. The code is as follows:[2]

(a) An educational representative is one authorized by his firm to visit schools, colleges and any other educational in-stitutions to display therein the books and/or materials produced by his firm for use in schools, and to assist the staff in evaluating their suitability.

(b) He enters any school, college or other educational institution under the authorization of the director of education and/or at the invitation of the principal, either or both of which may be withheld at any time. In certain areas the authorization of the director to the representative to visit schools controlled by the authority takes tangible form, i.e. a printed permit which is issued to the firm and which expires annually. The director is fully at liberty to refuse to issue or renew such permits and is not obliged to give his reasons for so doing. A representative may not visit any school controlled by such an authority without having in his possession a valid permit.

(c) It is accepted practice that the representative shall not

[1] Unsolicited Goods Act 1971.
[2] The author is indebted to the APER for permission to reprint the Association's code of conduct, and for further advice in preparing this section. The Association will investigate any complaint that one of its members has broken the code, whether made by a teacher individually, or through his local education authority or professional association. The address of the Honorary Secretary is at present: 3 Seavale Road, Clevedon, Somerset, BS21 7QB.

interview subordinate members of the staff without the approval of the principal, nor interview any pupil or student.

(*d*) The representative shall at no time attempt to canvass for orders or to take orders, or attempt to make a direct sale of any book or item of material either on or off the premises of any school, college or educational institution, except in so far as he has been instructed by his firm to visit authorized wholesalers or retailers for that purpose.

(*e*) It is accepted practice that the representative shall not normally make more than one visit in any one academic year to any school, college or educational institution.

(*f*) The representative shall at all times use his best endeavours to promote the sale of the books and/or materials published or manufactured by his firm, but none the less he shall answer to the best of his ability any questions relating to the books and materials, published or manufactured by a firm other than his own, put to him by members of the teaching profession.

(*g*) The representative shall not in the course of business call upon any member of the teaching profession at his private address unless expressly requested so to do by the teacher concerned.

The code was drawn up jointly by the Association and the Educational Publishers Council. The latter body is closely associated with the Publishers Association and, as all the principal educational publishers are in membership, it therefore has the approval of the representatives' employers.

The educational publishers' representative does not visit a school to sell books; indeed, the code prohibits him from direct selling. His primary function is to provide a service which enables teachers to discuss books and materials from different publishing houses in their own schools. This is of great advantage to the staff of a school: the representative can give them his full attention without distraction from other customers, and the whole staff of a department can make a leisurely appraisal together as to the best possible use of the limited resources at their disposal.

There is, however, another advantage to the teaching profession generally which should not be overlooked. As Professor Ivor Davies has pointed out,[1] we live in a world of rapidly accelerating change but this revolution has virtually bypassed education. 'After a long period of gradual and placid evolution, the conservative and traditional practices are gradually giving way. Progress, which has been so slow, is now accelerating to such an extent that an economy is now being built around education.'

In this dynamic situation teachers often complain that they cannot find the right books or materials. The representative is the publisher's ear to the ground, in the unique position of being able to feed back to his house the changing needs of teachers as he is confronted with them in discussion. He can prevent publishers and teachers from working in isolation, and so enable the production of material of the kind and quality required in schools.

Alone among education authorities, the ILEA will not authorize publishers' representatives to visit its schools. It is said that the Authority's own display in its equipment centre, the accessibility of many of the publishing houses and large bookshops, together with the London Head Teachers Association's annual exhibition, render this service unnecessary. Furthermore, the Authority seeks to protect heads from unnecessary disturbance and annoyance. This regulation does not apply to voluntary-aided schools unless the managers or governors have passed a resolution in these terms, as the Authority's regulations are not implied in the rules of management or articles of government.

Teachers must, of course, observe any rules applicable to them, and they should not admit persons wishing to sell articles to pupils, that is, to use the school as a market, unless it is definitely known that the authority has given permission in a particular instance. At least one authority is prepared to license ice-cream vendors to sell their wares in playgrounds.

To summarize, teachers should seek advice from the local education authority or their professional association before entering into any contract. If they feel at any stage in the course of

[1] I. K. Davies: *The Management of Learning* (McGraw Hill, 1971), page 20.

business that they are not being dealt with honestly, they should seek similar advice immediately. On the other hand, with the exception of schools to which the ILEA regulation applies, they need not be concerned about the admission of accredited publishers' representatives. In the very rare event of such a representative being in breach of his code, retribution will be both rapid and effective.

3 Other visitors

Unauthorized persons remain on the school premises as licensees[1] and, once the head's licence has been withdrawn, which can be done by asking them to leave, they become trespassers if they remain. If such visitors refuse to go, the request should be repeated, with a warning that the police will be called if necessary. If he deems it to be necessary, the head or his deputy may remove an intruder, but he may use no more force than is necessary to do so. It is far better, if possible, to wait for the police and ask them to remove the unwelcome guest, so that their evidence is available if required.

When unauthorized persons have entered the school on false pretences, and particularly when they have sought contact with the children, the local education authority should be informed immediately so that appropriate steps may be taken.

Parents are by far the most frequent visitors to a school, and they come for a wide variety of reasons. Generally speaking, this is to be welcomed, for it tends to produce a friendly atmosphere between staff and parents. It must, however, be borne in mind that parents have no right of entry to a school and that their presence is entirely at the discretion of the head. A parent, just as much as any other visitor, becomes a trespasser immediately that leave is withdrawn.

Under no circumstances should any parent be allowed to abuse a member of the staff, and such conduct should be reported at once to the local education authority. If an assault is threatened, the teacher may also wish to consult his professional association.

Difficulties sometimes arise when attempts are made to remove

[1] See pages 274–5.

the child of a broken marriage by the parent who has not been granted custody. Great tact is needed in dealing with a situation which can rapidly turn to the child's detriment. It is always wise to inform the authority so that, if the parent's conduct becomes persistent, arrangements can be made to restrain him or her.

It should go without saying that a pupil must never be released into the custody of a stranger.

The question of accidents to visitors has already been noticed.[1]

4 Complaints by neighbours

Much of what has already been said about other visitors applies to visits by persons who come to a school to make complaints about pupils. Such complaints should be received courteously, with a promise that they will be investigated. The names and addresses of pupils should not be given to the complainant as, in a case of mistaken identity, there may be serious results from such action. Under no circumstances should the visitor be allowed to hold an identification parade unless the local education authority has given permission for this to be done because of the gravity of the complaint in a particular case.

Complaints by neighbours that their property has been damaged by pupils should be referred to the authority's legal department. Care should be taken not to say anything which could be construed as an admission of liability in dealing with a complaint of this nature.

5 Police investigations

From time to time, police officers visit schools in connection with investigations which they are conducting into alleged offences. It is an offence to obstruct a police officer in the course of his duty, but the head of a school also has a duty to his pupils and their parents.

Interrogations carried out by the police should be in accordance with the principles laid down by Her Majesty's judges in the

---

[1] See pages 274-5.

'judges' rules'[1] which also deal with giving cautions and taking statements.

The present rules were adopted in 1964 by a meeting of all the judges of the Queen's Bench. They are designed to prevent investigations from taking a form which would render the resulting evidence inadmissible. They do not affect (a) the duty of every citizen to assist in the discovery and apprehension of offenders, (b) the fact that the police (except on arrest) cannot compel anyone to come to (or remain in) a police station, (c) the right to consult a solicitor privately at every stage, (d) the need to charge without undue delay, or (e) the essential need for all statements to be voluntary.

The administrative directions which accompany the rules include the following statement:

> As far as possible children (whether suspected of crime or not) should only be interviewed in the presence of a parent or guardian, or, in their absence, some person who is not a police officer and is of the same sex as the child. A child or young person should not be arrested, nor even interviewed, at school if such action can possibly be avoided. Where it is found essential to conduct the interview at school, this should be done only with the consent, and in the presence, of the head teacher, or his nominee.

As a rule the principle laid down in this paragraph is followed today in all investigations as it is realized that a visit by the police to a witness at his place of work may cause embarrassment or injury to his reputation.[2] Police visiting a school in the course of an investigation usually arrive in plain clothes.

Whilst a minor is in school the senior member of the staff present is *in loco parentis* to him and, except in certain circumstances, can refuse to produce the pupil for interrogation or to allow him to be removed to a police station. In cases where the

[1] *Judges' Rules and Administrative Directions to the Police* (HMSO, 1964).
[2] *Report of the Royal Commission on Police Powers and Procedure*, 1929.

police wish to interview a particular child, the pupil may be asked whether he has any objection to being questioned in the absence of his parents. If so, the police should be asked to defer the examination until they have an opportunity of conducting it in the parents' presence. If they refuse to wait, the head should be present *in loco parentis* throughout the interview. The matter should be recorded in the school annals, and the local education authority informed. If the head is a man, and a girl is being interrogated, a mistress should also be present. The head should not allow a pupil to be searched, except in the presence of the parent, unless the circumstances are such that it would be unreasonable to object.

If, on arrival, the police are armed with a warrant for search or arrest, the head must allow it to be executed; to resist would be obstruction. It is also not possible to refuse to co-operate if the police are acting under statutory powers which authorize them to bring a child in need of care or control before a juvenile court.

A head should insist on obtaining the instructions of his local education authority before allowing the removal of a child from the school or the holding of an identity parade on the premises. He should insist that written statements should be taken only at a police station with the consent of the parents.

The police may be informed of pupils' addresses.

6 School rules

In cases where negligence is imputed against the school, the defence is materially assisted if it can be proved that a school rule existed forbidding the conduct by which the plaintiff contributed to his accident or loss.

There is no need for the school rules to be codified or circulated to parents, although both these courses may be deemed desirable, especially when rules are of an unusual character. It is generally assumed that parents, in sending their children to a particular school, have implicitly accepted its rules, even though they have not seen them.

At least one local education authority has advised its teachers that it is not possible legally to compel pupils at a maintained school to wear school uniform, and the only pressure that can be brought to bear in this direction is through the medium of the school's *esprit de corps*.

In *Spiers* v *Warrington Corporation*[1] it was held, however, that to send a child to school dressed in such a way that it is known that he will be refused admission as a matter of discipline is, in fact, the same as failing to send the child to school at all. This decision has been followed in a number of cases, but the reported cases have all been concerned with the suitability of clothing without reference to distinctive uniform. So far as is known at the time of writing, no case involving disciplinary exclusion for failure to wear the school's distinctive uniform has been tested before the Courts. *Prima facie*, the Warrington case does not seem to exclude the possibility that a view sympathetic to the enforcement of uniform might be taken if a case were brought, especially in view of a number of comments (though admittedly *obiter*) that the discipline of the school must be maintained.

An interesting extension of this principle took place in 1965, when the Derby borough magistrates fined two parents for failing to ensure that their sons attended school regularly. The boys were sent home more than fifty times for having shoulder-length hair.[2]

The proposition that the school rules constitute part of the law of the land for the pupils of that school has been discussed in the introductory chapter.[3]

7 Homework

In sending children to school, parents delegate a portion of their authority to the schoolmaster, and are assumed to assent to all reasonable school rules. It is probable that the courts would decide, at least in the case of pupils of secondary school age, that a requirement that a child should do a moderate amount of homework is a reasonable requirement and that, where such a rule exists, a parent may not order his child to break it. A head propos-

[1] [1954] 1 QB 61. See also pages 26–7.
[2] Reported in the *Times Educational Supplement*, 29 October 1965.
[3] See pages 25–7.

ing to introduce homework in a school where it has not been the practice to require it would be well advised to seek the support of the governors (in the case of an aided secondary school) or the local education authority (in all other maintained schools), as the body responsible for the secular instruction.

It is surprising to find in a recently published book a statement that 'detention after school hours for not doing home lessons is not permitted, at least if the school is administered by a local authority under the Education Act 1944, since that Act does not authorize the setting of home lessons.'[1] This view is based on a case decided in 1884[2] in which it was held that the Elementary Education Acts 1870 and 1876 did not authorize the setting of lessons to be prepared at home by children attending a board school, and the detention of a child for not doing home lessons therefore rendered the master who detained the child liable to be convicted for an assault.

It must be remembered that this case was heard in the early years of compulsory education, when strenuous attempts were made to confine the elementary education given by the board schools within narrow limits. In the Cockerton judgment, some years later, it was held to be *ultra vires* the powers of a school board to provide at the expense of the ratepayers science and art schools or classes in day schools.[3] The Cockerton judgment galvanized Parliament into legislative activity on behalf of education at a speed which has never been equalled before or since. The result was the Education Act 1902 which abolished the school boards and set up local education authorities which, if they were the councils of counties or county boroughs, were empowered to establish secondary schools.

From their beginnings the new secondary schools introduced homework, following the practice of the ancient grammar schools, and punished their pupils for failure to perform the tasks set. The powers given to local education authorities by the 1944 Act are wide, homework was a well-established practice in 1944 and,

[1] H. K. Bevan: *The Law Relating to Children* (Butterworth, 1973).
[2] *Hunter* v *Johnson* (1884) 13 QBD 225.
[3] *R* v. *Cockerton*, ex parte *Hamilton* [1901] 1 KB 726; LCT 30.

if Parliament had wished to proscribe it or to make it unenforce-able as a matter of discipline, it would surely have done so in precise terms.

8 Modern disciplinary problems

Violence – It is frequently said, probably with some degree of truth, that violent behaviour in schools is increasing.[1] A clause in the rules forbidding the possession of dangerous weapons and substances by pupils on the school premises might reduce the risk of serious incidents.

Pregnancy – Happily, the pregnant pupil is a comparatively rare phenomenon, and the solutions to individual problems lie within the home and the supportive welfare services. It is certainly not for the school to cast blame. Nevertheless, it is generally undesir-able for a girl to return to her former school, if another is reason-ably available; and this is an even stronger consideration if she should decide to bring up the child.

Drugs – The mere possession of 'controlled' drugs, which include amphetamines, cannabis, heroin, LSD, methadone, morphine, opium and pethidine, is an absolute offence unless the person in whose possession they are found is lawfully authorized. It is also an offence to produce a controlled drug, to supply (or offer to supply) such a drug to another person, or to allow pre-mises to be used for producing or supplying such a drug.

The available defences to charges on drug offences are very restricted. They include prescription by a doctor, a licence to manufacture, or the removal of a drug to prevent the commission of an offence by someone else provided it was then destroyed or handed to a responsible authority.

Setting on one side the professional care of a teacher for the pupils in his charge, and having regard to the disastrous effects of the misuse of drugs, it is clear that a schoolmaster (and this applies with particular force to the head) runs considerable risks if he believes that drugs are being brought into the school, but does nothing about it.

[1] See pages 292–5.

Clearly, the parents of any pupil concerned should be brought in as quickly as possible. Any drugs found in school should be impounded immediately, and destroyed or handed to the police. No schoolmaster likes 'shopping' children in his care, but the arrival of controlled drugs in the school leaves him with no alternative, especially if he has reason to suspect that a 'pusher' is operating in or near the school. His first concern must be to protect all his pupils, and particularly to prevent any who are not involved from being drawn into the net of addiction.

9 School badges

Most schools have adopted an emblematic device for use on pupils' uniforms, and for display in other appropriate ways. These are usually known as school badges, although they do not conform to the strict definition of a badge according to the rules of heraldry.

In heraldry, badges are simpler and more primitive than arms and crests; they are not mounted on a shield as are arms, neither do they issue from a wreath as do most crests.

The right to bear armorial ensigns is authorized by letters patent which are issued by the Kings of Arms after obtaining a warrant from the Earl Marshal in respect of each grant.

The fee for a grant of arms and crest is £250 for private persons, or £400 for corporate bodies and, at the discretion of the Kings of Arms, for certain non-corporate associations of suitable standing.

Colleges, schools, and other scholastic bodies may now apply for the grant of a badge in addition to their arms, or to their arms and crest. If a badge is assigned in the same letters patent the additional fee is £90, but the fee for the grant of a badge in a separate patent is £110.

It should be borne in mind that many of the devices in use by schools would not be accepted for registration from an heraldic point of view, and the Kings of Arms would not be prepared to make a grant in respect of them until such designs were revised to conform to heraldic law.

In general, arms can be granted only to corporate bodies with perpetual succession, but schools are an exception to this rule, and a grant may be made to the owners or trustees for the use of the school.

Schools wishing to consider making an application for a grant should write to the College of Arms, Queen Victoria Street, London, EC4V, 4BT.

10 School magazines

Cases arise occasionally where a pupil submits previously published work as an original contribution to a school magazine. The editor should take every possible care to ensure that plagiarism of this kind does not slip past him. Under the Copyright Acts, the British Museum is entitled to be supplied with a copy of every book published in this country, and it has been held that this right includes school magazines. Such a copy must be delivered within one month of publication.[1]

Editors of school magazines are advised to read the chapter on copyright[2] particularly the section dealing with copyright vested in minors. It would seem to be the custom of the trade that material handed in by contributors is, by the act of delivery, licensed by the owner of the copyright for publication in one issue of the magazine. It is also accepted that no payment is made for such publication. This has the effect of transferring, free of charge, first serial rights to the school. The school can undertake no further publication of the work without permission from the owner of the copyright and in terms agreed with him. In the case of a minor such terms must be negotiated with the parent or guardian.

Editors must remember that it is an offence to stir up hatred against any section of the public in Great Britain distinguished by colour, race, or national or ethnic origins by publishing or distributing written matter (including any writing, sign or visible representation) which is threatening, abusive or insulting.[3]

[1] Copyright Act 1911, s. 15.
[2] See pages 344–69.
[3] Race Relations Act 1965, s. 6.

11 Care of property

A local education authority will not accept liability for the loss of personal property in a school, whether by pupils or staff. It is desirable to display notices to this effect at suitable points. Teachers who have personal items of value in a school are advised to insure themselves against possible loss.

If a teacher takes charge of property on behalf of a pupil, he may be liable in damages if he fails to exercise reasonable care in its custody. In such cases, reasonable care would amount to the degree of care which a prudent person would exercise with regard to his own property.

Occasionally a local education authority will make an *ex gratia* payment in respect of property lost through no fault of the owner. Professional associations carry insurance on behalf of their members, but claims are examined carefully, and often rejected if the owner has been careless, e.g. by leaving a handbag in an unlocked drawer in an unlocked room.

Householders' comprehensive policies may be so arranged that a stated percentage of the amount insured is covered whilst temporarily removed from the policyholder's house. A teacher who loses money in school, therefore, may be able to claim against his own policy, though as a rule this extension applies only to goods, and does not include money.

12 Lotteries and money-raising activities

Consideration of this matter falls into two distinct parts. School voluntary funds are raised in a number of ways, and some schools have used raffles as such a means. It is for the school to decide whether such a method is consistent with the principles which should be inculcated in the young.

If it is felt that such means are permissible morally, care must be taken to ensure that the method employed is permissible legally.[1] Raffles must be purely incidental to some other entertainment and the whole of the proceeds, after deducting expenses and a sum not exceeding ten pounds for prizes, must be given to a purpose other than private profit. Money prizes are forbidden.

[1] Betting, Gaming and Lotteries Acts 1963 to 1971.

All the tickets must be sold, and the result declared, at the entertainment to which the raffle is incidental.

The law relating to street collections, which includes door-to-door collections, requires that permission must be obtained from the police before such a collection is made. All collectors must carry an authority signed by a responsible person, and no person under the age of sixteen may act as a collector.

In all money-raising activities, care must be taken to see that the law relating to the employment of children is not broken.[1]

13 Television licences

One licence taken out by the school covers the use of any number of sets in the same block of buildings, provided they are installed for the use of the licensee or the general use of the pupils. It does not cover private sets owned and used by employees.

14 Tuck shop

A tuck shop is not taxable on its profits so long as it complies with the conditions of mutual trading, but it may be assessed in respect of investment income. If the investment belongs to the school, and the profit is used only for the benefit of the school, tax will possibly be avoided and it is therefore desirable to create some form of trust by which the investments are automatically handed over to the school.

Most tuck shops are relatively small concerns, but the position with regard to VAT should be verified if the turnover of the school's commercial enterprises shows signs of approaching £5,000 a year.

It is also important to ensure that the items offered for sale in the tuck shop are fit for human consumption. In 1971 a pupil took home some crisps he had bought during break at his infants' school. They were covered in green mould, and his parents reported the matter to the health inspector, who telephoned the headmistress to tell her she had committed an offence under the Food and Drugs Act. No prosecution followed in this case but, as responsibility for the quality of food offered for sale rests with

[1] See pages 198–201.

the retailer, the headmistress could have found herself in an embarrassing difficulty.

15 Vending machines

Problems sometimes arise over vending machines leased to schools on contracts without a termination clause. Some local education authorities have rules about the installation of electrical equipment without the clearance of its engineers: in such cases the authority must be informed before any contract is signed. The contract should also be examined by the authority or the head's professional association before signature. Such contracts frequently include an absolute liability to pay the rental for a fixed period. The risk here lies in economic inflation. The head is usually advised by the supplier on the price to be charged for various drinks, and the machine is adjusted accordingly. When the cost of new supplies to the school rises, the operation may become uneconomic unless the machine is readjusted to charge more.

In one case the fixed charge brought in only a minimal profit at the time of installation; when it became uneconomic the headmistress took the machine out of use, but the supplier failed to alter the charging mechanism in spite of repeated requests. When the head who had signed the contract retired, her successor was told by the supplier that she was bound by its terms, and faced with an account for more than £600 arrears of rental.

Properly costed, however, vending machines can be a blessing. Subject to the considerations outlined above, there is no reason why arrangements should not be made to include the provision of staff refreshments and cigarettes. Schools with girls on the roll have for many years installed machines to sell sanitary towels. The advantage of the machine is the time saved in setting up shop by people who are already busy.

16 Confiscation of property

Confiscation of pupils' property is a long-established practice in schools. Sometimes a teacher is exasperated because a pupil is misusing his personal property, or articles of high value are removed because of the risk of loss. Sometimes pupils bring things to school which are forbidden by the school rules; and, occasionally, pupils are found in possession of items which a prudent parent would consider they should not have, or which are plainly illegal.

The last-named categories might include the possession of cigarettes by a pupil under sixteen, contraceptives, flick-knives and drugs.

Teachers should remember that anyone who 'dishonestly appropriates property belonging to another with the intention of permanently depriving the other of it' is guilty of theft.[1] The law makes no exception in the case of confiscation by teachers, and schools should therefore design a suitable code of practice for dealing with such items.

A convenient classification would seem to be as follows:

Articles of small value – These may include comics, pen-knives and items of similar worth. It is good practice to ensure that these are returned not later than the end of the school week in which they are confiscated.

Articles of considerable value – There is a growing tendency for pupils to bring valuable property to school, including watches, jewellery, expensive pens, tape-recorders and record players. Long-playing records and tapes may also fall within this category. It is most unwise to keep these beyond the end of the school day on which they are confiscated. The question of care of other peoples' property is considered elsewhere,[2] and this applies to confiscated items. A teacher must take all reasonable care of pupils' property whilst it is in his possession and the longer he retains it, the greater the risk of loss. If such articles are kept in school overnight there is always the risk that they may disappear during a burglary. The teacher may then be personally liable.

Articles which pupils should not have – These may be returned to the pupils' parents.

Illegal articles – In certain circumstances it may be necessary to call in the police; in others the articles can be destroyed after explaining to the pupil why this is being done. Responsibility for

[1] Theft Act 1968, s. 1.
[2] See page 430.

dealing with property falling within this class should be exercised personally by the head, and the parents should always be informed.

17 Children's nightdresses

Regulations were made under the Consumer Protection Act 1961, and are primarily concerned with nightdresses offered for sale. Needlecraft departments would do well to impress the restrictions on the pupil's minds, and to ensure any garments made in the department conform to the standards laid down. This is of course, essential if it is likely that any of the garments might be offered for sale in any way.[1]

18 Use of private cars[2]

From time to time teachers are faced with the problem of getting a sick child to a doctor or hospital in circumstances where an ambulance or other official conveyance is not easily available. This raises an important point in connection with insurance, since teacher's cars are normally covered only for private use, that is, for social, domestic and pleasure purposes.

Most insurance companies and underwriters have inserted a clause which extends the definition of private use to 'official use by the policy holder in person'. This would appear to give some cover to a teacher using his car in such circumstances, but it must be remembered that an insurance policy is a contract which must be construed as a whole, having regard to all the facts in a particular case. A policy arranged through a scheme agreed between an insurer and a professional association would normally cover use by the policy holder in connection with his duties as a teacher, but not for any other business use. 'Official use by the policy holder in person' may be regarded as requiring the presence of the policy holder, but he need not necessarily be driving.

The underwriters of one of the teachers' policies have agreed that the policy is effective, even though the policy holder has lent the car to a colleague for use in connection with a school accident

[1] Children's Nightdresses Regulations 1964; see also British Standards Specification, BS 3121; 1959.

[2] See also page 126.

or emergency. The underwriters have not stated whether use in such circumstances is official or unofficial: but they would not regard the official use clause as having been breached.

Some education authorities have advised teachers against using their own cars in such emergencies, others have forbidden them to do so. At least one, however, has specifically stated that a sick child may be taken to a doctor or hospital in a teacher's own car, whether the teacher is authorized to use the car on the authority's official business, or not. The same authority has laid down that this procedure may be followed when a doctor has advised that a child should be taken home, and that the teacher may claim reimbursement on the basis of the appropriate mileage allowance.

Even though a local education authority may have advised teachers not to use their cars in this way, or even prohibited such use, a teacher is still covered for the use, in a private capacity, of a car which he has insured, provided that he accepts no fee or reward other than an official allowance.

If the authority has specifically stated that the practice is approved, the teacher is clearly acting within his official capacity, and any action arising out of an accident might lie against him and the authority as joint tort feasors. Teachers frequently carry children in connection with educational activities which may or may not be 'official' in the sense that he is 'required' to do so by his employer. A policyholder may not lend his car to a colleague to take children on school activities without specific arrangement with his insurers. This use is distinct from use in an emergency referred to above.

If a private motorist accepts any fee or reward for the conveyance of a passenger he violates the terms of a private car policy, but the policies issued under arrangements concluded between insurers and professional associations permit the receipt of an allowance for official use from the teacher's employers. An allowance of this kind does not establish 'hiring'. From December 1973, however, all motorists have been allowed to accept a contribution towards running costs, provided they do not make a profit.

It is by no means unknown for teachers to give children lifts to a games field, or to pick them up from a bus stop on the way to or from school. In such cases, especially since they often occur out of school hours, it is probable that such courtesies would come within the scope of private use, and the policy would provide adequate indemnity.

A policyholder whose car is insured under arrangements made between an insurer and a professional association is covered, no matter in what kind of school he is serving. The advantageous terms of his policy arise from his professional status as a teacher.

In general, car insurance policies do not distinguish between liability to passengers and liability to other third parties. The policy therefore covers claims made by a passenger and claims arising from the negligence of a passenger.

Every teacher would be well advised to make a careful study of the terms of his policy in this connection, and to remember that in the last resort the application of these conditions to a particular situation can be determined only by a court of law on evidence of the facts.

19 Minority groups

The law, as a matter of public policy, seeks to protect the rights of members of minority groups in this country, and the operation of the conscience clause in religious matters, as well as the provisions of the Race Relations Acts, have already been noticed.[1] Schools must observe the letter of the law in matters of this nature, and it is to be hoped that they will also promote the spirit which lies behind it. The promotion of harmony may well begin in primary schools with the unspoken acceptance of integration, for young children are less inclined than adults to accentuate differences. In secondary schools any teaching should be directed towards recognition of common humanity and an understanding and tolerance of differences.

The classroom is not the place for the promotion of a teacher's personal views; it is not a policy-making chamber, but a place where individuals work and play together. All pupils, whatever

[1] See pages 107–9 and 215–16.

their origins, have an equal claim on the teacher's care and professional skills.

The situation has changed considerably since the passage of the 1944 Act, largely because of the considerable number of people from overseas who have made their home in these islands. The integration of people from other countries is no new experience in the United Kingdom, but the two new factors are the arrival of many people whose skins are darker than those of the people who have been settled in this country in the past, and the fact that many of these new citizens come from a non-Christian heritage. With the exception of the Jewish people, this second element has previously affected only very limited areas of the country.

Two groups are selected here for consideration. The first has been represented in Britain for many years, but its cultural background and way of life have prevented it from seeking complete integration into the life of the people. The second, not previously living here on a large scale, is distinguished by differences both in skin colour and religion from the majority of United Kingdom citizens, and there are signs that it wishes to preserve its own identity and ethos.

Gypsies – Attempts to educate gypsy children go back almost two centuries. The difficulty has stemmed not merely from the wandering nature of the lives of the travellers, as they prefer to call themselves, but also from their desire to preserve their own culture. Travellers are well aware of the need for literacy in modern life, but they believe that the state system of education should be sufficiently flexible to allow their children to reap its benefits without destroying their way of life.

The National Gypsy Education Council was formed in 1969. Including both gypsies and non-gypsies in its membership with Lady Plowden as chairman, the purpose of the Council is to concentrate on the advancement of education for gypsy children and adults, and to collect and disseminate information.

The children of travellers are subject to the law relating to school attendance in the same way as all children. It is said, however, that educational welfare officers do little to persuade travellers who do not live on caravan sites to send their children to

438 MINORITY GROUPS

school and that headmasters have sometimes refused to have them. Children may of course be absent from school for not more than two weeks in a year to accompany their parents on their annual holiday,[1] and there are special provisions for children whose parents' work requires them to travel.[2] There is no equivalent in England and Wales to the Scottish law which sets out a minimum number of days in which the children of 'tinkers' are required to attend.

The travellers' way of life is based on the family and the extended family. Their children tend to view the strange life inside a building with mistrust born of their experience of free life out-of-doors, where there is little restriction on movement. Before all else, they need to become confident in a new environment. The National Gypsy Education Council[3] will be pleased to give advice to teachers.

Muslims – In the past Muslims have appeared to settle into the western way of life, and into school with comparative ease. In 1972 a father was fined for not causing his daughter to receive full-time efficient and suitable education, because he had refused to allow her to attend a co-educational school.

Towards the end of 1973 publicity was given to the story that a Muslim parent had sent his family back to Pakistan rather than allow his daughter to go to a mixed school. In the following January the Muslim Parents Association was formed in Bradford, where one in ten pupils belonged, at that time, to that faith. Bradford had been phasing out single-sex schools for some time, and officers of the local education authority said they had made concessions in dress and meals.

From puberty, Muslim girls are not allowed to mix with males who are not close relatives, and the stricter families from Kashmir regard the 'uncivilized exposure of the body', and acts 'encouraging demoralization' of Muslim children as unacceptable. An official of the Muslim Education Trust said 'The morals of society in Britain are not acceptable to us; we are planning our

[1] See page 209.
[2] See page 205.
[3] 61 Blenheim Crescent, London,W11 2EG.

own school because we believe prevention is better than cure. Education authorities only think about education. We are thinking of the moral and religious health of future generations.'[1]

It was said that the Trust was hoping to establish its own secondary schools on a voluntary-aided basis.

20 Parent–teacher associations

Many schools have parent–teacher associations and, properly organized, they can do much to promote a good relationship between the groups they represent. Many such associations have been of tremendous benefit to the schools to which they are attached, and have often raised funds for equipment and journeys which would not otherwise have been possible.

It should, however, be clearly understood that, in a maintained school, such a body has no executive power. Under no circumstances can it usurp the functions of the managers or governors and the head as laid down in the rules of management or articles of government.

Parent–teacher associations have grown both in number and strength in recent years, and their activities are by no means confined to money-raising. Discussions with the school staff and listening to visiting lecturers form part of the staple diet of many such bodies. In some cases they add weight to the views of the staff in negotiations with the local education authority, and help in fostering public interest in and developing public opinion on educational matters in their locality.

Many parent–teacher associations belong to the National Confederation of Parent–Teacher Associations[2] which encourages the development of associations and local federations. The Confederation was one of the founding bodies of the Home and School Council, and is represented on the Schools Council and a number of national bodies concerned with education. It works closely with the teachers' professional associations.

The National Confederation is in membership of the Confédération Internationale des Parents on which most European

[1] *Times Educational Supplement*, 11 January 1974. See also page 50.
[2] 1 White Avenue, Northfleet, Gravesend, Kent.

countries are represented, as well as Canada, Venezuela, the Ivory Coast and Senegal.

If difficulties arise from the operation of parent–teacher associations, it is not unusual to find their origin in inadequate planning in the early stages. Many of these snags could be avoided by the adoption of a constitution which defines the association's terms of reference clearly. Teachers and others concerned with the formation of an association would do well to consider using the draft constitution issued by the National Confederation, which is reproduced below with permission. Modifications may be made to suit local conditions, provided that the clauses which establish the charitable nature of the association[1] are included without alteration.

1 – The name of the Association shall be ....
....

2 – The objects of the Association are to advance the education of the pupils of the school by providing and assisting in the provision of facilities for education at the school (not normally provided by the local education authority) and as an ancillary thereto and in furtherance of this object the Association may:

(a) foster more extended relationships between the staff, parents and others associated with the school; and
(b) engage in activities which support the School and advance the education of the pupils attending it.[2]

3 – The Association shall be non-political.

4 – The President of the Association shall be the Head Teacher.[3]

[1] Nos. 2, 18 and 21.

[2] *It is essential that this clause be adopted without alteration.* This wording has been agreed between the Chief Inspector of Taxes, the Charity Commissioners and the Department of Education and Science as being acceptable for use by parent–teacher associations. Any variation could render an Association liable to income tax on their investment income.

[3] This clause is not essential. For example, some head teachers are chairmen of their associations.

5 – The names of the Vice-Presidents shall be submitted at the annual general meeting.[1]

6 – The annual subscription shall be (.........) per household. becoming due at the annual general meeting.[2]

7 – The management and control of the Association shall be vested in a committee which shall consist of the following:

The Head of the school and the following officers, who shall be elected annually at the AGM:

    1. Chairman
    2. Treasurer (parent)
    3. Secretary

Other members from the following sources – Parents representing the first and subsequent years. – Members of the staff of the school. – Members from friends of the school.[3]

8 – (.........) members of the said committee shall constitute a quorum for the Committee.

9 – Committee meetings shall be held at least once each term at such times and places as the committee shall direct.[4]

10 – The annual general meeting of the Association shall be held on (.........) of each year. At the annual general meeting the chair shall be taken by the Chairman, or in his/her absence by the Vice-Chairman of the committee. Additional meetings shall be held of the sub-sections of the Association, and these may be in addition to those called by the convenor from time to time.

[1] These are usually people the Association wishes to honour.

[2] A growing number of PTAs no longer have subscriptions, thinking they are restrictive and difficult to collect and administer. Where subscriptions are levied, the amount is usually 25p per family.

[3] This is a possible arrangement, and can be varied in many ways. For example, in some schools the Secretary is a member of the staff, appointed and paid for that duty. Again, while some schools have committee members representing year groups, others have class representation, or, more usually, election of those parents generally considered suitable.

[4] It may also be thought desirable to specify the frequency of ordinary meetings.

11 – (.........) members shall constitute a quorum at the annual general meeting.

12 – The committee shall have the power to co-opt up to (.........) members, and to appoint any sub-committee, and shall prescribe the function of any such sub-committee.

13 – A special general meeting shall be convened at the request in writing, to the Secretary, of *ten* members of the Association. Such a meeting shall be held within *thirty* days of the request. Agenda and motions submitted shall be circulated to all members.

14 – Casual vacancies on the committee may be filled by the committee by co-option. Any person so co-opted shall serve only while the person in whose place he/she is co-opted would have served.

15 – At the first committee meeting after the annual general meeting the committee shall elect a Vice-Chairman from among its members.

16 – Where a child leaves school during the year then the parent, being a fully paid member of the Association, shall be deemed to continue as such until the next AGM.

17 – Where parents no longer have children at the school, but wish to continue their interest in the school through the Association, such parents may be accepted as Friends of the School, on payment of the annual subscription, and shall be entitled to full membership with the exception that they may not hold office as chairman, secretary or treasurer, or serve on the committee.

18 – No alteration of the rules may be made except at the annual general meeting or at a special meeting called for this purpose. No alteration or amendment shall be made to the objects clause or dissolution clause which would cause the Association to cease to be a charity at law.[1]

19 – The Honorary Treasurer shall keep an account of all income and expenditure and shall submit accounts, duly audited, at the AGM. The banking account shall be in

[1] This is another *essential clause* that must not be varied.

the name of the Association and withdrawals shall be made in the name of the Association on the signature of any two of the following:

(*a*) Chairman
(*b*) Treasurer
(*c*) Secretary

20 – Two auditors, not being members of the committee, shall be appointed annually at the annual general meeting to audit the accounts and books of the Association.

21 – Any assets remaining on dissolution of the Association after satisfying any outstanding debts and liabilities shall not be distributed amongst the members of the Association but will be given to the school for the benefit of the children of the school in any manner which is exclusively charitable at law.[1]

22 – The Association shall take out public liability insurance to cover all its meetings and activities.[2]

23 – That any matter not provided for in the constitution shall be dealt with by the committee, whose decision shall be deemed final.

It must be realized that on all educational matters the head teacher has the ultimate responsibility. Should an association wish to mention this in its constitution, an additional clause could be inserted, e.g. 'The head teacher shall have the ultimate decision on all educational matters.'

21 Politics and law

As was stated in the preface, the main purpose of this book is to provide the practising teacher with an outline of the ever-widening implications of the law for his profession. To a large extent, therefore, it is descriptive of the way in which education is brought within the sovereignty of the Rule of Law. Law is

[1] This is another *essential clause* that must not be varied.
[2] Membership of the National Confederation of PTAs automatically provides this.

concerned with rights, but every right has a correlative duty: to avoid one's duty is frequently to deny someone else his rights.

Midway through the second half of the twentieth century, it is clear that principles and concepts once sacrosanct are being assailed. Moreover, the structure of society is changing more rapidly than at any time in history. It is inevitable that, in these circumstances, the law is being moulded to take account of developments of thought and structure.

At one time it was firmly held that a teacher should keep his political views to himself within the context of his professional activity: this has been challenged. It was once considered beneath the dignity of a learned profession to indulge in strikes and other industrial action: this has been challenged. The whole relationship between the schoolmaster and his charges has been based on the concept that one is *in loco parentis* and the others *in statu pupillari*: this has been challenged.

The segregation of powers is historically fundamental to English law. It is for the executive to implement the law, for the judiciary to enforce it, but the power to make it is reserved to Parliament. Only by delegation from the legislature may any other body or individual presume to create law. The essence of the wisdom of Parliament, enshrined in law, is distilled from public policy; and public policy is forged on the anvil of politics.

Since the last edition of this book was published, some hundreds of thousands of young people have been enfranchised by the lowering of the age of majority. The television cameras have brought the living, walking, talking images of policy makers into most homes and schools. In the industrial field the Rule of Law has been openly defied. In schools there has been a demand for consultation and participation by teachers, parents and pupils. Truancy, an offence at law, is publicly condoned and blamed on the schools. Teachers may be found who will approve, if not encourage pupil demonstrations.

These circumstances have imposed a testing time on educational institutions; and political activity, once confined to colleges and universities, has moved into the schools. Those charged with their direction find themselves caught between the lower millstone of demands for greater freedom and wider rights, and the upper stone of the law as it exists. Ever seeking to promote the claims of those who feel themselves under-privileged, the mass media have accorded much publicity to those who see the schools as an arena in which new liberties can be won. On the other hand, it is by no means certain that the great majority of the public would agree with some of the views so insistently expressed.

For the teacher, the dilemma lies in the uncertainty of the future. There is no indication, at present, of any change in public policy so settled that it is likely to issue in radical legislative action. Until it does, a teacher is well advised to work strictly within the framework of the law as it stands, and not as he thinks it ought to stand.

APPENDIX I

TABLE OF STATUTES

TABLE OF CASES

APPENDIX III

ADDRESSES OF PROFESSIONAL ASSOCIATIONS

The national associations whose names are included in this list are concerned with the professional status of their members. Those which are purely academic in character have not been noted.

Associations which are in membership of the Trades Union Congress are marked by an asterisk. The date of formation is given in brackets.

Association of Agricultural Education Staffs
Manor Farm East, North Cove, Brough, Yorkshire.

Association for Technological Education in Schools (1950)
Elgin Secondary Technical School, Carr Hill, Gateshead, NE9 5PA.

Association of Headmistresses of Preparatory Schools (1929)
Meadowbrook, Abbot's Drive, Virginia Water, Surrey, GU25 4QS.

Association of Teachers in Colleges and Departments of Education (1943)
3 Crawford Place, London, W1H 2BN.

Association of Teachers in Technical Institutions (1904)
Hamilton House, Mabledon Place, London, WC1H 9BH.

Association of Teachers of Domestic Science (1896)
Hamilton House, Mabledon Place, London, WC1H 9BJ

460

PROFESSIONAL ASSOCIATIONS

British Association of Organizers and Lecturers in Physical Education
23 Quadring Road, Donington, Lincolnshire, PE11 4TD

Faculty of Teachers in Commerce
12 Crampton Drive, Altrincham, WA15 oHH.

The Headmasters' Conference (1869)
29 Gordon Square, London, WC1H oPS

Membership of this body is limited to headmasters of schools which fulfil certain conditions. Generally speaking, the schools whose headmasters are in membership must be independent or direct grant, though there is provision for the election of a limited number of headmasters of other types of school when it is thought that their personal contribution to the thought and affairs of the Headmasters' Conference would be useful. In considering applications for membership the Committee will have regard to the degree of professional and administrative independence enjoyed by the headmaster, and the academic standards obtaining in the school as indicated by the size of the sixth form in relation to total numbers of pupils over thirteen who qualify for matriculation purposes in each year. Although there is no official definition of the term, it is commonly held that schools whose headmasters are within the membership of the Headmasters' Conference are to be recognized as public schools.

Incorporated Association of Preparatory Schools
138 Kensington Church Street, London, W8 4BN.

Independent Schools Association Incorporated
49 Gordon Road, Whitstable, Kent, CT5 4NG.

Joint Council of Heads (1944)
c/o Maxwelton House, 41-3 Boltro Road, Haywards Heath, Sussex, RH16 1BJ.

The committee deals with matters of common interest to members of the Head Masters Association, the Association of

Head Mistresses Incorporated, the Headmasters' Conference, and the National Association of Head Teachers.

Joint Committee of the Four Secondary Associations
29 Gordon Square, London WC1H 0PP.

This committee co-ordinates the work of the four associations of teachers in secondary schools, and deals with matters which are common to them all. Usually known as the 'Joint Four', it has no individual membership, the teachers who are associated with it being members of one of the constituent bodies which all have their offices at this address:

Incorporated Association of Head Masters;
Association of Head Mistresses Incorporated;
Incorporated Association of Assistant Masters;
Assistant Mistresses' Association (Incorporated).

The Assistant Mistresses' Association also admits women teachers in primary schools to membership.

National Association of Head Teachers (1897)
Maxwelton House, 41–3 Boltro Road, Haywards Heath, Sussex, RH16 1BJ.

This is an association of heads of all kinds of schools which are recognized as efficient by the Department of Education and Science.

*National Association of Schoolmasters (1919)
Swan Court, Waterhouse Street, Hemel Hempstead, Hertfordshire, HP1 1DT.

The Association exists to safeguard and promote the interests of career schoolmasters in all types of schools and colleges.

National Association of Teachers in Wales (Undeb Cenedlaethol Athrawon Cymru) (1940)
11 Gordon Road, Cardiff, CF2 3AJ.

National College of Teachers of the Deaf (1918)

Needwood School, Rangemore Hill, Burton-on-Trent, DE13 9RH.

The College was formed by the union of the College of Teachers of the Deaf and Dumb (1885) with the National Association of Teachers of the Deaf (1895). The Diploma, instituted in 1885, is recognized by the Department of Education and Science.

National Federation of Continuative Teachers' Associations

110 Bournville Lane, Birmingham, B20 1LN.

The Association exists to promote the development of adult and non-vocational education, and to protect the professional interests and status of part-time teachers in this field.

National Society for Art Education (1973)

37A East Street, Havant, Hampshire.

*National Union of Teachers (1870)

Hamilton House, Mabledon Place, London, WC1H 9BD.

This is the largest of the associations, and comprises in its membership teachers in every kind of school and college. The interests of the various groups are safeguarded by the formation of sections within the union.

Physical Education Association of Great Britain and Northern Ireland (1899)

Ling House, 10 Nottingham Place, London, W1M 4AX.

Professional Association of Teachers

24, The Strand, Derby, DE11 1BE.

The Association seeks to maintain high professional standards among teachers, and eschews all forms of industrial action.

*Union of Women Teachers (1965)

Swan Court, Hemel Hempstead, Hertfordshire, HP1 1DT.

The Union represents the interests of women career teachers in primary, secondary and special schools throughout the country.

The College of Preceptors

Bloomsbury House, 130 High Holborn, London, WC1V 6PS.

The College is the oldest society of teachers in England, and has always been noted for its pioneer work in many aspects of education. It received its Royal Charter in 1849 and, throughout its history, it has shown a high regard for the status of teachers.

The College is actively engaged in the field of higher professional education for serving teachers through courses and examinations. Qualifications awarded on the authority of the Royal Charter are Associate (ACP), Licentiate (LCP) and Fellow (FCP). The LCP is recognized for salary purposes as the equivalent of a university first degree by the Burnham Main Committee (Primary and Secondary). The title of Fellow is also conferred annually in March in a Charter list on a small number of persons eminent in education at home and overseas. The College's Regional Executives arrange a programme of short courses and seminars on various aspects of the teacher's work and, in particular, on school management studies.

The annual Joseph Payne and Sir Philip Magnus lectures are sponsored by the College.

Its publications include a bi-monthly digest of current educational literature, *Education Today*.

Membership may be either individual or corporate. All members receive all publications.

VOLUNTARY EDUCATIONAL BODIES

Baptist Union of Great Britain and Ireland
Baptist Church House, 4 Southampton Row, London, WC1B 4AB.

British Council of Churches Education Department
10 Eaton Gate, London, S.W.1.

Catholic Education Council
41 Cromwell Road, London, S.W.7.

Central Council for Jewish Religious Education
Woburn House, Upper Woburn Place, London, WC1H oEP.

Central Education Policy Committee (Anglican and Free Church)
69 Great Peter Street, London, S.W.1.
27 Tavistock Square, London, WC1H 9HH.

Church of England Board of Education
Church House, Dean's Yard, London S.W.1.

Free Church Federal Council Education Committee
27 Tavistock Square, London, WC1H 9HH.

Friends' Education Council
Friends' House, Euston Road, London, N.W.1.

Methodist Education Committee
25 Marylebone Road, London, N.W.1.

Moravian Provincial Board

Moravian Church House, 5 Muswell Hill, London, N10 3TJ.

United Reformed Church (Congregational and Presbyterian)
27 Tavistock Square, London, WC1H 9HH.

BIBLIOGRAPHY

1 Government Publications

A complete and up-to-date list of Government publications on Education will be found in *Government Publications (Sectional List No. 2): Department of Education and Science.* Another useful guide is the annual *Index to Department of Education and Science Circulars and Administrative Memoranda* which lists all current publications under these heads. All publications of this nature are obtainable from any bookseller or from the Government Bookshop, Holborn, London, WC1V 6HB.

2 Other Publications

EDUCATIONAL LAW

Taylor and Saunders: *Halsbury's Laws of England: Education* (Butterworth, 4th edition in the press). *Halsbury* is the standard lawyer's reference work, and a new edition, under the general editorship of Lord Hailsham of Marylebone, is being published between 1973 and 1982. Single volumes cannot, however, be purchased.

Taylor and Saunders: *The New Law of Education* (Butterworth, edition, with other relevant statutes). The standard work on the Education Acts 1944 to 1965, and the instruments and memoranda issued under their authority.

H. C. Dent: *The Education Act, 1944* (University of London Press, edition, 1968). A valuable summary which is constantly in process of revision, and frequently reissued to bring it up-to-date. Addenda have been inserted to include changes up to, and including, the Local Government Act 1972.

468 APPENDIX V

Alexander and Barraclough: *County and Voluntary Schools* (Councils and Education Press, 4th edition, 1967). An analysis of sections of the Education Acts which deals with the provisions of those sections as they affect the administration of different kinds of school.

L. B. Tirrell: *The Aided Schools Handbook* (National Society and SPCK, 2nd edition, 1969). A useful commentary on the law relating to, and the work of, these schools by a former Director of Religious Education for the Dioceses of London and Southwark. Though primarily intended for managers and governors, teachers interested in aided schools will find much useful matter here.

G. R. Barrell: *Legal Cases for Teachers* (Methuen, 1970). A collection of nearly 150 cases dealing with educational matters. Many of the cases touched on in this book are dealt with in more detail. Every effort has been made to present the cases in an interesting and relevant manner, without sacrificing legal accuracy.

Herb T. Appenzeller: *From the Gym to the Jury* (Michie, Charlottesville, Va, 1970). A fascinating introduction to the legal problems of Physical Education by the Athletic Director of Guilford College, Greensboro, North Carolina. It must be remembered that, though American common law is derived from its English counterpart, and though judgments from the English courts are quoted with approval in the United States, statutory modifications have led to some changes. Nevertheless, the family likeness is recognizable in this book and *mutatis mutandis* it contains much wise advice.

CHILDREN AND THE LAW

Clarke Hall and Morrison: *The Law Relating to Children* (Butterworth, 8th edition, 1972). The standard work on all aspects of this subject, monumental in its conception and meticulous in its presentation.

H. K. Bevan: *The Law Relating to Children* (Butterworth). A new, and conveniently arranged, work.

G. H. F. Mumford: *A Guide to Juvenile Court Law* (Shaw, 8th edition, 1974). An exceedingly valuable reference book which covers all aspects of the subject and is invaluable when heads have pupils who are in trouble with the courts. The book now includes a separate treatment table in respect of juvenile court procedure, incorporating an age table. This has been revised, and can be obtained separately.

L. Goodman: *Notes on Juvenile Court Law* (Barry Rose Publications, 9th edition, 1973). The most concise, yet authoritative, guide. This is an invaluable booklet for teachers whose pastoral responsibilities bring them into contact with the juvenile courts.

L. F. W. White: *'Where' on Parents and the Law* (Advisory Centre for Education). Useful notes by an educational administrator who was always concerned that people should be aware of their rights.

REFERENCE AND PROFESSIONAL

The Education Committees Year Book (Councils and Education Press). An annual directory of the local education service in the United Kingdom, and the official year book of the education committees.

Education Authorities' Directory and Annual (School Government Publishing Co). An annual directory of local education authorities and establishments.

J. L. Mellor: *The Law* (English Universities Press, 3rd edition, 1974). A concise introductory guide to some general aspects of the legal system.

Charlesworth on Negligence (Sweet and Maxwell, 5th edition by R. A. Percy, 1971). The standard work on this subject. The current edition devotes a chapter to negligence in schools.

R. E. Barker: *Photocopying Practices in the United Kingdom* (Faber, 1970). A valuable introduction to the legal problems posed by the development of a new technique, with some constructive proposals for the future.

National Council for Educational Technology:[1] *Copyright and
Education* (Working Paper No. 87, 1972). A statement by the
Council's Working Group on Rights, to which are added
statements by a number of bodies closely concerned with the
subject.

Handbook of School Administration (National Union of Teachers
2nd edition, 1972). A digest of regulations, together with some
professional advice.

Peter Newell: *A Last Resort?* (Penguin, 1972). A frankly abolitionist critique of corporal punishment.

Michael Carter: *Into Work* (Penguin, 1966). An appraisal of the
needs of the secondary school pupil as he makes the transition
from school to work.

English and Empire Digest, Volume 19 (Butterworth–Blue Band
edition, 1962). This volume, not easily obtainable separately,
contains a digest of many educational leading cases, with
references to the appropriate Law Reports. It may be consulted in the larger reference libraries.

The following pamphlets have been produced by the School
Journey Association of London, and are invaluable for those
planning such events. Free to members, they may be obtained
for a small charge by non-members from the School Journey
Association of London, 43 Cavendish Road, London, SW12
0BH.

Types of School Journeys
How to Promote a School Journey – Homeland
How to Promote a Continental School Journey
A School Journey to London

THE ORGANIZATION OF EDUCATION

H. C. Dent: *The Educational System of England and Wales*
(University of London Press, 5th edition, 1971). An authoritative account of all parts of the system, including the independent schools, by a former Assistant Dean of the Institute

[1] Now the Council for Educational Technology for the United
Kingdom.

of Education of the University of London, who had previously been Professor of Education at Sheffield. A leaflet setting out the provisions of the Local Government Act 1972 has been inserted.

Bernard Lawrence: *The Administration of Education* (Batsford, 1972). A review, partly historical, partly administrative, and partly visionary, of the educational system by a former Chief Education Office for Essex.

A. Griffiths: *Secondary School Reorganization in England and Wales* (Routledge, 1971). A valuable summary.

Comprehensive Schools (National Foundation for Educational Research, 1972). A survey of strengths and weaknesses.

Tyrrell Burgess: *Inside Comprehensive Schools* (HMSO, 1970). Commissioned by the Department of Education and Science, this book is a sympathetic account of the work of comprehensive schools.

London's Comprehensive Schools (ILEA, 2nd edition, 1966). An account of the development of comprehensive secondary education in London.

R. Pedley: *The Comprehensive School* (Pelican, revised edition, 1969). Part factual account, part apologia, by a leading protagonist of schools of this kind.

Robin Davis: *The Grammar School* (Penguin, 1967). A defence of grammar schools which provides a valuable record of their achievements on the eve of their disappearance.

Cheshire Education Committee: *The Secondary Modern School* (University of London Press, 1958). A symposium on the development of secondary modern education in Cheshire.

J. V. Chapman: *Your Secondary Modern Schools* (College of Preceptors, 1959). An exhaustive survey of the birth-pangs of these schools, and their position in the late 1950s.

W. Taylor: *The Secondary Modern School* (Faber, 1963). An appraisal by the Principal Lecturer in Education at Bede College, Durham.

John Partridge: *Life in a Secondary Modern School* (Penguin, 1968). A description of life in a Midlands secondary modern school in the early 1960s.

John Blackie: *Inside the Primary School* (HMSO, 1967). A personal account of primary schools written by a former HMI at the request of the Department of Education and Science.

David Ayerst: *Understanding Schools* (Penguin, 1972). Also by a former HMI, this book raises important questions about the present and the future of schools.

W. O. Lester Smith: *Government of Education* (Penguin, 1971). A survey of the external forces acting on schools at the present time, indicating the tensions between them, how they arose, and how they may develop.

HISTORY OF EDUCATION

John Lawson and Harold Silver: *A Social History of Education in England* (Methuen, 1973). An important account, which sets the development of English education against the background of the cultural, political and economic life of the country.

D. W. Sylvester: *Educational Documents, 800–1816* (Methuen, 1970); J. Stuart Maclure: *Educational Documents, 1816 to the present day* (Methuen, 2nd edition, 1968). Two essential quarries of original material for anyone who wishes to understand the development of education in England and Wales.

NEW

Barbara Bullivant: *The New Governors' Guide* (Home and School Council, 1974). A useful summary of the powers and functions of managers and governors.

INDEX

[1] *J* – Justice (Judge) *LJ* – Lord Justice of Appeal *LCJ* – Lord Chief Justice
LJC – Lord Justice Clerk (Scotland) *MR* – Master of the Rolls

480 INDEX

480 INDEX

JUDGES CITED (*contd.*)
Lush, *J*, 246
McCardie, *J*, 103
McNaghten, *J*, 141
McNair, *J*, 230
Mocatta, *J*, 247
Nield, *J*, 305
Ormerod, *J*, 47
Parker, *LCJ*, 48, 123–4, 207, 375
Paull, *J*, 398–9
Pearson, *Lord*, 237
Phillimore, *J*, 279–80, 287–8
Reid, *Lord*, 120
Sachs, *LJ*, 119
Salmon, *LJ*, 258–9
Scrutton, *LJ*, 245–6
Singleton, *LJ*, 270–71
Sumner, *LJ*, 118
Swift, *J*, 399
Ungoed Thomas, *J*, 49
Vaisey, *J*, 230 *n.*
Waller, *J*, 267
Walton, *J*, 277
Widgery, *J* (now *LCJ*), 248–52
Wightman, *J*, 402
Willmer, *LJ*, 234–5
JUDGES' RULES, 422–3
JUKE BOXES, 368
JUNIOR HIGH SCHOOLS, 53
JUVENILE COURTS,
absolute discharges, 386–7
age of criminal responsibility, 382
appeals from, 388
attendance centres, 385
attendance control, 389–90; *see also* Truancy
binding over, 388, 391
Borstal treatment, 388
care or control, 389–91
care orders, 384–5
child, defined, 379–80
compensation, 387, 391
conditional discharges, 387
constitution and procedure, 378–9, 383–4
detention centres, 385
doli incapax, 382
fines, 387
hospital and guardianship orders, 386
offences by juveniles, 382–8
place of safety, 382
protected child, 381
reports by l.e.a.s, 391–2

supervision orders, 385–6
young person, defined, 380–81

LANCASTER, JOSEPH, 217
LANGUAGE LABORATORIES, 367
LASERS, 190
Last Resort, A, 297
LATENESS, 213–14
LEAGUE FOR THE EXCHANGE OF COMMONWEALTH TEACHERS, 128
LEAVE OF ABSENCE,
accidents, 143–4
conferences, 149
days of obligation, 150
domestic reasons, 149
further training, 149
infectious illness, 143
maternity, 145
national service, 150
public duties, 150
pupils, 180–81
sports meetings, 150
superannuation, effect on, 159
tuberculosis, 144, 159
see also Sick pay
LEAVERS,
attainment of leaving age, 203
removal from roll, 174–5
school-leaving age, 202–3
Legal Cases for Teachers, 452–9, 468
LEGAL GUARDIAN, 381
LIBEL, 394–7
LICENCES,
employment of children in entertainments, 199–200
music and dancing, 335–6
Performing Right Society, 340–41
Phonographic Performance Ltd, 341–2, 362–3
stage plays, 333–5
television, 431
LICENSEES, 274
LOCAL AUTHORITIES, MEMBERSHIP OF, 111–12
LOCAL COLLEGES, 55
LOCAL EDUCATION AUTHORITIES, *see* Authorities, Local education
LOG BOOK, *see* School annals
LONDON ALLOWANCES, 135–6
LORD'S PRAYER, 220